CRUCIAL CHOICES – CRUCIAL CHANGES

THE RESURRECTION OF PSYCHOTHERAPY

AMERICAN MENTAL HEALTH FOUNDATION

IN COOPERATION WITH

INTERNATIONAL INSTITUTE FOR MENTAL HEALTH RESEARCH

ZÜRICH AND GENEVA

THIS VOLUME IS THE THIRD IN THE SERIES

THE SEARCH FOR THE FUTURE

VOLUME I

THE CHALLENGE FOR GROUP PSYCHOTHERAPY

Stefan de Schill, editor

VOLUME II

THE CHALLENGE FOR PSYCHOANALYSIS

AND PSYCHOTHERAPY:

SOLUTIONS FOR THE FUTURE

Stefan de Schill and Serge Lebovici, editors

Pertinent information about Volumes I and II
can be found in the appendix.

CRUCIAL CHOICES — CRUCIAL CHANGES

THE RESURRECTION OF PSYCHOTHERAPY

Stefan de Schill

DIRECTOR OF RESEARCH
AMERICAN MENTAL HEALTH FOUNDATION

an American Mental Health Foundation book

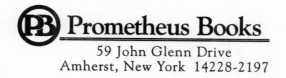

Prometheus Books

59 John Glenn Drive
Amherst, New York 14228-2197

Published 2000 by Prometheus Books

Inquiries should be addressed to
Prometheus Books
59 John Glenn Drive
Amherst, New York 14228–2197
VOICE: 716–691–0133, ext. 207
FAX: 716–564–2711

04 03 02 01 00   5 4 3 2 1

Library of Congress Cataloging-in-Publication Data

De Schill, Stefan
    Crucial choices—crucial changes : the resurrection of psychotherapy / Stefan de Schill.
        p. cm. — (The search for the future ; v. 3)
    Includes bibliographical references and index.
    ISBN 1–57392–812–7 (alk. paper)
    1. Psychotherapy. 2. Psychoanalysis. I. Title. II. Series.
RC480.5 .D465 2000
616.89'14—dc21   00–039009
                                                                                          CIP

Printed in the United States of America on acid-free paper

To our destiny we are chained –

for even the gods cannot alter the past.

ATTRIBUTED TO HERACLITUS

AMHF

The American Mental Health Foundation, organized in 1924, is dedicated to the welfare of people suffering from emotional problems and to the concerns of the elderly. The Foundation has devoted its efforts, with outstanding success, to bettering the quality of treatment and developing more effective methods, afforable even to low-income wage earners.

The Foundation's major therapeutic advances and improved training methods are described in its publications, considered by preeminent international mental health professionals to be of exceptional value for the essential improvement of psychotherapy and psychoanalysis. The Foundation, vitally interested in reaching the greatest possible audience for its findings, publishes in both the United States and abroad. Its publications appear in at least three languages.

None of the board members, officers, or professionals of the Foundation receives remuneration. Nevertheless, the costs of doing research, preparing publications and translations, and making the Foundation's findings known to the professions and the general public are very costly.

Because the Foundation has no endowment, all donations constitute a meaningful contribution to the public interest. Donations are tax-exempt.

AMERICAN MENTAL HEALTH FOUNDATION
1049 FIFTH AVENUE NEW YORK, NY 10028

CONTENTS

I. THE RESURRECTION OF PSYCHOTHERAPY

WORKING TOWARD CLINICAL EXPERTISE

In a war almost lost,
a battle almost won:

II. THE QUEST FOR AFFORDABLE
AND EFFECTIVE PSYCHOTHERAPY

At the end of the book, the reader will find
"Comments and Acknowledgments," and the indexes.
Preceding the indexes is an appendix providing information
about the other volumes in the series
THE SEARCH FOR THE FUTURE.

FOREWORD

HOPE – IF . . .

Monroe W. Spero

CHAIRMAN
PROFESSIONAL BOARD
AMERICAN MENTAL HEALTH FOUNDATION

Those who attempt to obtain everything at once will find little fulfillment. Morality may consist principally in the courage to make the initial choice in its behalf.

Léon Blum

Despite goodwill and effort by many individuals and organizations, including the American Mental Health Foundation, it has been a long time since we have seen major advances in psychotherapy that have actually benefited a significant portion of the patient population. In fact, many authorities with extensive experience, including some who are contributing to this volume, deplore the marked decline in quality of treatment, theoretical development, and psychotherapeutic training. There has never been a Shangri-la, but there have been times when hope for a better future stood on more solid ground.

It is futile to bemoan those problems or to brood over obstacles to success. Our difficulties, surprising though it may seem, are not attributable to a scarcity of realistic solutions. On the contrary, many answers are already here and waiting to be applied.

The goals of the series The Search for the Future are those of the Foundation. Representing a long-term effort, the series now comprises three volumes: THE CHALLENGE FOR GROUP PSYCHOTHERAPY, THE CHALLENGE FOR PSYCHOANALYSIS AND PSYCHOTHERAPY: SOLUTIONS FOR THE FUTURE, and the present volume, CRUCIAL CHOICES – CRUCIAL CHANGES: THE RESURRECTION OF PSYCHOTHERAPY. They present a broad range of informed perspectives and viewpoints and describe promising approaches for the improvement of mental health treatment and policy.

For the companion volume, edited by Stefan de Schill and Serge Lebovici, the Foundation carefully selected leading psychoanalysts and psychotherapists, representing a diversity of approaches, and asked them to write on the subjects that are within their expertise and that they consider to be of major importance for the future of psychotherapy. This is the first time that the work of these authors is to be found in a single volume, allowing an unprecedented comparison of their basic assumptions, their expectations for the future, and their proposals for improvement. When the papers of the invited authors were selected, no consideration was given to whether the views presented were in harmony with those of the Foundation.

The present volume, on the other hand, focuses on the studies and efforts of the American Mental Health Foundation during the last 45 years and on cogent related studies supporting its position. The basic problems of psychoanalysis, psychotherapy, and mental health in general are carefully examined to determine the extent to which the welfare of the patient is safeguarded and the quality of psychotherapeutic practice, writings, and teaching. Because outstanding clinical expertise in psychotherapy is required to define the problems correctly and to develop the unusual vision necessary to offer effective solutions, this volume gives much attention to the improvement of clinical expertise. The novel and substantive answers that the American Mental Health Foundation has worked out are presented with uncommon realism from the vantage point of its independent position.

In this volume Dr. Stefan de Schill describes the concepts and goals that have guided his efforts as the director of research of the Foundation for 45 years and, on the basis of that unique experience, discusses the changes considered to be of primary importance.

Since a considerable part of the two volumes is concerned with projects and findings that are the result of the efforts of the American Mental Health Foundation, a brief account of the work of the Foundation is in order.

The Foundation was established in 1924 by civic leaders, eminent jurists, psychiatrists, academicians in the humanities, and people of goodwill in government and business. Their goal was to improve the plight of the emotionally ill. Therefore the Foundation set as its priorities the development of more effective methods in psychotherapy and the protection of the public interest. In the following years the members of the Foundation pursued those endeavors throughout the country.

During the Second World War the acute need for better psychotherapeutic services and more qualified practitioners became urgent, and the Foundation increased its efforts in that direction. In

1942 its board, under the chairmanship of Professor Hermann Broch of Princeton University, began to look for a professional suitable to direct such an undertaking. The person not only had to be capable of generating valuable ideas for the advancement of psychotherapy, but also had to have shown considerable concern for patient welfare. The board members reviewed many applications, but it was not until 1947 that they found such a professional. Professor Otto Kauders, chief of the world-renowned Psychiatric Clinic of the University of Vienna, proposed Dr. Stefan de Schill, who had studied and worked with him. Other institutions where Dr. de Schill had subsequently worked gave laudatory recommendations.

After his appointment as director of research, Dr. de Schill set to work on the major challenges before him. With public interest a priority, he developed a comprehensive mental health program on national, state, and community levels. Seen from that viewpoint, the most serious problem was the need for affordable, effective treatment for the emotionally ill. Dr. de Schill was and is a strong believer in psychodynamic therapy and the great potential for its future improvement.

Professor Kauders, visiting the Foundation in 1950, found the program to be one of the most promising projects of its time. Furthermore, the program so impressed Richard Weil Jr., a pioneer in the field of mental health and president of the National Association for Mental Health, that in 1955 he resigned from that post to join the Foundation, and he subsequently became its president.

Many public-spirited people have expressed their appreciation of the Foundation's work. I will cite only two. "This Foundation," stated James A. Foley, the prominent New York judge, "is one of the finest examples of what American humanitarianism can achieve – a perfect blending of knowledge, charity, and hope." Dr. Otto Klineberg, former chairman of the Department of Social Psychology at Columbia University, former professor at the Sorbonne, and honorary president of the World Federation for Mental Health, wrote: "I have known Dr. Stefan de Schill since 1945 and have now been on the Board of the American Mental Health Foundation for over 40 years. . . . Encouraged by the dedication and accomplishments of this organization, I am confident about the most meaningful contribution the Foundation will make to the future of mental health."

The Foundation has as its goal the development of more effective methods of treatment. Most people in need of professional help can afford, at best, one session a week, which obviously does not allow sufficiently intensive therapy. The Foundation has made great progress in improving the effectiveness of individual and group psychotherapy, thus reducing the cost of therapy to the patient.

Among other therapeutic achievements, the Foundation has developed an intensive form of group psychotherapy in which members meet twice a week for a total of six hours. The method, if administered by expert therapists, is affordable and effective for many patients and thus answers an essential mental health need. It allows a drastic reduction in the frequency of individual sessions, and patients can be placed in groups at the beginning of therapy. It is applicable to many ambulatory patients, and even those with severe emotional disturbances not previously considered amenable to group therapy can now be treated in a group setting. Very satisfactory results have also been obtained in the treatment of the elderly.

The treatment form permits even modest-wage earners to pay their own way. The unwarranted interference in the treatment process by third-party insurance providers is often avoided when there is a reasonable fee that the patients can pay. As for patients who take advantage of the insurance coverage to which they are entitled, the modest cost of the treatment allows them to continue once their coverage is exhausted. On the whole, because of the low cost of the procedure, third-party payers are less likely to interject the habitual obstacles that, sadly, affect other treatment plans involving necessary but time-consuming reconstructive in-depth psychotherapy.

Over the past 40 years many Foundation publications have discussed this intensive form of group psychotherapy. One such publication, prepared by Dr. de Schill, has more than 80,000 copies in six editions circulating in the United States alone, a remarkable distinction for any text in the mental health field. Subsequent works on the method, widely acclaimed in Europe and the United States, have appeared in five major languages. Among them was THE CHALLENGE FOR GROUP THERAPY, edited by Dr. de Schill, which received unusual recognition in many countries. Its French edition was the first book on group therapy by a distinguished psychoanalytic society, the Psychoanalytic Institute of Paris. Those publications have been used by psychotherapists, psychiatrists, students, and other members of the mental health professions as well as by clinics, hospitals, university departments, training institutes, and social agencies.

Because of the Foundation's goals and policies, its public relations efforts have been different from those of other entities in the field. Rather than concentrating on raising funds, it has always sought, and obtained, the cooperation of foremost mental health professionals, here and abroad, and of government officials interested in the public welfare. None of the board members or officers receives remuneration. Since 1959 the research and publication efforts have been in conjunction with the International Institute for Mental Health Research of Zürich and Geneva, to which many of the foremost European mental health professionals belong.

From 1950 until 1971 the Foundation offered orientation sessions for people seeking psychotherapeutic assistance. Independently of that, the Foundation sponsored a nonprofit treatment and referral center for some 30 years. At this center all applicants for services had extensive initial interviews. Over 40 percent of the applicants had previously been in treatment. Many had discontinued treatment not because of dissatisfaction with their therapist but for other reasons, such as moving to another geographical area or having financial difficulties. Since it was important to obtain adequate information about prior therapy, those applicants received two or more interviews. The information obtained from the orientation sessions and the screening interviews, data from more than 6,000 patients, has been invaluable and cannot be found elsewhere. The findings from the interviews influenced Foundation policies in numerous ways. They are described in this volume by Dr. de Schill.

Because we wanted the present volume to offer unencumbered information, we asked Dr. de Schill to express his views of present problems and future solutions in the form of a detailed commentary rather than a scholarly presentation. His critical examination of basic shortcomings in contemporary psychotherapy and mental health practice is accompanied in each instance by his comments and descriptions of what clinical expertise tells us and what beneficial approach is indicated. Many highly experienced psychotherapists consider the resultant wealth of unique clinical material to be of outstanding usefulness.

So far, Dr. de Schill has invited Dr. Alexander Wolf, Dr. Stanley Lesse, and, after the latter's death, Professor Serge Lebovici to participate in the editorial work on planned volumes. About 90 of the foremost authorities in the United States and Europe have accepted our invitations to participate in those works.

As noted, a basic goal of the Foundation's program is to advance the public interest. Although challenging and stimulating, efforts toward that goal have often been the source of difficult struggles against vested groups. For instance, when the Foundation's first publication on intensive group therapy appeared in the 1950s, this treatment modality was little known in the United States, and the pioneering efforts of Dr. de Schill and others were sharply criticized. Those difficulties were minor, however, compared with the reactions to some of the Foundation's other efforts in the public interest. Controversies on community and national levels have arisen frequently over the years, and Dr. de Schill deserves much credit for speaking up without hesitation concerning matters that most would prefer to forget.

Generally, professional activities and publications within the mental health field are based on and perceived from the viewpoints of the psychiatrist and psychotherapist, even if they work in agencies or universities. But those activities and attitudes take on a different aspect when scrutinized by a foundation and its director whose main concern is to advance the welfare of the public and the patient.

About 30 years ago I joined the organization, and I continue to be extensively involved in its daily work. Like my colleagues, many of whom have served the Foundation since Dr. de Schill started his work 45 years ago, I have been impressed by his outstanding clinical expertise, his understanding of the human psyche, and his unusual concern for the emotionally ill. The dedication and efforts of this man have sustained the work of the Foundation. Our feelings are best expressed by the words of our previous chairman, who wrote on the first page of the Foundation's 1971 volume on group psychotherapy: "It was a privilege to witness the brilliant, always carefully thought-out ways in which Dr. de Schill, in his capacity as director of research of the American Mental Health Foundation, explored and experimented with the innumerable facets of individual and group psychotherapy, constantly seeking better theoretical formulations and techniques."

The practice and teaching of psychotherapy have deteriorated in the last several decades. Despite an enormous increase in the quantity of academic treatises on the subject, their quality has decreased. The mountains of nondescript books, articles, and computer printouts, hopelessly burying any quality work, are sad monuments to the status quo.

In contrast, this book addresses the fundamental problems and offers feasible, though necessarily difficult, solutions. The findings presented here are a realistic way out of the present predicament. They are crucial to the future of mental health.

PREFACE

TO TAKE ARMS AGAINST
A SEA OF TROUBLES
SHAKESPEARE

Needless Suffering, Available Answers, Overdue Improvements

You can serve a cause you believe in or you can serve your personality, but you cannot do both.

JEAN MONET

How we live is so far removed from how we ought to live, that he who abandons what is done for what ought to be done will rather bring about his ruin than his preservation.

MACHIAVELLI

In these pages we shall consider the future of mental health. At present, the name itself is its only asset. There is scarcely an area in the field that is not beset by formidable, almost insurmountable, difficulties. Since its inception in 1924, the American Mental Health Foundation has sought to deal with those difficulties by placing the patient's interest in the forefront of its considerations.

This book and its companion volume, THE CHALLENGE FOR PSYCHOANALYSIS AND PSYCHOTHERAPY: SOLUTIONS FOR THE FUTURE, approach the topic from two perspectives: (1) to present well-known authors who reflect contemporary thinking and attempt to map the future course of mental health and (2) to outline the American Mental Health Foundation's detailed investigation of basic problems in mental health and proposals for the alleviation of those problems. As this book will make apparent, the problems can be traced to a small number of important factors.

For over 45 years I have been the director of research of the American Mental Health Foundation. A more interesting position in the field is difficult to imagine. The task involves a great number of issues, ranging from the satisfying to the dismal.

One of the Foundation's two highest priorities is to improve treatment of the emotionally ill by finding ways to make it both affordable and effective. The cost factor is crucial, for the expense of psychotherapy severely limits its accessibility. Even patients who have insurance coverage are usually not allowed adequate treatment time. For those who do not have such coverage, the problem can be insurmountable. One cannot expect psychotherapists to work for reduced fees. Psychotherapy, if practiced diligently, is one of the most difficult professions. Furthermore, except for a small number of professionals benefiting from special referral opportunities, remuneration is comparatively modest.

Over many years the Foundation has been engaged in a concentrated effort to improve the effectiveness of individual and group therapy. That effort had to start with a thorough reevaluation of present-day practice from the perspective of clinical experience; throughout this book I describe the findings of that evaluation. A major goal was to develop treatment procedures that would enable even modest-wage earners to obtain effective therapy without undue sacrifice or help from third parties. As a result of those efforts, an intensive form of psychodynamic group therapy was developed.

Patients in interactive analytic group therapy meet twice a week in extended sessions. Satisfactory progress of a great number of patients has been obtained with the help of this method, whereas traditional group psychotherapy, consisting of a single session a week of the usual one-and-a-half-hour duration, had proven insufficient. Unfortunately, the battle is far from won. Owing to inadequate basic training, few therapists can acquire the skills to practice this sophisticated form of therapy. Thus, at the present time, only a tiny fraction of patients in need can be helped.

The shortage of qualified group psychotherapists is not merely due to insufficient training in this specialty; it is also a result of the difficulties in obtaining a desirable education in individual psychotherapy, which must precede group therapy training. In this volume I describe some of those problems, and John E. Gedo discusses them in his introduction. Inadequate instruction greatly diminishes the potential of talented students and eventually results in inadequate performance in psychotherapeutic work. Elucidating the deficiencies in psychotherapeutic training and practice by devising improvements is an essential part of the Foundation's work and a goal of this volume.

The other high priority of the Foundation is to advance the patient's interest by making essential improvements in the mental health care system. As an independent organization, the Foundation is not influenced by external pressures and can therefore play a unique role in the quest for progress.

Many people of goodwill, intelligence, and talent are engaged in psychotherapeutic work. Fundamental obstacles exist, however, in translating those assets into needed changes. Most practicing psychotherapists and faculty members at universities and training institutes are subject to restraints and pressures. They may depend on patient referrals, belong to professional associations, or be affiliated with treatment facilities. Even those with the best minds, who are sometimes professionals in positions of prominence, tread carefully to avoid discord and offense. And the need to make a living is a strong incentive for rationalizing. Vested interests in the mental health realm can present formidable obstacles for even conservative reforms.

Mark Twain described it well: "We have these unspeakably precious things: freedom of speech, freedom of conscience, and the prudence never to practice either of them." Rarely will you find among mental health professionals a Joan of Arc or a Semmelweis defending the interest of the public.

The Foundation's independence has often led it to take positions in principal areas of psychotherapy and mental health policy that differ from mainstream professional views. That is unavoidable if public welfare is the primary concern. But professionals who cherish psychotherapeutic work and are seeking to improve it will find that their interest actually coincides with the public interest.

Many of the Foundation's findings described in this volume may be surprising, even disconcerting, to some readers. Time, however, has shown that the fundamental positions the Foundation has developed over the years are valid. I regret the absence of other independent mental health organizations of importance with which we could have cooperated constructively.

An inevitable matter must be settled at the outset. Upon hearing about the preparation of this work, many professionals voiced the widely held opinion that money – much more money – was all we needed to solve most problems in our field. And mental health organizations frequently claim that with greater funding they could achieve extraordinary benefits for patients. The standard platitude is that "the patients will then be able to lead constructive and happy lives."

Such claims are more than suspect. We know of no substantive data to support them. In fact, even the financially well-off need exceptional good luck to find therapists who can help decisively and lastingly. The sad fact is that most patients who suffer deep anxiety and depression never obtain adequate professional assistance. We should not tolerate perpetuation of that dismal situation.

Although money is necessary in many situations, it is simply not the main answer in our field. Money cannot bring about better psychotherapeutic theory and practice. We need some entirely different approaches, and the purpose of this book is to present them.

Responsibility for the mental health situation clearly lies with the professionals and their associations. It is unconscionable to try to shift the blame for inadequacies onto an "uncomprehending government" or an "indifferent public" or "insufficient funds." As the Foundation predicted many times, the enormous sums of money channeled to professional entities on the basis of grandiose promises have produced meager results. Indeed, much of it has only perpetuated the very system that is the cause of the prevailing misery.

The considerable damage done by misdirected money frequently goes further than merely reinforcing an undesirable status quo. Money can be a formidable obstacle to progress. Stanley Lesse, the late coeditor of our companion volume and the former president of the Association for the Advancement of Psychotherapy, expressed a similar view (in the following, the term *psychiatry* refers mainly to psychotherapy):

> In a sea of money . . . men, institutions, and cultures have been known to become indigent and die. What is . . . the point where growth is stimulated without destroying the very projects that are being encouraged?
>
> Employment in large medical institutions (government or private) often encourages "me-tooism and watch-your-stepism" which are, in turn, antagonists and inhibitors of the free and original thinking that is necessary. . . .
>
> Huge sums of money have created some psychiatric research monstrosities. . . . There has been no definitive

evidence, thus far, that large sums of money can stimulate new ideas or significant research in psychiatry. . . .

The present clinical teaching may be greatly inferior to the older system in which clinically oriented practitioners were in charge of student instruction.

Furthermore, gratuitous theorizing in teaching has all too often replaced clinical expertise. The student . . . may never develop the diagnostic and therapeutic acumen that was enjoyed by students trained . . . decades ago. Money, in one form or another, has been responsible . . . for the development of this order of things.

Thus, as a matter of fact, while the number of academic courses demanded of the psychotherapy student has increased considerably, overall clinical expertise is markedly in decline.

It may well be that from "little clinicians," unhampered by administrative problems, intricate equipment, and not swayed by the current trend to espouse superficial facile treatment approaches, new ideas will come. At the turn of the century, it was with such men that the revolution in psychiatry was born.

Money has not as yet led to a significant improvement in psychiatry. Let us beware lest it build mausoleums for individual thinking and thinkers.

When Dr. Lesse wrote of "little clinicians" from whom new ideas were forthcoming in the past, and may be again in the future, he touched on a fundamental problem in mental health. It is given foremost attention in this volume.

Amid the incessant clamor for research funds, the statements of Professor Alex Müller, a Swiss Nobel Prize winner and a pioneer in superconductivity, are refreshingly honest and relevant. To an American reporter who remarked that the research must have cost millions, Müller replied: "Money is not what counts; ideas do. All we spent were some 80,000 francs" (about US$ 45,000 at that time).

We encounter a meaningful parallel to that when we consider the work of the American Mental Health Foundation; here too it was not money but rather the knowledge and talent of the experts who developed vast improvements in individual and group psychotherapy as well as substantive reform projects that were responsible for the achievements. As we shall see, enormous sums, governmental and private, have been and are being wasted on fruitless and self-serving endeavors in psychotherapy practice and education and on mental health projects. On the other hand, far smaller sums, unfortunately not available, would have helped the Foundation disseminate its valuable findings on an infinitely wider basis nationally and internationally.

This book is concerned with basic issues. It is based on my desire to give major attention to the interest of the patient. Thus it reflects and serves the objectives of the Foundation. Studies prepared with the public interest in mind must be critical of institutions, policies, and professionals, and I describe the findings here with frankness. To do otherwise would be meaningless. The solutions proposed here as necessary for substantial progress in the field of psychotherapy and mental health are twofold: (1) the elimination of approaches and methods that have been shown through documented and responsible inquiry to be ineffective or even destructive and (2) the implementation of ideas, developed by the Foundation over 45 years, that will result in major and decisive improvements to psychotherapy. The solutions are feasible and substantive.

These chapters – unlike my previous writings, which were mainly organized as psychotherapeutic presentations – also give major attention to the patient's concerns and interests. Although the volume devotes a great deal of space to examining the deficiencies in psychotherapy evident in the writings of many well-known psychotherapists, our intent is to go far beyond mere criticism. In each instance the shortcomings are contrasted with the facts of clinical experience. As a consequence, we present much useful clinical material not found elsewhere.

Many of the writings examined leave one with a marked uneasiness. One should not forget that we psychotherapists are mere repairmen. Even the best of us are far from being adequate, let alone perfect. Our craftsmanship does not come close to that of a philharmonic musician. Modesty, not grandiosity, should be the hallmark of a knowledgeable psychotherapist.

Some readers will note that I repeat certain short statements in different sections. The repetition occurs mainly in three instances. First, after examining the work of certain authors, I point out how misleading and damaging to psychotherapeutic practice and teaching those writings are.

Second, I repeat certain statements to avoid confusion. Many people read only the sections in a book that are of particular interest to them and thus miss explanations given earlier. In the first part of a book whose English title was THE CHALLENGE FOR GROUP PSYCHOTHERAPY, I stated that the goal was to improve group psychotherapy to such a degree that increased effectiveness would greatly reduce the total cost of treatment. Quite a few readers and reviewers who skipped that paragraph questioned the title.

Third, I repeat statements to clarify some pertinent facts for the reader; for example, that my chapters survey psychotherapy and its practices from the point of view not only of the psychotherapist but also of the public interest. Such a focus necessarily influences the choice of the material examined. Our critical examination of psychoanalytic and psychotherapeutic writings and practices attempts to evaluate the quality of present-day professional activity. Such a review provides an effective way to examine areas of basic importance, and shortcomings therein, and to point out requisite improvements.

In this volume, in accordance with the wishes of the board of the American Mental Health Foundation and based on my long experience at the Foundation, I describe my views on the main problems of psychotherapy and mental health and propose the specific solutions indicated. The board members felt that the overall goal would best be served if I wrote in the same informal language and manner I use in day-to-day contacts with colleagues at the Foundation. They also thought that in some instances where I made critical comments, it would not be necessary to identify the professionals and publications in question.

Many of the advances and reforms described here have been proposed by the Foundation to the mental health professions, the United States Congress, and various administrations since the early 1950s. Despite considerable effort by informed supporters, no proposal was accepted.

Instead, ill-advised policies have resulted in huge amounts of wasted funds, in squandered opportunities for progress, and in reinforcing an undesirable status quo.

To the many people who ask why our proposals for change are essentially the same as those we made some 40 years ago, the sad answer must be that the basic problems have not changed. In fact, the situation has deteriorated in a number of areas.

This volume is concerned with psychotherapy, primarily the problems of the nonpsychotic emotionally ill. Certainly all people so afflicted suffer. Many, however, such as the depressed and the anxious, are subject to some of the worst torment human beings can experience. Exiles from all happiness, they partake of life's sorrows and miseries, seldom of its joys. Restless and haunted, many cannot find solace even in literature and music. Even the presence of talent, intelligence, and humane qualities cannot mitigate their ever-present pain.

In his first session one of my patients described the agony of his chronic anxiety and depression: "The Chinese had a torture in which they cut open a man's belly, placed a large rat inside, and sewed him together again." And I cannot forget a statement by another patient: "The anguish and torment that other people suffer when experiencing personal tragedy I feel night and day." Another patient, a talented and sensitive writer, showed me a manuscript of his autobiography, entitled "Pretending to Be a Person." Like all his other writings, it was never published. A most fundamental and tragic problem still with us is the undeniable difficulty of treating the severely anxious and depressed with lasting success. That difficulty is frequently the cause of the resignation or indifference that can be found among many mental health professionals. In his introduction to this volume John E. Gedo discusses the situation, which he and other committed psychotherapists deplore.

We are presented with an intolerable situation – our failure to alleviate the ordeal of so many human beings destroyed by forces from within. But redress is possible, and it need not depend on the discovery of new remedies; rather, it depends on the necessary knowledge that is already available. Unfortunately, most of that knowledge is not found in the various modalities of training. To acquire it, the student has to set out on a protracted, frustrating search and engage in an unending struggle to separate the valid from the useless.

The reforms described in these volumes were developed with this conviction in mind: Our profession cannot ignore its responsibility for the emotionally disturbed. We must be unrelenting in our effort to bring about more effective treatment of patients and more knowledgeable teaching of students.

S.DES.

Jerusalem, my longed-for home,
When shall I come to thee?
When shall my sorrows come to end?
The joys when shall I see?

SONG OF MARY, 1601

Introductory Reflections

What Is Going on Here ?

> That it should come to this!
> SHAKESPEARE

As a consequence of the deterioration in psychoanalysis and psychotherapy, an ever-increasing number of people suffering from anxiety and depression are being deprived of much-needed help. Almost as discouraging is the fact that hoped-for improvements in psychodynamic therapy have little chance to be realized under current conditions. We have never even approached the potential of psychoanalysis and psychodynamic psychotherapy, either to help us understand the human psyche or to improve the lives of those who are suffering.

In their introduction John E. Gedo and Robert J. Stoller examine fundamental problems that have led to the decline of psychoanalysis and psychotherapy.

A TIME OF DISCONTENT
CONTEMPORARY PSYCHOANALYSIS
IN AMERICA

John E. Gedo

When this was written, John E. Gedo was Training and
Supervising Analyst, Chicago Institute for Psychiatry,
Abraham Lincoln School of Medicine, University of Illinois.

One of the gravest problems we face is the selection and training of psychotherapists. In this introduction John E. Gedo addresses major facets of the matter. I shall refer to his statements when we look at this topic in Part I. There we will examine how it is affected by the overall status quo in psychoanalysis and psychotherapy.

The current age of mass culture is inhospitable to most products of civilization; the psychoanalyst and the psychotherapist, like other practitioners who belong to the cultural elite, tend to be ignored – unless they can be turned into superstars. I have previously discussed the corrosive effects on true creativity of the pervasive pressure to conform to the demotic mainstream (Gedo, 1983). Here I would like to focus on a different aspect of those circumstances: the manner in which they have undermined and even corrupted our psychoanalytic institutions.

I believe that I am exceptionally informed about these matters as a result of extensive scientific and organizational contacts with the American psychoanalytic community. Over the years, I have had the opportunity to take an active part in the scientific programs of the American Psychoanalytic Association (hereafter the American) and 18 of its component local societies, of some branches of the Canadian Psychoanalytic Society, and of a number of psychoanalytic organizations not affiliated with the International Psycho-analytic Association. From an administrative vantage point, I have learned a great deal from six years of service on the Committee on Institutes of the American, where every training program is regularly reviewed in some detail. As part of that work, I participated in extensive visits to six institutes. Six years with the Committee on Research and Special Training and significant periods with the Committee on Scientific Activities and the editorial board of the JOURNAL OF THE AMERICAN PSYCHOANALYTIC ASSOCIATION have also provided me with valuable lessons about the status quo within organized psychoanalysis. Locally, I have observed the Chicago Psychoanalytic Society and the Institute for Psychoanalysis for three decades, have participated in their affairs at multiple levels, and have held the office of society president.

Today it has become evident that American social conditions do not favor the acceptance of psychoanalytic ideas. Thus Freud's most pessimistic intuitions have been substantiated; psychoanalysis has not taken root in

American soil without becoming denatured. In other words, Freud's aversion to America was not based simply on prejudice. On the contrary, his view must have stemmed from his deep appreciation of the place of his own thought within the great tradition of European ideas from Plato to Nietzsche – a tradition essentially alien to the pragmatic optimism of the New World (see Gedo, 1983, 1991).

For some decades after the 1930s, the influence of refugees from Nazism caused the development of psychoanalysis on this side of the Atlantic to take on a central European flavor. The intellectual leadership of Hartmann, Jacobson, Kris, and Loewenstein (or, in a vein of dissidence, of Horney and Radó) in New York, the Bibrings and the Deutsches in Boston, Waelder in Philadelphia, Alexander and Benedek in Chicago, the Sterbas in Detroit, and Rapaport in Topeka and Stockbridge, to name only a few of the more prominent émigrés, screened the actualities of the development of American psychoanalysis. Even more recently, a large proportion of influential analytic thinkers in this country have been of European origin – for example, Erikson, Kernberg, Kohut, Loewald, and Mahler.

Over 50 years have now passed since the outbreak of war stopped the flow of émigré intellectuals; even those, like me, who arrived as preadolescents have reached the twilight of their analytic careers. Hence we no longer have a cadre of analytic leaders, trained abroad and endowed with unchallengeable prestige, to counteract the impact of autochthonous mass culture on our discipline.

In a similar vein, Eissler (1965) excoriated such a reduction of our horizons as the "medical orthodoxy" of American psychoanalytic organizations. In the past generation a growing number of nonmedical analytic groups, including several training institutes accepted into the International Psycho-analytic Association, have produced graduates no less pragmatic in their orientation than are North American analysts with a background in psychiatry. Thus the retreat from Freud's standards did not result simply from the policy of the American, until a few years ago, of excluding nonmedical therapists from training; rather, the retreat seems to be an inevitable concomitant of making analysts out of contemporary mental health professionals of whatever background.

To be sure, the recruitment policies of the American before the recent abandonment of the medical monopoly proved to be disastrous at the practical level. As American psychiatry has increasingly espoused a reductionistic biological orientation, it has attracted a shrinking number of medical graduates, and those who do choose this specialty tend to be among the less able students. (Statistics about those matters are regularly compiled and published in periodicals devoted to medical education.) As a result of the unfavorable changes in psychiatry, the number of medical candidates for psychoanalytic training has steadily diminished, despite the increased geographic availability of analytic training centers. In many localities, institutes have been able to recruit psychiatric candidates only by sacrificing our nominal standards of competence. In every institute there are many "problem candidates" who have no hope of mastering the skills required to perform adequate clinical work. (I base that assertion on personal observation as a visitor on behalf of the Committee on Institutes of the American at six of its institutes and on careful review of site visit reports from all other programs under the aegis of this committee.)

At the same time, it has proved impossible to maintain higher standards for nonmedical candidates than for psychiatric ones. The initial proposal to monitor the admission criteria for that fresh source of psychoanalysts-in-training through an oversight committee of the American soon had to be abandoned in the face of widespread opposition from local groups. (I also served on that committee, the Committee on Nonmedical Clinical Training, for a number of years and witnessed the gradual erosion of its ability to screen out unqualified applicants.)

The deficiencies of unsuitable candidates generally manifest themselves early in the course of training. Nowadays, according to conventional wisdom, it is legally risky to fail the unsatisfactory students, although, in fairness to them, they should be advised to drop out. Instead, institutes generally allow them to exist in the limbo of interminable candidacy. They are finally granted a "compassionate graduation," with the not-so-secret proviso that their failure to meet the certification standards of the American will serve as the needed caveat to prevent them from practicing psychoanalysis.

In principle, all institutes approved by the International Psycho-analytic Association have the same minimal criteria for graduation. (The American requires a bit more: In addition to an analysis, ordinarily performed by a "training analyst," and the satisfactory completion of didactic work offered in a sequence of at least four years, the candidate must conduct at least three analyses for a minimum of one year each. The analyses must be regularly supervised by a faculty-appointed "supervising analyst," and at least one of the three must be brought to a satisfactory termination.) The minimal criteria are now periodically breached by allowing the analyses, either those of the analysts-to-be or those of their analysands, to be conducted in fewer than four visits per week; by providing less supervision than is necessary to ensure competent management of cases; or by graduating candidates who have not achieved a successful termination with any of their patients – presumably because the delay in reaching the goal is not attributable to any deficiency in the student.

The Committee on Certification of the American has chosen to do no more than check on the manner in which the minimal criteria have actually been met by reading narrative accounts (often supplemented with an oral interview with the applicant) of each supervised analysis. Briefer reports from the institutes, including information from the supervisors, are compared with those accounts.

Although such a certification procedure seems quite lax in comparison with the procedures in other disciplines, voices for egalitarianism and a larger membership have succeeded in eliminating certification as a criterion of eligibility for membership in the American. In other words, membership no longer implies anything beyond graduation from a local institute. About a decade ago, approximately half of such graduates were certified when they applied for membership in the American, although some who failed initially were subsequently approved if they submitted better case reports. (I am certain that that possibility led to the creation of a great deal of low-quality fiction.) At any rate, the ranks of the American have been considerably expanded by the ingathering of graduates who could not be certified.

It is difficult to blame the beleaguered faculty of specific institutes for the general debasement of the currency of their diplomas. All educational institutions must adapt to the needs of the students they are able to attract; the only alternative is to allow the institutions to collapse. Most of the individuals who staff psychoanalytic institutes, almost invariably on a volunteer basis that entails sacrifice in time and money, are in later middle age. They almost universally demonstrate an intense loyalty to their organizations – a commitment most likely to surface when an institute threatens to splinter into rival camps – so that they will go to great lengths to protect its survival. At a more personal level, they have scarcely any other option, for it is typically too late in their professional careers to develop alternative academic or intellectual commitments.

Part-time so-called clinical appointments in medical schools once constituted a career line of almost equivalent prestige. Over the past generation, however, the increasingly biological orientation of most psychiatry departments has contracted such opportunities for psychoanalysts, whether they have a background in psychiatry or in clinical psychology. At the same time, for the analysts who still serve medical schools as clinical faculty members, the shift of administrative support in other directions, as well as the poor caliber of many trainees in the programs, has considerably impaired the satisfaction to be derived from such activities.

Of course, psychoanalytic educators can always follow Candide and cultivate their private gardens – or private practices. But academicians are understandably reluctant to fall back to the position of mere providers of services. Moreover, the very fact of being members of the faculty of a psychoanalytic institute gives analysts an opportunity to develop private practices of an advantageous type – practices more focused on the performance of analytic work proper than on other forms of psychological therapy.

Periodic surveys of the professional activities of members of the American have consistently shown that among the respondents (who are more likely to be actively involved in analytic enterprises than are those who do not return the questionnaire), training analysts do much more analytic work than the remainder of the membership does. In the last survey I saw, those who were not training analysts averaged two analytic patients in their practice at any one time, while training analysts averaged five (including the two or three candidates that most training analysts treat). In other words, achieving training analyst status is the easiest way to obtain a steady supply of analytic referrals. In certain communities it may well be the only way. Of course, many observers feel that training analyses do not provide the conditions required for optimal analytic work. But that problem may be diminishing as a result of general acceptance of the rule that the analyst provides no information about his work to the institute.

All in all, then, we expect psychoanalytic institutes to provide instruction to most applicants *willing to pay,* in preference to persevering in self-defeating efforts to uphold the training standards proclaimed in their bulletins. To be sure, some exceptions do exist, particularly certain smaller training centers that accommodated themselves to a shortage of applicants some time ago, when local psychiatry departments turned against psychoanalysis. In a few such places a high-minded spirit of commitment to official standards led to the virtual disappearance of medical candidates. Before the abandonment of the medical requirement, those institutes limped along by obtaining waivers for training nonmedical academicians through the American's program for "research and special training."

When nonmedical clinical training through the American became established, the number of applicants to the research track naturally diminished to a trickle, because members of the mental health professions (psychologists, social workers, and nursing practitioners) found it much easier to pursue the clinical track. Since 1991 applicants to the clinical track with doctoral degrees have not been screened by a national committee, although such a committee continues to evaluate the credentials of those with master's degrees. It is remarkable that the expansion of the opportunity for analytic training has thus far attracted no significant influx of nonmedical applicants; it has merely restored each cohort of candidates to the modest numbers of more than a decade ago. *The vast majority of "psychoanalytically oriented" mental health professionals seem to be satisfied with a veneer of analytic terminology and a prudent avoidance of the rigors of a personal analysis, supervision, and so on.* Most of those I have confronted with the question of what discourages them from obtaining better training have claimed they cannot afford it. Many of those prosperous burghers, however, drive $40,000 automobiles.

Instead of lapsing into endless committee meetings devoted to the problem of creating old-style psychoanalytic candidates out of thin air, some institutes have devoted more and more effort to educational activities beyond what is euphemistically called the "core program," that is, the shrinking enterprise of training "professional" psychoanalysts. The new activities generally fall within the rubric of an "extension division," and they are justified as promoting an interest in psychoanalytic ideas in whatever segments of the public may be receptive: psychiatrists, social workers, teachers, cultivated laymen seeking to broaden their education. Thus, while the core programs of psychoanalytic institutes are stagnant, in many localities an increasing amount of effort has been devoted to the educational efforts of the extension divisions. I have the impression that clinical psychologists, for instance, have been less than willing to accept such second-class status – at least that was so as long as they were more or less barred from the "core program."

To my knowledge, people who have taken such extension division courses have thus far not presented themselves to the public as full-fledged analysts, but they are bound to do so shortly. After all, some of them are probably at least as competent as certain graduates of the weaker institutes, perhaps even of some of the institutes affiliated with the American. I make that assertion on the ground that courageous (or brash!) people have always been able to become capable analysts outside the establishment, most often through private consultation about their clinical efforts with respected senior colleagues. Such "bootleg" training has been prohibited by organized psychoanalysis, with expectably discouraging results. In France private enterprise has triumphed in that regard, and it may do so in many other places in the future.

At the same time, a number of centers modeled on Anna Freud's Hampstead Clinic have trained people of diverse vocational backgrounds to do child analysis. Although they are not eligible for membership in the International Psycho-analytic Association, they cannot be compelled to give up their patients when the children attain the age of 18, or 30, or 65. Furthermore, they have their own professional organizations and can hardly be prevented from multiplying their training centers. Moreover, some of the extension divisions of psycho-analytic institutes train people to do "psychoanalytic psychotherapy" with children, and it is difficult indeed to distinguish among this variety of more or less "analytic" professionals on the basis of formal credentials. Winners in the professional marketplace therefore tend to be those who inspire confidence (for whatever reason), thus creating for themselves a private referral network. Under the circumstances, how could psychoanalytic institutions resist the demand of would-be students of every sort to receive instruction at whatever level they desire?

It may seem odd to emphasize those "below stairs" developments in analytic education when the official news is the admission of hundreds of psychologists (and many other nonmedical professionals) to the institutes of the American and the establishment of more and more independent institutes under the aegis of the "psychoanalytic" Division 39 of the American Psychological Association. But the very fact that more applicants turn to those fragile new programs of uncertain standards than to the established institutes of the American (and the International Psycho-analytic Association) shows that "the pure gold of psychoanalysis" (as Freud proudly called it) is likely to be driven off the market by the various base metals offered as *easier alternatives*. Thus the prospects of American psychoanalysis as an intellectual discipline are not favorable.

Ten years ago the American's abandonment of the medical requirement for training did not seem possible. However desperate local institutes may have been to recruit candidates, none dared defy the national organization by overtly renouncing its policy – in other words, continuation of the medical monopoly embodied the wishes of a majority everywhere. The leadership of the American, at least those constituting its Board of Professional Standards, appointed a succession of committees that made a series of recommendations to relax the medical requirement, but the proposals did not meet with success until the American was faced with a lawsuit, brought by a group of psychologists excluded from its institutes, for "restraint of trade." Figures high in the federal judiciary told me that legal precedents made it unlikely that the American could successfully defend itself – in any case, such a legal battle promised to be so costly that opposition to the admission of psychologists evaporated.

The history of the controversy is worthy of note because it demonstrates that the interests of psychoanalytic educators conflict sharply with those of the membership-at-large of analytic societies. On the one hand, the institutes need students, and on the other hand, there is an oversupply of analytic practitioners in most major American communities. (The Boston-Washington corridor and the cities of the West Coast area seem to have reached the saturation point about 20 years ago; the major midwestern cities, perhaps a decade later. Only a few localities, where analysis was unusually slow to take root, still present real opportunities for willing pioneers.)

The surveys of private practice I have already mentioned substantiate the assertion that the United States does not need more analysts. Extrapolating from the raw data, it is clear that the average caseload of members of the American includes only around 12 to 15 hours of analysis per week – in other words, about 30 to 40 percent of their time is devoted to clinical activities. If training analysts are excluded from the sample, the figures are 5 to 8 hours (10 to 15 percent of their time). It is likely that the discouraging statistics would be duplicated among analysts who do not belong to the American (members of the Academy of Psychoanalysis – a medical organization not affiliated with the International Psycho-analytic Association – or of Division 39 of the American Psychological Association), as well as those who do not bother to respond to questionnaires.

Per contra, the discouragement that those numbers may lead to may be unwarranted. In every community one finds colleagues – including some of the youngest! – able to build exclusively analytic practices. Whenever I question them about how they have managed that feat, I invariably receive similar answers. They attribute their success to the establishment of a reputation for clinical excellence and to a wholehearted commitment to the psychoanalytic method as the treatment of choice in a broad range of personality disorders.

Whenever I ask colleagues – both successful analysts and those unable to obtain analytic referrals – about the probable explanation for the scarcity of analysts successful in establishing a fully analytic practice (or, at least, doing as much analysis as they desire), once again I receive remarkably consistent answers. Except for members of the mental health professions, patients ready to undertake psychoanalysis are very rare. Analysands are not born; they are created through careful preparation. To accomplish that task, the therapist who has been consulted must be convinced that he can do a better job for the patient if they jointly choose the method of psychoanalysis.

Candidates who finish their supervised experience with the conviction that they have become competent analysts often seek to achieve true *mastery* by acquiring as much analytic experience as possible. In my judgment, few practitioners do achieve mastery before completing 15 to 20 reasonably successful analyses – that is, before completing a decade or so of full-time analytic work. There are exceptions, of course, and some of the unusually gifted people are not satisfied with a career confined to the clinical aspects of psychoanalysis. Nonetheless, however gifted a colleague may be, I would hesitate to refer someone to an analyst who splits his time between analytic work and research or teaching if one ripened in the analytic trenches were also available. (It is true, of course, that a variety of circumstances, including aging, may, in the course of time, impair analytic capabilities.)

To repeat, an analytic clinician can blossom only through lengthy immersion in performing numerous analyses. Because of that, the psychoanalytic community tends to fracture into two groups, increasingly divergent in their characteristic career development. A minority of enthusiasts become increasingly involved with psychoanalysis proper (in the natural course of events, other things being equal, they achieve faculty and, ultimately, training analyst status at institutes), and a larger number have increasingly tenuous ties to psychoanalysis, despite holding analytic credentials.

We find ourselves, then, confronted with a paradox: Opposition to the broadly based recruitment of potential analysts is probably strongest among the segment of the psychoanalytic community that feels threatened by more intense economic competition – that is, by the very people who are least successful in maintaining an analytic practice. In my judgment, practitioners in that group are in any case condemned to the loss (or impaired development) of their clinical skills, caught as they are in the vicious circle of inexperience, lack of analytic self-confidence, and, inevitably, increasing resort to nonanalytic methods.

The opposition of that group to the expansion of the cadre of well-trained analysts was dictated by narcissistic needs. I am convinced that the presence in a community of a significant number of effective analysts will actually increase the number of patients who will seek analytic assistance. The most effective advertising for any method of treatment is word-of-mouth – the recommendation of a satisfied patient, particularly one whose improved adaptation is easily observable. We may also put the matter conversely: If the pragmatically oriented American consumer has turned away from psychoanalysis as a preferred method of therapy for personality disorders, the most important reason for that disaffection may well be that as actually performed by its practitioners today, *that form of treatment has not been sufficiently effective.*

The activities of graduate analysts cannot be monitored, but the unsatisfactory results of analyses performed by trainees have been widely reported (e.g., Firestein, 1978; Erle, 1979; Schlessinger & Robbins, 1983; Kantrowitz, 1987; Kantrowitz, Katz, & Paolitto, 1990). The damaging effects of poor work by trainees on the public reputation of psychoanalysis should not be underestimated.

Former patients who are bitter or discouraged or outraged about their analytic experiences often share their grievances with anyone willing to listen. Institutes are often more concerned with giving candidates every opportunity to "make it," whatever that may mean, than they are with protecting the patients whose analyses are botched by marginal students. It is by no means unusual to encounter candidates in good standing who have provoked more than a half-dozen patients into flight shortly after starting analysis with them. My experience as a visitor to various institutes where I have personally observed a score of ongoing supervisory sessions has led me to conclude that no more than 15 to 20 percent of the ongoing analyses about which I heard were conducted in a manner that had any chance of success. The supervisors were almost always aware of the candidates' unsatisfactory performance but seldom expressed skepticism about their suitability for the profession.

In the present context, however, I raise this matter not to argue for more stringent criteria of candidate selection and progression – although such policy changes are certainly desirable (see Gedo, 1984). I do so to examine the implications of *the all-but-universal lack of concern on the part of all participants for the lamentable outcome of most analyses* conducted under institute auspices (see, for example, the complacency described in that regard in Firestein, 1978). I should, in fact, put the issue more strongly, for lack of concern is the more benign form of official reaction to such failures. It is actually just as common to hear contemptuous statements about various qualities or behaviors of the patients who did not achieve a satisfactory analytic **result** – as if every analysand always got his just deserts.

Both attitudes – bland complacency and **self-exoneration** through blaming the patient – imply a conception of **psychoanalysis** as a healing procedure rather than a scientific one. That **attitude is** even clearer within French psychoanalysis, where the idea that our discipline is a branch of science is almost universally rejected; for the most part, our French colleagues seem to regard analysis as a form of art in the realm of human transactions.

It is characteristic of such belief systems that they are unaltered by the outcome of the performance of the prescribed ritual. The happy results attributable to chance alone suffice to confirm believers in their faith. Failures are invariably attributed either to insufficient attention to liturgical purity or to the unworthiness of the petitioner. Psychoanalyses carried out in that spirit are equivalent to medieval trials by ordeal; poor results mean either that the analyst did not carry out the task with the requisite sacred fervor or that the patient was irredeemably wicked.

Unfortunately, that spirit of esoteric ritual is widely prevalent within psychoanalysis, and indifference about the outcome of analyses conducted by less-than-competent candidates (or graduates, for that matter) is by no means the only evidence pointing to the corruption of its scientific essence. To cite one further indication of the presence of such regression to magical ideation, witness the widespread tolerance of the use of ready-made interpretive schemata – a tolerance of inadmissible dogmatism that is thrown into bold relief by the contrasting attitude or moralistic outrage that even minor proposals for technical innovation, however well-reasoned they may be, are likely to evoke. In other words, the outward *forms* of psychoanalytic therapy are viewed as sacrosanct by our cultists; at the same time, those subverters of scientific methodology silently lay claim to the esoteric wisdom of the guru or the Zen master (see Gedo, 1983).

Psychoanalysis conducted in the spirit of disavowed omnipotence may well have extensive therapeutic influence, but its beneficial effects in the adaptive sphere necessarily remain contingent on the continuing idealization of the analyst (or at least of psychoanalysis as a "movement"). The most familiar instance of that type of "cure" was Freud's original treatment of the Wolf Man (Freud, 1918); in that case, the therapeutic benefits disappeared about a decade after the analysis was terminated, when, in various ways, the patient learned about his analyst's fallibility (see Gedo & Goldberg, 1973; Martin, 1984). Professional psychoanalysts have the best opportunity, among "analyzed" people, to maintain therapeutic gains achieved on the basis of the magic of the discipline as a healing cult; they need only conceive of themselves as the inheritors of that magic. Kohut (1984) rightly emphasized that training analysis may serve the function of perpetuating such a priestly conception of the analytic role.

One often hears calls for restricting the application of the psychoanalytic treatment method to the narrow segment of the patient population consisting of those who can allegedly profit from the use of a "classical" technique – that is, from an exclusive resort to interpretation of intrapsychic conflicts that manifest themselves in analysis in the form of transference and resistance. Even if we granted the dubious claim that patients actually exist who require nothing more in the way of analytic intervention, adopting such a policy would amount to reducing psychoanalysis to a role of insignificance and relegating the vast majority of patients to nonanalytic therapeutic methods. The sincere devotees of our discipline who advocate such a program apparently value psychoanalysis as a numinous phenomenon, all the more precious for its rarity. Those analyst-shamans perceive the adoption of more complex analytic techniques, such as those that I, among others, have advocated over the past generation (Gedo & Goldberg, 1973; Gedo, 1979, 1981, 1984, 1988, 1991; Gedo & Gehrie, 1993), as the vulgarization or defilement of a sacrament (see Dewald, 1981).

In that connection, let me call the reader's attention to the fact that in the issue of PSYCHOANALYTIC INQUIRY devoted to a critical consideration of my work (Vol. 1, No. 2, 1981), none of the several commentators critical of my technical proposals deigned to comment on the implications of the successful results that I reported with cases that at least one reviewer acknowledged to have been exceedingly "difficult." To the contrary, the only critic who alluded to those results (Dewald, 1981) dismissed them with the cavalier claim that such happy outcomes can be obtained regardless of the type of therapy employed. Dewald failed to explain, however, why such ostensibly unexceptional clinical results are so seldom reported when the chosen form of treatment is the "classical analytic method."

At the moment, the political realities within American psychoanalysis have ensured the dominance of those doctrinaire attitudes. Moreover, the most important dissidence within the profession in recent years, the school of thought that Heinz Kohut called self psychology, has also been characterized by a religious fervor, fully as intense as that of the defenders of the traditional dogma. In these circumstances, one can only fear that our Valhalla will founder. This is, indeed, the twilight of our profession in the New World.

Freud (1927, 1930) dared to hope that psychoanalysis might play an essential role in the preservation of high culture by positing human values that might be acceptable to large populations. The passage of more than 60 years has undermined the basis for Freud's optimism; psychoanalysis has turned out to be unwelcome in every area of the world. In North America the resistance to its message has penetrated the psychoanalytic community itself, so that depth psychology has been watered down and replaced by mythic variants, in the manner I have described in this essay.

Perhaps psychoanalysis demands too much of people. As Waelder (1960) observed, it "presents a constant challenge to complacency and mental laziness and perpetually interferes with wishful thinking." But this doctrine, offering neither salvation nor faith, does not seem sufficiently inspiring to stem a rising tide of primitive religiosity. Plato's view that the masses need myths and slogans for their edification appears to apply even to the majority of psychoanalysts.

Rieff (1966) was the first to declare that psychoanalysis would be undermined by the inability of its adherents to preserve a scientific outlook. "The analytic movement," he wrote, ". . . has been ruined by the popular (and commercial) pressure upon it to help produce a symbolic [sic] for the reorganization of personality, after the central experience of [religious] deconversion." As Rieff saw it, the mutation of the psychotherapies into religion began with the defections of Adler and Jung from psychoanalysis. Freud alone continued to insist that psychoanalysis should be judged on the basis of its explanatory power, thus affirming his loyalty to the tradition of post-Baconian science. In contrast, the secessionists returned to a prescientific system. Their major aim was not to *know* but to *cure*. Their apostasy has now triumphed within psychoanalysis proper, with the devastating results I have described.

Freud developed a psychology that views much of human behavior as a compromise between instinct and culture. His recognition of the relative intractability of human nature has always been intolerable to philosophical meliorists (see Gedo, 1984). Optimistic splinter groups have repeatedly arisen within the field, adopting philosophies close to Dewey's operationalism or, as Rieff (1959) earlier put it, to faith in social engineering. Those purveyors of cheery platitudes labeled Freud a philosophical pessimist. Rieff effectively refuted the charge, pointing out that a view of personality that conceives of conscience as emerging from instinctual roots and trusts in the prudence and rationality of the ego is not a tragic one. As the critic of the passions and of the irrational conscience, psychoanalysis is mankind's tutor in prudence and compromise. Although the only explicit aim of the psychoanalytic procedure is self-cognition, it is understood that deepened self-knowledge will lead to self-control (see Friedman, 1988).

Thomas Mann ended DOCTOR FAUSTUS with the despairing cry, "When, out of uttermost hopelessness . . . will the light of hope dawn?" Might psychoanalysis still contribute to the consolidation of modern culture through the propagation of the scientific value system? Almost 400 years ago, in his "Novum Organum," Francis Bacon observed, "By far the greatest obstacle to the progress of science and to the undertaking of new tasks and provinces therein, is found in this – that men despair and think things impossible." We must not despair. It may still be possible to fulfill the hope that psychoanalysis will enable mankind to achieve a new triumph of humanism.

REFERENCES

Dewald, P. (1981). Revision: yes. Improvement: no. *Psychoanal. Inq., 1.*

Eissler, K. (1965). *Medical orthodoxy and the future of psychoanalysis.* New York: International Universities Press.

Erle, J. (1979). An approach to the study of analyzability and analyses: The course of forty consecutive cases selected for supervised analysis. *Psychoanal. Quart., 48.*

Firestein, S. (1978). *Termination in psychoanalysis.* New York: International Universities Press.

Freud, S. (1918). From the history of an infantile neurosis. *Standard Edition, 17.* London: Hogarth Press, 1955.

Freud, S. (1927). The future of an illusion. *Standard Edition, 21.* London: Hogarth Press, 1961.

Freud, S. (1930). Civilization and its discontents. *Standard Edition, 21.* London: Hogarth Press, 1961.

Friedman, L. (1988). *The anatomy of psychotherapy.* Hillsdale, NJ: Analytic Press.

Gedo, J. (1979). *Beyond interpretation.* Hillsdale, NJ: Analytic Press, rev. ed. 1993.

Gedo, J. (1981). *Advances in clinical psychoanalysis.* New York: International Universities Press.

Gedo, J. (1983). *Portraits of the artist.* Hillsdale, NJ: Analytic Press, 1989.

Gedo, J. (1984). *Psychoanalysis and its discontents.* New York: Guilford.

Gedo, J. (1988). *The mind in disorder.* Hillsdale, NJ: Analytic Press.

Gedo, J. (1991). *The biology of clinical encounters.* Hillsdale, NJ: Analytic Press.

Gedo, J., & Gehrie, M. (1993). *Impasse and innovation in psychoanalysis.* Hillsdale, NJ: Analytic Press.

Gedo, J., & Goldberg, A. (1973). *Models of the mind.* Chicago: University of Chicago Press.

Kantrowitz, J. (1987). Suitability for psychoanalysis. *Yearbook of Psychoanalytic Psychotherapy, 2.* New York: Guilford.

Kantrowitz, J., Katz, A., & Paolitto, F. (1990). Follow-up of psychoanalysis five to ten years after termination: I. Stability of change. *J. Amer. Psychoanal. Assoc., 38.*

Kohut, H. (1984). *How does analysis cure?* Ed. A. Goldberg and P. Stepansky. Chicago: University of Chicago Press.

Martin, J. (1984). The fictive personality. *The Annual of Psychoanalysis, 12.* New York: International Universities Press.

Rieff, P. (1959). *Freud: The mind of the moralist.* New York: Viking.

Rieff, P. (1966). *The triumph of the therapeutic.* New York: Harper & Row.

Schlessinger, N., & Robbins, F. (1983). *A developmental view of the psychoanalytic process.* New York: International Universities Press.

Waelder, R. (1960). *Basic theory of psychoanalysis.* New York: International Universities Press.

A Mark of Decline
The Abuse of Language
in Psychoanalysis and Psychotherapy

Robert J. Stoller

When this was written, Robert J. Stoller was Professor of
Psychiatry, Department of Psychiatry, School of Medicine,
University of California, Los Angeles.

An honest tale speeds best plainly told.

SHAKESPEARE

Humpty Dumpty found the easiest way:
words meant whatever he decided!
The history of psychoanalysis is strewn
with broken eggshells.

S.DES.

This part of the introduction is concerned not with semantics or style but with fundamental problems that reach the very heart of the deep malaise affecting psychoanalysis and psychotherapy.

Originally I thought I would have to write about these matters myself. Later I came across the writings of Robert Stoller and Nathan Leites. No one could have addressed these issues more inclusively and intelligently than those two men. Their criticisms are constructive and indicate necessary remedies.

These criticisms first appeared in 1971. Despite their exceptional significance, they were received in silence, except for a few acknowledgments that the profession should redeem itself in the future. Nothing has changed, however, and the situation discussed by Drs. Stoller and Leites has continued to deteriorate. On the basis of their previous work, we asked them each to contribute to the introduction to this volume. Unfortunately, we cannot include Nathan Leites's contribution here.

When dealing with matters of the unconscious, we must insist on the use of clear and relevant language in all writings, theoretical and clinical. We must not tolerate any facile obscurantism, achieved by aping the terminology and image of science. Only then can clinical work, thought, and writing be meaningful. We will continue to investigate those matters in great detail in Part I.

A barren superfluity of words.

SAMUEL GARTH

The man who thinks clearly, writes clearly.

BOILEAU

I greatly welcome this opportunity to express, once more, my thinking on a matter of primary concern to me.

If this introduction frightens psychoanalysts, as it should, psychoanalysis could be refreshed, something it badly needs.

Although most analysts are deeply concerned about the present state of analysis, they hope that the tree itself, still growing vigorously, can be properly shaped by trimming and pruning a piece of theory here and there. This pruning, it is suggested, should take the form of improving procedures for selecting candidates, improving the atmosphere in which training analysis proceeds, improving the curriculum, getting psychoanalysis more into the community (or out of it), improving techniques of graduate education so that more members will participate, changing criteria for membership in analytic associations (or holding the line against such changes), improving public relations (possibly even by keeping watch over what is said in public media about psychoanalysis), modifying theory (ego theory, for example, or Kleinian concepts), and even modifying technique (or fighting to prevent modifications). Behind these suggestions lies the belief that the issues, while real enough, are irritants on a fundamentally sound science.

Other analysts, who do not believe all is so sound, feel analysis has been wounded from outside – that society, as it changes, is unwilling to live in the heady atmosphere of truth required of the person committed to analysis; or else they suffer a gentle sadness and forbearance, most gratifying of pains, as they contemplate the inability of others to recognize the truths of psychoanalysis. At worst, it is said, it is the sick or villainous who wound us. But only if we band together, confident in the goodness of our intentions, can we hand our torch to the select of the future.

Agreeing with the foregoing (including even the incompatible opposites), I disagree, believing that none fully accounts for the trouble psychoanalysis is in. I think that the trouble is our trouble, the sickness our sickness, and that the return to health will not come by modifying society or our position within it, by modifying our educational methods, or by further distilling our theory.

If the problem is really ours, not the problem of those outside, the task of debriding psychoanalysis will be difficult and painful, as is the shifting of character structure in our patients. Here, too, the voice of reality will have to be strengthened in the psychic functioning of this rationalizing, intellectualizing, brilliant, imaginative, and creative patient – who does have a good prognosis if not permitted to think he can analyze himself, or worse, permitted to insist there is nothing so askew as to require fundamental treatment.

The first step in this reformation could be confrontation, wherein we are forced to look at and beyond the rationalizations, denials, and fantasies that "improve on" reality – where we are shown what we really are doing.

Few professionals have the expertise to detect, and the courage to critically dissect, hollow theorizing and faulty clinical observations and conclusions. While in this volume Stefan de Schill applies his remarkable clinical acumen to such a task, Nathan Leites takes quite a different approach: his logic is the scalpel with which he dissects the language of the theoreticians. Leites does this as it has never been done before. He does it not by bringing new data or theory to psychoanalysis, but by simply, insistently, maddeningly, relentlessly arguing for the application of good sense to psychoanalytic thinking. Leites yearns for clarity above all else; he does not complain because the findings of psychoanalysis are incomplete, the treatment techniques still being discovered, or its theory unfinished. What pains him is that analysts do not say what they think, or worse, do not know what they think.

Most of us know that psychoanalysis was founded and still founds itself daily on observation. While this is the core of an optimism for the future of psychoanalysis as theory and practice, as research tool and contributor to an understanding of man's psychology, this optimism is minuscule as compared with that of analysts who say that psychoanalysis is now a science. They may believe so because, valuing science, they would like to be scientists; or because of some inflated idea that every psychoanalysis is an experiment; or because consensual psychoanalysis is an unrelenting search for precise observations as uncontaminated as possible by bias or faulty methodology. I believe it is especially the last that gives the sense of conviction that one is a scientist if an analyst.

Why are analysts so damned insistent on being considered scientists? Artists do not claim to be, and yet their careers are honorable. They stir us, cure our pain, and, on occasion, overturn history. All that should be satisfying, but not for us analysts. What we must be, apparently, is scientists. I believe this means that we would rather be right than good.

And that is the essence of science: to be accurate (right). A field becomes a science when it develops techniques that have feedback mechanisms to guarantee an ever-increasing accuracy. Those well-known thoughts apply to the ideal of analysts – but not to their performance so far. What troubles me is that, while analysts idealize precise observation, predictability, control of variables, sharing of data with others to rule out misperceptions and misinterpretations, laboratories for the creation of models, and methods for correcting defects, none of these exists in psychoanalysis. More than that, the analyst not only seems to miss them but, when an attempt is made to introduce them, is apt to feel that they are unnecessary – or even harmful – to his "science."

One has to be careful, of course. Science is not a terminus at which one arrives, but a process moving toward infinity. Each of the sciences has shaped itself in the past with the criteria just mentioned, only to find itself in a tighter and tighter bind of orthodoxy in which only the known was proved, so that there was no way out except by an "unscientific" explosion of intuition (Kuhn, Koestler). So, thank you, but I know already that science is not an absolute. That is still no excuse for saying that anything we choose to call a science is one because it shares with science the quality of "tentativeness." Not even good intentions make a field a science. Fenichel's (1945) phrase in this regard is just right: "By opposing the idea that 'mind is brain' and by emphasizing strongly the existence of the mental spheres *and the inadequacy of physical and scientific methods to deal with it, he* (Freud) *won this terrain for science.*" That is right: he won the terrain for science. But it still has to be populated by science. *Of course, whether one labels psychoanalysis a science or not has no importance.* The purpose of this discussion is not to apply a label but to get at what should underlie it: are the methods of inquiry now favored by psychoanalysis likely to lead to the answers to our questions?

No field accepted as a science

1.   has such a high amount of reference to authority to bolster an argument
2.   can demonstrate so little of its data to others
3.   has a higher ratio of theory to observation
4.   prefers as much to refine concepts by reference to other concepts rather than by observations
5.   uses metaphor and analogy so profusely
6.   has such disagreement among peers about so many key words
7.   strings together to such an extent one unproved statement after another, using devices such as "it seems," "probably," and the like to arrive at a conclusion worded with the same assurance one would use if one had strung together a series of demonstrable facts to arrive at a new conclusion
8.   has such a lag in publication (proving that what is "new" is not new enough to cause editors to rush).

The *psychoanalytic writer is an essayist, not a scientist*; there are few scientific papers in the literature, but many, many essays.

We all agree that at the beginning of the process called science is precise observation; yet we also agree that observation must be refined and synthesized, for it is blind without concepts that unify and focus. Conceptualization has the power to improve observation and prediction, but it fatally attracts intellects to exalt their concepts and so distorts their vision, that is, to propagandize. This is too often true of some analysts, who, with only minimal data, attempt to soar, powered by theory alone. The speed with which some leave observations behind and begin theorizing can be so fast that one suspects that, with an extreme of efficiency, facts would become completely superfluous.

The temptation to theorize without data is increased by the privacy and trust without which analytic treatment cannot proceed. As a result, no analyst has ever reported what he observed, nor has anyone else seen it. What science can make *that* claim? This is not our fault.

What is our fault is that so many of us do not admit to regretting it. Some have argued cutely that in astronomy and theoretical physics one also cannot observe or experiment directly; but that is about all that psychoanalysis and such fields have in common, for the latter have been much more intent on precision about *whatever* evidence is required in any given case than analysis has been. To act in science is to be implacably oriented to returning to events, perhaps not right away but after a measured span of indirection. There is no such adamant drive in the psychoanalytic credo. (There was in Freud.)

Might there not be something wrong if, after 40 or more years of labor on ego psychology, there are no accepted definitions of such words as ego, ego functions, self, self-representation, identity, ego identity, self-identity – no way to know precisely which properties in the real world (i.e., behavior) an author has in mind when he uses one of these words? That there were problems in definition when ego psychology moved into focus 40 years ago was fine. That these problems are still unsolved – for all the back-slapping about advances in theory – indicates disorder.

Our marvelous pneumatic vocabulary; reading the psychoanalytic literature is like reading art criticism. If an author uses these words, will you know what he is talking about? – *libido, narcissism, cathexis, internalization, instinct, active, passive, neutralization, psychosis, neurosis, acting out, identity, ego identity, self-identity, ego adaptation, aggression, fixation, homosexuality, conscious, unconscious, countertransference, incorporation, phallic phase, fetish, psychic apparatus, masochism, introjection, insight, hysteria, identification, projection, bisexuality, psychic energy, castration anxiety, instinctual drive, drive, need, sexuality, sexualization, self, self-image, self-representation,* and even *psychoanalysis.* These terms are our "science," and in some manner they refer to events in reality. They are terribly important, for they grope to make sense of the most complicated of realities, psychic functioning. My point is not that it is useless to develop a technical vocabulary but, rather, that the way this vocabulary develops is leading us to "mythology disguised as reporting."

Astonishingly, on one hand, analysts declare they do not agree on the meanings of these words, and on the other, they continue to use them. To accept such a vocabulary is to walk on water. One wants to cry out, as Moses does in the joke when St. Peter, thinking to imitate him, steps on the waves and sinks: "Fool! Step on the stones."

What kind of business is it where a worker can build his reputation on inventing a word or redefining an old one?

Where would we be without "cathexis," "psychic energy," "libido"; suppose each author were forced, at the point where he would have used such a concept, to use instead simple descriptive words, immediately related to the events for which the Greek or Latin is applied? Why did psychoanalysis ever think that writing in the erudite style adds substance to one's thoughts? Yes, most ideas are more acceptable when made decorative, as in poetry, where ideas are often subordinate to style and beauty. In addition, psychoanalysis, like all of psychology, is the child of philosophy and, rather old-fashioned, still prefers stately ponderousness ("sentences of large scope and low cost") to modest clarity. Some analysts seem to believe that portentousness demonstrates profundity, objectivity, and scientific attitude. How else can one explain the universal habit among analysts of talking about "the" mother and "the" father when the clinical data being reported would justify saying "his" mother and "his" father? Let us hear what Leites has to say about that:

> In contemporary psychoanalytic thought, words often do not function as they do in the sciences, namely, as vehicles to designate events. Psychoanalytic writers frequently employ words as though to obscure their meaning. Sometimes writers use esoteric words as though their meanings were self-evident or as if a word had a standard meaning of which only nonspecialists would be ignorant. Or a writer may offer an obviously incomplete definition that applies to another word not meant to be a synonym of the first; by keeping a word's definition implicit, the writer can easily adopt a definition that is quite different from the word's ordinary usage and then violate it. A writer may prefer an uncertain definition. Some writers use highly charged words inappropriately because those words are more easily accessible than is real insight. Other writers may consider a multiplicity of definitions for the same word. After all, the

word is so important that it must have many meanings! Similarly, one expects an important event to be designated by several words, which may then diverge into other usages.

It then comes to be taken as normal that one cannot be sure what a colleague means when he uses the words of our common language.

As if they were events, words may be thought of as inexhaustible targets of exploration. A precious word will be a home for many things, will be rich in facets. When a writer proposes that a wide variety of phenomena be called by the same word, he apparently assumes that they all share a property, yet what that is may not be obvious or specified. With a large word, I can glide from one sector of its vast referent to another and envisage something different from what my colleagues see; then, perhaps, I can engage in exciting, riskless, and indecisive combat with them.

I am not alone in admiring Leites. Ralph J. Greenson wrote:

> The writings of Nathan Leites are evidence of his excellent grasp of psychoanalytic theory and literature. The keenness of his mind, the rigor of his thinking, his impeccable logic, are wonderful tools for uncovering inconsistencies, redundancies, and errors in psychoanalytic thought. He is not afraid to subject the most prestigious and influential contributors in psychoanalysis to his microscopic scrutiny. He insists upon psychoanalytic theory's being cogent, logical, and stripped of all pretentious nonessentials.
>
> Dr. Leites is not easy to read, but if one is seriously interested in clarifying basic psychoanalytic concepts, his critical examination provides the best approach available.

Leites's insistence on clarity and precision in psychoanalytic thought and writing extended over a period of many years. A few months before his recent death, I asked him what had been the impact of his efforts. His answer was clear and precise: "None!"

The inexorable conversion of hunch to hypothesis to theory to law to "concrete observation" is frightening. If only the words would stay

put and concept remain concept. That they all too often do not contributes to the odd atmosphere one sometimes senses when reading at
the highest level of psychoanalytic thinking. (We could as well be talking now of anthropologists, historians, sociologists, political scientists,
and others. But of course we shall not.)

Too frequently, an analytic author strings together what he
believes to be one proven law after another, while I get the impression
that each affirmation, so taken for granted by the author, is really the
title of an experiment yet to be performed, any one of which would be
a revolutionary contribution to the world of science if only it could be
demonstrated. When these run one upon the other without hesitation
or uncertainty, the effect is deafening. Take the following:

> The first form of anxiety is of a persecutory nature. The
> working of the death instinct within – which, according to
> Freud, is directed against the organism – gives rise to the
> fear of annihilation, and this is the primordial cause of per-
> secutory anxiety.
>
> Furthermore, from the beginning of postnatal life (I
> am not concerned here with prenatal processes), destructive
> impulses against the object stir up fear of retaliation. These
> persecutory feelings from inner sources are intensified by
> painful external experiences, for, from the earliest days
> onward, frustration and discomfort arouse in the infant the
> feeling that he is being attacked by hostile forces. Therefore
> the sensations experienced by the infant at birth and the
> difficulties of adapting himself to entirely new conditions
> give rise to persecutory anxiety. The comfort and care given
> after birth, particularly the first feeding experiences, are felt
> to come from good forces. In speaking of "forces" I am using
> a rather adult word, for what the young infant dimly con-
> ceives of as objects, either good or bad. The infant directs his
> feeling of gratification and love toward the "good" breast
> and his destructive impulses and feelings of persecution
> toward what he feels to be frustrating, i.e., the "bad" breast.
>
> At this stage, splitting processes are at their height,
> and love and hatred as well as the good and bad aspects of

the breast are largely kept apart from one another. The infant's relative security is based on turning the good object into an ideal one as a protection against the dangerous and persecuting object. These processes – that is to say splitting, denial, omnipotence, and idealization – are prevalent during the first three to four months of life.

One usually can see clinical data behind the jargon but is never sure just what the observations are. Granted, it is impossible to reproduce any moment of a psychoanalytic hour. Still, that is our problem, and if we do not solve it, we remain outside of science, and our statements, no matter how positively phrased, can be accepted by others only as possibilities, not as laws. When we listen to a patient, the slightest inflection, pronunciation, hesitation, drawing in of breath, or even shift of a finger can change a meaning. *These* are our observations, and in being reported, they are susceptible to our distortions. We all know this, and it should make us modest.

Unashamed theorizing is an occupational hazard of psychoanalysts. Perhaps our practicing in the midst of fantasies and wishes must be balanced by "noble" thoughts. Perhaps our practicing in the midst of bewildering detail makes us yearn to leave this disorder for theory that reduces the confusion. And yet, as we create such theory in words of seeming clarity (which, however, are secretly known to be vague), our language will permit the infiltration of hidden wishes. Perhaps we ease the strain of refraining from – and yet still immersing ourselves in – our patients' infantile drives by replacing daytime deprivation with evening indulgence. Not that this indulgence is as instinctual as what our patients would get us into, but nonetheless, we may feel a right to omnipotent speculation after a day's work at renunciation.

In the daytime practice, one is aware of the limitations of his powers, but at night he can regain his magnificence. By day, he is at times silent in his creative puzzlement, humbly subordinated to his patient's facts; at night he becomes lord of concepts. By day, he swims, resisting the undertow from the patient, which can endanger the analysis; at night, with his theory, he is back on shore.

The daytime analyst is humble; the nighttime writer, grandiose. The daytime analyst is attacked; the nighttime theorist, the attacker.

Pressure built up in the daytime is released at night. If one had to be as scrupulously skeptical at night as he is during the day, he would have to be his own attacker, and one needs relief from that. In our practice we try very hard to say what needs to be said exactly right so that our patients can comprehend and not be bullied into agreeing. If only the same care were taken in developing theory as in making just the right interpretation.

At this point we again differ from the true sciences: the distance between the narcissism of the first creative thought and the demonstration of the validity of the general rule is far greater there. In true science the creative moment may occur in the same way as in psychoanalysis, but thereafter the rules of the game are different: in the sciences after one makes his claim, he states what can be done to prove the claim wrong so that the theory can be related to evidence. Then a decent interval of time passes in which the test is made, and all the world can see if the theory has withstood the test.

I think a rivalry has existed between writers and psychoanalysts, the result of their arriving at similar insights by both similar and different techniques. Both use observations of the external world shaped by introspection, but each uses different language to report his findings. I am biased and think the writers (the good ones) tend to do better. Novelists, poets, and essayists will throw away in a phrase an insight over which we sweat for a whole paper, if not a book. And for all our pomposity about communicating, the writer is clearer, briefer, simpler, and no less profound. Not only that, he reaches us; our own discussions rarely do. Even when correct, we are tedious.

If we refrain from excessive intellectualization, we can commit ourselves more heavily to observations – not only to making them but to developing better techniques for communicating them to others for verification and to being able to judge better others' reports of data. Gardner Lindsay is worth quoting in this respect:

> There is only a tiny quantity of research existing today that is directly relevant to the theory [psychoanalytic] and is considered of reasonable merit by trained investigator and clinician alike. True, there is a considerable bulk of "psychoanalytic research" but it consists largely of delimited,

semi-experimental studies that are frequently so remote from the operations implied by psychoanalytic theory as to strain the credulity of the most sympathetic reader. . . . Or else the research consists of clinical reports or observational accounts that are faithful to the theory and its implied method, but are accompanied by so many empirical flaws as to provide evidence only for the devotee. . . .

Formal problems within the psychoanalytic theory are many and manifest. The investigator who wishes to use psychoanalytic theory as a proposition mill to grind out empirical predictions is destined not only to encounter little encouragement from his peers and a maximum of frustration from the slippery world of reality, but also to find little solace in the theory itself. The absence of a clear and explicit axiomatic base, the scarcity of adequate empirical definitions, the ever-abundant surplus meaning, the metaphorical excursions, and the almost nonexistent syntax – all of these could be explored at length. Their presence, however, is undeniable. Almost no one would deny that the theory at present is in a very crude state of development and looks scarcely at all like any theory we would hope to possess eventually. Indeed Nagel, distinguished philosopher of science, was recently moved to characterize psychoanalytic theory in the following terms: "The theory is stated in language so vague and metaphorical that almost anything appears to be compatible with it. . . . In short, Freudian formulations seem to me to have so much 'open texture,' to be so loose in statement, that while they are unquestionably suggestive, it is well-nigh impossible to decide whether what is thus suggested is genuinely implied by the theory or whether it is related to the latter only by the circumstance that someone happens to associate one with the other."

It seems to me that revision of the theory at present can be justified by results secured within the "context of confirmation" rather than the "context of discovery," and this implies empirical control, experimentation, statistical analysis, and other tools of analytic reasoning.

It is a lamentable fact that the distinction between competent observation and controlled experimentation is seldom appreciated by those working within a psychoanalytic framework. Freud himself never appreciated the difference.

Each time clear-cut observations are introduced into the argument, the effect is profound. To be sure, given observations will usually not resolve all arguments for which they are pertinent; multiple interpretations will still be possible. But these then call for further observations to decide among them, and even if it is not immediately feasible to make them, orienting oneself on them confers a new quality on theory. It is exhausting to think that we are still fussing about this.

An example: For how long has the discussion of the development of female sexuality been turning round and round, in and upon itself? And what strange assertions have sprung from the minds of male psychoanalysts regarding what is happening in the anatomy and physiology of that most feminine experience, a woman's sexual excitement. (What had to happen supposedly happened because theory demanded it, not life.) Not only did none of us collect data on female sexual excitement as Masters and Johnson did; but we rarely admitted that our assertions left unclear which observations could decide the issues. In contrast, while the relationship between female genital excitement and mature femininity is not settled by the work of Masters and Johnson, their research has produced a shift in the level of the discourse; beliefs have become questions that are now open to study.

Likewise the work of Mahler and others in observing infants. How can we have believed that we could *know* what went on in a particular mother-infant relationship if our information came from the history gradually revealed in an analysis and the myriad expressions of the transference manifested by this now adult patient, removed from those events by so many years and so many defenses? We really thought that we were magicians, that the ordinary procedures of science were unnecessary for us. Could we be so astute, so imaginative, so blessed by the gods that we could not only make out the dim outlines of the mother-infant or father-infant but could build substantial theories of growth and development without minute observations of parents and their infants?

Once again, we do not yet have many answers, but once again we can be hopeful because we are developing procedures that will make available, not simply more speculation, but answers, approximations.

Of course, not everything will be answered; of course, many theoretical questions will be left uncertain; of course, we will freeze this new methodology and its implications into a new orthodoxy that others will have to break open. But whatever may make the future of psychoanalysis viable, we will now have access to the findings and even the theories of nonanalytic workers.

Leites suggests that Hartmann did this years ago by permitting the obvious to become acceptable to psychoanalytic theoreticians. "One may proclaim truths that common sense has presumably never doubted, but that were (as a rule, implicitly) denied when analysis was young. One may do so without either recalling the earlier denials or what has made for their cessation: the arrival of evidence or the onset of sobriety." And I wonder, how often has one read in an analytic paper, "I was wrong" or "I made a mistake"? That Freud did so has become more a matter of deification than identification. While that thought is saddening, one can just as well say that the resistance of psychoanalysts is no more severe than that of any other committed group and that, sooner or later, we will accept anything, even the obvious.

For example, Rapaport says of Hartmann's epochal Ego Psychology and the Problem of Adaptation:

> The concept of "conflict-free ego-sphere" is perhaps Hartmann's most important single contribution among the many in this rich and sweeping paper. This concept actually condenses two ideas: (*a*) ego-development has conflict-free as well as conflictual sources; (*b*) though any of these conflict-free sources, and any of their maturational products, may at various times become involved in conflict, they form the nucleus of that group of structures and functions within the ego which is at any given time "conflict-free."

The influence of that monograph on subsequent psychoanalytic history has been perhaps more important than that of any other single work in the last 50 years: Hartmann shifted the course of psychoanalysis.

Yet even in 1939, psychologists might have shrugged at such an announcement, for, using a different language but *the same observations,* they had long known these two ideas and felt hurt that analytic writings ignored their work.

My purpose is not to defend academic psychologists; that would be presumptuous. Besides, I do not wish to; their obstinate refusal to recognize the role of conflict and unconscious fantasy is a historic blunder easily as fascinating as, and by an order of magnitude more stultifying than, our not taking account of nonconflictual forces sooner.

As to why it took 40 years after THE INTERPRETATION OF DREAMS before a major work would open psychoanalysis up to "the obvious," here is Hartmann:

> The close connection between theory and therapeutic technique, so characteristic of psychoanalysis, explains why the ego functions directly involved in the *conflicts* between mental institutions commanded our interests earlier than others. It also explains why other ego functions and the process of coming to terms with the environment – except for a few pertinent problems which played a role in psychoanalysis from the beginning – did not become the subject matter of research until a later stage of our science. Psychoanalytic observation has frequently come upon facts and considerations related to these other ego functions, but rarely subjected them to detailed study and theoretical reflection. I believe it is an empirical fact that these functions are less decisive for the understanding and treatment of pathology – on which psychoanalytic interest has been centered so far – than the psychology of the conflicts which are at the root of every neurosis. I am not inclined, however, to underestimate the clinical importance of these functions, though here I shall deal mainly with their theoretical significance, and even with that from only a single point of view. We must recognize that though the ego certainly does grow on conflicts, these are not the only roots of ego development. Many of us expect psychoanalysis to become a general *developmental psychology*: to do so, it must encompass these other

roots of ego development, by reanalyzing from its own point of view and with its own methods the results obtained in these areas by nonanalytic psychology. This naturally gives new importance to the direct observation of developmental processes by psychoanalysts (first of all the direct observation of children).

The last two sentences are especially gratifying, but in the years that have passed since this monograph was written, very few of "these other roots of ego development" have been encompassed in the heralded general developmental psychology; in fact, the resistance of psychoanalysts to such "encompassing" has been fractious indeed.

Freud and the early analysts had to establish their radical findings and defend them against the brutal simplicities of the philosophers and academic psychologists.

While studying learning theory, I have found that essential aspects of the development of masculinity and femininity cannot be accounted for only by considering conflict, the permutations of anxiety (especially castration anxiety), and the issues surrounding the oedipal conflict and its resolution. There is no question that the latter, with which we are familiar from our patients, shape the final forms that masculinity and femininity take. Yet I was surprised that some of the earliest and most fixed gender qualities (for instance, the sense of maleness or femaleness) can be established in a nonpainful, nonconflictual manner. Still, not having good enough data, I am forced to manage primarily by means of theory and so am struggling to decide to what extent these processes might be viewed from the perspective of learning theorists. There are extensive data showing that masculine and feminine behavior can be powerfully and permanently influenced by parents' attitudes "shaping" or "moulding," that is, by parents' reinforcing certain behavior with high rewards. (We already know that the business of "positive and negative reinforcement" is permanently memorialized in the identifications and other fixed modes of function that we call the superego.)

We need not consider these issues, which have been important to psychologists for the last half-century or more, superficial any longer. It is not that the academic psychologists' studies were inadequate, though how pathetic that these workers could not include *fantasy* as a variable in their theories. That is their problem. I am concerned with ours: we have failed to the extent that we did not absorb nonanalysts' studies of nonconflictual sources of personality development. Although it was necessary early in analysis to concentrate on the unconscious and on the id, and although a study of the history of psychoanalysis can make us understand the motives for that concentration, that does not mean it was not a mistake. Happily, we need not be in a hurry; it is impressive enough that once the first discoveries were consolidated, Freud could move more and more to study the surfaces of the mind (surfaces are not necessarily superficial, except in geometry). *But, still, one may complain that 70 or more years is a long time to wait for "the ultimate conquest of the obvious."*

Our drifting in dispirited theory could be ending. The willingness to generalize to laws of nature from a few observations is less likely now to give one the feeling of sailing with an acrobat's grace. *It is not satisfying to be fleeced by a theory that purports to explain most things.* We may be forever limited in what we understand; we may never know precisely what goes on inside an infant's psyche. *But it will be a relief to mark out our limitations.* If not, we shall continue fruitless arguments, for instance, about whether infants at three months have fully formed fantasies, as the Kleinians insist, or whether infants are incapable of such fantasies, as the rest of us insist, both groups not only without proof but also – and *this* is a graver matter – without techniques to get proof.

If psychoanalysis is a science, it must furnish instructions on how to prove or disprove propositions. Try this:

I keep seeing how much we take for granted, how many undemonstrated affirmations are compacted along with data in our analytic vocabulary, how I do not know if Hartmann, for instance, means the same as I think he does.

Another example:

> Let us now consider more closely the relation of the function of thinking, the foremost representative of the internalization process to the tasks of adaptation, synthesis, and differentiation. In this connection we will have to disregard much that we know about thinking, for

instance, its being energized by desexualized libido, its conjectured relation to the death instinct, its role as helper (rationalization) or opponent of the id, its dependence on the cathectic conditions, its facilitation or inhibition by superego and by drive – and affect – processes, and so on.

Hartmann says we *know* these crucial things about thinking. But, please. Wait.

Suppose, for instance, one takes the position that he does not know yet that thinking is energized by desexualized libido; he requests the data that others know so that he too can know. Suppose one says he has never been shown any part of the real world that can be measured, or even merely made manifest for a flickering moment, that energizes thinking (except carbohydrates, enzymes, and the like – and they are no more libido than they are death instinct). Suppose one says that he cannot grasp what form desexualized libido would take in the real world so that it demonstrated its existence. (Electricity is still a mystery to us; we do not know what it is, but the lights go on when the current – whatever that is – flows – whatever that is.)

Suppose one says that even if there were a "thing" called libido, he cannot imagine either the nature of the process "to desexualize" or in what form a product of that process would materialize.

(John 20:29. "Jesus saith unto him, Thomas, because thou hast seen me, thou hast believed: blessed are they that have not seen, and yet have believed.")

It simply is silly to disregard such questions *by reference to authorities* with whom you agree but who also do not know the answers, or by dismissing the questioner, or by suggesting that someone else at some future time will take care of the grubby details of demonstration.

Yet most analysts, in vibrant self-satisfaction, would agree with Rapaport, who says, "Dr. Hartmann's work demonstrates . . . a cardinal requirement of the scientific method . . . namely his unswerving insistence upon precision in methodology, and upon logical consistency in theory." When inside the system, one may not even know there is a set of rules. Inside the system there seems to be no system, and one feels he is free.

How will we, then, accept at face value a statement about some fundamental aspect of human psychology, when it is reported that "this paper is based on experience gained from the more or less profound analysis of X cases," when the author cannot help but leave us unclear about what is the analysis practiced moment by moment in the unique situation of that analyst's personality and that patient's personality; and what do we do about the "more or less profound," since lack of profundity (incompleteness) is the argument each of us can throw at the other in order to discredit the other's observations and conclusions? Or, another typical psychoanalytic comment:

> There is, I believe, no clinical observation to confute the idea that the intensity with which a child is desired is entirely dependent on the intensity of the preceding wish for a penis; therefore, one may say that the stronger the wish to have a penis, the stronger will be the subsequent wish to have a child; and the more difficult it is to bear being denied a penis, the more aggression there will be in the reaction to the thwarting of the wish for a child. Thus arises a vicious circle that often obscures the state of affairs for analysts; we find repeatedly that the very women whose violent psychic conflict was occasioned by the castration complex (i.e., by penis envy) are the ones who also have an ardent feminine wish for a child.
>
> There is no question about it: after the revolution things will be duller.

Once we are in principle dedicated to observation, we shall be in less danger from the single case study. The single analytic case is probably the most powerful source of original ideas in the history of psychology. *Unfortunately, in psychoanalysis the excitement generated is not always tempered by our seeking confirmation from enough other cases.* It depends, to be sure, on the nature of the conclusion drawn (e.g., Columbus discovering America). For certain conclusions, one need find only one occurrence for it to be validated, but other judgments require more. (Thus, to say that X may be found without a specific hereditary cause, one needs only one set of identical twins, one who has X, the other who

does not, both biologically identical in those factors essentially related to
X.) Since by now we have enough theory to explain any finding, we are
in special danger if we do not confirm an impression with other data.

For instance, in my research, the first boy studied in depth had a rare
condition (childhood transsexualism) but was found to be extremely active
and fearless. We were all struck by this finding, and we attempted, successfully, to explain it by theories already developed regarding the special
mother-infant relationship found in boyhood transsexualism. The finding
was fascinating, its fit with theory gratifying. The second such boy had the
same trait, and so we were even more pleased.

The next 10 failed to show it.

We just must restrain our enthusiasm and wait for those next 10
or 1,000 or however many the statisticians tell us are necessary for a
sense of conviction to be transformed into the validity of assertion. On
the other hand, there are very few discoveries indeed in human psychology that have been made by statistical techniques; on the record so
far, their generative power is low. Still these techniques do act as a marvelous conscience.

But as galling as is the habit of generalizing from the single case,
it hurts even more to realize that once a psychoanalyst has learned his
theory well, he need never see another patient and yet will hardly be
at a disadvantage with his colleagues in using the theory or in creating
new theory. Theory is now a perpetual motion machine.

What psychoanalysis needs is a good editor.

REFERENCE

Fenichel, O. (1945). *Problems of psychoanalytic technique*. New York: Norton.

PART I

THE RESURRECTION OF PSYCHOTHERAPY

The three basic factors in daily existence are utterly incomprehensible to us: time, because it is eternal; space, because it is infinite; and our consciousness, because it defies all explanation.

S.DES.

WORKING TOWARD CLINICAL EXPERTISE

Dull is he of soul
to pass by a thing of majesty.

WORDSWORTH

STATEMENTS TO MARVEL AT:

There are no homeless people in New York!
MAYOR ED KOCH
PRESS INTERVIEW, BUDAPEST, 1988

This boy will never amount to anything!
FREUD'S FATHER

There was no holocaust!

Dreams have no meaning!
FOR NAMES, SEE CHAPTER

In the foreword and introduction to this volume renowned psycho-analysts, with extensive experience and knowledge of present-day psychoanalytic affairs and literature, expressed their concern. Their descriptions of serious problems that are increasingly crippling psychoanalysis and psychotherapy provide a basis for understanding this section and place it in its proper context.

For those of us who consider the potential of psychodynamic therapy to be unquestionable and who seek its further development, the present stagnating trends, and their underlying causes, are distressing and, indeed, unacceptable. For that reason, the first part of this chapter critically examines the writings of well-known professionals on the fundamental aspects of treatment, enabling the reader to understand their views and abilities.

Essentially, psychotherapy endeavors to understand and change the emotional forces within an individual. Dreams are a manifestation of feelings; the two are inextricably linked. To understand fully a patient's feelings, and to see them in the proper perspective, we need his dreams. To comprehend his dreams, we need his feelings.

Many professionals who consider that focusing on feelings and dreams is a tool of primary importance in psychotherapy agree that it is in that area that the failings of a psychotherapist become readily apparent. As part of our examination of fundamental and pervasive deficiencies in the profession, in this chapter we will give considerable attention to that area.

Other basic topics in psychotherapy are also scrutinized here, and ample material unrelated to dreams is presented in an attempt to evaluate the present status of psychoanalysis and psychotherapy.

In this chapter, of necessity, many examples of ignorance and pretense by widely acclaimed authors in the field of psychotherapy are offered. The examples demonstrate what we must avoid and what is false. It is not important that the American reader may not recognize the European writers, and the European reader may not recognize the

American writers. What is important is that the examples demonstrate what is wrong.

At present, although our best experts are well able to recognize fallacies and shortcomings, our knowledge of what is valuable and effective is still limited. A large area necessary for the understanding of the human mind and the unconscious remains open for exploration and experimentation.

As we gain enlightenment step by step, we increase our ability to develop more effective psychotherapeutic procedures. In this chapter I point out facts and factors that indicate avenues to be explored.

In writing about psychotherapy, one would ordinarily organize the subjects in a sequence dictated by one's own perspective. The structure of this chapter, however, is a compromise. The order of the subjects is based to a large extent on the requirements of our examination of professional shortcomings. That study had to precede our efforts to correct present problems and propose viable solutions. When examining those deficiencies, the attempt is made, in each instance, to contrast the problems described with a more productive clinical approach.

Regrettably, the repetition of certain statements appears unavoidable. The assertions of quite a number of the authors examined here are misleading and even harmful to psychotherapeutic practice and teaching. That needs to be pointed out whenever it occurs. At any rate, beauty of prose is not within the compass of this writer, and thus the additional affront to elegance of style will be of slight consequence.

A. FROM THE CLINICAL VIEWPOINT: SHORTCOMINGS IN PSYCHOTHERAPY

Dream interpretation before Freud was far from perfect, witness this quote from the Bible (Daniel 2):

Now in the second year of the reign of Nebuchadnezzar, Nebuchadnezzar had dreams; and his spirit was troubled and his sleep left him.

The king gave orders to call in the Chaldeans, to tell the king his dreams. So they came in and stood before the king.

And the king said to them, "I had a dream, and my spirit is anxious to understand the dream."

Then the Chaldeans spoke to the king in Aramaic: "O king, live forever! Tell the dream to your servants, and we will give you the interpretation."

The king answered to the Chaldeans. "The command from me is firm: If you do not make known to me the dream and its interpretation, you will be torn limb from limb, and your houses will be made a rubbish heap.

"But if you declare the dream and its interpretation, you will receive from me gifts."

The Chaldeans conferred with each other and then told the king that they would need to reflect upon the dream.

The king said, "I know for certain that you are bargaining for time.

"If you do not make the dream known to me, there is only one decree for you. For you have agreed together to speak lying and corrupt words before me until the situation is changed."

The Chaldeans answered the king and said, "There is not a man on earth who could explain the matter for the king.

"Moreover, the thing which the king demands is difficult, and there is no one else who could declare it to the king except gods."

Because of this the king became indignant and very furious, and gave orders to destroy all the wise men of Babylon.

One of our teachers in Vienna used to refer in jest to the above quote. He would state that although that law had been decreed over 2,600 years ago, he considered it still to be one of the best. He felt that protecting public health interests by insisting that psychotherapists master their craft, including becoming proficient in the understanding and interpretation of dreams, was eminently fair. Scrupulous application of the law, he used to say, would eliminate many unqualified practitioners, regardless of their professional background.

Notwithstanding the wisdom of that biblical text and the commentary on it, in the next section I propose alternative solutions that would likewise result in considerable professional improvements, as dream interpretation in the twentieth century, despite Freud's contribution, has suffered from even greater confusion and ignorance.

1. FALLOW FIELDS – SPREADING DESERTS

Dreams, as the representations of feelings, are possibly the most neglected and abused major area in the psychotherapeutic domain. It is an area in which advocates for quality in psychotherapeutic work can frequently detect the pervasive cancer afflicting the profession.

Over the years, I have discussed the topic of feelings and dreams with many psychotherapists. But the number of professionals who show interest in the therapeutic use of dreams, and who are proficient in that craft, diminishes constantly. They all agree, and their consensus is disheartening, that what was once described as the Royal Road to the unconscious and to its understanding is traveled by relatively few – and often badly at that. As it is a matter of much importance, that conclusion deserves careful examination.

Although I selected the subject of feelings and dreams because it lends itself readily to an evaluation of a therapist's expertise, my comments and explanations will, I hope, provide an added benefit, convincing the reader of the value of dream study. During the many years of my work at the Foundation and at the Institute in Switzerland, I discussed the subject with innumerable psychoanalysts and psychotherapists, many of whom were candidates for employment at our affiliated treatment center. Quite a few showed genuine interest in the clinical aspects of the subject but admitted considerable ignorance. Among them were many who stated that they had been guided by dogmatic indoctrination in the matter. At any rate, when made aware of the value of dreams in psychotherapy, many enlarged their practical work along those lines. They invariably reported that both the quality of their practice and their own understanding were much enriched. I am not alone in that experience. Emil A. Gutheil, Ralph R. Greenson, and others have spoken of their satisfaction in having convinced many colleagues and students of the invaluable contribution the study of dreams brings to psychotherapy. Furthermore, I have known a number of professionals who had studied with Walter Bonime and who reported, with much gratitude, the same experience. On the other hand, many colleagues expressed considerable regret, even anger, that the study of dreams had not been an adequate part of their training, particularly in view of the fact that considerable time and importance had been given to inconsequential material.

The professional literature on dreams is scant in comparison with that on other fundamental areas of psychoanalysis and psychotherapy, and only a disappointingly small proportion of the publications on dreams are of value. Few professionals are comfortable and expert in dealing with dreams. Some are frank to admit that; others deny the importance of dreams in psychotherapeutic work; and still others delude themselves into believing that they are experts in dream interpretation and everything else.

Even in writings about the major aspects of psychoanalysis and psychotherapy, one can discern only a superficial treatment of feelings and dreams, or even a complete avoidance of the topic. Many writers merely acknowledge Freud's views as the final word and let it rest at that.

The writings of an author concerning feelings and dreams, or the absence of such writings – perhaps more than any other topic in the field of psychotherapy – provide us with considerable understanding of the author's thinking and work.

a. THE VOICE OF THE EXPERTS

There is something fascinating about science. One gets such wholesome returns of conjecture out of such a trifling investment of fact.

MARK TWAIN

Twain's justifiable sarcasm was directed at scientists who promote themselves unduly with exaggerated claims and unfounded statements. He might well have spoken of a considerable number of psychoanalysts and psychotherapists and, indeed, professionals in all the "behavioral sciences." Robert J. Stoller, in his introduction to this volume, describes the situation convincingly.

So that we can evaluate the quality of contemporary literature on feelings and dreams, we shall review some reports and writings that indicate the level and scope of professional thought in the field.

To begin, the opinions of some well-known researchers and psychotherapists are of particular interest. These experts in dreams were recommended by academic and professional sources to Dr. Daniel Goleman, a mental health professional and writer specializing in psychological matters. He is also a staff writer on those topics for the science section of the NEW YORK TIMES, where the article I am going to discuss appeared some time ago. It is still one of the best overviews of professional opinions on the subject of dreams. In the report Dr. Goleman relates the viewpoints of these experts on the usefulness and validity of dreams as a tool in psychotherapy. His report aroused considerable interest in professional circles.

One reason for my choosing this particular article for discussion is that Dr. Goleman, not I, selected the professionals. Therefore I cannot be accused of choosing only authors who bolster my arguments.

As later in this chapter I comment on some of the opinions and "findings" reported, each paragraph in this section is numbered for easy reference.

G1. The first paragraphs refer to the views of Freudian, Jungian, and Gestalt therapists. Goleman states that they all agree: dreams do have meaning, even if disguised. However, those therapists frequently disagree on their interpretation.

G2. Goleman then reminds us that according to classic psychoanalytic theory, dreams are caused by upsetting impulses. He cites Professor Morton Reiser of Yale, a former president of the American Psychoanalytic Association, who explains that dreams are disguised so that the impulses do not disturb sleep. In the case of nightmares, however, the impulses are too powerful, and sleep is disrupted.

G3. Those opinions are opposed by many neuroscientists, who assert that dreams are essentially mental nonsense of no psychological significance whatever. For instance, Dr. Francis Crick of the Salk Institute, a Nobel Prize winner, and Dr. Graeme Mitchison of Cambridge University assure us that the only function of dreams is to purge the brain of unnecessary connections made during waking hours. They argue that newborns have a great deal of rem sleep, indicating dreaming, in spite of the fact that babies do not have the psychological conflicts and "upsetting impulses" declared by Freudians to be the cause of dreams. They also assert that infants and adults alike need to get rid of those burdensome connections. They warn that attempting to remember dreams, as psychoanalysts ask their patients to do, is quite damaging, because it actually reinforces this poisonous waste, the links, instead of eliminating it. They state that the purpose of dreams is to forget.

G4. Goleman continues with the views of psychologist and computer scientist Dr. Christopher Evans, who, in his 1984 book LANDSCAPES OF THE NIGHT, states that dreams do not have psychological meaning but "are the brain's equivalent of a computer's inspection of its programs, providing a chance to integrate the experiences of the day with the memories already stored in the brain."

G5. Dr. Evans's reasoning is not accepted by two brain researchers at the Harvard Medical School, Robert McCarley and Allan Hobson, who assert that random signals from a dream generator in the brain stem are sent to higher brain centers, which then use them to create a coherent story. Consequently, dreams have no psychological meaning, and the bizarreness is not a disguise but is characteristic of random brain activity. They state that "dreams are ambiguous stimuli which can be interpreted in any way a therapist is predisposed to. Their meaning is in the eye of the beholder – not in the dream itself."

G6. In fact, that dreams are meaningless is an opinion voiced these days by a considerable number of mental health professionals, regardless of their discipline. A favorite argument of those holding such negative views is that different psychotherapists, even those who adhere to the same school of thought, give widely different interpretations to the same dream material.

G7. The article again mentions Professor Reiser of Yale, who believes that dreams have meaning but agrees that the work of the Harvard people refutes Freud's idea that a dream is instigated by a disguised wish. Professor Reiser states, "We can no longer say that dreams are instigated by wishes – rather that the mental apparatus exploits the rem (dreaming) state of the brain for cognitive problem-solving and memory functions."

G8. Goleman adds that views such as Reiser's stem "from a growing body of evidence that seems to show that dreams serve a major role in psychological life."

G9. The next professional quoted, Dr. Rosalind Cartwright, a psychologist at Rush–Presbyterian–St. Luke's Medical Center in Chicago, contends that dreams are connected with adjustment to major life crises and are safety valves allowing the dreamer to deal with upsetting psychological issues.

G10. The last researcher mentioned in the article, Dr. Martin Seligman, a University of Pennsylvania psychologist, holds that while dreams consist largely of random visual hallucinations and unrelated feelings activated by the brain's dream generator, those "elements are woven into a cognitive fabric that goes on continuously, day and night. . . . [The] raw stuff may be random, but subconscious motivation may influence the way we integrate the elements of the dream." He affirms also that the stream of thoughts operates in much the same way during the night as during the day.

Before those statements made by experts fade from mind – as most of them should – let us review them briefly, not only to set the record straight but also to establish points of reference to be used later in the discussion on the essence and functioning of dreams.

The reader should remember that in this book I was requested not to present academic papers but to outline in a personal manner my views based on years of work in an organization devoted to defending and advancing the public interest. While taking the point of view of a custodian of the public interest does not affect the essence of the criticism, it strongly affects the scope, style, and language used. Academic "protocol" and the etiquette governing "scientific" altercations provide formidable protection, even for those pronouncing the most outrageous and self-seeking inanities in the behavioral sciences. Anyone who has obtained an academic degree in this domain has the freedom of the land.

A single aspect highlights the seriousness of the problem. It has been said that a fool can ask more questions than a wise man can answer. To paraphrase, a fool can make more inept points in a short "scientific" paper than a wise psychotherapist can answer in a thousand pages. With innumerable meaningless papers and books around, we would need thousands of informed professionals merely to answer part of the scientific-sounding inanities. What, then, can we do? Non-resistance to the tidal wave of such publications has merely encouraged its ever-accelerating pace. The professional truly interested in the welfare of patients knows that insistence on the quality of professional work and writing is essential to maintain the quality of training and treatment. Few effective measures remain to stem the tide of irrelevant or misleading literature. One such measure is to slash through the Gordian knot whenever required, ignoring any outcries of "ad hominem, ad hominem."

To those who feel that some of these statements are unwarranted, I sincerely suggest that they suspend judgment until they have finished reading this section.

Now we return to the article under review. First, let us deal with the statement *that dreams are disguised so that they do not disturb sleep* (G2). That statement is frequently encountered in the literature. It should be taken with a very large grain of salt! Why? Because what we repress is hidden from us and so is disguised far more in our waking state than when we dream. It is disguised because of repression, not to protect sleep. Therefore the disguise is closely related to the status of the unconscious of the person at a given period in his life and is not necessarily the benevolent protector of sleep. Dreams follow their own merry – and not so merry – ways and could not care less what happens to sleep.

This hypothesis is also supported by the fact that dreams of people in deep hypnosis, where the likelihood of awakening is practically nil, show precisely the same disguises as they do when these people dream in normal sleep.

There are, of course, other factors besides repression to explain why dream imagery can be so strange or incomprehensible. One factor is that dreams may delve deeply into the unconscious and thus into very early, primitive levels of impression and memory. If therapy proceeds satisfactorily, the dream language tends to become clearer and less strange; the disguise, more transparent.

Recently the view that dreams do not protect sleep has also been proclaimed by the dream laboratories, although the assertion has a basis different from mine. At any rate, as interesting as it is, the question of whether disguise exists to protect sleep is of only minor relevance to us here. Our concern is the importance of the dream as a psychotherapeutic tool in understanding a patient's psyche.

The statement by Crick and Mitchison (G3) that *the only function of dreams is to purge the brain of unnecessary connections made during waking hours* betrays utter ignorance of all clinical psychoanalytic evidence. Those not versed in the psychology of dreams cannot, and should not, make any statements about the essence and function of dreams. The realization of the value of dreams as helpful in understanding the human psyche and its disturbances can come to expert psychotherapists only after prolonged clinical work. There is simply no other way to obtain such knowledge.

To reach accurate conclusions, the procedure to be applied must be the reverse of the one described in the article: Only expert psychotherapists with extended clinical experience in dreams can advise neuroscientists about which of their findings may be valid and of interest in the psychological area. In spite of all the "scientific" claims and clamor by the mechanical minded about rem sleep and non-rem sleep, and the importance of the type of sleep to the nature of dreams, nothing of significance has been added.

Furthermore, determining whether dreams have a specific purpose requires sophisticated answers by sophisticated experts. There is no place for irresponsible and unfounded claims. When we examine these matters later in this chapter, it may come as a surprise that knowledgeable answers can be surprisingly simple.

Equally irresponsible are the statements by Crick and Mitchison, namely, that *the purpose of dreams is to forget* and, consequently, that the request by psychotherapists that their patients remember dreams is actually damaging to the patients. It embarrasses me to point out the obvious, that many dreams occur again and again over the years, bringing up our inner problems, and do not allow us to forget them! In addition, if recollecting dreams is so poisonous, how do patients undergoing psychotherapy improve, whereas before they had been "ill"? Some of the aforementioned professionals may argue that other aspects of psychotherapy have such a curative potency that they can overcome both the emotional illness of the patient and the poisoning of the dream recall. Alas, much to my chagrin, psychotherapeutic intervention has no such powers. We have to work arduously and patiently to achieve progress – and are deeply grateful for each inch of progress – fervently hoping the patient will not slip back.

The statements by Evans (G4) and McCarley and Hobson (G5) deserve to be answered with equal harshness. We shall examine them in detail at a later point. They assert that dreams have no meaning. Evans also says that dreams are there to integrate day-to-day experiences with memories already stored. The fact is that many dreams show little residue of the previous day's "outside" events, or no residue, but reveal a current, inner focusing on meaningful matters of the past. Wide variations can be found, depending on the psychological structure of the dreamer.

Furthermore, the difference between imagery and dreams must be stressed. To answer McCarley and Hobson's assertion that dreams can be interpreted in any way therapists choose, I say that the opposite is true: Each dream is a unique statement by the individual and deals with distinct facts of his psyche. If therapists give different interpretations to the same dream, it is only because they do not have the superhuman perspicacity of McCarley and Hobson. Therapists must therefore toil, seeking to discover in the darkness of the unconscious what it attempts to hide. It is likely that experienced and open-minded therapists gifted in dream interpretation, and given the necessary data on a patient's history, including his associations to a dream, will arrive at similar conclusions.

The struggle to lessen our patients' pain, to make them improve bit by bit, is difficult enough as it is. Dreams are a most important tool in that endeavor. For professionals to discourage and mislead students, as well as emotionally ill people, is irresponsible and reprehensible. What would one think of a physician who broadcasts assertions that all antibiotics are useless, their benefits existing only in the minds of some foolish professionals of dubious intent? Yet "scientific" journals will publish similarly worthless material when it comes to the so-called behavioral sciences.

The "scientists" who take potshots at the validity of dreams (and please note that their "brilliant" explanations often contradict each other) assert that we misunderstand the nature of dreams and that dreams are merely random electrical impulses or some similarly meaningless activity. I assert that those people are unable to perceive psychological meaning and that their own lack of perception is reflected in their "theories" of the functioning of the human mind.

Owing to that lack of special sensitivity, mechanically minded researchers are unable to interpret meaningfully the data they collect and, what is more, to select for their experiments the questions that would have some meaning. Without those necessary premises, research projects are valueless. We discuss that in detail and offer specific proof later in this chapter.

It is necessary to repeat this over and over again: A sine qua non of the scientific approach is credible testing of the predictability of the specific subject matter. Let the "scientists" who deny the meaningfulness of dreams predict the next electrical impulse or burp. The term "random" provides an easy alibi for their inability to do so. I make that absurd request because similar demands are made of psychotherapy by a number of those scientists. Later statements in this chapter will examine the problem of relating psychotherapy and science.

Many of the "experts" we have cited engage in all-embracing general statements about the nature of dreams. Such generalizations are worthless, for there are many kinds of imagery and dreams that show many different characteristics, emanating from different levels and different areas of the psyche of the dreamer. It takes an expert psychotherapist to deal properly with such a complex matter and to grasp the significance of a dream.

We must not forget that the research activities within behavioral science, too often poorly conceived, planned, and executed, involve a tremendous amount of manpower and expenditure for salaries, equipment, administration, and the like. Later I will discuss some of those projects. As available manpower and funds are limited in our sector, that research is being carried out at the expense of good patient care and training of those who would be suitable for such difficult work.

The topics in paragraphs G6 to G10 will be addressed, along with other material, later in this chapter.

In a brief illustration from a book written by a practicing psychotherapist, Goleman elucidates further problems in the understanding of dreams. He is very interested in the variations resulting from different training and from the therapist's personal temperament.

The author of the book speaks about a woman who is apparently dissatisfied with her analyst's ability to interpret dreams. To find more suitable professional help, she presents the same dream to three other therapists. She is exceedingly disappointed that each therapist offers vastly differing interpretations.

The dream is as follows: "I was lying on a bed in a room, alone apparently, but with the feeling of turmoil around me. A middle-aged woman enters and hands me a key. Later a man enters, helps me out of bed, and leads me upstairs to an unknown room."

To me, this dream appears to be a construct – that is, not a real dream but one purposely created to evoke comments by the various psychotherapists questioned. If so, whoever produced it should be congratulated. It is clear, simple, and lends itself well to the purpose of eliciting responses. The basic elements and symbols would be heartwarming to an eager psychoanalytic trainee, especially as he would feel that they were easy to interpret.

The author then relates the different interpretations of the dream given by the three therapists. He explains that the differences are indicative of both the formation and the emotional characteristics of the interpreting therapist.

— No. 1: "The turmoil represents your unrecognized erotic impulses, which can be directed toward either a woman or a man. These figures actually represent your therapist."
— No. 2: "The dream shows your passivity: you are reclining, you take what is handed to you, and you are led away to another realm."
— No. 3: "When you confront your turmoil, it reveals itself as an older woman, who symbolizes your fear of growing unfruitful. But in her you find the creative key which becomes the man who leads you to the part of your psyche where you can be productive."

I cannot resist joining in the fun, so here goes:

— No. 4: "The turmoil you report is within you, as each dream is a picture of our inner emotional world. The turmoil is linked to your feelings toward others, and you are attempting to solve the problem by turning to the positive, constructive mother image. (That is just my way of describing this particular area within you.) I say 'constructive' because she does give you the key, and thus permission to move ahead. Now, with such permission granted, your next scene shows the direction in which you really want to go."

A gentle hint about a sexual component could be added, but as this is the patient's first session with me, I delicately refrain from it.

I hope you agree that my interpretation is quite good. Unfortunately, it is not at all! All four of us committed a heinous crime. The minimal punishment should be loss of our professional licenses.

There may be elements of truth in those interpretations. But as any student of psychotherapy knows, to proceed correctly, a therapist should be familiar with the childhood background of the patient and his subsequent history and have become acquainted with his dream patterns by hearing at least a dozen of his dreams.

After the patient has told his dream, the therapist should ask for the patient's feelings and associations for each part of the dream. The patient should also be asked if he can associate any part of the dream with an event during recent days, in case the event stimulated a sensitive area within the patient's psyche.

Obviously, the more sensitive and repressed a specific area is, the more the patient's associations will be "off target"; that is, they will not point clearly to the core of the matter. Yet, even then, often unbeknownst to the patient, much will be revealed over the course of time. The experienced therapist, with caution, tact, and patience, will circle closer and closer to the target.

Although asking those necessary questions would not seem an undue burden for the analyst, in too many instances they are not asked. The more experienced analysts, to whom thorough procedures are second nature, complain that many analysts today are satisfied with the "instant interpretation" of dreams, the content of which they may share with the patient. It is usually the inexpert therapist who is cocksure of his instant analysis of a dream, as well as of his other, equally superb, psychotherapeutic achievements. Seasoned therapists, competent in the handling of dreams, may concur in their evaluations of such an unsuited practitioner but do not seem to have the courage to send him to vocational counseling to be recycled. Our present system tends to foster a negative selection of candidates for psychotherapeutic training.

Erik H. Erikson stated, correctly, that the immediate recognition of standard symbols may induce the analyst to believe that he has understood the dream when, in fact, he has not. Yet Erikson, in spite of condemning this "dictionary type," simplistic translation of symbols of the manifest dream into standard latent "meaning," did engage routinely in another type of "dictionary" misconduct. That will be explained later. (I will also discuss later in this chapter Freud's views on dream symbols.)

Leon L. Altman complains that while younger analysts "understand dreams easily enough," they do not know how to integrate the dreams with their patients' problems. There is something very disturbing in that statement, particularly as it comes from one of the few writers who strongly emphasize the importance of dreams. The problem is that Altman obviously believed that those therapists understood dreams merely by being familiar with cliché interpretations.

Dreams are representations of the patient's psyche and thus also of his problems. The superficial, instant interpretation, using "standard meanings" for each symbol, is frequently misleading and of dubious value. The result is an illusion of understanding, a pseudounderstanding. The misuse of psychoanalytic textbooks as dictionaries for quick and easy "translations" of symbols is a disservice to patients. All too frequently dreams are misinterpreted. Rash and naive statements reflecting textbook learning and dogma are rampant. With dreams, there is a great deal of safety in safety, even for the competent therapist. We must not forget that dreams are highly individual productions.

It is important that I not be misunderstood. What I am complaining about is the many therapists who translate, without hesitation, the symbols in each dream into a definite underlying meaning. Certainly there are some dream symbols, such as an umbrella, for which the first thought that comes to a therapist's mind may well prove correct. But even with such symbols – and they are not that numerous compared with the rest – it pays to ask for associations as additional details are revealed. I have often been surprised in that respect. Of course, when there is a frequently repeated pattern in the dreams of a patient, some basic understanding comes even before associations are used. An experienced and gifted therapist, who will readily recognize underlying meaning and significant trends, may be able to dispense with asking for associations and feelings about dream portions that appear routinely in a particular patient's dreams and have been previously explored.

A brief illustration of repetitious patterns: In his initial session a man in his 40s talks about feeling inferior to other people and about other feelings of insecurity. His dreams are usually quite unpleasant. In them, he is often lost in the streets. When he dreams of himself in a room, it is usually dismal. A recurrent theme is of lamps that do not function and that, despite desperate efforts, he cannot get to work. In the next session the patient associates the ordeals with the lamps to his serious impotency problems and to his many fears, including fear of the dark.

While we have seen a pattern here that is coherent and recognizable, most dreams are far more complex. It takes an experienced and knowledgeable therapist to detect and sort out the meaningful parts so that the emotional forces within his patient's psyche are revealed. A therapist with insufficient acumen will not be able to put the material presented by the patient to good use.

Certainly there are dream symbols that occur more frequently than others, such as the key in the dream cited earlier. Even in such instances, however, the analyst should ask the questions mentioned, as the additional details obtained may improve his understanding of the dream and clarify the direction in which the true answer will be found. Useful information will be forthcoming to the extent resistance permits. There are a great number of possible meanings for each dream symbol; the meaning depends on the psyche of the dreamer. To demonstrate the wide range of meanings a single dream symbol may have for various patients, I have selected the image of the Statue of Liberty. The list, of course, is necessarily incomplete:

- a strong mother figure
- a threatening mother
- a protective mother (in all its varieties)
- as dreams can invert the gender of a dream symbol when its meaning is psychologically disturbing, a father, brother, or other male image
- a phallic symbol (here again there are many variations)
- a symbol of hope (and here we have to find out what hope)
- a symbol of liberty (liberty from whom or from what? liberty to do what?)
- a symbol of rejection that stops the patient even from hoping
- a pretty girl with a nice figure, beckoning him to follow.

A colleague reading that list told me about a homosexual patient who had dreamed that the Statue of Liberty was his mother, who forcefully pushed the torch up his backside. The man was also an enema addict.

Again, any of the foregoing perceptions of a single symbol can have many different connotations. Take the "protective mother" as an example. While it has a friendly, positive meaning for some patients, it elicits the greatest number of pejoratives in others. Still other patients have even different reactions. The variety of possible interpretations of this apparently simple symbol highlights the need to proceed carefully.

Clearly, a therapist cannot be certain of the correct meaning of a dream symbol unless he asks the patient for associations. Only by hard work, by delving into the patient's associations and seeking to explore his childhood, can one discover the unique meaning of a patient's dream.

By proceeding correctly, the therapist will frequently be able to gain considerable insight into the areas of a patient's resistance and the strength of each of those particular resistances. The therapist may become aware of a patient's blocking out associations and feelings to certain parts of the dream; he may observe that the patient is not producing associations at all, is merely brushing them off, or is presenting a reaction that is obviously not the expected one in view of the knowledge previously gained about the patient's psyche.

Along with Greenson I deplore the statement by the majority of the participants in the Kris Study Group of the New York Psychoanalytic Institute (Waldhorn, 1967) that dreams are merely one of the various communications in psychoanalysis and not a privileged one. I wonder if "the other communications" can really pinpoint areas of resistance as graphically as dreams do and indicate the strength of such repression as well. The problem here lies not with the dream but with the lack of necessary know-how of the professionals.

To illustrate the intricacies of dream interpretation and its dependence on the orientation of the analyst and whether or not he uses associations, I present a short dream of a patient in his 50s. His dream relates to his younger sister, whom he describes as "a lovable, sensitive, and gifted person, but unable to survive on her own in this harsh world." Consequently he supports her in every way he feels necessary. He states that it gives him much satisfaction to do so but that he worries about her a great deal, particularly about what will happen to her when he is no longer around.

The patient's dream:

> Near where my sister lives is a small movie house that plays a better class of pictures than most. It has a canopy supported by two slim poles, planted on the edge of the sidewalk. In my dream I see my sister bumping into one of the poles, and she seems rather hurt in one eye. The movie house is different from the real one; it is smaller, the canopy

is much narrower, and it gives a very shabby impression. The information on the movies is merely on handwritten notices pasted to the wall.

At the end of a luncheon meeting I read the dream to a prominent psychoanalyst and asked him for his interpretation. He did not ask me for associations, but he was aware of the facts about the patient.

The analyst's interpretation was that my patient had sexual feelings toward his sister. Those feelings were represented by the pole. The patient feared that his feelings would cause her harm, and he also considered them "shabby."

My own understanding of the dream, only partly communicated to the patient and based on previous communications and the patient's associations and feelings to the dream, was the following: Very deprived of love in his childhood and still a lonely man, and single at that, he gave all his love to his sister as if she were his only child. He worried greatly that her dreams for a happy marriage – her greatest desire in life – with all that marriage entails, including its sexual aspect, had never materialized and that the resulting hurt, though not expressed, was the reason for her frequent melancholy. The movie house, which had become so dismal, represented that disappointment well. Further therapy might have offered greater insight, but soon after the dream occurred, the patient, regrettably, had to relocate to another part of the country.

A therapist can look at a dream from a number of perspectives. For instance, he may wish to concentrate on the transferential aspects. But there can only be one correct interpretation of a dream, not two and not several. The reason is that we are dealing with a unique individual who, in producing his dream, makes a unique statement and creates a unique product that has an intrinsic meaning, in the same way that a writer writes a novel or a composer writes a piece of music. As the resistance may hide the true meaning, dreams are frequently confusing, even incomprehensible, to the therapist. The therapist must keep in mind that although he may have some hypotheses about the meanings of such dreams, in no way are those hypotheses certainties, and depending on the need of that particular moment in psychotherapy, he may or may not venture some remarks to that effect to the patient.

The symbols selected by the dream are significant and appropriate metaphors, and so are the other elements in a dream. A meaningful process can be detected in dream after dream after dream. The process is quite different from that imagined by impulsive neuroelectricians. And speaking of imagining, we must stress the difference between imagery and dreams.

Now I would like to tell an anecdote that is true, even though it may seem unbelievable. I will not mention names, but all the names of people, publications, and other sources referred to in this chapter are known to our editorial staff.

In the early 1950s I conducted a survey for the Foundation to determine specific patterns in the dreams of sociopaths and to confirm my contention that such dreams must be understood, and interpreted, in a very different manner from the dreams of neurotics. It is difficult to collect an appreciable number of such dreams, as true sociopaths rarely seek treatment. In those days, however, psychotherapy was still described as a possible miracle cure, and some sociopaths sought treatment, often to become more successful and aggressive in their sociopathic endeavors.

Anyway, I went out of my way to meet colleagues who might have access to such patients. I had lunch with the president of one of New York's largest psychoanalytic training institutes, quite orthodox in its orientation. This man was described by one of Freud's early and well-known followers as his most gifted student. During the course of our conversation I remarked that my interest in dreams was probably linked to the fact that I did not have much difficulty in understanding them. The man's response was surprising. He gave me an ice-cold look and said with great conviction, "The only people who are good at dream interpretation are schizophrenics." Well, according to that, there were only two categories in which Freud could be placed: either he was an inept interpreter of dreams, or he was psychotic.

b. The Bookish Theoric

SHAKESPEARE

b1 Dr. Faust and Little Moritz

If there is but little water in the stream, it is the fault not of the channel, but of the source.

St. Jerome

He is not only dull himself, but the cause of dullness in others.

Samuel Johnson

While "little (kleiner) Hans" is still known to students of psychoanalysis, "kleiner Moritz"* was a figure of still wider influence in the early days of that discipline. Despite trite and improbable statements that history would eventually and unfailingly give credit where due, "kleiner Moritz" does require a biographical rescue.

One of the bonds that used to hold the Viennese together was an enjoyable addiction to jokes, usually quite witty, often ethnic, and mostly sarcastic about others, as well as themselves and their own group. Forming part of this tradition were imaginary figures such as

---

* No connection with "Max and Moritz," two malicious boys who were the literary creations of Wilhelm Busch, an author whose work Freud enjoyed reading. Freud used those two names in criticizing Adler and Stekel. The choice of the name Moritz for a loudmouthed nitwit is somewhat of a puzzlement. The best-known bearers of the name were highly intelligent and successful statesmen and soldiers: Duke Moritz of Saxony, prominent in the 16th century, and, some 200 years later, Moritz, Marshall of Saxony. Equally well known were Moritz, Regent of Orange, and the idealistic poet Moritz Count von Strachwitz.

"kleiner Moritz," around whom innumerable anecdotes were created. "Kleiner Moritz" was presented as a loudmouthed boy, aged about 12, a pretentious little know-it-all who always blurted out inane and simplistic solutions for even the most complex matters. Thus it was sufficient to say someone was a "kleiner Moritz," and everybody knew exactly what you meant. Sometimes, for emphasis, the term would be used in the original context: *"Wie der kleine Moritz sich das so vorstellt!"* Roughly translated: "Oh my! How simple this dumb kid assumes this to be!"

In retrospect, it seems to me that it was the most frequently heard name in the psychiatric world in Vienna during the first half of the 20th century. It was bestowed fairly and democratically, and with much gusto, on colleagues of other theoretical persuasions, as well as one's own, with utter disregard for age, academic status, race, or religion. Freud was no exception.

Soon readers will begin to sense why the revival of that personality is a pressing necessity.

Let us continue to examine how the topic of feelings and dreams is faring in psychotherapy publications and how the literature is indicative of the level of competence of each psychotherapist scrutinized.

There continues to be a relative paucity of material on dreams. A survey conducted in 1992 showed, for instance, that in what is probably the most widely known psychoanalytic journal in the United States, only two papers dealing directly with dreams had been published in the prior three years. They were neither exciting nor original. Another well-known psychoanalytic journal, read mostly on the East Coast, printed just two articles concerning dreams in six years. A long-established national psychotherapy journal carried not a single article on dreams in eight years. The editor of the quarterly journal of a large national psychotherapy organization could not even remember when the journal had last published a paper on the subject.

Those facts must have some significance. True, journals reflect their editors' thinking, but editors also keep in mind the needs and interests of their readership. Because of the influence of editors on the dissemination of information, their competence on the subject of dreams is important to us here. Consider two examples on the negative side; both happen to be editors of journals with strong psychoanalytic emphasis, and both are trained analysts. It is easy to cite similar cases in more eclectic psychotherapy publications.

The first editor is a dedicated, likable therapist who frankly admits to a complete inability to understand dreams. Does that admission imply an equal inability to understand emotions? That question will be dealt with later. At any rate, the journal is extremely intellectual, and its papers – often esoteric and similar to literary essays or theoretical speculations – tend to intellectualize when discussing clinical matters.

The second editor is not in psychotherapeutic practice and is considered to have little competence in the matter of dreams. That shortcoming is, of course, also reflected in the papers selected. This journal, even more widely read in the United States than the other, presents more clinical material than the other, but, curiously, there is a general tendency for its papers, often quite intellectualized too, to miss the point entirely.

Some may wonder how such situations are possible. Three explanations are most frequently heard: (1) that the majority of readers are not discerning enough to know the difference, (2) that those who have the acumen will continue to subscribe to the journals to keep abreast, and (3) that editors, once appointed, can build a base of support. Professionals covet being published and will, in return, sustain an editor who helps them.

Equally discouraging is the choice by publishing houses of editors responsible for the selection of works in our field. Many of those editors are not practicing psychotherapists. Study of publishers' catalogs all too often reveals a considerable lack of expertise by those responsible for the selection of publications and an inability to distinguish the valuable from the mediocre or worthless. The editors play it safe; they follow the mainstream trends and tend to prefer authors, no matter how dull, who hold academic positions of importance. Consequently the titles and the content are repetitious, abstract, and intellectual. Theoretical topics abound, and works of clinical value are rare. With some notable exceptions, the calamitous deficiencies of many journal editors and editors employed by publishing houses are just as prevalent in the United States as in Europe.

Many analysts, particularly older ones, believe that writings on feelings and dreams, because of the difficulty and subtlety of the subject matter, will show up the psychotherapeutic insufficiencies of the writers or editors. Obviously, the quality, or lack of it, of the psychotherapy literature has an enormous influence on psychotherapeutic practice and training.

> Dreams are often most profound when they seem most crazy.
>
> FREUD

> Narrow-souled people and narrow-necked bottles: the emptier they are, the more noise they make when pouring it out.
>
> POPE

Let us consider some papers by well-known academicians. The first article under consideration was not so much chosen as forced upon me. It was by far the most extensive on dreams to appear in any of the major journals over a period of many years. Almost 100 pages long, it takes up most of the issue of the journal in which it was published, a privilege not accorded to other papers by this particular editor for a long time. Clearly the editor considered the paper to be of exceptional significance, possibly because it would present to a largely psychoanalytically oriented readership an unfamiliar perspective on a different world, namely, the approach to the subject of feelings and dreams by a major section of academic psychology. I, however, give the article considerable space for a different reason: It is a perfect example of the sterile and valueless academic matters our psychotherapy students are forced to ingest before they are allowed to enter the study for their future profession. If a knowledgeable and talented student dares to object, he creates serious obstacles to his graduation.

As I will later refer to some ideas and statements mentioned, the following paragraphs are numbered.

P1. The writer, a professor* at a well-known university, starts out by stating that a "peculiar ambiguity in Freud's thinking handicapped his theory of dreams." He then mentions Freud's division of dreams into three categories, as proposed in "On Dreams": "dreams which

---

* Please keep in mind that paragraphs P1 through P18 reflect, unless otherwise stated, the professor's views and not mine.

make sense within the context of our mental life; dreams which are clear, but do not seem to fit into our mental life; and lastly, dreams which are not clear at all, and seem confused and bewildering."

P2. The professor then states that in THE INTERPRETATION OF DREAMS Freud (1900) took quite a different view of dreams: that basic dream thoughts are quite rational but that the transformation of such unconscious thoughts, the dream work, is completely different, and not comparable to waking thought. In AN OUTLINE OF PSYCHOANALYSIS Freud (1940) reformulated that statement: "A dream, then, is a psychosis with all the absurdities, delusions and illusions of a psychosis."

P3. The professor continues by declaring that although Freud did not carry through with the establishment of categories, or styles, of dreams, if he had done so, he would have ended up with "a theory quite different from the one known to us."

P4. The professor goes on to say that the views of Freud and of such authors as Spence and Gordon, describing the typical manifest dream as "unorganized and nonsensical," were contradicted by Snyder, who asserted that the majority of dreams are entirely "credible as descriptions of waking events" and that dreams that were characterized by "bizarreness and incredibleness" were quite uncommon. The author then asserts that while an autonomous ego is now more widely considered as reality – rather than the previous focusing on the id-ego battle – it has not been explained how a mind, liberated from instinctual bondage, does its dreaming. The author says that *it is precisely that task that he is undertaking in his present paper.*

P5. The paper continues with the assertion that in the 1950s the discovery of two types of ocular mobility (rem and non-rem) during sleep "initiated a new era of dream research." The author discusses studies that emphasize the importance of the rem periods and criticizes various classifications of dreams by others, including Freud. Here and further on he devotes a great deal of space to Foulkes's criterion of "two kinds of dreams," which Foulkes himself separates into "dreams" and "thoughts."

P6. The professor, conceding that most people have a mixed style of dreams, proposes a division of the types of dreams into "logical" and "bizarre." He claims that the basic question is no longer, "Why are dreams so different from our waking thought?" but rather, "Why do we have two kinds of thought?"

P7. The next section attempts to examine the "styles of dreams," beginning with a chapter entitled "Mental Effort and Primary Personality Variables." The author declares that the theories of Freud and Jung, as well as those of most other authors, are unable to confront the question of the heterogeneity of dreams. The author affirms: "The authors, Freud and Jung included, were mistaken here. Some (manifest) dreams are, indeed, curious, or even bizarre, and not comprehensible, but others are well constructed and meaningful." He reemphasizes his claim that the proper division of dreams is into "logical" and "bizarre." He asserts that "logical" dreams are generated during periods of high mental effort, and "bizarre" dreams, during periods of low mental effort.

P8. Citing a number of studies, the professor concludes that the "majority of dreams reveal a mix of styles, with a minority reporting only logical, or only bizarre, dreams." Later he states that Freud's explanation of the peculiar nature of manifest dreams as the result of conflict between wish and anxiety would be acceptable only "if all dreams were similar, and everybody dreamt bizarre dreams. . . . However, people have both bizarre and logical dreams." To explain why people dream in one style or another, the professor declares that the difference must be due to "primary personality variables."

P9. In the next chapter, entitled "Primary Personality Variable Scanning," the author asks how many such primary personality variables might actually exist. He first cites Eysenck, who claims there are only two, and then follows by mentioning the works of Cattel, Thurstone, Kretschmer, Kibler, Enke, Witkin, Klein, Gardner, and Schlesinger.

P10. A chapter on cognitive structures ends with the author's formulating another basic tenet of his theory: that during non-rem sleep, reasoning allows for logical ideas, but during rem sleep, the lesser mental effort of the dreamer is not capable of that. The author then states that the only question that remains to be answered is why some people have only logical dreams, and others, only bizarre dreams.

P11. The professor feels that understanding three different aspects of cognitive structure, of which tolerance versus intolerance of incongruities is the most important, will help us comprehend the differences in dream styles. Much space is then devoted to methods and graphs measuring differences in how various individuals deal with contradictory information.

P12. The author next turns to what is, to him, a fundamental question: *how to distinguish between logical and bizarre dreams*. He offers six representative examples. The first three dreams are classified as bizarre:

—   *Dream i*. The dreamer sees himself sitting on a broomstick that moves faster the louder he and others sing. There is also a village where bears behave exactly like people.

—   *Dream ii*. The dreamer describes a friend who is joking around in a parking lot and lies down, in jest, in front of a bus. The bus moves backward, so its wheels do not touch the friend; nevertheless the friend is crushed.

—   *Dream iii*. The dreamer and others are twice suddenly uprooted from one place to a completely different scene.

The next two dreams are defined as logical:

—   *Dream iv*. The dreamer is at school with a friend. There is also a big fair. The dreamer sees another girl and wants to introduce her to her friend but gets separated from her. The dreamer's sister and brother are with her. They all buy stick horses and a hat. They then go to the dreamer's dorm and put the horses and hat down.

—   *Dream v*. The dreamer is pregnant and happy about it. She goes to a department store to purchase baby clothes.

The sixth dream is a "constructed" dream that the author briefly mentions to provide an example of a moderately bizarre dream. In it, a cat suddenly turns into a rabbit.

P13. The next dozen or so pages contain graphs and tests concerning the focus and modes of conceptualization. The author concludes that not all dreams are bizarre and that half are well-constructed, plausible stories. Thus "any theory of dreams that purports to uncover the hidden reasons for the bizarreness of all dreams has, in fact, failed, for it overlooks the fact that every second dream is not bizarre." Bizarre dreams occur during rem sleep, when the dreamer is not able to muster as much mental effort as in non-rem sleep. He claims that as the PPV scanning tests show, dreamers who have only logical dreams are mentally alert enough not to tolerate any violation of logic; the opposite is true of those with a pronounced tolerance for incongruities.

P14. The professor affirms that the existence of two styles of dreams invalidates Freud's theory, which, he insists, has many other flaws. The professor claims that he is "paving the way for the reconsideration of the whole body of our ideas on dreaming."

P15. The author continues to insist that the very existence of logical dreams undermines Freud's theory and the concepts of primary process and repression and casts doubt on the value and efficacy of using associations. The author ponders the problems of establishing the correct meaning among many possibilities, the problems caused by "contraries" (symbols that for purposes of disguise, may be the opposite of the real essence of the dreamed-about factor) and "overinterpretation" (fusing two or more underlying emotional factors into one symbol). The two parenthetical explanations are mine, but it is likely that they are what the professor had in mind.

P16. The professor doubts that an interpreting therapist can discover the essential underlying dream thought. He cites J. W. Reeves, who declared that the criteria for distinguishing the essential dream thoughts "have not yet been formulated and, to the logically minded outsider, this is a key problem in validation. . . . Psychoanalysts would make a vast contribution to general psychology if they were able to describe such cues more adequately than seems to be the case at present."

P17. Similar criticisms are leveled against Jung. The professor states categorically that "interpreting a dream by the methods of free association or by amplification has no advantage whatsoever over any other method. As far as scientific validation is concerned, our interpretation of a dream, of whatever kind, is not above the level of a guess. No matter how ingenious a guess is, a guess it remains."

P18. By now the professor's viewpoints are clear. The remaining 20 or so pages of the paper are devoted to his criticism of Freud's stance on the unconscious, on the mental apparatus, and on repression. The professor demonstrates his erudition by quoting from Kant, Descartes, and Aristotle, and he concludes by stating: "Freud . . . did not succeed . . . in substantiating his attempt to prove the existence of an unconscious mental system. . . . This essay was an attempt at imbuing the study of dreaming with the ideas of cognitive psychology."

The professor attempts to establish the indisputable superiority of his own theories over Freud's and of cognitive psychology over psychoanalysis. Thus, after a century of unscientific hocus-pocus, the true structure and essence of dreams has been illuminated.

As stated, I have given this paper so much attention because it received an unusual amount of space in a widely circulated psychoanalytic journal. Even more important, it is a perfect example of the extent to which academic teaching in the mental health sciences can deviate from even the most basic psychological reality.

I need comment only briefly on the many claims made by the professor, for they can be countered by any psychotherapist even minimally experienced in working with dreams. In the section on rem in this chapter I shall look particularly at the professor's statement (P5) that the discovery of two types of ocular mobility during sleep "initiated a new era of dream research." Here I should like to point out that nothing has resulted so far from any such research that has added to our understanding of the meaning contained in dreams.

The cornerstone of the professor's theory is his contention that the division of dreams into "bizarre" and "logical" is the very basis for understanding the psyche of the dreamer (see P6 and P7). However, in his quest to detect the structure of the patient's psyche and the forces active therein, the expert psychotherapist focuses on each dream's uniqueness. It is a meaningful endeavor – something utterly lacking in the professor's cognitive approach. Dreams emanate from various levels and "locations" in the psyche, the emotions in the dreams being imbued with different degrees of strength and inhibited by repressions of varying force. The dreams in which therapists are interested come from the deeper levels, where the forces of childhood reign and send us their signals. Any therapist worth his salt looks to dreams for clues that, when linked to the patient's early years, help clarify the patient's psychological development.

No particular importance should be attached to whether or not a dream appears to be "bizarre" or whether or not a person can tolerate incongruities (see P11). What may appear "logical" to the uninformed may well have arisen from very deep levels, in which case, the "logical" story of the dream is not based on nearness to the waking state but is due to particular childhood associations linked to specific emotional material buried in the dreamer's unconscious.

The only relevant issue is the value of a given dream in revealing to us the deeper forces at play and in helping us trace their origins; whether or not a dream is bizarre or the dreamer can tolerate incongruity is totally *irrelevant*. Those issues are as meaningful as classifying books according to the color of their binding.

To illustrate, I have constructed two brief dreams, one "logical" according to the professor's viewpoints and the other "bizarre." Both give precisely the same message. Even though the dreams are "constructed," the dream elements are all taken from dreams of actual patients suffering deep anxiety.

—   *Dream a.* I am in a room. I look in the mirror. My face has a sickly color. It looks drawn, really terrible. I feel very lonely. I am desperate to get out of this place, to go somewhere, anywhere. I look for my jacket but cannot find it. I do not dwell on that fact. I am now walking in the streets. They are rather dismal and unfamiliar, and it is getting darker. I feel awful. Then I spot a blond girl on the other side of the street. I realize she is the girl I adored from afar in school when I was a boy. I am very anxious to see her closer. As I start to cross the street, there is an increasing drone. It comes from a fast-approaching truck. I notice it only at the last moment. It is too late. As the truck is about to hit me, I wake up.

—   *Dream b.* I see an ugly dog in a prison. The color of the dog is a dirty, disgusting green. The dog whines and howls and wants to get out. I cannot see the prison walls, but I know they are there. In its attempts to get out, the dog raises and lowers and raises himself vertically along the invisible wall, scratching against it. The whole situation feels intolerable to me. The right ear of the dog is missing, but when I look again, it is now the left one. I do not dwell on that.

It is me. I know I am in a dark forest, even though I cannot see any trees. I feel unhappy and lost for a long time. Then I see in the distance something yellow and shiny, and I very much want to approach it. I feel like crying as I move toward it. There is a horrible noise. I look up. A huge, dark figure is bearing down on me to kill me. I wake up in terror.

It is not every question that deserves an answer.

Publius

To support his theory, the professor cites (P16) another "behavioral scientist," J. W. Reeves, who claims that psychoanalysts have failed to establish the necessary criteria to define "essential" dream thoughts and that they should give us precise clues to nail them down once and for all, as it would be a "vast contribution to general psychology." I see him visualizing a big box of butterflies on pins, all neatly labeled.

The terms Reeves uses, and his all too frequently found academic and intellectual approach, betray his utter ignorance of the human psyche. The generalizing theorizers pretentiously and naively assume that one can "nail down once and for all" the "essential" elements in order to arrive at a general psychology. The facts, however, are completely to the contrary. People are not factory products. Each individual is a vast, unique universe, and it takes an intelligent and expert psychotherapist to explore it. The "essential" dream elements are those that represent the highly specific emotional structure and forces of the individual. What does Reeves expect as an answer? The questions he raises are on such a level that to answer them would be embarrassing.

Having subjected the reader to the professor's ponderings, I shall devote only a few paragraphs to the next example. The paper is by Donald P. Spence, a psychologist and professor of psychiatry at Rutgers Medical School in New Jersey. The article is just over 20 pages, but one could easily devote 1,000 pages to refuting practically all the statements therein. The paper is proudly entitled "Toward a Theory of Dream Interpretation." This time I shall let the reader be the judge. Only a few statements from the article follow, but they are sufficient to prove my point.

Professor Spence complains about the absence of "general laws" and thus the "general absence of reversibility." That is, he contends that having arrived at the latent content of a dream, one should be able to tell this content to a third party, who, with the help of Professor Spence's "formula," can reconstruct the original, manifest dream. Later in the article the professor actually proceeds to do just that. The Great Houdini comes to mind. Alas! The fact is, he chose for the feat a dream of Freud's, of which he had, of course, the original, manifest dream.

It takes an unbelievable ignorance of the nature of the human psyche to assume that knowing the latent meaning, one could reconstruct the manifest dream. Even the simplest dreams involve a myriad of elements specific to the dreamer.

Here is an example: A man in his late 50s, married for some 30 years and deeply in love with his wife, was informed by her physician that she may have only one more year to live. This is his dream:

> I am alone, and I find myself in a dismal resort. I return to my hotel, and it is just as desolate and miserable. I discover that my room is merely a shabby lounge separated by a low partition from the lobby. I want to shave, but there is no sink with hot water. Then I discover that my suitcase with all my belongings has disappeared. I complain to the desk clerk, but he is very rude and completely disinterested.

We know the reason for the dream, but no one could reconstruct the manifest dream.

Professor Spence severely criticizes psychoanalysts for "their hunger for details," that is, associations. He asserts that their hunger is symptomatic of "the essential poverty" of psychoanalytic explanations, meaning interpretations. Proclaiming that what analysts do is characterized by an "absence of general laws," he claims that they have no "general theory of interpretation" and no "general principles."

Here again, Spence, like so many academicians, whether psychologists like him or not, demonstrates an utter lack of the psychological knowledge that expertise in psychotherapy confers. He lambastes as "poverty" the quest of the analysts to acquaint themselves with as many details as possible of their patients' psyche, a quest that is necessary if we are to do justice to the immense richness of the inner world. To satisfy his desire for general laws, theories, and principles, perhaps Spence should turn to the study of amoebas, an enterprise that would be more commensurate with the level of his thought.

Later Spence argues that "until we have a test for distinguishing relevant from irrelevant associations, we will be plagued with an inadequate theory of interpretation." One wonders to whom the "we" refers.

Professor Spence continues by explaining that there are two kinds of understanding. The weaker one is "I understand how you feel." The stronger one is "I understand what is wrong with the carburetor." "This rests on general principles," he says. He then states that traditional dream analysis, as practiced for almost the last 100 years, may provide us with the weaker form of understanding but contributes very little to the stronger.

To achieve his lofty goals, Professor Spence advises, "We must partition the dreamer's associations into a primary set, that is the presumed causes of the dream, and a secondary set, that is not having any significant relationship to the creations of the dream."

I have saved for last the pièce de résistance: how do we find the most meaningful of the meaningful – the "primary set"? Professor Spence divulges the ultimate secret: "They should all come from the same time period in the patient's life – as a working hypothesis, let us take the 24 hours preceding the dream" (!!!).

Will multitudes of therapists take Professor Spence's pronouncements to heart and sternly advise their patients to refrain from annoying them with tedious, valueless associations covering their childhood years?

It is a sad testimony to the status quo of mental health, and of academic teaching in particular, that men like Spence are admitted to the rank of "professionals" and, far worse, are allowed to teach at the university level. The disinformation and inanity emanating from such people is a disaster to their students. Not only are the students badly misled, but one can also be sure that such "teachers" will eliminate the psychologically gifted students and favor those inclined to sterile intellectual speculation. That, however, is merely one of the factors contributing to the widespread negative selection of trainees in the field of psychotherapy. The resultant damage to patient care is tragic.

It is significant that the professor cites two men, Reeves and Spence, who are just as alienated from even a minimal understanding of the workings of the human mind as he is. They are representative of the many mental health professionals who were able to enter the profession but who lack the sensitivity and talent necessary to grasp psychological matters. As shown, those people attempt to fill the gap with obtuse scholarly speculations, dwelling on the unessential and meaningless. True talent in our field is uncommon; facile and pretentious intellectualization is not. Understandably, in our system of interconnected systems, the scholastic interlopers have become a formidable force, an immense threat to knowledge and the public welfare.

It is inconceivable that a professional with any expertise in psychotherapy would have delineated the problems and posed the questions in the manner those three academicians did. Their sterile approaches and viewpoints are proof of utter ignorance of the nature and workings of the human psyche and thus of psychotherapy. Unfortunately their shortcomings are widespread, and expert clinical instruction is exceedingly hard to come by. The consequences for student training and ultimately for patient care are disastrous. All too often we encounter the following situations:

- Gifted and intelligent students are eliminated, and intellectualizing students, who have no criteria and judgment for psychotherapy, are favored, both at universities and at training institutes.
- After becoming aware of the incompetence of their teachers, the ludicrousness of the course material offered, and the paucity of valid clinical instruction, talented and discriminating students abandon their psychotherapy training.
- The majority of students who remain, believing that what they are being taught is all the information available, are unaware of the rich body of psychotherapeutic knowledge and clinical expertise that exists.

Dedicated students in other disciplines are likely to obtain a decent to excellent education, varying with the specific circumstances. It is only psychotherapy students who encounter major difficulties in finding quality instruction, personal analysis, and supervision. We, of course, need theory. But theory can be devised only by those with outstanding psychotherapeutic acumen, and it must evolve out of clinical expertise. Unfortunately it is most often the mental health professionals lacking those qualities who engage in freewheeling theorizing. They need to fill the gaps caused by their inability to comprehend the human psyche. Scrutiny of their writings reveals those shortcomings. We must beware of professionals who build grandiose, intellectual theories wrapped in scholarly language but who do not, and cannot, give proof of clinical understanding. When I speak critically of academicians, I refer solely to those people. It may be true that "a rose is a rose is a rose," but a psychotherapist is *not* a psychotherapist is *not* a psychotherapist. Some are; many are not!

For well over half a century, I have been asking this: How is it that people without the slightest talent for our profession, with no sensitivity for human feelings and thus no sensibility whatsoever to comprehend dreams, can infiltrate our profession in such great numbers, become teachers, and have their writings published? They are the people who train psychotherapists and other mental health professionals, thus creating greater masses of the incompetent to be let loose on the patient population and perpetuating the ever-increasing deterioration of treatment and education.

From the first day that I became a director of the Foundation and thus had some kind of forum, I have publicly called attention to the consequences of this situation. Would we allow blatantly incompetent surgeons to operate? Or to teach medical students worthless surgical procedures? Would we not insist that those responsible be deprived of licensure? Applying the same ethics to the mental health field, however, is contrary to present-day thinking. For every expert witness supporting such a complaint, there would be dozens of professionals testifying on the side of the defendants. If you doubt that statement, remember the days when lobotomy was rampant.

Ours is the only area in public health where, under the guise of "science," such a situation is tolerated to such an extent and can be comfortably rationalized with impunity. What makes the situation particularly discouraging is that although many competent and devoted psychotherapists are fully aware of the problems, they do not challenge the status quo.

Let us recall the title of this section: "Dr. Faust and Little Moritz." One may wonder why Dr. Faust was mentioned in the same breath as his opposite, the obnoxious know-it-all. Faust's intelligence and integrity made him realize that in spite of his constant search, he knew far too little. Those who struggle for meaning and understanding see in Faust the symbol of their sorrow and their aspirations. Freud cherished Goethe, cherished Faust.

I brought in the noble Faust for needed comfort, a counterpoint of courage and decency, to overcome the sadness caused by the ignorance and pretense we have encountered along the way. Faust says:

> Philosophy have I digested,
> The whole of Law and Medicine,
> From each its secrets have I wrested,
> Theology, alas, thrown in.
> Poor fool, with all this sweated lore,
> I stand no wiser than I was before.
> Master and Doctor are my titles;
> For years now, without repose,
> I've held my erudite recitals
> And led my pupils by the nose.
> And round we go, on crooked ways or straight,
> And well I know that ignorance is our fate,
> – And this I hate.*

GOETHE

* Translation by Philip Wayne.

b2   Curiouser and Curiouser

Even much learning does not teach understanding.

Heraclitus

If you talk enough, you will become a leader, even if you do not know what you are talking about. An extensive study conducted by Dr. Cabott L. Jaffee at the University of Tennessee's Department of Psychology demonstrated that female students who monopolized discussion but who were hardly ever correct in their statements were selected as leaders of their groups far more often than were the quiet girls, who were frequently correct.

The experiment was designed to ascertain the effect of quality and knowledge evinced in speech versus mere quantity of words as the decisive factor determining selection for group leadership.

Ordinarily a paper on psychotherapeutic matters should focus on what one believes to be valuable and useful. Here, however, I must seek out the negatives and deficiencies so that they may be identified and solutions proposed. I am not concerned here with the theoretical positions of the writers we discuss. My focus is solely on matters of clinical concern. Although experienced clinicians keep in mind various theoretical positions, the more expert the psychotherapist, the more his understanding of the problems of each patient is based on clinical material. If there are unanswered questions, one should admit that one does not know. To use theory to force an answer, to fill a gap, even though there is no clinical evidence for a valid connection, is a frequent practice but poor therapy.

Up to this point in the chapter, we have been marveling at creatures from outer space. We shall now go in the opposite direction to take a look at our inner circle, that is, psychoanalysts and psychotherapists. One would hope that after being forced to deal with a tedious enemy from without, this look within would be entrancing and joyous. Alas, it is not! We are going to encounter the enemy within, a master of many insidious wiles.

My disappointment should not be misconstrued. For over half a century and in several countries, I have encountered many, many teachers and colleagues with whom it was a joy to discuss our work and whose clinical acumen widened my view. Clearly the innate giftedness and humanity of those knowledgeable men and women, many of whom are unknown to the professional community, enabled them to overcome inadequate instruction and a faulty system.

While books on mental health do not usually contain detective stories, this one does. Who are the villains to be tracked down?

Over 50 years ago Otto Kauders, a friend and professor of psychiatry, used sarcasm – dear to the Viennese – when he severely criticized the methods of certain practitioners, whom he described as having "the soul of a peddler and the acumen of little Moritz." In case the reader needs to refresh his memory as to the prototype of that now ubiquitous species, he is referred to the beginning of the previous section, "Dr. Faust and Little Moritz." Many years later Gustav Bychofski also deplored the very same procedures and asserted: "No matter how disguised by high-sounding, scientific verbiage, they are nothing but bargain-basement populism. And if such shoddy approaches are taught to students, or otherwise disseminated, the consequences for patient care are dismal." Both men felt that those approaches constituted the major threat to the cause of psychotherapy.

To provide the best possible care, responsible analysts and therapists seek optimal understanding of each patient, often an exhausting task. It becomes even more difficult when a patient cannot afford the desirable number of weekly sessions. Less dedicated professionals are not likely to make the required effort. They seek shortcuts to avoid the tedious search for relevant facts and details in each person's psyche. That is the reason for the multitude of labor-saving and thought-saving approaches: the easier and simpler, the better.

One example from the distant past can serve as an illustration: lobotomy. In its time, lobotomy was acclaimed by many who used "scientific" justifications and was criticized by few. Understandably, some engaged in the procedure out of despair; too many, however, did so for less-than-altruistic reasons. While assurances were given that lobotomy was being applied only in the most desperate cases, the facts prove otherwise. All too frequently, the "surgery" was administered haphazardly in the practitioner's office, merely by introducing a long needle below the eyelid into the brain (for a clear and sober account see Valenstein, 1986). Compare that procedure with the cautious approach followed by the Food and Drug Administration for the protection of the public before approving medications, even when they have been tested and used for years in Europe.

Dr. Joseph Wilder, a fellow of our Foundation, was one of the few urging more restraint in the application of lobotomy. His requests were ignored. Criticism of the lobotomy practitioners, no matter how sound, was decried as unseemly and ad hominem. Thus, while the professionals stood by, thousands of patients were mutilated physically and mentally. Only when the consequences became all too evident did the practice fade from the scene.

Here we will search the literature for telltale clues to practices and theories in psychotherapy that, like lobotomy, simplify matters but sacrifice quality. Much simplification is achieved by moving the focus away from the patient, thus avoiding the difficulties of thorough therapeutic work based on clinical realities. As a substitute for an individualized approach, we are offered generalizations, which translate into gimmickry, and grandiose "theories" alien to clinical evidence.

We shall examine a considerable number of those approaches as they apply to individual psychotherapy. Group psychotherapy has been blessed with "group process," to be discussed later in this book. All those ingenious attempts to simplify make generous use of rationalization. All make life much easier for the "therapist," and if he is a teacher, grateful students should be plentiful. A "movement," or even a "school of therapy," may result.

In the following pages I shall attempt to substantiate those critical statements by examining the literature for practices and theories that advance patient care – and those that do not.

In selecting the writings for our critique, I used three criteria:

1.   The situation described evinces a considerable lack of understanding, or even ignorance, of clinical knowledge.
2.   The writer is well known and occupies a position of prestige,

thus representing in some way the status quo in psychotherapy.

3.   The deficiencies described can be recognized in many prac-
      ticing psychotherapists (including many of those who
      applied to, or were actually employed at, a clinic sponsored
      by the Foundation for over 20 years).

The clinical factors discussed here represent the areas in which
clinical expertise is frequently missing, that is, the knowledge essential
in day-to-day therapeutic practice.

Overall, one notices a marked reluctance to discuss practical clinical matters. The attitude is that they are elementary stuff that everybody knows and that there is no need for their detailed discussion. The
preference is for lofty, but safe, intellectual discussions, replete with
theoretically and dogmatically spiced comments that cannot be verified
by clinical data. Sweeping statements abound, either about a specific
patient or about broader issues. (The introduction to this volume by
Robert J. Stoller describes that situation cogently.)

I shall now continue my review of some representative writings
on feelings and dreams, focusing on the degree of their authors' comprehension and mastery of the subject matter as it affects the quality of
patient care.

Even though we are concerned here with present trends and their possible effect on the future, let us nevertheless take a quick look at the past
to see if the present downtrend was foreseeable.

To start, let us take a look at a volume of the venerable ANNUAL
SURVEY OF PSYCHOANALYSIS from the 1950s. I chose volume 5 (1954)
at random. While the work has over 600 pages, it is disappointing to
note that only 30 pages are concerned with dreams. That is certainly
not the fault of the editor, John Frosch, who cheerfully states, "The
recently renewed interest in dreams resulted in the publication of
more than a dozen papers in 1954." Dr. Frosch showed exceptional
talent; in many instances, his editorial comments were far more cogent
and clearer than the papers in the volume. But as even the ever-polite
Frosch admits, most of the papers in the section on dreams are routine.
I shall touch briefly on just three.

The first paper, by Erik H. Erikson, contains a few statements of interest to us. I quote them without comment:

> With advance in the technique of analysis, the exhaustive analysis of dreams is all but a lost art.

> Early overtraining of the student analyst can do much harm in that the immediate recognition of symbols, verbal double meanings, etc., may induce the analyst to reach a premature closure in his conviction of having "understood" the dream.

> Different schools of dynamic psychology and different analysts manage to provoke systematically different manifest dreams, obviously dreamed to please and impress the respective analysts.

Another paper, by Charles Fisher, reports on experiments extending the previous work of Pötzl. I quote only one sentence – the only sentence in italics in Frosch's paper on dreams: *"The dream cannot compose a new visual structure any more than it can a new speech."* A look at Fisher's original paper reveals that the italics are Fisher's, not Frosch's. Moreover, in the summary Fisher writes, "It was suggested that the dream cannot create a new visual structure any more than it can a new speech."

In any event, Fisher was utterly wrong. Dreams frequently create new visual images and new speech, the same way artists and writers do. I will illustrate his error with a dream I have used for years to illuminate a number of points.

I am very familiar with the history and all the data necessary for the psychotherapy of the dreamer, a former patient of mine. He was a psychology professor, quite conscientious, intelligent, frank, and well meaning. He was not a happy man.

In the dream, which relates to a situation preceding it by some 15 years, he finds himself in a room he does not recognize. That is of no importance to him, but the following scene is: The professor is with three junior faculty members for whose work he is responsible. Two are merely onlookers in the dream. The third is a young assistant, whom the professor later describes as "glib, shifty, varying from adulation to 'catty' hostility, and a sociopathic liar, often successful in inveigling others."

In the dream the professor is discussing routine matters. The telephone rings, and the assistant picks it up. Hearing what the assistant says to the other party, who is a patient at the university clinic, the professor realizes that the assistant has acted contrary to instructions and has bungled a situation involving the patient.

After the telephone conversation ends, the dreamer addresses the assistant in a gentle way, hoping to avoid the kind of nasty scene usually created by the assistant at the slightest hint of criticism. He tells him that something apparently went wrong with the plans for that person and asks the assistant a question to get some indication of what the problem was. The assistant, who has obviously felt on the defensive from the moment he answered the telephone, as usual responds instantly with a counterattack and snaps, in a vicious tone: "Not now. My stomach hurts like crazy."

Reporting the dream, the patient commented, "It was quite clear that he wanted to make it obvious that my questioning him was completely unwarranted and most unfair, quite upsetting to such a perfect worker as he, and thus the cause of his incapacitating stomach pain. This guy always played up to evoke sympathy from others, in this case, the two other staff members present."

In the dream the professor feels that the patient who phoned is being victimized by the assistant's negligence and that something ought to be done to remedy the problem. He turns to the assistant again. So as not to aggravate the situation, and even though he knows the original plan, the professor says diplomatically and matter-of-factly: "Look, this is important. Can you refresh my memory as to what our original plan was? I do not have the notes in front of me." The assistant snaps back, "I thought you didn't."

Here again, the professor states that the implication is clear that the assistant's remark was addressed to the other two faculty members and implied that the professor was grossly negligent in not having the papers in question right there. Of course, the professor states, it would not have been possible to have the papers there, inasmuch as the particular problem arose unexpectedly owing to the telephone call.

I do not present this dream to analyze it but so that the dialogue between the professor and the assistant can be scrutinized. The professor insisted to me that even though the dream accurately mirrored the constant annoyances created by the assistant, the incident never occurred, nor did he and the assistant ever exchange those particular remarks. He said that the dream, however, accurately described the assistant's unbelievable capacity to come up, in a split second, with malicious answers that effectively slanted any situation to his advantage and to the detriment of any "adversary."

Clearly, not only is new dialogue created in dreams – and that is why I selected this example – but dreams can create dialogue alien to the dreamer's personality. The professor remarked that in his waking state he could never have produced, even with enormous effort, the snappy answers of the assistant. He stated that in the dream, as in reality, the answers of the assistant shocked him, leaving him stunned and often unable to answer adequately and with immediacy.

The retorts suggest a mentality contrary to that of the professor. Common wisdom in psychotherapy holds that all personalities in a dream represent facets of the personality of the dreamer, albeit some of them hidden. Here again, we have a convenient, facile, pseudoexplanation, repeated again and again. The fact is that the assistant's character was not part of the character structure of the professor.

Another example: A patient, an employee in a large office, dreamed of being harassed and verbally attacked by another worker whom he described as a very nasty homosexual. In the dream, the patient is frightened and upset by the incident. On the face of it, many psychoanalysts would understandably assert that the aggressive figure in the dream represents the patient's own homosexual feelings, which he fears. In this case, however, such an obvious interpretation would be recognized as incorrect, were all the other material presented by the patient taken into consideration.

A third dream is typical of those with inferiority complexes. The patient, a man in his 40s, relates:

> I invited an attractive girl to the theater to see a comedy. She sits on my left. During a funny scene she laughs heartily. A handsome young man sitting in front of me turns around, looks at her, and starts talking to her in a joking, self-assured manner. She is obviously quite pleased and responds, openly flirting with him. She gently places her hand on his arm. I

feel miserable and do not say anything.

The young man represents the idealized male image the patient would fervently like to be.

The key to understanding all three dreams lies in two fundamental facts:

- A severe, cruel superego is at the origin of the dreams of the patients, who are subjected to frightening, hateful, and humiliating experiences.
- The unconscious has an uncanny capacity to create instantly, and without effort, any number of scenarios representing inner emotional states. Those scenarios may vary from desolate barrenness to high drama. The creative activity of the unconscious in dreams often exceeds by far the imaginative capacity in the waking state.

We need to shed some of our shibboleths about dream work. "Producing" the dream involves elements and operations within our psyche that have so far not been touched on in the literature. We shall have to look at the Shakespeare hidden within us, who is always creating new works.

The next paper to be discussed is symptomatic of one of the major faults of the psychoanalytic movement from its very beginning: over-simplification and overgeneralization. In some cases they are accompanied by statements that give the impression of a psychoanalytic textbook gone wild. A number of papers on myths and mythology also fall into that category. One wonders how such articles find their way into serious professional publications.

The author of the paper, Alfred Winterstein, asserts that the feeling of astonishment in a dream is most often based on the surprise a child feels at the first sight of the genitals of the opposite sex. Are there no other surprises of psychic importance that may suddenly appear in dreams? Surprises can pop up in dreams at any time, such as when something repressed suddenly breaks through; it may be minor or major, temporary or lasting.

But the best is yet to come. Editor Frosch, ever tolerant, states, without batting an eye, "The author concludes with the speculation that the primary astonishment at the sight of the opposite sex may find its lifelong continuation in the philosophical 'astonishment at everything' which Aristotle felt to be the source of all philosophizing." Thus, for all of us who search for truth, philosophically, spiritually, or scientifically, the proper emblems to be proudly placed on our flag and to be engraved above the entrance doors of our abodes, have at long last been revealed.

At any rate, do not forget Winterstein, as he will surface once more, briefly, but without his surprising genitals.

You may recall a book on dreams by Erich Fromm, published in 1951. The title, THE FORGOTTEN LANGUAGE, speaks for itself. One of the main chapters in the book is "The Art of Dream Interpretation." Fromm is correct; a much-forgotten art it was then – and still is.

Also in 1951, Emil A. Gutheil's illustrated HANDBOOK OF DREAM ANALYSIS was published. It was a colossal effort that touched on a huge variety of facets of the topic. The bibliography included more than 800 publications in eight languages, covering a period of 50 years. At that time it had some influence in reviving interest in dreams among psychotherapists.

Not very reassured by what we have found thus far, let us turn to articles and books published more recently. I shall comment on some concerned with our topic. In several instances, for brevity, I present only a few representative passages from the writings. I would have preferred that an independent party make the selection, so that I could not be accused of bias. Later in this chapter, when I briefly review the writings of seven contributors in a recent work, we shall find precisely such an independent choice.

Let us start by taking a brief look at two authors frequently considered experts on the topic of dreams.

Stanley R. Palombo

Earlier I mentioned the statement by Crick and Mitchison wherein they declared that the purpose of dreams is to forget. Now we encounter the opposite position. In a paper entitled "The Adaptive Functions of Dreams" Stanley R. Palombo (1978), a training analyst at the Washington Psychoanalytic Institute, states that dreaming serves an adaptive function. Frequently citing Arlow, he says that that is accomplished by matching old information with new, enabling it to be entered in the permanent memory structure, an "internal reordering and updating of experiential data that has already been registered in previous waking experience."

Like so many other writers, both Arlow and Palombo make sweeping, categorical, abstract statements that can be neither proved or disproved. Only when writers become explicit and speak about clinical facts can one pin them down and ascertain their competence. Here is a pronouncement by Palombo: "When a dream, in which old and new experiences are unsuccessfully matched, awakens the dreamer . . ." And interpreting several dreams of a patient, he writes: "The unconscious meaning to the patient . . . was that he removed Father's corpse from the inside of Mother's body," "anal impregnation fantasy or dream," and "the noisy refrigerator was clearly a screen memory from another primal scene experience." Perhaps, from now on, the refrigerator will never seem the same! And if there are children at home, it had better be covered up.

Contrary to the first assertion, "not matching" per se will not awaken the dreamer. Regarding Palombo's interpretations, you will find nothing in the patient's dreams or associations to justify those simplistic assertions. Unfortunately, such baseless interpretations are made far too often. They are a sorry travesty of psychoanalytic acumen.

We must wonder what such "therapy" will do to a patient with serious emotional problems – all in the name of psychoanalysis!

In the early 1970s I became aware of the efforts of Robert J. Stoller, an experienced clinician devoted to the improvement of psychoanalytic therapy. He was engaged in a systematic and exhaustive critical examination of the shortcomings of psychoanalysis in many areas. Until his recent death we stayed in contact and kept each other abreast of our critical efforts. Stoller's perspicacious work cogently and thoroughly covers many topics of psychoanalysis I can only barely touch on. Outstanding among them is the question of whether psychoanalysis can be called a science. After careful examination he concludes that it cannot. To a great extent our writings complement each other. I strongly urge any reader interested in the constructive criticism of psychoanalysis to acquaint himself with Stoller's writings. His ideas can be found in his introduction to this volume, as well as in Colby and Stoller (1988).

My complaint against Palombo's writings also applies, of course, to those of many other psychotherapists. As Stoller wrote in Colby and Stoller:

> Because of the way analytic reports are written, we cannot tell how analytic treatment goes about affecting patients, why it works, and why it does not. Yet, who begs that we correct the situation of vague reporting? Most often, we are not told what was communicated or what words the patient and the analyst said to each other. Regarding analysts' formal reports, we know that our colleagues, friendly, neutral, or inimical others, are often untouched, unconvinced by the writings of other analysts and therapists. How about bad theory, mistaken observation, little consensus, little trust in the reports, the failure to make ideas clear to others, and to report findings clearly?

When people asked old man Luther for details of his past, he would invariably answer: "I do not remember too well. Go ask Erikson. He does!"

S.deS.

Erik H. Erikson

How a vociferous purist – and self-proclaimed saint – like Erik H. Erikson can actually have committed cardinal sins is evidenced in his writings. Erikson considered human existence in terms of common denominators and life stages. It is true that we all have certain things in common and that we pass through phases linked to our age. Although Erikson wished to incorporate those general factors in the body of psychotherapy, the fact is that they are not matters that can be, or should be, addressed by psychotherapy. They apply to "normal" people, as well as to all the others.

Because Erikson was such a gifted writer, the reader is tempted to read on without ever pausing for a critical evaluation. But since we are dealing here with psychoanalytic works and not literary essays, the yardstick to be applied is quite different. Writings in our field should use responsible restraint and abstain from inundating us with easy, general explanations applicable to everyone. They should provide us with the fullest possible specific description of the psychodynamics, different for every individual. Thus when writing about one's own patients, one must offer a detailed and accurate report and stay close to the clinical data. Writing about those who have not been one's patients and about whom one does not have firsthand information – which is Erikson's specialty – requires even greater prudence if the author is honest and responsible. Freewheeling fiction, all too frequent in psychotherapy, has no place here.

That said, let us discuss two analytical works and biographical statements by Erikson: the first about Martin Luther, the second about Freud.

Erikson's (1958) YOUNG MAN LUTHER reads like an eyewitness account – but even more than that. An eyewitness can merely describe external events and facts. Erikson, however, not only does that, but also intrepidly describes, step by step, all the psychological events taking place within Luther's psyche. A single brief quote is representative of his approach:

> His scruples began to eat like moths into the fabric of monkhood which before had felt like a well-woven protection against his impulses. He thus became susceptible to the alliance of erotic irritability and hypersensitivity of conscience which brings identity diffusion to a head. He attempted to counter this alliance with the redoubled use of monastic methods, and consequently found himself estranged from all three.

If one can convince oneself to consider this book merely as a freely conceived biographical novel, it makes for interesting and enjoyable reading.

The same cannot be said for another of Erikson's (1954) best-known papers: "The Dream Specimen of Psychoanalysis." Here Erikson does not engage in the generalizations about life stages, on which he so often dwelled. Rather he tries to teach us what he describes as the state-of-the-art method of "exhaustive dream interpretation" that he has devised for all to follow.

First, Erikson rightly condemns facile, instant, dictionary-type interpretation, where one symbol is declared to have a definite, latent meaning (see also my comments on that subject earlier in this chapter). He then employs Freud's "Irma" dream to demonstrate his ideas. Erikson uses Freud's associations and comments for his own elaborations. But serious trouble is inherent in his choice of Freud's dream as a demonstration object. Although Erikson obviously believes that he is giving a pedagogic display of analytic thoroughness and brilliance, the following questions point to what separates his effort from valid and credible analytic procedure: Would you ever consider telling a patient not to come anymore to the analytic sessions but simply to mail you his dreams annotated with his associations? Would you consider such a procedure to be as valid as the usual analytic session?

If your answer is no, then you cannot condone Erikson's procedure. There is an important difference between the notes of a person's associations to a dream and the exploration of dream associations in the analytic session. Owing to resistance, a patient may slide over the most significant associations and dwell on those of lesser importance. A competent analyst, to the extent that it is advisable at a given stage of analysis, will discreetly focus the patient's attention on his significant associations and the key points of the dream for further exploration. Thus the analyst's presence is essential, even if the dreamer is Freud.

To expand on the Irma dream and to call such an enterprise a lighthearted attempt at speculation and fantasy would certainly be a permissible literary exercise. What Erikson indulges in, however, as the next pages will confirm, is heavy-handed and blatant mischief.

To provide valid instruction on the subject of dream analysis, a knowledgeable analyst would select a meaningful dream of one of his patients and present the patient's psychological history, prior developments in therapy, and associations to the dream. The analyst would follow with his comments, indicating which ones he made to the patient and which ones he did not. Furthermore – and this is a crucial part of such a report and a major cause of Erikson's failure – the analyst would describe to us the development of the patient's transference and explain how the transference is manifested in the dream under examination, as well as in other dreams the patient has had. Only such a method can be considered responsible workmanship.

Professionals with expertise in dreams will find Erikson's article questionable and disappointing for a second reason. Trying to find a brief example to substantiate my second criticism, I encountered an obstacle: in this extensive paper Erikson not only deals with a single dream but also dwells at great length on each point. To avoid an accusation of citing out of context, I would have to quote two or more pages and then devote at least five pages to their examination. That is not possible here.

I did, however, find a brief passage in Erikson's discussion of the Irma dream that substantiates my argument. Although the report of the dream was originally written in German, the excellent translation by Erikson allows clear understanding of the matter. (The reader may wish to read this curious paper himself.) The day before Freud's dream, a colleague had told him about the not-too-satisfactory condition of Irma, one of Freud's patients. Sometime before leaving on vacation, Irma had found an interpretation by Freud to be unacceptable.

In this part of the dream Freud reproaches Irma for being to blame if she still has pains, as she did not accept his "solution." Irma responds by complaining that her pains are unbearable; she is "choked by them." Freud, startled, looks at her. She appears to be quite ill, and he wants to look into her throat, but she is hesitant. Quoting Freud: "She offers some resistance to this, like a woman who has a set of false teeth. I think, surely, there is no need for her to resist like this." The official translation continues: "She doesn't need them [the teeth]." As Erikson notes, that translation is incorrect. In German: *"Sie hat es doch nicht nötig."* The meaning is unequivocal: She does not need to be so bashful, as a woman with false teeth might be.

Now we turn to Erikson's interpretation of the passage, because of its implication for dream interpretation. The basic tendency reflected here occurs over and over again, often magnified, in Erikson's writings. Erikson correctly, though too briefly, translates the German text into "She does not need it" and adds, "meaning her resistive behavior." He then continues, citing an extended colloquial version of the same phrase: *"Das hat sie doch gar nicht nötig, sich so zu zieren."* That is the same meaning as "There is no need at all for her to be so bashful (hesitant)," since there is nothing to hide (such as false teeth).

But now the trouble begins. Departing from Freud's statements, Erikson proceeds with his own associations and thoughts on the dream. He asserts that the meaning of the quoted phrase, and thus its proper (though freer) translation, should be "Who is she to put on such airs?" Erikson then continues:

> This expression includes a value judgment to the effect that a certain lady pretends that she is of a higher social, esthetic, or moral status than she really is. A related expression would be the protestation brought forth by a lady on the defense: "Ich hab das doch gar nicht nötig, mir das gefallen zu lassen"; in English, "I don't need to take this from you," again referring to a misjudgment, this time on the part of a forward gentleman, as to what expectations he may cultivate in regard to a lady's willingness to accept propositions. These phrases, then, are a link between the associations concerning patients who resist "solutions" and women (patients or not) who resist sexual advances.

We have here three clear assertions by Erikson about Irma:

1. that she has pretenses to higher status
2. that she has an "I don't have to take this [sexual advance] from you" attitude
3. that her resistance to accepting Freud's dictum is linked to women's resistance to sexual advances.

So what is my second reason for complaint? It is Erikson's blatant misuse of a dream, and complete disregard for the clinical facts, to bolster his theoretical speculations. There is nothing whatsoever in Freud's dream or associations to justify Erikson's three assertions.

Moreover, remember that Erikson always inveighs against "dictionary" interpretations. There are three kinds of such interpretations. All represent decisions imposed by the analyst without the benefit of the patient's associations and therefore without the desirable confirmation.

The first kind of dictionary interpretation occurs when the analyst assumes that a given dream symbol has a fixed meaning, for example, a horse represents father.

In the second type the analyst, referring to a supposedly key word in the patient's dream, claims that the word stands for a similar-sounding word that holds the real meaning. Examples would be "bed" standing for "bad," "horse" standing for "hearse," or, as we shall later encounter in our discussion of Morton F. Reiser's (1991) book, "suntan leading to tannic acid." Gustav Bychofski expressed the belief that most of "the dreams that were never dreamt," meaning those invented by the authors themselves to show analytic "brilliance," use such gimmickry.

The third type is perfectly illustrated by Erikson's second assertion, that her attitude is "I don't need to take this from you." That statement can in no way be linked to the dreamer, Freud. It is merely one of many contexts in which the word *"nötig"* (necessary) may be used. Freud is fortunate that Erikson did not pick another meaning, also listed for this word: the pressing need to have a bowel movement.

What, then, about Irma's hesitation in the dream? Right after mentioning her hesitation, Freud continues recounting his dream as follows: "The mouth then opens wide, and I find a large white spot on the right, and elsewhere I see extensive grayish-white scabs." Rather than speaking with the certainty that Palombo, Erikson, and later on Shengold do, I venture the following possible interpretation: Freud felt disturbed and guilty about Irma's complaint. The hesitation of Irma's image in his dream is simply caused by Freud's own momentary hesitation to face the unpleasant, ugly feelings and facts.

That Erikson is a widely read, influential author explains much of my concern regarding his writings, namely, the danger to thorough, individualized work in psychotherapy that generalizations and irresponsible and facile assertions cause. Moreover, Erikson, as demonstrated by his analysis of the Irma dream, was teaching inadequate approaches based on purely intellectual procedures, far removed from clinical evidence. Interpretation based on dictionary meanings of a given word is merely one of many such abuses. Once more, we should be troubled by the consequences to teaching, and thus to patient care.

Harold P. Blum

Now let us see what a longtime editor of the AMERICAN JOURNAL OF PSYCHOANALYSIS has to say about dreams.

Harold P. Blum (1976), in an interesting article on the changing use of dreams, shares my opinions that "laboratory sleep and dream research have added very little to psychological understanding, or to the clinical significance, of the dream in therapy. . . . In recent years there has been very little evolutionary change in the clinical use of dreams." Blum contrasts the view of those who consider dreams to be merely one of several clinical communications available with the view of those who accord the dream an exceptional status. Blum explains that the absence of evolution is due to "Freud's masterful conceptions and insights into the dream [that] have been so rich and relatively complete that new additions to dream theory have been very limited."

In this relatively short article Blum makes an amazing number of brief dogmatic statements about the nature and function of dreams. It would take a sizable volume to scrutinize all of them. Here I shall note only a few, those that clearly indicate his traditional positions, including his notion of phallic women. It is not clear whether they are the same as those who appear nightly on New York cable television.

Here are some of his statements:

> It is doubtful that a patient who never dreams can be analyzed.

> The traumatic dream is still puzzling and may not be identical in origin and function to the usual dreams which serve wish-fulfillment.

> The dream may be used to widen self-understanding . . . but this is an ego adaptation and not an intrinsic function of the dream.

Ralph R. Greenson

The monograph of the Kris Study Group of the New York Psychoanalytic Institute (Waldhorn, 1967) is also particularly discouraging. Let us hear the competent voice of Ralph R. Greenson (1970) on some of the key points of the study group's conclusions:

The psychoanalytic literature in recent years reveals that a number of psychoanalysts believe that either the dream has declined in clinical importance over the last forty years, and is of no special value for psychoanalytic theory, or they use techniques which indicate that they have disregarded Freud's theory and methods of understanding and of using the dream in clinical practice. I am also impressed that some influential psychoanalysts contend that this downgrading of the significance of the dream in clinical practice has come about because (a) the structural theory was introduced; (b) Freud's great work on dreams has discouraged attempts at emulation or elaboration; and (c) Freud's concept of the topographic theory has become useless.

Greenson continues:

Most of the members of this group appear to have concluded that (i) the dream is, clinically speaking, a communication in the course of analysis similar to all others, (ii) it does not provide access to material otherwise unavailable, (iii) it is simply one of many types of material useful for analytic inquiry, (iv) it is not particularly useful for the recovery of repressed childhood memories.

Greenson then states categorically, "I disagree with every one of the conclusions stated above." And he is not alone; Greenson relates that a section of that group, with Leon Altman as its spokesman, opposed many of the majority opinions.

At the end of this section I will discuss what I believe to be the major cause for so disappointing a situation.

While perhaps not obvious to outsiders, therapists who attach considerable importance to dreams tend to have a great affinity for each other and a sense of separation from those who do not share their convictions. Addressing them, they feel that an entire dimension is missing and that their words fall on barren ground. Here is a fine example of that point from Greenson's paper. Toward the end of the Kris monograph, the study group presents its conclusions concerning a patient's dream:

Such axiomatic procedures as the desirability of working with transference elements before nontransference material or affect-laden before nonaffect-laden material, or the necessity of drawing the patient's attention to evident omissions or to an addendum, were all mentioned. The consensus was that these were best considered as tactical maneuvers, subordinated to an overall strategy of the conduct of the analysis, which would, of course, change with the progress of the treatment.

Greenson replies:

In my opinion there is no place for axiomatic procedures in trying to do psychoanalytic therapy. It is true that some of us follow certain time-tested technical guidelines in beginning the exploration of such oft-recurring clinical constellations as may occur in associating to dreams, or in free association in general. These approaches are tools for investigation. *I find the concept of an 'overall strategy of the conduct of the analysis' an impressive, high-sounding phrase but, in reality, with the present state of knowledge, this overall strategy is at best loose, subject to frequent changes and revisions, and full of unknowns. Only psychoanalysts with preconceived and rigid theoretical notions are sure of an 'overall strategy.' And they also have prefabricated interpretations for all types of patients, and disregard the fact that each individual human being is unique.* (Italics added)

By way of illustration, Greenson cites Eissler's criticism of Alexander and his disciples for their preconceived plans for treatment in each case. Eissler thought that their paramount concern was to validate their hypotheses.

Greenson also reminds us that Freud had the humility to say that we should let the patient determine the subject matter of each session and pay attention to the patient's dream content and free associations.

I share Greenson's conviction that it is necessary to emphasize the vast chasm, and the differences in theory and technique, that separate the analysts who insist on the exceptional importance of the dream from those who do not. He emphatically declares, "One cannot carry out genuine analysis in sufficient depth if one does not understand the structure of dream formation, *as well as the patient's and the analyst's contributions to the technique of dream interpretation.*"

Greenson continues:

> I realize that no clinical demonstration of the value of dream interpretation will change the opinions of those who are predominantly devoted to theory conservation or theoretical innovations. Their theories seem to be more real to them than the memories and reconstructions of their patient's life history. Working with dreams is not only an enlightening experience for the patient, but it may be a source of new clinical and theoretical insights for the analyst, if he has an open mind. Furthermore, there are some analysts who have no ear or eye for dreams, like people who find it hard to hear and visualize the beauty of poetry, or like the tone-deaf who cannot appreciate the special imagery and language of music, or those who have no facility for wit and humor. Such analysts will lower the importance of dream interpretation, no matter what evidence you present. Finally, there are analysts who, for some other reasons, have never had the opportunity to learn how to listen to, understand, and work with dreams.

It was uncharacteristic of Greenson to mention unspecified "other reasons," as in the last sentence of the foregoing quotation. The motive for such reticence became clear when he answered my question on the subject. He stated that in a great number of instances the candidates' analyses were woefully inadequate, partly because the training analysts were not competent to familiarize the candidates with the essentials of dream interpretation and to demonstrate their expert usage. Many friends of mine have had the same complaint. It is the rare candidate, however, who dares request a referral to another training analyst.

It is difficult to estimate the proportion of therapists who emphasize the use of dreams, as many professionals in our field do not write.

The number of nonwriting "prodream" analysts one personally knows largely depends on the company one keeps. I can, then, speak only from my personal experience: The proportion of therapists who do attach special importance to the analysis of dreams is notably larger than I would have assumed from merely looking at the existing literature.

André Haynal

We tend to forget that many of the earlier authors attached great importance to dreams for their potential in the exploration of human emotions. One can find a wealth of cogent observations in many of their writings. I was reminded of that fact while reading a moving account of Ferenczi's struggles in André Haynal's THE TECHNIQUE AT ISSUE (1988). I shall cite only a few of Haynal's remarks: "Whereas Freud used dreams to explore the unconscious, Ferenczi stressed their communicative value. . . . He links the transference experience to the patient's childhood situations and not to an abstract psychological framework." A little later Haynal quotes C. Reverzy-Piquet speaking of "the priority which Ferenczi assigns to experience. The care he took to avoid dogmatism and to preserve independent thought and freedom of action, made him suspicious of theoretical systems which he countered *by stressing the importance and value of subjectivity. . . . It resulted in a method inseparable from clinical observation and experience"* (italics added). And Haynal again: "Sensitive to distress and suffering, Ferenczi always oriented his efforts towards care and healing, in other words, towards therapy." The reader will notice the congruity of Ferenczi's positions and priorities, voiced some 80 years ago, with my own convictions expressed here. While many things will have to change in psychoanalysis and psychotherapy, those fundamentals must not.

Ernest Hartmann

Because he was such a well-known researcher in this field, a brief comment on Ernest Hartmann is in order. As he gave much of his life's work to the topic of dreams, one would hope to find helpful material in his writings. The titles in the table of contents in SLEEP AND DREAMING (Hartmann, 1970) are certainly most attractive. The contents, however, are a different matter. A paper by Helen B. Lewis deals, more than any of the others, with a matter of interest to us, and her chapter is fairly representative of the standard of the book. Lewis attempts to delineate the effect of sleep research on the handling of dreams in psychoanalytic practice. Drawing on sleep research, she asserts that rem sleep provides a "parking space" for dreams, some of which emanate from the unconscious and some of which do not. She does not recognize that we cannot separate any function of a human being from the unconscious. Moreover, Lewis, like the great majority of sleep and dream researchers, is unaware of the vast difference between dreams and imagery. She never mentions imagery. More about that difference later.

Equally unfortunate is a 1976 paper by Hartmann purported to be on the changing use of dreams in psychoanalytic practice. Actually, the paper does not deal with that topic at all. Rather it attempts to explain the functioning of dreams in the context of neurology, specifically in terms of the theories of the neurologist Hughlings Jackson. Hartmann, quoting Jackson, writes: "Any neurological illness involving damage to the so-called higher centers produces two kinds of symptoms: it reveals or unmasks something of the underlying 'lower' structure, and it also tells us something of what has been *removed*" (italics added). The entire article is devoted to compressing all explanations on the essence and functioning of dreams into that single concept. The results are dismal. Now, some 20 years later, the concept has still not made an impression on sleep laboratories psychotherapy.

Finally, I would like to mention two recent publications. The first one, THE DREAM IN CLINICAL PRACTICE, edited by Joseph Natterson (1993), is actually a softcover edition of a 1980 publication. It has some 30 contributors. The second volume, DREAM READER: PSYCHOANALYTIC ARTICLES ON DREAMS, has been assembled with much diligence and care by the editors, Toni M. Alston, Roy C. Calogeras, and Heinrich Deserno (1993). It has over 50 contributors. In view of the paucity of writings on the subject of dreams, all such books are of value. They force us to evaluate each contribution and thus to sharpen our thinking. We hope to be able to discuss the merits and the fallacies of a number of the articles in those two books in a future volume, DREAMS AND THE MODIFICATION OF THE SELF.

KOHUT'S MANDALA

The title of this section may appear to be an acute case of strange bedfellows – and indeed it is. What is the reason for this unholy marriage?

Owing to my fascination with dreams, I have always been on the lookout for the special kinds of dreams that some others speak about but that are unknown to me. I am thinking here particularly about the mandala dreams, so frequently reported on by the Jungians, and Kohut's self-state dreams.

To those should be added dreams that fall into the domain of parapsychology, such as telepathic and precognitive dreams. Among colleagues who have called attention to those particular dreams are Gardner Murphy, Emanuel K. Schwartz, Jan Ehrenwald, Ian Stevenson, Nandor Fodor, and Jerome D. Frank. And we know of Freud's long-standing interest in the matter.

In the three-hour group sessions conducted at the Foundation, dreams are routinely reported. To them we may add the dreams related during private sessions. Consequently we have an unusually large number of dreams available for scrutiny.

Of all the dreams related to me, in not a single one did anything even faintly resembling a mandala appear. I hope that I will be forgiven, but it is understandable that eventually, and with regret, I concluded that the mandala exists only for patients of Jungian analysts. I say "with regret" because it would be a welcome addition to our world. However, the night after I looked through my meager notes on this subject and came to that conclusion, I dreamed about a beautiful round velvet tablecloth with a lovely design. Perhaps Dr. Jung was trying to alert me to my erroneous ways.

As far as ESP is concerned, the results were almost as poor as the search for the mandala: a single short dream. The patient, an elderly, lonely man, dreamed of a particular doll. When he visited his family the following Sunday, his little niece had a new doll identical to the one he had seen in his dream.

I am coming now to the principal reason for this section on unusual dreams. We have spent considerable time insisting on the desirability of asking for free associations for all dreams, without exception. I was therefore surprised by statements by Kohut (1977) in which, discussing the connection between self-disintegration and self-state dreams, he asserts that those dreams do not require free associations.

In spite of my best efforts to be open minded and learn something new, among the thousands of dreams I have heard, there was not one that I was able to place in the category of Kohut's self-state dreams, dreams that would not benefit from free associations. Kohut asserts that these dreams strengthen the dread of dissolution of the self and that asking for free associations will merely provide imagery that is, at best, on the same level as the manifest dreams.

Kohut's favorite example of dreams where no associations need to be requested is dreams of flying. Many dreams of flying have been reported to me over the years, and I dealt with them routinely, asking for associations and feelings. Without exception, I found them to have different meanings for different patients, but each one was congruent with the specific psychological structure of the patient. All I can say is that it would never have occurred to me that these dreams belonged to a completely different category or that associations to them would yield nothing.

For Freud, dreams of flying — far from being linked to a sense of impending doom — return the dreamer to the early joys of swinging and rocking and lead him from there to pleasant sexual sensations and possibly orgasm. That may explain why we have more Freudians than Kohutians.

THE NIGHTMARE

Oh, I have passed a miserable night,
So full of ugly sights, of ghastly dreams,
That, as I am a Christian faithful man,
I would not spend another such a night,
Though 'twere to buy a world of happy days.

SHAKESPEARE

My dreams are always disagreeable—mere confusions—losing my clothes and the like. The same dreams go on night after night for a long time. I am a worse man in my dreams than when awake, do cowardly acts, dream of being tried for a crime.

THOMAS CARLYLE

The pain to which you were ordained
grows in your sleep beyond belief,
Thus, hopelessly to illness chained,
to become well, to find relief:
rot you must first!

LENAU

My last night was a night of horrors, as three nights out of four are, with me. Oh God! when a man blesses his loud scream of agony which awakens him, night after night, night after night – it is better to die than to live.

S. T. COLERIDGE

In principle, dreams and nightmares should be treated in the same work, because nightmares are dreams and are subject to the same ground rules. The author should first explore all pertinent aspects of the subject of dreams and only then move on to deal with nightmares.

In practice, however, the topics are occasionally dealt with separately. In some cases the reason is space; the author has reams of material to present on the nightmare. In other cases the author, unable to come to grips with the topic, sees a vast chasm between dreams and nightmares. It is interesting to note that despite his interest in dreams, Freud never analyzed a nightmare.

John E. Mack

NIGHTMARES AND HUMAN CONFLICT, by John E. Mack (1974), provides more valuable and insightful comments on dreams than many of the writings dealing exclusively with dreams. Mack is an intelligent and sensitive clinical observer who writes clearly, even when engaged in theoretical considerations. He calls attention to many questions that have not been answered.

Referring to the clinical material, Mack agrees with Charles Fisher (1954) in doubting that nightmares serve any adaptive functions or figure in the mastery of anxiety. His comment that severe nightmares occur frequently in non-rem periods reminds us that too many authors mistakenly assume that dreams occur in the rem stage only. That assumption may be due to the lack of attention given by dream laboratories to the non-rem phase. To understand nightmares, Mack stresses, one must seek the link between current anxiety-provoking situations and anxieties experienced in early, threatening events.

One of the weightier points Mack presents is his warning that when neuroscientists or mental health professionals attempt to translate biological hypotheses, including those based on rem experiments, into psychological terms, *"they are pursuing a discourse on an entirely different level. It is important to avoid the pitfalls from shifting too readily from the use of terms such as adaptation and integrity in their physiological sense to applying them in a psychoanalytic or metapsychological framework"* (italics added).

That kind of damage does not originate with neuroscientists alone. While expert clinicians, well grounded in their knowledge, do not engage in such mischief, there are always some less endowed therapists and behavioral scientists only too eager to demonstrate how "modern" they are. Of course, the trends have varied over the decades. The present fashion is to imbue one's writings with the concepts and jargon of neuroscience and the sleep laboratories. The resultant pretentious hi-sci pronouncements frequently run counter to all clinical evidence. The cognitive psychology professor discussed at the beginning of this chapter is an illustration of such an approach.

In another excellent example Mack criticizes Ephron and Carrington, who declare that the rem period serves a homeostatic function, promoting cortical efficiency and thus readiness for adaptive responses. The same authors then affirm the existence of an "ego-reintegrative process in the dreams that mobilizes emotional responses and memories and integrates them into images of special meaning for the dreamer." We may admire Mack's gentlemanly and understated chiding of those professionals for their assertions. But we must not forget that such baseless statements will influence therapists and students and may ultimately cause considerable damage to those in treatment. The last thing psychotherapy needs is to become a garbage dump for professionals from other disciplines.

Henry Kellerman

The Nightmare: Psychological and Biological Foundations, edited by Henry Kellerman (1987), includes many papers by different authors. Here a difference is made between night terrors, which occur during non-rem sleep, and nightmares, which take place in the rem period. Those who are fascinated by dreams can find some interesting clinical material and theoretical speculations in this book, even if it does not enlarge our present understanding of the meaning of dreams.

I was much interested in a chapter by Daniel P. Juda, entitled "The Nightmare and the Criminal," in Kellerman's book. Although it may seem absurd to lament a lack of sociopaths, the reader may recall from earlier in this chapter a few words about the Foundation's efforts to obtain the dreams of sociopaths. While I have a number of such dreams (but no nightmares) from my own practice (see de Schill, 1971), the few dreams obtained from other sources were not of any use; closer scrutiny of the case histories and clinical data made it evident that the individuals were not true sociopaths, even though they had criminal records. There are frequent misdiagnoses of sociopathy, and criminal offense is not necessarily the most salient indication. There are far more sociopaths who do not get embroiled in legal difficulties than sociopaths who do.

Juda states:

> The dreams and nightmares of criminal offenders evidently have never been studied. A computer search of the literature failed to uncover a single publication in which the dreams or nightmares of a criminal's experiences were investigated. Charles Fisher has also confirmed the absence of studies in this area. The lack of research is both surprising and unfortunate.

I fully agree with that complaint and hope that a clinician with sufficient expertise will surprise us with an exciting study. It would be a most significant step toward progress in psychotherapeutic understanding. The great problem here is, of course, obtaining *valid* dream material.

F. Strunz

An extended, well-organized paper (in German) on nightmares by F. Strunz (1955) contains some interesting facts and provides a number of references not mentioned in the better known literature. Among the many works discussed by Strunz is one item I thought to be curious: a proposition by J. O. Wisdom (1949) to consider dreams the fulfillment of needs rather than wishes, and consequently nightmares as an expression of "needs" of the superego. I consider such a formulation inappropriate and specious; needs should be considered exclusively from the point of view of the individual. Otherwise we end up discussing such childhood traumas as the need of the nails to grow and the need of the nose to be blown. Beyond that, to differentiate between the wish and the need, both within the unconscious, is fruitless, just as in the primary process such a distinction would be an impossibility.

Since we are speaking of nightmares, I will recount an unusual one that should delight any orthodox analyst. A young, highly intelligent South American woman who was not in therapy reported a frequently recurring dream that she insisted on calling a nightmare. When I pointed out to her that a nightmare involves only negative feelings, which wasn't the case here, she protested, repeating that the dream was indeed a nightmare. As a matter of fact, when she was a child, the impact of the dream was so strong that even after she had awakened, it completely possessed her mind for considerable time. The dream is as follows: The woman senses a strong, threatening presence that terrifies her. She cannot see anyone. She cannot make out whether the presence is male or female. At the same time, she also has a very comforting, reassuring feeling, as if someone were holding her in a gentle, warm embrace.

James L. Fosshage and Clements A. Loew
Let us now leave nightmares behind and return to the literature on dreams in general. This curious book, DREAM INTERPRETATION: A COMPARATIVE STUDY (Fosshage & Loew, 1987), contains papers by seven authors, each representing a different psychotherapeutic orientation. For our purposes, the book has the advantage that the authors were selected not by myself but by a third party not committed to our critical pursuit. The basic idea of the book is challenging: One of the editors, Fosshage, presents six dreams of one of his patients, Martha, a 33-year-old single woman. The first dream dates from the second month in therapy; the intervals between the others range from six months to two years. The seven contributors offer their interpretations of the six dreams. And that is where the trouble starts.

The case history presented is extremely short, about two pages, and the associations to dream 1 are only eight lines long; to dream 2, seven lines; to dream 3, five lines; to dream 4, four lines; to dream 5, two lines; and to dream 6, a line and a half.

Thus a potentially interesting experiment was destroyed before it even started. To have sufficient clinical material for evaluation, the case history and clinical data should have been six to ten pages long, and the associations should have been about the same number of pages. I am puzzled that the invited authors even agreed to work under such impossible conditions. Fosshage, of course, had access to the necessary material; the lady had been his patient for years.

With all those handicaps, what is left? With so little clinical material at hand, one cannot consider the presentations of the authors, except Fosshage, to be valid attempts at interpretation. It is up to the reader to call them free associations, fantasies, or whatever. I will not refer to the interpretations of the Jungian or Gestalt therapists because their comments happen to be, in each instance, too far removed from the approaches examined here.

The first paper, said to represent the Freudian approach, is by Angel Garma, a well-known analyst, a graduate of the Psychoanalytic Institute in Berlin now practicing in Buenos Aires. Here is a quote from his paper: "Her obesity probably stems from her infantile submission to her real parents and also to her internalized parents. Her surrounding fat would appear to signify her parents surrounding her physically, thus impeding a mature contact with her environmental objects." Now, at last, we comprehend why Mae West became a symbol of ascetic isolation.

In the case history of Martha, Fosshage states: "She had a phobic fear of cockroaches. . . . Her initial fears began when she was a child living in an apartment which was infested with roaches." But forget that fact of the patient's childhood. Garma elucidates:

> In dreams and other fantastic tales, insects often represent siblings or a fetus. Martha's fear of cockroaches may have had the same meaning. Her phobia may have come from infantile fears which arose from fantasies of sexual play with her brother and sister, which she felt were disgusting. Cockroaches are disgusting animals that look for food and hide in holes (vagina or anus).

After those useful hints for the next visit by the exterminator, we turn to happier matters.

Here are Garma's comments on two passages in the first dream. Regarding the open jacket of a young man, which reminds Martha of the therapist's sport coat, "This represents the therapist's penis, which he exhibits." And regarding a passage in a dream where the therapist offers a helping hand in a potentially dangerous situation, "orgiastic acceptance of the genital relationship which the therapist is suggesting in the guise of a manual caress or even of mutual masturbation."

We can only assume that the other therapeutic approaches used by this analyst are of the same quality as his dream interpretations. Unfortunately, those examples of "analytic interpretations" are indicative of the level of the therapeutic work of far too many practitioners.

Representing the cultural approach, Walter Bonime prudently calls his presentations "interpretative hypotheses." Bonime's reflections on Martha's dreams attest to his sensitivity; he is an old pro working his way cautiously but expertly on a problem for which he has far too few clues.

Next comes the "object relations approach," in a chapter by John H. Padel, a London psychoanalyst with impressive professional credentials and affiliations. In one of the dreams, Martha attempts to kill one of the feared cockroaches with a spray. There are no associations given. A single interpretation is sufficient. Here is Padel: "It represents the sense of power she had felt, both in urinating and masturbating."

The phenomenological approach is covered in a chapter by Medard Boss and Brian Kenny. Boss started his training analysis with Freud and for many years has been a professor at the medical school of the University of Zürich. Kenny is an analyst at the Boss Foundation, also in Zürich. Theirs is a perceptive clinical approach that does not allow for inane dilettantism in interpretations. In spite of the skimpy data provided, they manage to create an opus in which the voices and melodies could possibly represent the drama in Martha's psyche.

The last dream interpretation is Fosshage's. He starts with this statement: "In order to provide for a meaningful comparison among the various approaches to Martha's dreams, I will attempt to set aside the considerable knowledge of Martha derived from her analysis and to restrict my formulations and comments to the dreams, limited associations, and case material presented in Chapter 1." Those are strangely naive words coming from a psychotherapist. No such mental separation can ever be achieved.

I will abstain from comments on his interpretation and merely quote some examples from the book explaining his theoretical views on dreams. They were already expressed in an earlier paper, "The Psychological Function of Dreams: A Revised Psychoanalytic Perspective" (Fosshage, 1983). Here we encounter another shortcoming in what could have been a project of some interest. When engaging in theoretical considerations and speculations, Fosshage frequently uses a highly convoluted and sterile "scientific" jargon, as can be seen in the following quote. Later in this chapter I shall touch on his proposition and others encountered previously.

> The primary process principles of condensation and symbolization, rather than processes primarily providing a disguising function, are redefined as organizational principles that reflect, respectively, a combination of imagistic mental elements involving similar thematic experiences and a particular imagistic configuration that captures and expresses thematic and affective meaning.
>
> In keeping with this reconceptualization of primary processes, I have proposed that the supraordinate function of dreams is the development, maintenance (regulation), and when necessary, restoration of psychic processes, structure, and organization.

b3   THE NEW MAJORITY: ACADEMIC POPULISM

Will you, won't you, will you, won't you, tell me what you do?

FREE, AFTER LEWIS CARROLL

Earlier I spoke of the need to obtain the associations of the patient to his dreams, even if a dream appears transparent to the therapist. Scrutinizing today's writers for their use of dreams, I was puzzled when I came across LOVE'S EXECUTIONER, ten case histories written, as the dust jacket states, by a master psychiatrist. I had just received an offer from Brooks/Cole Publishers to purchase five videotapes for a price close to $1,000, wherein a master would teach me how to conduct group psychotherapy. I was informed that the cost must be considered a bargain, since a free instructor-practitioner booklet by the master himself was included, and that the price would soon be raised. Of course, after so many disappointments I was truly glad that at long last, I would be able to report on two new masters. On closer inspection, the two masters turned out to be one, Irving D. Yalom, professor of psychiatry at Stanford University. Many other books have been written by him.

There are special reasons why Yalom's writings are scrutinized here at length. As stated, I am attempting to determine trends indicative of the quality of the profession. While copy on the dustcover is frequently written by the author, endorsements by professionals are another matter. The number of exuberant endorsements by well-known professionals appearing on the dust jackets of Yalom's many books is amazing. The same holds true for the reviews of his books in professional journals. Such testimonials certainly reflect the level of psychotherapeutic acumen of the professionals who write the endorsements – and that is precisely what I am attempting to evaluate here. The decisive factor for our scrutiny, however, is a survey reported in the AMERICAN JOURNAL OF PSYCHIATRY and quoted on the dust jacket of Yalom's (1991) book on group psychotherapy. The journal describes the book as "one of the ten most influential psychiatry publications of the decade, and it was one of the very few judged to be of seminal or lasting value."

In the United States Yalom's books are among the most widely read publications in our field and have received wide professional praise. To judge purely by numbers – and thanks to the enormous American market – he is probably the most widely read contemporary author in psychotherapy. In the behavioral sciences, as in politics and many other areas, however, being widely known, or even applauded, bears no relationship to being professionally competent. We must find criteria better than mere acclaim to arrive at conclusions about a professional's level of quality and acumen. For the longest time, Freud had only a few admirers.

Nonetheless our task here is to examine the present trends. Whether we like it or not, there is a second reason we must give so much attention to Yalom's writings: His approach is highly representative of that of a considerable proportion of American mental health professionals, many of whom are in academic teaching positions, and it is spreading to other parts of the world.

Let me quote Yalom from his book on group therapy (1991):

> During the past decade I have addressed approximately twenty-five thousand therapists in lectures on workshops on group therapy, and have asked the audience about their primary therapy orientation: Freudian analytic? Interpersonal? Behavioral? Gestalt? T.A.? Existential? Without exception, between 30 percent and 60 percent of the audience identified themselves as existential in orientation.
>
> Even therapists who nominally adhere to other orientations are surprised when they look closely at their techniques and their basic view of the human situation, and find that they are existentially oriented. Most therapists who consider themselves psychoanalytically oriented inwardly eschew or, at best, ignore much of the fundamental analytic theory.

Although Yalom's assertions are somewhat tainted, and although we must consider that he speaks only about the one therapist in four who is interested in group psychotherapy, we have no reason to assume that the theoretical orientations of the other 75 percent of mental health professionals are vastly different from those counted by Yalom. Here we are examining the reasons for the popularity of Yalom's approaches. If we are ever to improve psychotherapy, such scrutiny is sine qua non.

Let us now return to LOVE'S EXECUTIONER and its ten case histories. The first nine cite only three dreams, and there is no mention of free association. The last case history, "In Search of the Dreamer," does contain a welcome surprise. It is based entirely on the dreams of the patient who is the central figure in the story. The author describes the patient as exceedingly dull, without even a trace of insight. His dreams, on the other hand, are surprising from the very onset of therapy; they are short, neat, transparent as crystals, and highly meaningful.

The interesting theme of the case history is the reason for its title. After each dream Yalom presents its "message." The messages tell Yalom unequivocally not only what the patient is experiencing in his hidden psyche but also how the therapist must proceed. Strangely, like the dreams themselves, the messages are short, neat, transparent as crystals, and highly meaningful, and they fit the dreams like a glove.

Here are just a few of the passages in which the author refers to the superior guidance received by the dreamer's unconscious:

> The voice . . . had created those astonishing dreams. Buried somewhere within Marvin's walls was a dreamer tapping out an urgent, existential message.

> At the same time, as I was conducting this gentle, somewhat concrete therapy with Marvin, I was also engaged in a fascinating discourse with the dreamer. . . . While Marvin and I strolled, and casually conversed on superficial levels, the dreamer drummed out a constant stream of messages from the depths.

That passage indicates that the dialogue between therapist and patient was conducted at the surface level and did not, at least at that point, bring in associations to the deeper level represented by the dreams.

> I remember beginning every hour . . . with anticipation about my next communiqué from the dreamer.
>
> The dreamer was advising me how to proceed.
> Regardless of his motivation, his [the dreamer's] advice was sagacious.
>
> By the time six months had gone by, I still had no deep fondness for him (the patient). This was very strange, since I adored the dreamer: I adored his courage and his scorching honesty.

And so forth.

Many of the messages are existentialist in nature. The author too is an existentialist. That presents us with this question: Is the *unconscious* existentialist? That would certainly be a deplorable ingratitude to its discoverers.

There is no indication that Yalom ever uses associations to the dreams. To clarify that point, I turned to his highly praised compendium on group psychotherapy (1991). While essentially a reference book covering a wide range of topics, it is strongly imbued with the views and bias of its author. The largest section, devoted to the "here and now," contains some 70 pages; the second largest, on encounter groups, 48 pages. I could not determine whether associations were asked for. The author speaks about "detailed investigation" and "discussion" of dreams but does not explain those terms.

There are, however, a number of revealing statements on how the author uses dreams, both in individual therapy and in group therapy. Here are two quotes for consideration:

> The number and types of dreams that patients bring to therapy are largely a function of the therapist's behavior. Your response to the first dreams presented by patients will influence the choice of dreams subsequently presented.

> Generally, the individual therapists will use dreams to explore the *current theme* in therapy. (Italics added)

The first quote contains two statements requiring comment. First, any expert psychotherapist will be careful not to engage in any "behavior" or "response" that may influence or stifle the unencumbered flow and content of dreams. Second, the psychotherapist cannot affect the essence of the dreams presented; a patient suffering from severe anxieties will not bring in joyous dreams. Moreover, the elements of transference in dreams are related to the dreamer's emotional structure, which was formed in childhood.

The second quote conceals disastrous advice. No therapist should restrict a patient to a *single* "current theme." Rather, the task at hand is to uncover that which has been covered, so that the knowledge may be used for the purposes of therapy. At any time, dreams may give us a view of a number of "themes," that is, facts and forces in the patient's psyche. As they are part of the patient's unique personality, the "themes" are necessarily interconnected. The therapist must always keep the strength of each theme, its visibility, and the extent to which it is connected to, or disconnected from, other relevant themes under consideration. Workmanship cannot allow for facile gimmicks such as single-theme therapy. A patient is, after all, a complex human being, not a telephone answering machine. What a therapist says and does depends on the various relevant themes of which he is becoming aware, as well as on his acumen in knowing what can be safely and advantageously said and done at a given stage of therapy. Most pertinent here, again, is Freud's admonition that we should let the patient determine the subject matter of each session and follow the patient's free association (see also the section on Greenson).

Yalom's three statements are in gross contradiction to the position he takes in the case history "In Search of the Dreamer." There he praises the wisdom of dreams and claims to depend entirely on their guidance for the conduct of therapy.

Most of the work that psychodynamically oriented psychotherapists engage in when working with dreams is omitted from LOVE'S EXECUTIONER. In nine of the ten case histories, hardly any attention is given to dreams. In the rare instances where dreams are discussed, systematic use of free associations to each dream is ignored, and there is no linking of dream contents, manifest or latent, to the past of the patient. The result is a barren procedure, stripped down to less than the minimum requirements, easy to apply and easy to teach – delightful for master and apprentice but catastrophic for the patient.

In the prologue to the ten case histories, Yalom, a gifted writer, speaks movingly about the unfulfilled desires of patients; in fact, of all people. He calls it "destiny *pain,* existence *pain."* I quote:

> I believe that the primal stuff of psychotherapy is always such existence pain and not – as is often claimed – repressed instinctual strivings or *imperfectly buried shards of a tragic personal past.* In my therapy with each of these ten patients, my primary clinical assumption – an assumption on which I based my technique – is that basic anxiety emerges from a person's endeavors, conscious and unconscious, to cope with the hard facts of life, the "givens" of existence.
>
> I have found that four "givens" are particularly relevant to psychotherapy: the inevitability of death for each of us, the freedom to make our lives as we will, our ultimate aloneness, and finally, the absence of any obvious meaning or sense to life. (Italics added)

The reader will recall a well-known and wise remark by Freud, who, when asked whether a patient who had terminated psychoanalysis would from then on be happy, said that the person would still be subject to all the emotions and events all men experience. Yalom, we are glad to learn, can do much better; he will free us of the pains caused by the four "givens," which, to be sure, are inherent parts of each individual's life.

Earlier in this chapter I stressed the danger of generalizations. Yalom speaks of a "primary clinical assumption" that he applies a priori to *all* patients. In his group therapy book (1991), he repeatedly states his belief that there is no need to search for the "buried shards" of each person's past. Not only that, he denies the value of such a search: "There is considerable question about the validity of our assumptions about the relationship between types of early experience and adult behavior and character structure."

Yalom emphatically asserts that the core of the human problem is crystallized by asking a *single* question: "What do you want?" He continues: "So much wanting, so much longing. . . . Many things remind us that our wants can never be fulfilled. . . . 'I want, I want' is heard through these tales." And then, pointing toward the positive: "I hope to demonstrate, in these ten tales of psychotherapy, that it is possible to confront the truths of existence and harness their power in the service of personal change and growth." That is eloquent and inspiring oratory indeed, similar to what is heard from television evangelists.

Many people are unconcerned about the four "givens," and many do not consider, as Yalom declares, life to be meaningless. Who, then, are the people most affected by the "hard facts of life" that Yalom considers the core of our psychological problems? They are the people whose unconscious is filled with "broken shards" and has been torn by inner tortures since those early times when Yalom's givens were still nonexistent for them. They deserve better professional help than a "common denominator" approach that operates largely by use of transference and suggestion, avoiding the labors that psychodynamic therapy requires. Understandably, simplistic approaches never fail to recruit a multitude of enthusiastic followers.

For Yalom, the "I want" is the core of the problem. But even if one were to accept that premise, the psychotherapeutic solution can be found in one direction only, and it is not the one he recommends. Let me quote Schopenhauer, who wrote about the unconscious many years before Freud: "A man can determine what he wants to do, but he cannot determine what he wants." For those "wants" are circumscribed by specific forces, unique to the individual and operating deep within his psyche.

Even though some of the observations made here are based on Yalom's book on group therapy, I did not place this discussion in the group therapy chapter in this volume, because we are dealing here with fundamental matters relevant to all therapy.

I had hoped that my arguments would prove the fallacy of Yalom's generalizing approach to dreams, to psychotherapy as a whole, and specifically to group therapy. But not so. All my efforts came to naught when I came across the following passage in his group psychotherapy volume: "Throughout, I have stated that group therapy is a highly individual process. Each patient will enter, participate in, use, and experience the group in a uniquely personal manner." But that statement is in direct contradiction to the claimed supreme rule of the four "givens" applicable to all, as well as to Yalom's emphasis on group process and the group-as-a-whole treatment approach.

That brings us to an important basic point. Yalom's extensive reference book speaks about many trends in group psychotherapy, and even devotes considerable space to lesser and marginal approaches. However, for a long time the two fundamental but opposing positions in group psychotherapy have been held, on the one side, by advocates of the individualized analytic approach and, on the other, by those who focus on the group process. In his writings Alexander Wolf explains cogently the differences between the two positions and why they cannot be combined in practice. Yet Yalom does not even mention the existence of individualized orientation in group therapy, which focuses on the transference and psychodynamics of each group member and is called analytic group psychotherapy or, sometimes, psychoanalysis in groups.

Occasionally Yalom claims that he too favors a highly individualized approach. In reality and in practice, however, his own description of his work with patients definitely contradicts such a claim.

It is unheard of for a reference book on group psychotherapy not to include a section on the eminently important group analytic school that had such a decisive role in its evolution. But we encounter that very omission when Yalom writes about the origins and development of group psychotherapy; he rewrites history with a vengeance.

To understand what is happening here, one must examine Yalom's attitude regarding thorough analytic procedure. I already briefly mentioned his assertion that it is useless to investigate the past of the patient to discover the origins of his psychological problems. Here again is Yalom:

Too often, explanation is confused with "originology" (the study of origins). I have discussed already that an explanatory system may effectively postulate a "cause" of behavior from any of a large number of perspectives. Still, many therapists continue to believe that to find the "real," the "deepest" causes of behavior, it is necessary to refer to the past. This position was staunchly defended by Freud, a committed psychosocial archaeologist.

And what are Yalom's views on Freud and psychoanalysis?

Keep in mind that classical psychodynamic theory is based explicitly on a highly materialistic view of human nature. It is not possible to understand Freud fully without considering his allegiance to the Helmholtz school, an ideological school that dominated Western European medical and basic research in the latter part of the nineteenth century. The basic Helmholtzian doctrine was simply stated: No other forces than the common physical-chemical ones are active within the organism; that, in those cases which cannot at the time be explained by these forces, one has either to find the specific way or form of their action by means of the physical-mathematical method, or to assume new forces equal in dignity to the chemical-physical forces inherent in matter, reducible to the force of attraction and repulsion.

Freud never swerved from his adherence to this postulate and to its implications about human nature; many of his more cumbersome, more relentless formulations, for example, the dual instinct theory, the theory of libidinal energy conservation and transformation, were the result of his unceasing attempts to fit human behavior to the Helmholtzian rules.

History is in the eye of the beholder. Later we shall see how McCarley and Hobson (1977a) present us with a completely different history of the theories that principally influenced Freud. Their version neatly supports their own theoretical assertions. Helmholtz is not even mentioned.

Throughout his writings Yalom presents Freud and his followers as simpleminded mechanics who, because they obstinately follow a single track, are ignorant of the richness and scope of the human psyche made obvious to us by Yalom's pervasive insight. In creating a Freud who never was, Yalom builds a straw man that he can burn.

Not only does Yalom abstain from referring to the analytic school within the group psychotherapy movement, but he also avoids mentioning the vast influence and contribution of analytically oriented therapists in that domain, and particularly their emphasis on the individual, his transferences, and his dreams. To set the record straight, one would need to write a monograph. Here I will refer only to four therapists.

Yalom scarcely mentions Paul Schilder, an eminent psychoanalyst whom he calls D. Schilder, and S. R. Slavson. Slavson was the founder of the American group psychotherapy movement and of the American Group Psychotherapy Association. He was the association's president for many years, and his numerous books had immense influence on the advancement of group psychotherapy. Yalom similarly gives short shrift to Alexander Wolf, the outstanding pioneer who established much of the fundamental structure and ground rules of psychodynamic group therapy. Wolf has written over 120 truly competent books and articles on group psychotherapy, addressing all its important and relevant issues. Yalom mentions none of that and refers to Wolf as a pioneer only when briefly discussing him in connection with two technical matters, one of them concerning sexual relations between group members. It would be like writing a book on the history of music in which the only reference to Mozart was that a type of candy had been named after him. Another pioneer who has done much for the group movement, Emanuel K. Schwartz, is not mentioned at all. And so on.

Yalom consistently states that his approach is "ahistoric," meaning that he does not feel it necessary to refer in treatment to the patient's past. Yet, as always, one can find contradictory statements he makes merely to protect his flanks. He says, for example, that "there will be frequent excursions into personal history" and that one can "use the past for help in understanding the individual's mode in relating." Those are fundamentals of the analytic approach, but in fact nothing like them can be found in Yalom's descriptions of his therapy sessions.

We must wonder why Yalom keeps silent on the analytic movement in group therapy and its pioneers and yet claims that its most relevant characteristic, the focus on the individual, has been his own
"throughout." Likewise, many related approaches that guide his
practice, or so he claims, are also the result of the work of psychoanalysts. We will shortly encounter another example of that pattern when
we examine his "here and now."

Yalom's statement that focus on the individual is the primary requirement in group psychotherapy represents the analytic position and seems
to invalidate all my complaints regarding his superficial and group-cen-
tered approach. But aimlessly turning pages in his book, I find myself
staring at the following: "The therapist's choice should be based on one
primary consideration – the needs of the group." As well as: "The content
of the problem was intriguing *and the group spent forty-five minutes discussing such aspects of justice versus mercy"* (italics added).

The first quote once more emphasizes the group-as-a-whole
approach and directly contradicts Yalom's assertion paying lip service to
the primacy of the individual. One fact emerges clearly: No matter how
often Yalom claims to follow various approaches, in practice, and in blatant contradiction to those claims, he basically applies the simplistic
group-process method.

By including in the written description of his practice a multitude
of existing approaches, he not only believes himself to be on the safe side
but also hopes to impress colleagues and students as a virtuoso, masterfully handling a vast array of instruments. No wonder that nationwide
publicity campaigns always refer to him as a "master." However, his talent in writing, storytelling, and public relations – considerable though
it may be, as evidenced in his case histories and activities – bears no relationship to psychotherapeutic substance.

The vast difference between Yalom's description of the high-
sounding, sophisticated approaches and theories presumably applied in
his group work and what actually happens in his groups is readily
apparent in his own reports. The last quote is as good a proof as any. I
repeat: He says that a problem was intriguing and the group spent 45
minutes discussing justice versus mercy. Elsewhere he mentions that as
a consequence of a remark made early in a group meeting, the balance

of the time was spent on an intellectualized debate of "the virtues versus the dehumanizing aspects of parenthood." Condemnation of such proceedings simply cannot be harsh enough. What we are seeing here is something akin to a high school debating society. It is completely alien to psychotherapy.

Badly neglecting the individualized approach, involving the examination of transferences, dreams, and the patient's history, the described sessions clearly demonstrate an emphasis on global group events that in no way constitute group psychotherapy, not even of the shoddiest kind. Yalom's groups last 90 minutes. Time in psychotherapy is precious. It is the therapist's responsibility to ensure that it is used judiciously. (The reader will find a clear description of what work in a group should consist of in the present volume.)

One would think that Yalom's above statements were definite proof of how barren his approaches are. However, Yalom insists that he engages only in the finest therapy approaches: "The therapist's task is to . . . steer the group members away from discussion of outside material, and focus their energy upon their relationship with one another." That happens to be a fundamental of analytic group therapy, even though Yalom somehow forgets to mention it and forgets to do it.

The pages where those quotes are located are supposed to deal with group process and the "here and now." More confusion is to be found here: Much of what Yalom describes is really transference interaction by the individual members. The transference, as used in the analytic session, individual or group, is always in the "here and now." At Yalom's hands, most of the required work is eliminated, with the result that most of the meaning is lost. His comments, while interesting, remain on a surface level, attempting, in essence, to make the patient aware of distortions and misconceptions in his interpersonal interactions. No attempt is made to elucidate his transference reactions by linking them analytically to his past. Once more, a valuable psychotherapeutic tool, namely the psychodynamic use of the patient's transferences, is stripped down to a pitiful mockery that is, of course, easy to teach and to learn.

It seems ludicrous to have to explain the necessity of uncovering the psychological history of each patient. With the ever-growing influence of the shortcut artists, however, the embarrassment of having to give elementary explanations cannot be avoided. I offer a brief dream of one of my patients.

The dreamer, a highly intelligent man in his early 70s and thus distanced by many years from his childhood, first stated that he would have to see a certain man in the near future, that the man was basically a friendly person but that he, the dreamer, was annoyed because the man had selected an inconvenient meeting time.

In the dream he saw himself in a narrow room with the man, who behaved in an uncharacteristically obstructive and negative manner, which distressed the dreamer. The man walked back and forth, and the dreamer felt intimidated by him. At the same time, the dreamer was desperately looking for some much-needed items but was unable to find them. He woke up with a feeling of fear, hopelessness, and emptiness.

While relating the dream, the patient suddenly realized that the room in the dream was the one in which he had spent most of his childhood. His free associations were not productive, and he was mystified by the behavior of his acquaintance in the dream.

The salient point is the part the patient blocked out, even though he had repeatedly mentioned it in earlier sessions: Adjacent to his room was the living room, where his father would walk up and down at night. The father was short-tempered and strict, a formidable obstacle to any self-expression by the child. The patient told me how, in helpless terror, he would listen to his father's footsteps.

Without going into the details, unnecessary here, of how that knowledge was used therapeutically, I must emphasize that one thing is certain: Without prior exploration of the patient's childhood, the meaning of the dream would have remained hidden.

Many years ago in American medical journals, advertisements appeared that publicized small booklets with the title "How to Become a . . . in Ten Minutes." They would mention a medical specialty, for example, gynecologist. There were about 20 different versions, one of them for aspiring psychiatrists. The psychiatry booklet was well written and offered easy-to-learn shortcut approaches. Here, too, transference, childhood history, and dreams were badly neglected. But would anyone want to consult a therapist trained in this fashion? Fast-food hamburger places train youngsters in two hours to prepare the food, but they do not claim to be gourmet restaurants. Yalom's approach could easily be taught in such a booklet. A renowned professor of psychiatry compared Yalom to a man who dismantles a Mercedes and then holds up one of its wheels and shouts, "See what I have created!"

Yalom is by no means the only one to hustle a stripped-down version of simplified, instant psychotherapy training, such as his $1,000 video for training in group psychotherapy. Many others, some preceding him, others imitating him, have attempted to create facile forms of therapy. But Yalom has by far the most followers. They have invaded psychotherapy like a swarm of locusts.

Although Yalom pays lip service to the importance of dreams and the need to explore them in depth, what he does is quite the opposite. He neglects to elucidate the latent-dream content by searching for the link to the patient's early history. As far as his practice of group psychotherapy is concerned, the scrutiny of dreams is practically impossible. By wasting much of the 90 minutes in immaterial discussions, insurmountable obstacles are created to the presentation of dreams by the group members. Actually, even in analytically oriented groups, the limited time available represents a major and frustrating problem. The only effective way to overcome it is to extend group time significantly. (The reader can find more information on that matter in the group therapy chapter in this volume.)

> The merry-go-round, what a delight,
> So much fun –
> And the price is right!
>
> VIENNESE SONG

Why, the reader may ask, is this section entitled "The New Majority: Academic Populism," when it deals essentially with just one author? The answer is simple. In this chapter I discuss a great number of authors, many of them in academic positions of responsibility. Among those criticized, important common denominators are evident, even though the authors are as diverse in their approaches as Spence, Grotjahn, Karasu, and Yalom. Each of them has been successful in academic life.

What do I mean by "populism"? It is the avoidance of dealing squarely with issues, usually difficult and complex, by offering glib answers and easy solutions. In the mental health professions populism is manifested by one or more of the following:

- advocacy of facile treatment approaches
- application of speculative, generalizing theories (despite the academic and "scientific" language, theorizing is easy; it applies to all)
- using readily available precepts rather than clinical effort in treatment (for example, assuming that a noisy refrigerator in a dream must represent the primal scene).

Those practices, whether carried out within the confines of Yalom's philosophy, or in the name of psychoanalysis, or otherwise, damage patient care. Much of the time, in spite of claims to the contrary, the concepts employed are distant from clinical facts and lack psychological and clinical acumen. Their abstractness permits endless discussion and precludes proof or disproof.

If the theories advanced were valid, the psychological structure and dynamics of the human psyche, and consequently the many forms of emotional illness, would be far more uniform than they are. Theorizing permits easy generalization and avoidance of the task of achieving an understanding of each individual patient. In his introduction to this volume Robert Stoller cogently remarks that quite a number of theories, seriously considered by many, are actually based on poor observation. Moreover, very few of those who boldly set forth their views about psychoanalysis actually have the necessary number of psychoanalytic patients to enable them to back up their theoretical generalizations. Also in the introduction, John Gedo remarks on the paucity of cases where psychoanalysis is actually performed, and I believe the number is even smaller than Gedo estimates. Many write about psychoanalysis, but few actually practice it.

I have pointed out the easy, populistic approaches to be found in a lot of professional writing, teaching, and patient care. The fact is, however, that clinical talent is not common, clinical expertise is hard to come by, and clinical work is difficult and demanding.

We need theory. But it must evolve from psychotherapeutic experience. The less expert the psychotherapist is, the more he depends on learned precepts or theory to patch up his lack of understanding. Fortunately, that does not apply to all academicians.

At some point in Lewis Carroll's THROUGH THE LOOK-ING GLASS, Tweedledum and Tweedledee lead Alice to the place where the King is sleeping. To her astonishment, they tell her that His Majesty is dreaming about her.

Then Tweedledee exclaims, "And if he left off dreaming about you, where do you suppose you'd be?"

"Where I am, of course," says Alice.

"Not you!" Tweedledee retorts contemptuously, "You'd be nowhere. Why, you're only a sort of thing in his dream!"

"If that there King was to wake," adds Tweedledum, "you'd go out – bang! – just like a candle!"

"I shouldn't!" Alice exclaims indignantly.

"Well, it's no use your talking about waking him," says Tweedledum, "when you're only one of the things in his dream. You know very well you're not real."

"I am real!" says Alice and begins to cry.

c.   Heaping Stones and Rolling Eyeballs

> Dreams really have a meaning and are far from being the expression
> of a fragmentary activity of the brain, as the authorities have claimed.
>
> Freud

> A collection of facts is no more a science than a heap of stones is a house.
>
> Poincaré

I would like to remind the reader that this is not an academic paper but a review of professional activities in the mental health field undertaken at the request of a foundation devoted to protecting the public interest. This approach results not in a less accurate evaluation but, quite the contrary, in a more comprehensive one.

More than any other areas of health care, two stand out for their professional disregard of the patient's welfare: nursing-home care for the aged and therapeutic assistance to the emotionally ill. While in the first deficiencies are easily observed by a dedicated investigator, in the behavioral sciences the causes of harmful situations and practices are often subtly disguised by the mantle of accepted professional and "scientific" conduct.

Our responsibility here is to seek out such shortcomings and abuses, to point out clearly and incisively the practices that are detrimental to adequate student training and desirable patient care, and to formulate concrete proposals for improvement.

We now have four decades of the sleep laboratory behind us. On one hand, behavioral scientists have written numerous papers on that research, and many consider it extraordinarily important. On the other hand, such seasoned psychotherapists as Harold P. Blum have correctly noted that none of those studies increases understanding of the meaning of dreams.

As related earlier in this chapter, Professor Morton F. Reiser of Yale, a former president of the American Psychoanalytic Association, affirms that a neurobiological investigation carried out at Harvard refutes Freud's theories regarding dreams. We shall return to that shortly.

Neurological and biological research, if competently conducted, is undeniably necessary and of interest to psychotherapists concerned with sleep and dreams. While many researchers, such as David Buchholz of Johns Hopkins, approach the task with imagination and responsibility, others, as we shall see, do not.

Here we will not enter into the question of which sleep laboratory studies have validity in terms of the physiology of sleep. We will focus solely on the aspects that are of interest to psychotherapists, specifically the findings of rem and non-rem sleep that are of consequence to our work with dreams. (We use small letters for *rem* on purpose.)

Our coverage includes an exploration of (1) what is being done in the sleep laboratory relative to dreams and how it affects psychotherapeutic care of patients, (2) the literature dealing with the feasibility of incorporating sleep laboratory findings into psychotherapy, and (3) what should have been done – but was not.

The Study of Dreams in Sleep Laboratories

The proliferation of sleep laboratories, both in the United States and in Europe, has resulted in a new branch of "meter readers," technicians engaged in studying physiological responses. Even though they have neither a psychotherapy background nor clinical experience with dreams, much of their work is concerned with sleep stages wherein dreaming occurs and with dreams themselves.

The abundance of sleep laboratory studies of dreams is matched only by the redundancy of the investigations conducted by some of these "new" behavioral scientists. The level of their work is evident in some of their most frequent research projects. These studies attempt to ascertain the presence of color in dreams, the presence of bizarreness, the continuity and discontinuity of content, the pleasantness or unpleasantness, and the presence of the dreamer and other people in the dream. A Harvard study (Hobson et al., 1987) combines two of those elements by dividing the "bizarre features" into three categories. Quoting the abstract:

The unusual aspect of dream consciousness which has been called dream bizarreness may be defined as impossibility or improbability in the domains of dream plot, cognition and affect. The bizarre features of dreams may be divided into three broad categories: discontinuities, incongruities and uncertainties. Discontinuities are interruptions in orientational stability; incongruities are inappropriate syntheses of mismatching plot elements; uncertainties are confusions of distinct conceptions. Dream bizarreness appears to be the manifestation of *some* state-dependent cognitive process which is *probably* rooted in rem sleep neuropsychology. (Italics added to highlight the "precision" of this scientific study)

To quote from an Italian laboratory report:

[Dreams] were scored for interrelated contents, using Clark's system of analysis of paired units, which operates by matching linguistic features. Results showed that interrelations in morning report pairs are as frequent as in night report pairs, maintaining the same linguistic characteristics and with little transfer of contents from one MSE (mental sleep experience) to another.

The multitude of such titles as "Recurring Themes and Images in a Series of Consecutive REM Dreams" reflects the repetitiousness of such investigations.

One of the more comprehensive texts describing the work of sleep laboratories is LE SOMMEIL, by Jean Michel Gaillard (1990) of the University of Geneva. In contrast to many others, Gaillard allows for the possibility that psychological factors influence dreams. His book provides an interesting overview of the research done in Europe and in the United States and Canada. Even though many sleep researchers claim otherwise, the paucity of their findings on dreams is evident here; after thousands of experiments carried out over many years on two continents, this book of some 320 pages contains only nine pages on dreams and three more on nightmares.

Contrary to the dogmatic assertions of many sleep technicians who claim that dreams have no meaning and that dream interpretation is fiction, or even fraud, Gaillard admits to the limitations of reaching such conclusions on the basis of sleep research.

Gaillard speaks of the special attention warranted if a "significant" word is found in the dream report of the sleeper. He specifies that a significant word is any substantive, adjective, or verb, excluding "to be" and "to have," excluding any words describing the mental state of the subject, such as "I am not sure . . ." and "I believe it was . . . ," and excluding any statement that is a comment on reality. Reports containing at least one significant word are independently scored by two judges using a rating scale devised by Gaillard and M. Phelippeau. Among the items rated are unreality, presence and participation of the dreamer, pleasantness or unpleasantness, verbal and physical aggression, and sexuality.

The breakdown of dreams into word elements does as much violence to the meaning of a dream as would the same technique applied to a passage from Shakespeare. With the end of Wundt's laboratory more than a century ago, that kind of atomized investigation had seemingly come to an end, only to be reborn in the sleep laboratory.

Occasionally the assertion is made that the dreams of "normal" people do not have any content that would lend itself to understanding, whereas the dreams of neurotics might provide some information on the dreamer. That assertion is simply not factual! To the contrary, everyone who has a mind, a childhood, and emotions can have meaningful dreams.

General assertions by neurobiologists and sleep researchers that dreams are quickly forgotten for nonpsychological reasons are contradicted by the following two facts:

1. A great number of dreams are well remembered; many are reported in psychotherapy sessions and elsewhere.
2. Patients in a hypnotic trance who are instructed to dream that night and to remember the dreams almost invariably do so.

The first fact is occasionally acknowledged and mentioned by a few researchers; the second one never is.

There are, of course, a vast number of other experiments and activities at the sleep laboratories that I could mention, but doing so would not advance the aim of this chapter. Here I want merely to single out practices of relevance to psychotherapy so that we may evaluate the quality of such professional work.

Behavioral scientists, such as the "professor," who proclaim the outstanding importance of their sleep studies maintain a convenient silence on a number of salient facts. For example, they imply that the rem period invariably produces dreams, whereas some reports reveal that 18 percent of male subjects awakened during rem sleep cannot report any dreams, and other studies report 25 percent. Furthermore, a correlation between eye movements and dream content has so far not been conclusively verified. Eye movements can also be discerned in people who have been blind from birth and have only narrative, not visual, dreams. In fact, on the basis of the enormous number of studies conducted over many years and in many places, a hypothesis is gaining ground that most of the ocular movements during the rem period are a stereotyped function, quite independent of dreaming. Be that as it may, these, as well as some purely technical data referring to sleep and its related phenomena, are interesting but have no bearing on our topic.

The sleep laboratory studies dealing with dreams are at best naive; at worst, outrageous. Repeating innumerable investigations, even in the name of "pure science," to determine again and again presence of color, number of people present, pleasantness or unpleasantness, bizarreness, and the like, seems more than suspect.

True, in the name of "pure science" experiments are legitimately conducted in virgin territory without any connection to practical applicability. But the scientists conducting them have expertise in the domain they are probing. Unlike those investigators, a great many of the sleep researchers and other behavioral scientists who make negative or erroneous statements concerning dreams have obviously not bothered to acquaint themselves with the vast body of professional knowledge accumulated over a century of intensive investigations. Their procedure is like classifying books according to their cover rather than their content. I used that comparison earlier in this chapter when reporting on the repeated assertion of the "professor" that the most important aspect of cognitive structure is "tolerance versus intolerance of incongruities." He attempted to substantiate that claim by studies of how various individuals deal with "contradictory" information.

As stated, I consider it a deplorable indication of professional ignorance to link bizarreness in dreams to tolerance or intolerance of incongruities. Bizarreness in dreams cannot be used to determine personality factors. In "true" dreams the symbols that seem bizarre are not incongruous but follow a meaningful sequence. Thus we should distinguish between imagery – which some analysts call dreaming – and true dreams. True dreams have a definite meaning.

From the point of view of psychodynamic therapy, bizarreness is of no relevance whatsoever as far as the meaning of a dream is concerned. Bizarreness depends on many factors; for example, the level of the psyche from which the dream emanates, the emotional areas that are involved, and the associations that are brought into play. Earlier in this chapter I presented two dreams as illustrations. One dream was supposed to be "logical"; the other, "bizarre." The two dreams, even though immensely different in language, story, and imagery, have precisely the same meaning.

The elaborate experiments to pinpoint "significant" words and to discover "continuities" have been utterly in vain; there is no way to find significant words and continuities by the procedures used in sleep laboratories. Determining what is significant requires a skillful psychotherapist well acquainted with the repressed material and the childhood background of the patient in question. Only such a therapist would be able to determine which parts of a dream are relevant and if there is thematic continuity in a number of dreams.

Those very themes will most likely appear in *different* forms, symbols, or actions in subsequent dreams. It is naive to think that a "significant word" alone can be a clue to any relevant issue; whatever the "significant" word represents in one dream may show up in a different shape and form in subsequent dreams, even though the underlying meaning is precisely the same. The "presence of the person" – namely the dreamer – presents a similar problem, since he or she may appear in various disguises.

Here the sleep technicians, disregarding established, fruitful procedures evolved from knowledge of the nature of dreams, claim to have created their own method of investigating the "significance" and "meaning" of the dream. Yet none of them is able to explain how their simplistic methods could, by any stretch of the imagination, bring even minimal results. It comes, of course, as no surprise that no meaningful findings were established.

Such pretense to scientific procedure would not be possible in any domain except the behavioral sciences. For a cogent review of this matter, I refer the reader to Robert J. Stoller's introduction to this volume and to Colby and Stoller (1988). For instance, the "investigators" speak, by and large, as if all dreams were of the same category. That approach is the equivalent of writing extensive "scientific treatises" about the bicycle, the sled, the hovercraft, the jet plane, and the Swiss alpine train as one and the same, merely calling them vehicles. Those researchers disregard the wide differences in quality, essence, and meaning. The differences in the nature of dreams, the various levels and domains of our unconscious from which they emanate, and thus their different functions and meanings are utterly unknown to them. There are many forms of imagery, and in dreams the matter is infinitely more complex.

Some professionals with a psychodynamic background, perhaps wishing to be "thoroughly up-to-date," allow dubious physiological data to imbue their writings. Or, even worse, they use such studies to manufacture attention-seeking "discoveries" by combining sleep laboratory data with psychodynamic theory and therapy. In the next section we look at authors who claim that they have succeeded in creating such a cocktail and other writers who declare that to be impossible.

THE LITTLE MORITZ TWINS

The first problem we shall address is the undue influence of overvalued physiological data on psychodynamic thinking. Let us consider, as an example, the work of Robert McCarley and Allan Hobson because it is so widely quoted and accepted by many mental health professionals, certainly a sad testimony to the lack of discrimination and competency of so many psychotherapists. This statement, mentioned earlier, of Morton F. Reiser of Yale University refers to two studies of McCarley and Hobson (1977a, 1977b) of the Harvard Medical School: "I tried to indicate that we can no longer say that dreams are instigated by wishes – rather that the mental apparatus *exploits* the rem (dreaming) state of the brain for cognitive problem-solving and memory functions" (italics added).

The following comments are in order:

1. The work of McCarley and Hobson does not lend itself to valid conclusions on dreams. A paper of several hundred pages would be needed for a full analysis of their work and dubious claims. Let it suffice to say that they do not have the slightest comprehension of the difference between imagery and dreams. It is indicative of the quality of their studies when they imply that dreams have no meaning and can be interpreted in any way a therapist wishes. That is about as valid as someone declaring that the French language does not exist because he does not know it.

2. Wishes and other emotions, such as fear, can indeed be the basis for a dream. Emotions do not "exploit" dreams but are the creative force forming them.

3. Any conclusions about whether wishes cause dreams should have been based on the far more solid grounds of clinical acumen and experience. This subject will be discussed in the following section.

4. As I said earlier, Reiser's remark that dreams are disguised in order not to disturb sleep is contrary to clinical evidence.

In view of the fact that McCarley and Hobson are so frequently cited, additional comments regarding their claims are necessary.

Recently we have witnessed two "scientific" claims impugning Freud's integrity and expertise. Both have attracted considerable attention in the ranks of behavioral science.

In 1984 Jeffrey M. Masson claimed to have uncovered scandalous circumstances related to Freud's versions of the seduction theory. His insinuations start with references to occurrences in the year 1895. We are not concerned here with his assertions. But, as we shall see, the years 1890 and 1895 seem particularly promising to the self-appointed Freud detractors. Yet, in the long run, those are years they will prefer to forget.

At the beginning of one of their two papers, McCarley and Hobson state that they *were surprised to discover the origins of the major tenets of psychoanalytic dream theory in the neurophysiology of 1890"* (italics added). Their supposedly earthshaking and surprising "discovery" is constituted by their claim that the work of Exner, the prestigious Viennese neurobiologist and physiologist, had an overriding influence on Freud and was the true basis not only of his concepts in neurobiology but also of all his psychological thinking. Why were they so "surprised" to discover the influence of the neurophysiology of 1890 on Freud?

Freud has always given foremost attention to the interrelationship between physiological and psychological aspects, as have all who have written about his work. Surely that cannot be the "surprise" McCarley and Hobson refer to. Given Freud's strong interest in neurophysiology, it had to be neurophysiology as it existed at the time. It could not have been otherwise. So, again, that cannot be the surprise. What could the mysterious surprise be?

It is this: Referring to the major work by Exner, the one that is supposedly the source of Freud's thought, McCarley and Hobson state, *"Because of these relationships and interests, it is quite likely that Freud knew about Exner's 1894 book and Freud himself seems to have indicated that this was the case"* (italics added).

Now let us put two and two together. McCarley and Hobson assert that

1. Freud based his clinical and theoretical writings primarily on Exner's thoughts and work
2. Freud *never* acknowledged the true source of his wisdom.

It is certain that Freud was familiar with such an important work by Exner, one of his teachers at Vienna University. In those days the number of experts in physiology was exceedingly small.

We can now understand why McCarley and Hobson say that they experienced great surprise upon "discovering" the hitherto secret source of Freud's wisdom and the "origins of psychoanalytic dream theory." The "surprise" calls attention to the importance of this discovery of theirs, a historical feat matched only by the findings of Jeffrey Masson.

I have already mentioned the absence of clinical knowledge of one of the "twins," Hobson, when I pointed out the striking fallacies of his paper on bizarreness. I purposely selected points that I could answer briefly, as some substantive questions would require too much space. Here are two illustrative quotations from McCarley and Hobson:

> The dream process is thus seen as having its origin in senso-rimotor systems, with little or no primary ideational, volitional or emotional content.

> The random, but specific, nature of the generator signals could provide abnormally sequenced and shaped, but spatiotemporally specific, frames for dream imagery: the clustering of runs of generator signals might constitute time marks for dream subplots and scene changes.

Here, again, we note their failure to distinguish between imagery and dreams and to realize that there are many different types of dreams. In the face of all the evidence, they deny the basic elements that cause our dreams and manifest themselves in them: the emotional forces in our psyche and their interplay. Should it really be so difficult for anyone with the slightest bit of sensitivity to see that, for instance, there are connections between childhood events and dreams? The patients of competent psychotherapists, most often after a single demonstration, are fully aware of that and become eagerly involved in the exploration of such connections. How is it, then, that we do not find any such recognition in these two professionals who, after all, had the benefit of exposure to the literature of psychotherapy and the presence of expert psychotherapists at their university?

As for the second quote, it is not "the clustering of runs of generator signals" that constitutes "time marks for dream subplots and scene changes" but simply the logic of action and reaction of emotional forces. A simple example: A man with marked inhibitions has many dreams about attractive women. However, as he gets to a point of intimate closeness, there is a disruption or the scene changes. That happens every time the man has sexual dreams. According to McCarley and Hobson, however, he is likely to have faulty clustering of generator signals.

I have already explained that McCarley and Hobson's view of random activation of images is shown to be invalid by the fact that "true" dreams have a definite and cohesive meaning that clearly mirrors events in the individual's emotional history. Furthermore, dreams that have repetitive content and meaning definitely could not occur if only random brain activity were present.

McCarley and Hobson immerse us in an ocean of "electronic" data, presented as the basis for a great number of conclusions on the nature of dreams. By and large, to anyone who has clinical expertise, the conclusions appear to be either non sequiturs or nonfactual.

To elaborate on my assertions, I found, not without difficulty, three *quotes using clear language:* "We *believe* that the two processes emphasized in this paper – activation and synthesis – are major and important advances in dream theory" (italics added). "The idea that dreams reveal wishes is also *beyond* the direct reach of our new theory" (italics added). "The new theory cannot *yet* account for the emotional aspects of the dream experience" (italics added).

It is not uncommon for "behavioral scientists" to use language that is slippery and whose truth or basis in fact is next to impossible to pin down. Another ploy, also frequently used by McCarley and Hobson, is first to make strong, definitive statements about their "findings" and then to follow them with innumerable qualifiers and escape routes, such as "we believe," "not yet," "maybe," "perhaps," and the like. I wish Dr. Nathan Leites were still among us. He could have dealt with McCarley and Hobson in a decisive manner.

At any rate, let us now return to the three quotes from McCarley and Hobson, starting out with the second and third quotes. The authors state that the idea that dreams reveal wishes is "beyond" the scope of their theory. I want to state categorically that any "dream theory" unable to include wishes or feelings is utterly worthless. In actuality, feelings should be *at the core* of any valid assessment of the nature of dreams. The "cannot yet" in the third quote is an attempt to gloss over their fallacy.

McCarley and Hobson's understanding of wishes and feelings is practically nil. To substantiate that statement, I present a simple, recurrent dream of one of my former patients. The dream is not disguised, nor does it carry any hidden sexual connotation. The patient, who had artistic and aesthetic tendencies, was brought up in a very attractive home. At the age of 50, he was forced to live in a rather shabby, small apartment, as he had no money-making skills. In sporadically recurrent dreams he saw himself living in an attractive, spacious apartment. As short and simple as those dreams were, they destroy the entire basis and structure of McCarley and Hobson's theories.

An old psychotherapeutic technique consists of telling a patient to dream again about the content of his latest dream, or at least of a part of it. The technique is particularly useful when the meaning of the events is not clear to either the patient or the therapist. Often such a recommendation results in a new dream dealing with the same subject matter, even though the imagery is likely to be different.

McCarley and Hobson assure us that dreams are the result of *random* impulses of the brain. When studying the contents of the follow-up dreams, however, one is impressed by the meaningful links of these dreams with the prior ones. Of course, the proof furnished by such induced dreams is not needed. Many people, at some time in their lives, have repetitive dreams that show identical or similar images and the same basic theme. Furthermore, many dreams dealing with childhood problems show the rooms and dwellings where the child lived. The building stones of the dream are thus carefully selected and not random at all.

One of the causes of certain repetitive dreams can be traumatic situations that extended over many years. A patient who was a poor student would have terror-filled dreams about examinations, even long after obtaining his college degree. The dreams would reoccur when he had anxiety-provoking experiences. An elderly New York resident also experienced repetitive dreams. For over 26 years he had been severely harassed by a brutal and criminal landlord who tried to push him out of his apartment. The persecution stopped when the building was acquired by a new owner. Even many years later, however, he had frightening dreams in which he saw himself evicted and homeless. In both cases, the specific scenarios of the dreams were dictated by specific facts and emotions, the opposite of random mental activity.

And now a comment on the first quote. McCarley and Hobson claim that their discoveries are "major and important advances in dream theory." Such self-aggrandizement is preposterous, and the opposite is true. It is inexcusable for academicians to propagate untenable fabrications that undermine confidence in approaches of proven therapeutic value. Unfortunately, most psychotherapists, both those who are well grounded in their craft and those who are not, abstain from criticizing other professionals, even when unfounded claims cause major damage.

To a large extent, McCarley and Hobson's papers are an exercise in beating a dead horse. They give a distorted description of Freud's thought without proper consideration for its inseparable psychological aspects. There have always been psychiatrists, neurologists, and psychotherapists who, while interested in Freud's psychological insights, do not subscribe to most of his neurobiological hypotheses. And as McCarley and Hobson admit, many psychoanalysts have expressed their theoretical and intellectual misgivings concerning Freud's postulates, also faulted by McCarley and Hobson.

Much space in McCarley and Hobson's papers is devoted to criticism of Freud's (1895) "Project for a Scientific Psychology," specifically, his views on the function of neurons explained in that paper. Those views, however, were consistent with biological knowledge of those days. Are we supposed to blame Freud for not being clairvoyant enough to base his work on our present-day knowledge of neurology?

Maybe, as their next "surprising" project, McCarley and Hobson will try to disprove Galen.

Now let us turn to a weightier matter. McCarley and Hobson try to convince us that their study was based on the minute scrutiny of what they claim to have been Freud's rigid and narrow hypothesis regarding dreams and their origins. They focus on the most orthodox aspects of Freud's theory but omit important later statements by Freud that would damage their case against him. We know, for example, that in 1925 Freud made a meaningful addition to his 1900 book THE INTERPRETATION OF DREAMS. Since McCarley and Hobson refer to later editions of Freud, they cannot claim that they are aware only of his very early work.

I am quoting from the well-known English translation by A. A. Brill, which preceded the *Standard Edition* version, and shall limit myself to citing the important core statement by Freud:

The dream is fundamentally nothing more than a special form of our thinking, which is made possible by the condition of the sleeping state. It is the dream work which produces this form, and it alone is the essence of dreaming – the only explanation of its singularity. . . . That the dream should concern itself with efforts to perform the tasks with which our psychic life is confronted, is no more remarkable than that our conscious waking life should so concern itself.

No wonder McCarley and Hobson never mention that fundamental statement. Those few sentences invalidate their pretense of having based their criticism on an exhaustive examination of Freud's theories. Of course, many analysts have disregarded that statement, as well as other aspects of Freud's thought and work, if they considered them inconvenient.

The following quote by McCarley and Hobson concerning dream generation not only is a demonstration of the fine art of confusing apples and oranges but also attempts to deliver the deathblow to such concepts as the "unconscious" and "repression":

For D [dream] generation there is also no need to postulate the existence of the unconscious as the psychic subsystem or collection of neurons necessary for the storage of the energy of repressed wishes, and there is nothing to suggest that the concept of repression is in any way germane to controlling the activity of the pontine cells responsible for D generation.

Interestingly, McCarley and Hobson, after making such bold claims of "novel discoveries," were fully aware of the need to protect their flanks. In their summary of one of their two main papers, the categorical claims are nowhere to be found. We find instead ten timid propositions, each cautiously preceded by "may," "might," "could," "assume," or "perhaps." It would have been prudent for McCarley and Hobson merely to speak about their own hypotheses, right or wrong, rather than present us with claims of "sensational discoveries" on the nature of dreams. (For comparison, I call the reader's attention to W. W. Meissner's more responsible paper, "Dreaming as a Process.")

It is fun to note how each of the dragon slayers who wish to disprove Freud neatly tailors his own version of history to suit his endeavors.

We have already reported in detail Yalom's criticism of Freud's "highly materialistic view of human nature," based on his complete "allegiance to the Helmholtz school." Now let us look at the same part of history as narrated by McCarley and Hobson. As I discussed earlier, they "were surprised to discover the origins of the major tenets of psychoanalytic dream theory in the neurophysiology of 1890." Thus they give primary importance to the influence of Exner; Helmholtz does not exist for them. On the other hand, Exner does not exist for Yalom.

If there is any topic that has been explored over and over again, it is the factors that could have influenced Freud's thinking. Rather than present my own thoughts on that matter, I refer the reader to Peter Gay's (1988) monumental effort to evaluate such influences. His unprejudiced account does not substantiate either of those two claims.

By turning to the early days of psychoanalytic history, over a hundred years ago, McCarley and Hobson might just as logically have tried to write a volume dissecting Freud's early belief that nasal surgery was of help in solving sexual problems.

The field of psychotherapy is beset with countless problems. Although we have a solid body of knowledge and valid, proven methods, practitioners and teachers who have mastered the craft are woefully lacking. Too many professionals and students are not aware, or only vaguely so, that valuable knowledge and skill do exist. Yet unknowledgeable teachers are capable of reaching a vast academic audience. When they discredit one of the most important tools of psychotherapy, they do irreparable harm to patient care and student education. If McCarley and Hobson were interested in the truth, they would have spent an hour or two of their time in presenting this issue to an experienced psychotherapist, who would have demonstrated convincingly that dreams relate to a person's psyche and childhood.

In this chapter we are examining procedures and practices in the mental health professions. Thus we should note that McCarley and Hobson, as well as Yalom, are certainly not the first of the simplifiers to rewrite history, eliminating important facts inconvenient to their pretensions.

While reading about Yalom's activities at Stanford University, I also obtained information on the work done at Stanford's sleep laboratory. A significant part of the laboratory's studies was devoted to a technique called lucid dreaming, based on the discoveries, investigations, and thinking of Kilton Stewart. I do not include lucid dreaming in my examination, because in this book we are concerned only with the traditional quest of detecting meaningful material in dreams.

Stewart was a very talented and original psychotherapist who, like his friend Nandor Fodor, gave paramount importance to dreams. Stewart became well known for his reports on the Senois, a primitive pygmy tribe of the Pacific. He was the first to describe the tribe's habits and approaches to dream interpretation. The Senois, according to Stewart, purposely reshaped their dreams to achieve psychological improvement and serenity. His best-known book on the subject is PYGMIES AND DREAM GIANTS (1954). Margaret Mead, the foremost anthropologist of the period, highly praised the insight and importance of this work.

Older therapists may remember that techniques similar to those described by Stewart were recommended in PSYCHOANALYSIS AND THE WAR NEUROSES, by K. Abraham, S. Ferenczi, E. Simmel, and E. Jones (1921). It is not clear from the text if those gentlemen were also Senois.

The best known of the books based to a considerable extent on Stewart's thinking and work is LUCID DREAMING, by Stephen LaBerge (1985). Although LaBerge describes those techniques as he applied them at the sleep clinic at Stanford, he never actually mentions Stewart. LaBerge does, however, start his book by stating: "Originality, it has been said, is merely unconscious plagiarism. Because the ideas in this book derive from so many sources, I have not always been able to remember whom to credit." His memory lapse is particularly regrettable, in view of the fact that LaBerge is also coeditor, with Jayne Gackenbach, of another volume, CONSCIOUS MIND, SLEEPING BRAIN: PERSPECTIVES ON LUCID DREAMING. An extensive introductory chapter, written by another author, is entirely devoted to Senoi dreams and makes reference to the seven publications by Kilton Stewart that are fundamental to this matter.

I hope that these historical reminders will help render Dr. LaBerge's unconscious more conscious, his waking state more lucid, and his conscience more active.

A careful examination of sleep laboratory data does not substantiate the claims of the "meter reader" specialists, nor of the many behavioral scientists, such as the "professor," who affirm that it is the rem state that *causes* dreams.

To explain, I present a simple comparison: The waking state does not cause a person to double-check his bank balance, or to write an intricate letter, or to read his newspaper. The waking state is merely a state in which such activities can take place. Other examples of the vast number of mental activities are daydreaming and seeing imagery.

The same situation applies to the rem stage of the sleep state, a fact unrecognized by the self-appointed "experts" on dreams; the rem stage is merely a stage in which the many different kinds of imagery and dreams *may* take place but do not always do so. It is not surprising that the "blank spaces" account for only about 18 percent of the rem stage in men. Compare how often your mind is blank in the waking state. All we can safely say is that the mind is active in various forms in various mental states. The rem stage does not *cause* the dreams and is not the only stage wherein imagery and dreams take place. In short: In the rem stage dreams are possible; in deep sleep they are not.

The use of an academic degree to claim expertise in an unrelated area in which a professional has no familiarity is unconscionable yet common among the so-called behavioral scientists. Sadly, psychology and psychotherapy have become garbage cans of academic entrepreneurs.

Are my views particularly original, showing special acumen? Not in the least. Many knowledgeable colleagues who are in prominent positions and well known for their writings not only share these views but also have contributed valuable suggestions for inclusion in this book. I only wish they would make their opinions known, instead of keeping their silence. It would be a testimony to courage and morality in our profession.

We shall now address the question, mentioned at the beginning of this section: Have the sleep laboratory studies affected the psychotherapeutic care of patients?

The answer is yes, but not in the way one would have hoped. The negatives far outweigh the positives. Furthermore, we have not seen any contribution that could be considered to have a positive impact on the meaningful interpretation of dreams.

The following analogy illustrates my point: We know that certain medicines reduce high blood pressure and that salt intake increases it. What would we think of a physician who advised his patients to do just the opposite of what is indicated? Precisely the same problem is encountered here. Many physiological investigators have insisted that the use of dreams in psychotherapy, one of its important tools, is unscientific and ill founded, that its benefits are an illusion, or even a hoax. Such irresponsible assertions have undermined the confidence of patients and students, the most vulnerable group, and have placed a dangerous excuse for superficial practices in the hands of inadequately trained, mechanistically inclined mental health professionals. Thus psychotherapists who are content to apply simplistic procedures are only too glad to find a "scientific" justification for shoddy workmanship and, in particular, for their failure to engage in competent dream interpretation.

One more problem caused by the sleep laboratories must be added here. It is in the time-honored tradition of the other disciplines of "behavioral science," and it is not unlike the practice in Eastern Europe when it was communist; factories churned out mountains of worthless goods merely to provide salaried work. I have already spoken of the endlessly repetitious and trivial dream investigations that merely accumulate meaningless data. Funds, public and private, are limited in mental health. The last thing we want is one more pork barrel at the expense of improved student training and needed patient care.

CAN SLEEP LABORATORY FINDINGS
BE FRUITFULLY INCORPORATED INTO PSYCHOTHERAPY?

Among the numerous papers addressing the uses of sleep laboratory findings in psychotherapy, the five reviewed here are fairly representative of divergent positions.

> They fly through the air with the greatest of ease, These daring young men on the flying trapeze.
>
> LEYBURNE

Ramon Greenberg and Chester Pearlman Jr.
On the whole, psychoanalysts have not shown much enthusiasm for sleep laboratory findings, as the research hardly ever examines the psychodynamics of dream content. It is understandable, however, that with the research on rem sleep, professionals with some background in psychoanalysis and psychotherapy would sooner or later attempt to fill that gap. If done with the necessary know-how and sophistication, such efforts may yield data of some interest.

Let us look at a paper by two professors in Boston, Ramon Greenberg and Chester Pearlman Jr. (1975). The paper is modestly entitled "A Psychoanalytic-Dream Continuum: The Source and Function of Dreams." I am puzzled by the hyphen in the title but perhaps it was placed there to show us what a continuum is. The authors state: "A series of experiments in our laboratory has led to the conclusion that rem sleep is involved in information processing in the service of emotional adaptation." Further announcements advise us that emotionally significant waking experiences touch on conflictual matter from the past, arousing affects that set in motion either adaptive or defensive mechanisms; that rem sleep deprivation impairs such operations; and that greater emotional excitation of the individual before sleep – the authors call it "awareness of aroused conflictual material" – leads to a greater "pressure" to dream.

Having surprised us with such "novel" information, the authors proceed to further exploits. The question they address is "whether dreams are fortuitous creations with no significance beyond their current, dynamic meaning, or whether they exemplify a more fundamental process of adaptation." Why do the authors attach so little importance to the dynamic meaning, and how can a dream possibly be called "fortuitous"?

The authors then attempt to investigate the psychodynamic relationship between the dreams of a psychoanalytic patient in a sleep laboratory on nights before and after psychoanalytic sessions. The authors describe five such dreams and give us the benefit of their interpretations. As the dreams were written down in the dream laboratory, no associations by the patients are available, and thus the interpretations lack substantiation.

I will now cite a few passages from their summary discussion. "We found that the manifest content contained many meaningful residues from the presleep analytic hours." Using the Irma dream for their argument, they state, "What Freud did not include . . . were the important day residues"; "We can now see that Freud's formulation of latent content was related to feelings he was struggling with in his relationship to Fliess, but because he was apparently unaware of the *important* day residue of the Irma dream . . . "; and, "In summary, this study has demonstrated the continuity of mental life in waking and sleeping (dreaming) states. The view of rem sleep (dreaming) as an adaptive mechanism helped to organize material collected during an ongoing psychoanalysis."

First, in many instances the authors report the obvious, or already known, as if it were their scientific discovery. Second, I have the same objection as I raised about Erikson: The authors attempt to analyze the patient's dreams, as well as Freud's Irma dream, without the necessary associations presented in the analytic session. Third, the "analytic" interpretations of the five dreams, supposedly supporting the authors' conclusions, are not at all plausible and are obviously bent to prove the authors' assertions.

Later in this chapter I will discuss the authors' claim that dreams serve an adaptive purpose, an assertion also made by many others.

The fish dies because he opens his mouth.

SPANISH PROVERB

David M. Berger

David M. Berger's (1981) "Psychoanalysis, Dreaming and the REM State: A Clinical Vignette" was a presentation to the annual meeting of the Canadian Psychoanalytic Society in June 1980. In the preamble Berger states: "This presentation examines the effect of the discovery of the rem state on the role of the psychotherapist. . . . The tentative findings from the rem laboratory concerning the function of dreams are shown *to fit nicely with the use to which dreams have been put by psychoanalytic therapists*" (italics added).

Berger based that remarkable discovery on a single dream reported by one of his patients: "I had a dream in which I was going round and round. As if I were caught up in a whirlpool." Berger states that the patient experienced a sensation of dizziness in the dream.

Berger begins his argument by relating this dream to the positions arrived at by investigators in the area of rem research. McCarley and Hobson, for example, have put forward an activation-synthesis hypothesis of dreaming. Emphasizing the isomorphisms between the physiological activation of desynchronized sleep and the psychological events in dreams, they suggest that the sensation of dizziness in dreams results from pontine stimulation of the vestibular system.

Berger further relates that the patient mentioned his dislike of coming to the hospital for his session and also feeling faint when arriving for a previous appointment. Berger states: "I suggested to the patient a possible similarity between the faintness he described and the sensation of dizziness in the dream. . . . I suggested further that the dream may have been telling us something about the way he felt about coming to the hospital."

Berger continues: "This therapeutic intervention, it seems to me, would be equally valid, whether one conceptualized dream formation in pre-rem terms or in rem terms, because it sidesteps the whys of dreaming and focuses on the content."

As psychotherapists, we are constantly taking notice of remarks by our patients that, unbeknownst to them, are far more revealing than their reports of what they consider important. Thus, unbeknownst to Berger, we learn a lot about him when he calls his rather trite remarks concerning an obvious similarity of feelings a "therapeutic intervention."

Berger then explores painful childhood situations with the patient linked to a stay at a hospital and a feeling of drowning and dizziness at the onset of anesthesia.

Berger continues by mentioning that in dreams an unconscious conflict is pressing for discharge and threatening to disrupt sleep, and therefore the energy of the conflict is dissipated with the help of a dream, thus preserving sleep.

I have already asserted, when discussing a similar statement by Morton F. Reiser, that solid clinical observation shows that dreams do not protect sleep. Even when I was still a psychotherapy student, it took neither much acumen nor vast experience to note that the dreams of patients suffering from anxiety would, again and again, disturb their sleep.

Berger reviews the positions taken by the sleep laboratory researchers and then returns to expand on the patient who had the "dizziness" dream. He reports that in a subsequent session the patient remembered having had a "whirlpool" dream by the age of four, after a fall from a tree, even before the anesthesia experience.

Certainly, there is nothing to be criticized in Berger's relating various theoretical positions, nor in his describing in a case history the gradual remembrance of childhood episodes. However, in his conclusion Berger states that "there is much in psychoanalytic theory consistent with, and of value to, rem dream research, and there is much in rem dream research consistent with, and relevant to, psychoanalytic theory." That assertion is identical to the one he makes at the beginning of his paper, namely: "The tentative findings from the rem laboratory concerning the function of dreams are shown *to fit nicely* with the use to which dreams have been put by psychoanalytic therapists" (italics added).

I have shown that statement to a number of psychoanalysts who are knowledgeable in both physiology and psychodynamic therapy. Their attitude was to shrug their shoulders and say "So what?" Their response is understandable; how could they get excited about all those papers that they consider inadequate?

I, however, find myself in a less accommodating position, and it is with good reason that I selected Berger's paper. Let us return to the two last quoted statements. A reader may think they are bland, friendly remarks, a conciliatory bow in both directions. After all, Berger does claim a "nice" new discovery, attesting to his exceptional talent as a thoroughly modern expert in neurophysiology, as well as in psychoanalysis.

Not so, in my opinion. Once published in a professional journal, even the most incompetent statements become part of the body of "behavioral science" and are quoted again and again in other papers. No matter how wild and irresponsible the assertion, it gradually assumes the aura of scientific fact and academic respectability. It is certainly far more comfortable to let papers pass, such as those by Greenberg and Pearlman, or the present one by Berger. It is precisely such a "collegial" attitude, however, that has turned mental health into a wax museum of horrors. As I have stated over and over, their influence on student training and patient care is pervasive.

Having made those statements, I would like to justify them.

There is nothing in Berger's paper that supports his claim of having discovered the mutual benefits that psychoanalysis and rem findings bestow on each other.

Berger relates an extremely brief dream in which the patient felt dizzy and the subsequent psychodynamic exploration of that feeling through the scrutiny of childhood incidents. He links that psychodynamic effort to the "positions arrived at by investigators in the area of rem research," and mentions the work of McCarley and Hobson, who suggested that "the *sensation of dizziness* in dreams results from pontine stimulation of the vestibular system" (italics added). Thus Berger investigates the "dizziness" by psychoanalytic procedure and links it "nicely" to the statements on dizziness made by McCarley and Hobson.

However, Berger selected an extremely short dream that can be summarized by the word "dizziness." While it is easy to pick out a "one-word dream" and attribute all kinds of meanings to it, such manipulation could not be made with a more substantial dream. Moreover, dreams that have dizziness as part of the story are actually rare, and no link to the dizziness in dreams postulated by McCarley and Hobson can be established.

I have already stated that McCarley and Hobson evidenced deplorable ignorance in the matter of imagery and dreams by insisting that dreams have no meaning and can be interpreted in any way a therapist wishes. We now encounter a second statement by those two experts that has no validity. They speak blithely about the "sensation of dizziness in dreams." I would like to ask: What sensation of dizziness in dreams? There is no such thing in the vast majority of dreams. If they are referring to the occasional dizziness when waking up, that is just as likely to occur when no dreams preceded the awakening.

Morton F. Reiser

Morton F. Reiser's (1991) book MEMORY AND BRAIN: WHAT DREAM IMAGERY REVEALS is pertinent to our subject matter. On the dust jacket prominent academicians offer their rave endorsements. Reiser's initial concept for the book is alluring. The follow-through, however, is beset by problems. Nevertheless, for those interested in these matters, the book may offer some stimulation to their thinking.

I have selected a few significant passages from the book and will comment on its underlying trend and main characteristics. Reiser's intention is to use what he calls a dual-track approach to establish the links between "the psychoanalytic side largely from Freud's seminal discoveries and from my own clinical work . . . and the neurobiological side . . . looking specifically into psychoanalytic and neurobiological aspects of memory . . . making use of cognitive psychological research and cognitive neuroscience."

Let us look at the premises for Reiser's claims to having established convincing links between the neurobiological and the psychological factors affecting the human mind. To a large extent, Reiser bases his neurobiological considerations on the work and theories of McCarley and Hobson. If my criticism of their assertions, presented earlier in this section, is valid, then Reiser's theorizing is fallacious. On the basis of their assertions, Reiser states that it is not wishes that cause the dream; the dream merely "exploits" the rem stage. As stated, according to McCarley and Hobson's proposition, the dream is not caused by emotions but uses the random signals as building material, weaving them into a story. The fact is, however, as mentioned before, that many dreams dealing with childhood events picture the appropriate childhood surroundings, such as the actual rooms and dwellings at the time. In other dreams people in the dreamer's life appear in their habitual environment; for example, a physician may be seen in his real office. As previously mentioned, all such dreams are therefore properly put together and factually accurate; they are not based on random elements. One does not have to be a student of psychotherapy or neurobiology to be aware of such simple facts.

Reiser's psychological premise is equally weak. From among other questionable approaches, Reiser selects, as a demonstration for this project, Freud's dream of the botanical monograph. In discussing Erikson, I have already remarked on the shortcomings of using the dreams of nonpatients for important demonstrations. Basic to Reiser's attempt are the data drawn from Freud's dream. By using a dream of Freud's rather than of a patient, a therapist can, consciously or not, more easily manipulate the limited dream material to prove his point. For a project like Reiser's, and for the purpose of demonstrating his procedure, it would have been far more desirable to use a dream of one of his patients. By presenting the many associations and responses of the patient, he could perhaps have convincingly traced the memory and effective connections. Moreover, those links – and that is what Reiser's book is about – could have been tested by further work with the patient and particularly by scrutinizing the material in other dreams.

We know that far more significant data are yielded when patient and analyst explore dreams together than when a person merely writes down his thoughts and associations. That is true even if he has much insight and is as meticulous as Freud. The value of data gathered in therapeutic sessions is superior for many reasons, including the analyst's ability to reduce the patient's resistance to focusing on sensitive parts of the dream, which he might otherwise have glossed over. Unless we are only paying lip service to the basic analytic truths we proclaim to believe in, we must surely adhere to them in our own work, even though doing so requires far more effort. The additional data that results will have to be taken into account, making it considerably more difficult to present a credible hypothesis.

At the beginning of the book Reiser, referring to the human psyche, admits, "We can never know what is in there: the real stuff of our beings, what it is doing and why." Later the tone is quite different, as illustrated by the following quotations from the end of the book. Speaking about his work, Reiser rejoices:

> Are these really to be regarded as minor revisions? Certainly they are neither few nor trivial. They are important and necessary in order to bring the model into balanced conformity with contemporary, cognitive neuroscience and psychoanalysis. In this sense, they are major, additive revisions.
>
> The goal rather has been to evaluate the fit of the postulated mental mechanisms with cognitive neuroscience and with psychoanalytic observations, thereby to achieve a balanced, contemporary psychobiological model of the dream process. I think that the goal has been achieved. We have accomplished what we set out to do. The modified, or revised, model does make it possible to formulate a new psychobiological view of the dream process that is both balanced and contemporary.
>
> This book stands as an example of both the promise and the limitations of one individual effort – as competent as could be expected under current conditions – to deal, in depth, with one selected sector of mind/brain functions.

The reader may not find cause in Reiser's book to justify such euphoria. If the task he attempted is to have validity, its psychological and neurobiological premises need to be solid. To detail the premises, and the many other related points presented, would not be difficult but would take a voluminous tome, as the work touches on many disciplines. Such an effort is not necessary, however, as the validity of the work can be judged by scrutinizing its basic assumptions.

Thus I shall limit myself to alerting the reader to the points that provide a representative picture of Reiser's reasoning. His book is of interest because it presents some of the topics that will need to be addressed in any future study of this kind. Its enormous weakness is caused by his considerable neglect of the important role of emotions. His approach to describing our inner life is skeletal and one-sidedly cerebral and gives complete primacy to the workings of the memory. His charts bring to mind computer diagrams.

In contrast, I would like to give a simple illustration of the important role played by the emotions. A man with inferiority feelings looks up to men who appear emotionally strong. Such people, even though they may be from the distant past, appear in his dreams if they are suitable figures for the drama the dreamer's unconscious wants to present to him. The unconscious selects that particular image because it provides the desired feeling. Thus the unconscious casts the figures like the director of a play, to match the emotions of the dreamer.

In spite of some objections, Reiser is happy to accept McCarley and Hobson's assertions, which, as I have said, ignore or contradict clinical evidence. Actually, McCarley and Hobson, when speaking about their "findings," tend to be more cautious than Reiser, preceding their claims, for example, with "may," "might," "could," and "assume."

Analysts with strong cerebral, mechanistic inclinations will naturally favor such procedures. They frequently use one of the three "dictionary approaches" to dream interpretation that I described when criticizing Erikson's "analysis" of the Irma dream. Let me refresh the reader's memory on one such approach: The analyst, referring to a supposedly key word in the patient's dream, claims that a similar-sounding word actually represents, or refers to, its real meaning. For example, "bed" stands for "bad"; "horse" stands for "hearse"; or, as in Reiser's book, "suntan" leads to "tannic acid."

Reiser's choice of metaphors used in explanations shows the same tendency. The following is a fine example of the level of Reiser's understanding of the human mind: He attempts to explain how "a picture stands for a word that, in turn, connotes a meaning or idea." He shows us, side by side, two drawings: one of a tie, the other of a knee. He then explains: "The dual mental operation of first naming each of the drawn images, and then combining the sounds of 'tie' and 'knee' to form the word 'tiny' produces a word stimulus that is capable of evolving a recognizable meaning."

Such intellectual gimmickry and all the dictionary approaches have this in common: They are general and not based on clinical observation focusing on the individuality of the patient and his specific psychodynamics. Their application is most often inappropriate and eminently forced. These approaches are a favorite tool of analysts who are unable to understand an individual patient's emotional structure.

As the book progresses, a knowledgeable reader may feel increasingly uneasy about the assertions relating to the two areas Reiser attempts to link. (In comparison, a less ambitious study within this domain – Meissner, 1968 – is on more solid ground throughout.)

The following quote illustrates Reiser's perspective of the human mind and his hope of the way in which understanding of it can be brought about: "The idea of understanding the mind exclusively in terms of brain function represents a distant and, perhaps, impossible dream." One man's dream is another man's nightmare.

In his epilogue Reiser insists not only that future investigators must be expert in psychoanalysis and neurobiology but also that their education "cross other disciplinary boundaries . . . to allow for the degree of understanding of the methods, data, and concepts required for meaningful collaboration and conceptual divergences. New patterns of training would have to be established for such collaboration." So far so good.

But then he lists his requirements for specific areas of expertise that the future investigator will need to master:

> Only universities could embrace the full range of disciplines that would be involved in seeking integrations across the multiple interfaces that could be involved: molecular genetics, molecular biology, cell biology, neurophysiology, neuroanatomy, neurochemistry, neuropsychopharmacology, all branches of psychology including psychoanalysis, computer science, sociology, anthropology, earth sciences, political science, history, and the humanities.

Obviously, his requirements would present a formidable obstacle. I would suggest that a more feasible solution can be found by viewing the matter more realistically.

While it is true that the disciplines listed by Reiser are taught at universities, a parliament of scientists could not bring about Reiser's dream. For his edification, let me present a cogent quote from Sanford

Ellberg, formerly dean of the graduate division at the University of California, Berkeley: "You must remember that a great university is a place where nothing is ever done for the first time."

Reiser's writings, like those of many others in our field, project a much oversimplified, largely mechanistic universe. Hence his desire to understand the mind primarily in terms of brain functions. In the final summary of the book, Reiser quotes Jonathan Winson, who proposes "associating recent events to past memories, and evolving a neural substrate to guide future behavior." Does that explain to Reiser the extraordinary creativity of men like Shakespeare and Mozart, or of any dream?

McCarley and Hobson, as well as Reiser in his own way, focus on the less important and elevate it to the primary. It is like attempting to describe men by merely describing their socks.

Having taken that necessary detour, let us now return to the endeavor to clarify further any existing, significant connections and relationships between biological and psychological factors.

The key investigator of such a project need not be an academic centipede or an expert in microneuroimmunology. He does, however, need to have a substantial qualification: outstanding acumen and expertise in psychotherapy. There is by now a sufficient body of knowledge in psychotherapy for us to be able to separate the wheat from the chaff when the data are presented to us. Just as a talented musician can easily detect false notes, the expert psychotherapist can determine which "findings" from other disciplines are valid when the touchstone of psychotherapeutic knowledge is applied.

We can proceed in that way when considering the various professional views on the rem state in relation to dreams. As described in this chapter, such opinions range from the ludicrous to the well informed. As we will see, conclusions arrived at by competent professionals can be fruitfully used in planning future investigations. Interpretation of the data obtained from other disciplines is not unmanageable. Unfortunately, the greatest difficulty may lie in overcoming the obstacles caused by mental health professionals themselves and in obtaining cooperation and understanding. The nature of such obstacles varies, of course, from project to project and from place to place. Nevertheless, let us review two illustrative situations where such problems occurred.

I proposed a small number of relatively simple yet meaningful projects to the sleep laboratories of two well-known universities. I will describe the projects a little later, in the section entitled "What Should Have Been Done – But Was Not." Both laboratories rejected the proposals almost immediately. (I should mention that my proposals did not include my participation in the projects.)

It was not difficult to ascertain that resistance to the projects by the sleep researchers was caused primarily by their fears. The investigators were concerned about having to operate in an unfamiliar – that is, psychological – area and thus opening themselves to criticism for their lack of knowledge. Furthermore, in spite of their lip service praising the value of the proposals, one could not discern any real interest on their part. It was obvious that some of them were loath to share, even temporarily, the hegemony of their domain. In short, the overall attitude of the sleep researchers was that the proposed projects were simply an inconvenience to be avoided.

The second illustrative situation is a well-known academic endeavor that became a victim of professional obstructionism. The consequences were far reaching because of major damage to the public interest. We are speaking of the formidable opposition to one of Robert S. Wallerstein's projects: the creation of a vastly improved training program for mental health professionals. The main reason for the hostility and insistence on maintaining the status quo was the mental health practitioners' fear that a better-trained professional discipline would be a definite threat to their own privileged positions. The story of the events is disturbing and poignant. It has been published under the title THE DOCTORATE IN MENTAL HEALTH (Wallerstein, 1991). Anyone undertaking an interdisciplinary project would do well to anticipate similar obstacles and consider ways of assuaging professional fears.

Let us return to Reiser. Reading his book, one cannot fail to notice a striking fact. The work of psychotherapists, except for Yalom and his ilk, also demands linking the patient's emotions with memories of past events. A rich tapestry, representing the patient's unique universe, is created. Month after month, as work progresses, new colors and thought-provoking details are added. In contrast, Reiser's project brings to mind an image of gray, poorly connected, or forcibly linked, wires. Three factors contribute to that disappointing impression: the very nature of neurobiology, the sterility of Reiser's approach, and the pervasive oversimplification that characterizes the project.

It can be argued that without such oversimplification Reiser could not have undertaken this project. To answer that point, I refer to criticisms I have made here of other facile approaches. Just to mention a few: certain forms of group therapy, shoddy dream interpretation, outcome research, and psychoanalytic process research strategies. All those approaches have disastrous results. One of those results is vastly misleading information. Too often, valueless projects that cannot withstand scrutiny by expert psychotherapists are represented as remarkable academic and scientific wisdom.

Even though there is little hope that we can rid ourselves of those pretentious endeavors, it would be far better, and more honest, not to engage in any project requiring oversimplification to such an extent that most of the pertinent facts either are not included as components or are reduced to nonsensical simplicity. In good literature one would never describe the personality of an individual by merely depicting his garments, but that is a common occurrence in the behavioral "sciences."

Our profession, like all professions, has its share of brazen opportunists. When the Soviet Union fell apart and the putsch failed, hard-line communists became, overnight, vociferous reform democrats – and got away with it. We see a similar scenario in brain research.

Serious brain research by competent specialists has produced valuable findings. Some of it has brought us closer to the understanding of heretofore incomprehensible phenomena, like the way we form our language. But as we have demonstrated, many poorly endowed and poorly qualified mental health professionals rushed to jump on the bandwagon, trying to outdo each other with proclamations and writings to convince us, and perhaps themselves, that their thought and research are state-of-the-art. Hanging a cat by its tail to the tongue of a bell will get the desired attention, but it fails to demonstrate a harmonious interplay of two systems.

To contradict Reiser's approach to dreams, I would like to present a simple, run-of-the-mill dream in which the elements are selected by the logic of emotions. Practically any dream can be used to demonstrate that fact.

The dream is from a sensitive and cultured man in his mid-40s who is forced to work in a dreary and demanding job not at all commensurate with his talents and inclinations. There are strong negative forces in his psyche that militate against him in his waking state and his dreams.

The dreamer sees himself at an oceanside resort, perhaps in the Caribbean. It is a huge, modern, cheap-looking hotel that obviously caters to mass tourism. The ocean can barely be seen in the distance. Hundreds of tourists are milling around. They are the kinds of people he would much rather avoid. Feeling urinary pressure, he looks for a toilet but cannot find one. He feels increasingly depressed and lost. He is glad to see a friend whom he admires for his strength and equanimity. However, when he approaches the friend, the friend makes a biting, derogatory remark. The dreamer feels crushed and wakes up.

All the dream elements follow the logic of the dreamer's emotional setup. First he wishes to escape the dreariness of his daily drudgery. He tries to escape to an attractive place. But, as always, his unconscious denies him such relief and gratification. The place is dreadful, and he cannot even find the men's room. In his despair, he tries to find support, and the image of his friend is created. Alas, the negative forces within his psyche also turn that image against him.

Over the years, many have tried to design a model that would correlate the functions of the mind with those of the brain and body. In Reiser's book the reader will need to watch out for two major shortcomings that afflict many such attempts: (1) Many pertinent facts, inconsistent with the grand design, are simply left out, and (2) other facts are conveniently bent into a splendiferous "novel" hypothesis. As stated, we are here confronted by unsatisfactory premises; an overly academic, cerebral approach, emphasizing the mechanical; and insufficient attention to the causative role of emotions in the formation of the "links" that Reiser hopes to find. His shortcomings are also obvious in the transcripts of his remarks in analytic sessions, the report of one of which follows. I was relieved to find that there exists at least one person who shares my response to Reiser. In the following passage Reiser presents, with a touch of humor, an exchange with a patient during a therapy session:

MR: When we first spoke of your feeling of having been thrown out of the Garden of Eden, the image of a painting came into my mind. (*I identified and described it.*) I find myself thinking of it again, and believe we can learn from it. Adam and Eve were expelled because they had acquired sexual knowledge. I think it's time to add to what we already understand. It is not just the idea of having a baby – it is also the idea of sex, of making a baby that contributes to making you feel so bad.

Eve: Is it time to go? I'm glad August will give me a break from this.

In this chapter we scrutinize many samples of writings in psychotherapy. Where the criticisms are brief, the reader may not find them convincing. On the other hand, it would be impractical and tedious for the reader were we to examine all such samples at length. Thus I have limited the extended scrutiny to a relatively small number of papers particularly representative of major trends. Frankly, the least enjoyable task in preparing this chapter was reviewing the incredibly large number of books and writings that, while most often not treating it as their main topic, give some consideration to the role of rem sleep and its relationship to dreams. As I have said, far too many mental health professionals, trying to show that they are thoroughly up-to-date on the newest "scientific" discoveries, hasten to climb on the bandwagon – in this case, the rem bandwagon. Consequently, we are offered some unappetizing and scrambled dishes of pieces of neurobiology, psychotherapy, and naive theorizing, served with an abundance of hi-sci verbiage.

It is therefore a relief to turn to investigators who write on the subject soberly, without exploiting neurobiological and sleep research findings for self-promotion. Because in this chapter we are concentrating on the negative influences in mental health, I shall mention the meritorious only briefly, taking the work of two such authors as examples.

First we turn to S. Gabel's (1985) "Sleep Research and Clinically Reported Dreams: Can They Be Integrated?" Gabel agrees with Blum that rem research has hardly been able to contribute to the clinician's task. Toward the end of his paper, Gabel states:

Employing clarification, amplification of symbolic material, personal meanings, limited association, and some understanding of developmental processes, dreams can be interpreted along lines that do state the positions and conflicts of the dreamer; that dreams do reflect and symbolize problems the dreamer faces in his or her everyday life; and that one can discern adaptive and defensive functioning in the stories and contents of dreams.

Certainly there is nothing new here, but in this day and age we have to be grateful for each professional who writes about dreams without demolishing the topic one way or another and who has enough expertise and integrity not to join the rem faddists in the pretense of ultramodern know-how.

Another author who has arrived at the same conclusion is J. M. Porret, of the Department of Child and Adolescent Psychiatry at the University of Lausanne. In his (1987) paper Porret arrives at his conclusions not only on the basis of his investigations at Lausanne but also by scrutinizing the writings of a great number of European and American researchers. In his summarizing statement Porret reports that research convincingly disproves the illusion that the model underlying psychodynamic therapy and the model on which electroencephalographic investigations are based allow for any overlap.

WHAT SHOULD HAVE BEEN DONE – BUT WAS NOT

So far, in the voluminous literature dealing with rem, we have not found a single instance where sleep laboratory research was used intelligently and fruitfully in the service of psychotherapy. On the surface that seems hard to understand, because, as the suggestions that follow indicate, some possibilities come easily to mind. We will look at several reasons for the neglect a little later, but I mention one of them now: To obtain solid results, the work cannot be done by the sleep laboratory technicians alone; *it requires the active participation of a psychotherapist with considerable experience and acumen in matters of dreams.*

One needed investigation would bring to the sleep laboratory patients who are undergoing psychodynamic therapy but who state that they are *not* dreaming. Without dreams, the task of the therapist is extremely difficult. In fact, as I noted earlier, Harold P. Blum believes that without dreams, psychoanalysis is impossible. In a sleep laboratory one could look for answers to a number of interesting questions: Do they really not dream? If they do dream, what are those dreams specifically, and do the dreams reveal the reasons the patients forget them? Will the patients now become aware that they dream and from here on be able to remember their dreams and bring them to therapy sessions?

A visit to the sleep laboratory could similarly benefit specific patients who show the two following characteristics: insufficient progress in their psychotherapy and only rare occurrences of remembered dreams. The increased number of dreams collected would be sure to be an asset in their therapy.

I have already spoken of the patients who dream because while they were in a hypnotic trance, they were requested to do so. They too should be the subjects of a sleep laboratory investigation.

In all those instances interesting data could be gathered, such as the differences between the dreams recounted after the subjects are awakened and those reported to therapists in regular sessions. Some patients may forget, upon awakening on their own in the morning, dreams dealing with a particularly sensitive topic.

One of the least-documented areas in psychotherapy is the dreams of sociopaths, as I have mentioned before. There is no doubt that the sleep laboratory could play a useful role here. I have already advanced my conviction that the dreams of sociopaths should be interpreted quite differently from the dreams of others, and we need to have many more sociopaths' dreams if we want to strengthen our hypotheses in this area. However, we encounter a preliminary problem. I wrote earlier in this chapter about an author who was interested in this matter but naively stated that he could not obtain dreams of convicted "criminals." One has to be careful not to confuse sociopathy and criminal conviction. Most convicted criminals are not sociopaths, and most sociopaths are never convicted; they may live happily ever after and hold prestigious positions, even in the professional world.

Another area in which competent investigation is practically nonexistent is that of non-rem dreams. By "competent investigation" I mean scrutiny of those dreams of a specific patient by his psychodynamic psychotherapist, who must be thoroughly familiar with the patient's background and psychological structure. The therapist could then compare the dreams with those obtained during the rem period. Other valuable projects that would need the participation of psychotherapists of considerable acumen would scrutinize the dreams of so-called normal people, that is, those with limited emotional disturbance, and the dreams of people falling into specific clinical categories.

It is inexcusable that such work – the need for which is obvious and the benefits from which would be immediate – has been avoided because it requires some additional and sophisticated effort. The incredibly poorly designed, virtually identical dream investigations by sleep laboratories have been carried on and on in the name of pure science for almost 40 years. I have seen no tangible results, in terms of scientific or therapeutic advancement, that those repetitious "dream investigations" have achieved.

As far as my simple proposals are concerned, any psychotherapy student, from any background, could have proposed them, as long as he had some acumen in clinical work and some interest in the welfare of his fellow man.

I would now like to present some specifics on how the investigations proposed should be carried out. I shall limit my recommendations to the proposal concerning patients currently undergoing psychodynamic therapy and claiming not to dream. Some of the suggestions made here can be applied to the other proposals.

The project should either be under the supervision of a psychodynamically oriented psychotherapist with a considerable acumen and experience in dreams or have the collaboration of such a psychotherapist. The not-so-easy first step would be to locate patients who claim that they do not dream. To ensure that one is not dealing with a temporary condition, one should select patients who state that they have not dreamed for at least five years. Furthermore, so that one can obtain meaningful information from any dreams collected, the patients should be undergoing treatment with psychodynamically oriented therapists with proven expertise in understanding dreams. I suggest that ultraorthodox psychoanalysts not be included, as they tend to interpret dreams automatically in a classical, schoolbook manner. That kind of interpretation would be destructive to our second goal: to discover, from the dreams obtained, why the patients were unable to remember dreams. One of the causes may be memories that are so distasteful or frightening to the patient that he is blocking out all dream recall.

The next point is important but may be somewhat difficult to achieve. Ideally, it should be the patient's own therapist who questions him after he is awakened, for he is familiar with the patient's psychic makeup. Although I doubt that any therapist would be willing to spend two or three nights at the laboratory, the procedure could be done by phone, the questions and answers being recorded and the material examined in the next therapy session. As one can see, I would gladly sacrifice the therapist's sleep for my curiosity.

There are yet more obstacles, which, as stated, I have learned about from bitter experience. It would be difficult to find a sleep laboratory director willing to venture out of his comfortable niche and involve himself in an experiment that, even though of definite therapeutic value, would make more demands on him. Furthermore, as sleep laboratories use their budgets only for their own programs, financing these projects, inexpensive though they are, is an additional problem. Here is one solution: Given the importance for a patient's psychotherapeutic progress to investigate his dreaming, or not dreaming, as the case may be, the sleep laboratory experience would be part of the psychotherapy and thus covered by insurance.

The appalling chasm between what should be done and what has been done is indicative of the poverty of professional thought and acumen in our field. Equally appalling is the absence of any professional interest in applying new findings in the service of patient care rather than creating facile, sterile, self-perpetuating opportunities for academic employment in teaching and "research."

Minds that have nothing to confer find little to perceive.

WORDSWORTH

d. Dreams and the Feeling for Feelings: Talent versus the Imitation of Science

LIA FAIL

False men using mask of truth,
Their face so bland,
Their talk so smooth,
Betrayed is our land!
Arise, o voice,
Arise, o voice,
Arise the truth to hail!
The stone first whispers,
The stone shouts loud,
The stone called Lia Fail.*

SEAN FARO

*The stone upon which Joseph rested his head when dreaming his prophetic dreams. It was later brought by the "lost tribes" to Tara, in Ireland. Whenever the wisdom of dreams is misused, mutilated, or maligned, the powers of this ageless, living stone surge like a tide to destroy the infamous offender.

What Others Have Said about the Dream

Try as you might, you will always see yourself as "seeing."
Methinks, we dream to keep on seeing.

GOETHE

And now from the Vast of the Lord will the waters of sleep
Roll in on the souls of men,
But who will reveal to our waking ken
The forms that swim and the shapes that creep
Under the waters of sleep?

SIDNEY LANIER

When most I wink, then do my eyes best see.

SHAKESPEARE

It was the wise Zeno that said, he could collect a man by his dreams. For
then the soul, stated in deep repose, betrayed her true affections: which,
in the busy day, she would rather not note. . . . The best use we can make
of dreams, is observation: and by that, our own correction or encouragement. For 'tis not doubtable, but that the mind is working in the
dullest depth of sleep.

OWEN FELLTHAM

We should show life neither as it is nor as it ought to be, but as we see it
in our dreams.

CHEKHOV

Friend, many dreams . . . may be borne out, if mortals only know them.

HOMER

I say: "My bed will comfort me and ease my sleep." But You frighten me
with such terrifying dreams that I would choose death rather than these
pains.

JOB

There ain't no way to find out why a snorer can't hear himself snore.

MARK TWAIN

We hold these truths to be self-evident.

JEFFERSON

There is meaning and depth in our dreams for those able to understand. When psychotherapy increasingly mirrors the stranglehold of barren minds, there is need to value the few sources that still flow.

In this chapter I am trying to present an overall picture of current psychotherapeutic trends and know-how; in short, to evaluate professional quality. In earlier sections I recounted what various behavioral scientists have to say about dreams. Having criticized several authors, I want to present data derived from clinical experience to clarify my negative comments.

PSYCHOTHERAPISTS AND DREAMS

I have stressed that a full understanding of the nature of dreams can be arrived at only by first approaching them from a purely psychological point of view. The only professionals qualified to arrive at valid conclusions about dreams are experienced psychotherapists with outstanding acumen in comprehending dreams. Only they can assess the validity of findings from other disciplines. They can determine, as we have seen when examining the work done in sleep laboratories, that claims made about dreams may be lacking in verity and substance and may contradict clinical facts known to psychotherapists. All attempts by other professionals to approach the topic from their perspectives have proven incomplete and one-sided at best, misleading and inane at worst.

Of course, not many psychotherapists have the required expertise. Nevertheless, now we have a solid body of knowledge of what dreams are and what they are not. The problem is that much of that knowledge is not accessible to the profession and to students. Misconceptions abound, and teaching is ruefully inadequate.

I have pointed out that psychotherapists and psychoanalysts who only inadequately comprehend clinical realities have no firm ground and no reliable yardstick to use in distinguishing between truth and falsehood. Compensating for and rationalizing their short-comings, some of them cling to theory, dogma, and authority, wrapped up in high-sounding, "scientific" language. Others are swayed by trendy, simplistic, or mechanistic information coming from other fields. Obviously, none of those approaches, no matter how widespread and commonly accepted, has enriched our psychological understanding of dreams.

I used the word "simplistic" on purpose, even though the approaches proposed by such professionals appear, on the surface, highly complex. Morton Reiser, for instance, suggests that to comprehend human psychology, one must have academic expertise in more than 50 disciplines and subdisciplines. But as Poincaré said, "A collection of facts is no more a science than a heap of stones is a house." A person's ability to understand is in direct proportion to his depth. Such depth provides the guiding light. If it is lacking, no amount of book knowledge, facile theorizing, or "scientific" pretense can lead to any accomplishment except self-glorification.

When I refer critically to academicians, I am pointing solely to the mental health professionals who, occupying academic positions and not being well grounded in the understanding of the human mind and psychotherapy, make uninformed pronouncements. Being teachers, they cause considerable damage.

We must never lose sight of the fact that all the factors that result in inferior knowledge of psychotherapy also result in inferior patient care, causing unnecessary and prolonged suffering for many. Looking the other way, perhaps under the guise of "professional ethics," is comfortable and avoids a tidal wave of problems. It is also unconscionable.

To gain a meaningful first impression of an author with whom I am not familiar, I check the index and look up what he has to say about feelings and dreams. I am interested less in his expertise in interpreting dreams than in his approach to the whole subject. I know of no other topic that can reveal as quickly so much significant information about an author. Of course, we must be careful not to equate expertise in dealing with dreams with overall psychotherapeutic proficiency.

> Disagreement about a dream's understanding
> Causes many a friendship's ending.
>
> WILHELM BUSCH

Let me categorize psychotherapists by the role that dreams take in their professional work:

1. psychotherapists who have a considerable interest in dreams and are much guided by them
2. psychotherapists who have some interest in dreams but do not accord them a position of special value in their work
3. psychotherapists who have little interest in dreams and do not use them in their work
4. psychotherapists who consider dreams to be of no value.

Strangely enough, it is the psychotherapists in the first category that do the most damage. We find here a great many psychodynamically oriented psychotherapists who, not having sufficient expertise in dream matters, enthusiastically superimpose inappropriate, often blatantly ridiculous, "psychoanalytic cliché" interpretations on dreams. In this chapter I have already cited a number of those psychotherapists. Nothing could be more exasperating to knowledgeable professionals and eager students. Much damage is thus done to the cause of psychotherapy, because many of the offenders hold prestigious teaching positions.

We should, however, respect the attitude of the psychotherapists who, while aware of the importance of dreams, are intelligent enough to realize that their talent in that direction is limited. Not every music lover needs to play an instrument.

A number of factors could have played a role in forming psychotherapists' views concerning dreams. Outstanding among them is a lack of talent and sensitivity that prevents some of them from grasping the essence of dreams and their messages. Others may not have had the good fortune to have come across a competent teacher or analyst to arouse their interest. Some may even have concluded that dreams are meaningless because of the nature of their own dreaming. Many people who are not at the moment undergoing psychotherapy may not experience "true" – that is, meaningful – dreams but mostly imagery; some analysts use the term "dreaming" instead of "imagery." Or people may have **dreams that,** possibly owing to repression, are extremely choppy, subject to **frequent** interruption such as switching from dream to imagery **and back.** Such dreams do not make sense to the dreamer, and that fact **may lead** him to conclude that dreams are meaningless. It is interesting to note that patients in intensive psychotherapy, individual or group, invariably bring in meaningful dreams.

It is impossible to give percentages for each category of psychotherapist. To judge from the literature, the number of psychotherapists who are truly expert on dreams seems small. Yet if we speak personally with therapists, the number seems to be considerably larger. I will always remember an old psychiatrist who was brilliant in interpreting and handling dreams but never wrote a single line about them.

A factor that has greatly contributed to widespread stagnancy in the area is that, like Harold Blum, a majority of analysts feel that Freud's views on dreams are the final word. That opinion is evidence of the lack of clinical expertise and of the rigidity of the training. The indoctrination of those many professionals and the resulting consensus embolden them to make pronouncements that are "politically correct," from a dogmatic viewpoint, but inane, far removed from clinical reality. I have presented a number of such statements in this chapter.

Some psychotherapists rationalize their negativism about the importance of dreams in therapy. Ignorant of how to deal with dreams, they declare dreams to be of minor value, or no value, in treatment. To declare that dreams are unimportant, however, is akin to saying that thoughts and feelings are unimportant. All three emanate from our mental apparatus and are intimately interlocked.

The value of dreams in psychotherapy is twofold: they provide the psychotherapist with exceptional information on the patient's psyche, and their expert interpretation is a unique therapeutic tool.

We now turn to four difficult questions:

- Can a therapist who is not proficient in the understanding and handling of dreams be effective?
- Can a therapist who excels in the interpretation of dreams be inadequate?
- Can a therapist fully understand a patient's emotions without understanding his dreams?

—   Can a therapist devise valid theory without understanding
     emotions and dreams?

We will be able to throw some light on those issues when I examine the topic of talent later in this chapter. Some comments can, however, be ventured here.

Because dreams are part of most people's lives, it would be inappropriate and arbitrary to exclude them from the material that ought to
be examined in therapy. When there is such an omission, whether
because of the therapist's inadequacy or because of his personal orientation, the therapy is lacking in a vital area.

As for the need for true proficiency in dream interpretation, the
view of professionals has changed remarkably over the last decades.
Until the 1950s, psychodynamically oriented psychotherapists would
say that such an ability was indispensable. It is difficult to know if their
statements were sincere or if they were merely paying lip service to
official thinking. Now most professionals in our field attach only minor
importance, if any at all, to the role of dreams. Frankly, those are not the
analysts I would choose for friends. If Blum is correct in his statement
that a patient who does not dream cannot be analyzed, then a patient
who has dreams but whose therapist is unable to deal properly with
them is not receiving valid therapy.

As I have often mentioned, it is understandable that Freud,
starting almost from scratch, needed to explore not only a vast range
of theoretical possibilities but also a multitude of therapeutic techniques. Some of those procedures are no longer employed by the
more capable therapists, but unfortunately there are many therapists
around who strictly follow chapter and verse. That is particularly
true if it makes their work easier, as does the use of analytic clichés in
dream interpretation.

We know, for example, that Freud would frequently present to
patients his thoughts about their problems and try to convince the
patients of their validity, particularly when it came to dreams. The Irma
case is one example. How strongly Freud believed in the feasibility of
such an approach was demonstrated as late as 1937, when he affirmed
that if, as frequently happens, the analyst cannot retrieve the repressed
memory, he can convince the patient of the veracity of his construction

by means of a properly conducted analysis. Such a "technique," still used more frequently than one would suspect, has to be employed with considerable subtlety lest it adversely affect the patient.

Let me digress for a moment. We have dealt a great deal with the bizarreness of dreams, but, as the following two examples demonstrate, psychotherapists can be just as bizarre.

The first is a psychology professor and psychotherapist who in the 1940s or 1950s got it into his head that to be able to analyze a dream, one must obtain the patient's associations to every single word, including "and," "but," "however," "with," and so on. That ludicrous procedure was somehow supposed to result in an end product that revealed the meaning of the dream.

Just as bizarre is the assertion of Calvin S. Hall (1966), the great collector of dreams, that 85 percent of dreams basically present three dream figures, a man, a woman, and the dreamer, and that jealousy is frequently the underlying theme of the dream action. Hall estimated that his "finding" supported Freud's theory on the omnipresence of the oedipal situation. Hall's assertion is simply inaccurate. Whether you take the dreams of people undergoing treatment or not, the variety of action plots and the number of people present is enormous. Neither the experience of professionals who have analyzed many dreams nor the scrutiny of works by authors such as Gutheil (1951) and Bonime (1982), who present a great number of dreams, lends credibility to Hall's surprising claim.

The role of the specific sensitivity and the talent to understand dreams is all-important. I have seen patients in group psychotherapy who had no psychotherapeutic training whatsoever but showed outstanding talent in comprehending the dreams of other group members and, moreover, asked the right questions to obtain meaningful associations and self-reflection.

The quality of an analyst's understanding, interpretation, and use of dreams in the therapeutic session is in direct proportion to his clinical aptitude. We should be suspicious of authors whose writings are devoted mostly to theorizing but who show no evidence of clinical expertise and comprehension of dreams. I am convinced that the greatest damage to psychoanalysis is perpetrated not by poorly informed outsiders but by poorly suited practitioners of our craft. I hope that the samples in this chapter are convincing proof of the widespread malignancy. It was that malignancy that called for the solutions advocated later in this chapter.

FREQUENT MISCONCEPTIONS, OLD AND NEW

Many statements that turn up in the literature are treated as gospel, without any examination of their validity. We encounter a variety of positions, such as that dreams are the protectors of sleep, that dreams always represent sexual wish fulfillments, that dreams are not wish fulfillments but have adaptational functions, that dreams never have any surprises, that dreams never contain any new material, that dreams are always sexual, and that dreams always contain important day residues. It should be obvious, however, that there are many forms of imagery and dreams, and such generalizing statements constitute a fallacy by oversimplifying matters.

The dreams that psychotherapists are interested in are those that are indicative of a person's specific emotional structure and functions. The clues thus obtained confirm that such dreams have meaning. That is not a hypothesis; it is a fact.

As stated, Harold Blum asserts that we have learned little about dreams since Freud's time because Freud's insights were such that nothing could be added. Let me repeat that Blum is wrong. In spite of Freud's remarkable accomplishment in providing us with the fundamentals for the understanding of dreams, he is also the source of a number of misconceptions. Working in virgin territory with little material for comparison, Freud had an enormous handicap in trying to understand the nature of dreams and how to use them advantageously in therapy. I will discuss that matter and the various misconceptions later in this section. However, the final reason that satisfactory literature on dreams is sparse is simply that too few qualified writers have been forthcoming.

Let us look briefly at the frequently heard but unwarranted assertions mentioned before.

"Dreams are the protectors of sleep." As stated earlier in this chapter, the unpleasantness or anxiety present in many dreams and nightmares does not justify the assertion that dreams protect sleep. The hiding of disturbing inner facts that causes the disguises in the dream is also operative in its own way in the waking state. It is part of our mental life, attempting to protect the individual at all times, and is not a specific function of the dream.

Here is another type of dream that does not protect sleep: A person seeks sexual gratification in the dream, but because of his inner restraints, he meets with obstacles and frustrations. There is no soothing protection there for the hapless sleeper.

Although authors frequently separate dreams and nightmares, nightmares are, in fact, based on the same fundamentals as dreams.

"Dreams represent sexual wish fulfillments, and all dreams are sexual." Although some dreams are sexual, many are not at all. If a man who has been fired from his job dreams that he is desperately crawling along a steep, slippery roof, the dream can hardly be considered a primarily sexual one, castration anxiety notwithstanding. It is easy to see in that extreme example; however, innumerable other dreams are also nonsexual.

Many dreams that are wish fulfillments need not be sexual ones. For instance, a nature lover who is forced to live in a big city may find himself in a beautiful countryside in his dream. Other dreams tell stories, apparently to entertain the dreamer, without any sexual content. The variety of dreams that a person has can be enormous, depending on his makeup.

"Dreams have an adaptational purpose." That assertion has become fashionable of late. As dreams reflect a person's emotional and mental functioning at a given time, the conscious or unconscious striving for adaptation may be operating in the person in the dream state. But adaptation is no more a basic function of dreams than are any other human strivings and feelings that permeate the psyche, in both the waking and the dream state.

If dreams were merely adaptational, with a positive purpose, then severely self-destructive people simply would not dream. But they do, and their dreams are as destructive as their thoughts. There isn't even a trace of the frequently vaunted "adaptation," unless one insists that the dreams occur to make the person adapt to hell.

Innumerable nondestructive dreams also have no adaptive purpose whatsoever. To state that dreams occur solely for adaptation is as valid as saying that all thoughts serve that aim.

"Dreams never present anything new and never have surprises." The statement that we dream only what is already known to us, that is, previously registered memory impressions, is utterly without basis and surely reflects on the barren minds of those making such an assertion. I do not say that facetiously; those making statements about dreams necessarily rely on self-observation and insight.

No one with clinical expertise would make such a claim. New situations, scenery, towns, houses, streets, rooms, furniture, people, and animals appear constantly in dreams. Some people are far more creative in dreams than they ever will be in the waking state. To deny that dreams are creative and innovative is as valid as saying that Mozart and Shakespeare only reproduced already existing works. Surprises, even major ones, do occur in dreams. Some people dream entire "plays" with involved plots and surprises, sudden events that they watch like a movie. The reader may joyously remember Alfred Winterstein's explanation of the cause of all surprises occurring in dreams.

"Day residues are always present." It is true that as a matter of routine, one should look for day residues, which may provide a meaningful connection. However, in many dreams one cannot find any trace of such residues. We have to be careful to distinguish between unconscious mental activity related to matters of which one has been consciously aware and unconscious mental activity that has no relationship to such matters. Since the writers who claim that day residues are always present refer only to the former kind of mental activity, their all-encompassing claim is not factual.

Psychotherapists should not be surprised that many dreams are unrelated to external events. Too many professionals feel more comfortable with tangible, "real" outside events than with internal events. However, the underground rivers of our unconscious mental activities have a life and a logic of their own. Since they are the source of our dreams, the stimulus for a dream may be connected solely to the inner events.

"The sleep laboratory has revolutionized our knowledge of dreams." Over the years, we have been bombarded by "scientific" hype asserting that "outside" (meaning physiological) discoveries have changed and improved our understanding of dreams. As explained earlier in this chapter, such understanding is still based solely on psychological factors.

DREAMS IN PSYCHOTHERAPY

I will refer to only a few seldom-mentioned facts to clarify some of my prior criticisms. A dream can be easy or difficult to understand. But we should be careful when we speak of a particular dream as being easy to understand; often our comprehension is incomplete. Although some people who are not psychotherapy patients occasionally have understandable dreams, particularly when their emotions are aroused, such dreams are far more frequent with patients. It can be said that the dreams of a patient, as he makes progress in therapy, gradually become clearer.

I have constructed some dreams as simple illustrations of such progress. Of course, they are only one possibility out of many. At the beginning of treatment, an anxiety-ridden patient may dream that a huge truck is converging on him with a frightening roar, and he may wake up in a panic. In dreams objects such as trucks indicate a greater degree of disguise and symbolization than actual people. Later in the therapy the danger symbol will become personalized, and the patient may dream he is threatened by a giant policeman who accuses, arrests, and then imprisons him. The patient feels guilty and helpless.

A dream in the next phase may show the patient less crushed and even protesting, although feebly, against his arrest. Sometime later he may dream about a similar situation and see himself with an attorney to defend him. Then may come a period when the patient himself vigorously argues his innocence. In the next phase he is being attacked by a gangster, no longer an authority figure. Note that at this stage the "dangerous" figure is the outlaw, and no longer is the patient being arrested or accused. The next stages will, it is to be hoped, bring recognition of the "attacker" as a figure from the patient's childhood, and thereafter dreams may occur where the patient will fight back to an ever-increasing degree, eventually with success. Finally, the patient's dreams should contain few threats, or none at all.

Many dreams of patients and nonpatients alike reveal much significant information without analytic work. Even the therapist not engaging in interpretation can be aided in his work by scrutinizing the patterns and events of the manifest dreams. They are often more meaningful than the verbal communications of a patient. Of course, the unconscious of a patient about to enter therapy, or already in therapy, tends to focus on the emotional problems he wants to overcome and thus helps render the dreams more intelligible.

I am in the habit of asking people, whenever feasible, about their dreams, whether or not they are in therapy. Starting with the easy-to-understand dreams, I present here those of a 19-year-old girl who was not in therapy and had no intention of undergoing treatment. She was composed, self-assured, intelligent, attractive, and well dressed. Her dreams, however, were a different matter.

She explained that practically all her dreams were unpleasant, that people in her dreams would say nasty things to her. She also recalled two sexual dreams, both involving an "ugly, revolting" boy in her class to whom she "would never even come close in real life." She also stated that she was not sure if she had orgasms during intercourse with her boyfriend. She felt that sex was to give him pleasure, not to seek her own. Both the dreams and her statements pointed to the emotional problems that, if she had been in therapy, would have clearly indicated to the therapist which path to follow.

Such dreams are revealing even without further free association. As I mentioned earlier, free association is always desirable, as it may bring in additional, sometimes even surprising, information. There are, of course, situations where the use of free association is limited or impossible, for instance, when the session has been crowded with other material.

Now let us turn to dreams that present difficulties for the therapist's understanding. I will offer only a few simple illustrations.

First are dreams that appear to be understandable but in reality require a far more extensive knowledge of the patient's background and psychodynamics than the therapist possesses at that time. Here many sins are committed, both by the cliché analysts and by analysts with insufficient expertise. Among the dreams that tend to be misunderstood are those that allegedly demonstrate the latent homosexual tendencies of a patient. This is an area where many therapists jump to facile conclusions. What seems obvious to them may not be the underlying truth.

Let us consider the occasional dreams of a patient in which he sees himself intimidated by an aggressive, powerful man who apparently wants him to submit to sexual acts. The feeling in the dream is of considerable fear, disgust, and hatred for the aggressor. The free associations are in the same vein. Many analysts would immediately interpret such dreams as proof of the patient's repressed homosexuality coming to the fore and distressing him.

Not necessarily so. This anxiety-ridden patient suffered from many dreams in which he was the victim of aggression by all kinds of bullies, authority figures, and the like, who tortured him in one way or another. To say that the aggressor in the dream represents repressed homosexual feelings in the patient is as valid as asserting that dreaming of a disheveled black man who attacks him on the street indicates the patient's repressed desire to be a disheveled black man. The unpleasant images were merely part of the vast armamentarium with which the patient's unconscious could torture him. Furthermore, nothing in the patient's clinical material indicated homosexual inclinations.

"Homosexual" dreams, therefore, must always be studied in the context of other dreams and the patient's clinical history.

Another patient who occasionally had repugnant "homosexual" dreams also had other frightening, punishing dreams. Among them was a recurring dream that he found particularly revolting. In it someone threw decayed animals at him. Are we going to tell him that they represent his repressed, sodomistic tendencies?

The assertion that all images in a dream represent the psychological facets of the dreamer is incorrect. It does indeed happen that the dreamer appears in the guise of another person. However, much of the time the various dream figures are created as actors, necessary to present the inner drama the dreamer is experiencing at the moment.

There are dreams in which a man has sexual contact with a woman for whom he has friendly feelings but, as questioning reveals, no sexual desire at all. It would be wrong to suggest, on the basis of his dreams, that his sexual feelings for the woman must exist but are repressed, possibly because she represents his mother. Instead, perhaps the image of that particular woman was used for sexual purposes in the dream merely because she was the last one seen or because she was not a threatening figure.

Other dreams that lend themselves to misinterpretation are those in which a patient dreams that someone has died. Care has to be exercised not to jump to the conclusion that the patient harbors a death wish against that person.

Here is another brief example of the complexity of dreams and the need to evaluate them in the context of a person's life history and psychological development: A man in his 40s who had many emotional problems and was sexually under par presented dreams in which he would have liked to come sexually close to women. After a few limited steps in that direction, however, the action in the dreams invariably changed, and there was nothing but frustration. After a few months in therapy, the patient remembered that when he was an adolescent, even though he was extremely neurotic and anxious, he had satisfying dreams of intercourse with lovely girls; the dreams always resulted in ejaculation. Obviously, at that age his biological strength succeeded in overcoming his neurotic inhibitions. To see psychological facts in the context of the patient's life history is of major importance in therapy. Yalom, however, states that such historical exploration is useless; he prefers to spend the group's time discussing such fascinating topics as justice versus injustice.

Many nonpatients report that their dreaming consists mostly of fragmented, fast-changing imagery, almost impossible to remember. That may also hold for a few patients, particularly if they are alcoholic or of an advanced age. A patient who, after 11 years of interruption, had recently reentered therapy could recall only dreams that were in complete disarray, in incomprehensible pieces, about which he could not freely associate in any meaningful way. It would have been premature to reach any major conclusions on the basis of that problem. A conversation with his former analyst, with whom he had undergone treatment for about five years, revealed that the patient had had, on the whole, intelligible and meaningful dreams.

Another patient, in therapy for years, routinely remembered her dreams. About six years after terminating therapy, she says, she stopped dreaming, and for the last 13 years she has been unable to remember any dreams.

Some patients, though very few, may bring in dreams that, even though they are coherent, seem so alien to them that they might as well have been dreamed by someone else. That is more likely to occur with patients who come only once a week or less. For a long time free association may be fruitless, and relating the dreams to the patient's present or past may be impossible. There may be similar difficulties with patients who, while they do not feel that their dreams seem to have emanated from another person, do experience frustration in relating to their contents. Of course, there is just as much difficulty with patients who cannot remember having had any dreams. To overcome the aforementioned problems, the patients would have to receive more intensive therapy.

Some confusion can arise with patients who have spent a considerable time with Freudian or Jungian analysts who have used standard interpretations characteristic of those orientations. If the analyst insists that the patient concentrate on his individual feelings, reactions, free associations, and memories, then phallic mamas, penis envy, peculiar-looking archetypes, and the like, tend to disappear, and the patient's own miseries are at last free to emerge.

Great attention must be given to the character structure of the dreamer. A dream that would indicate progress for an anxious patient, such as a display of strength in a controversy, must be interpreted differently if it has been dreamed by a sociopath. In that case, it would merely mean that the antisocial pattern is maintained. I will clarify that point later on, when describing a useful working construct, the arc of guilt. Furthermore, the psychotherapist must not be misled by the emotions in the dreams of a sociopath. If concern and sorrow turn up, they are related to the dreamer, and not to others.

An important, but often neglected, part of psychoanalysis is leading the patient gently toward recognizing the difference between the father and mother images in his dreams, on the one hand, and his real father and mother, on the other. When such insight takes on recognizable forms, the analyst has to clarify those discrepancies and attempt to determine why they occurred. The analyst indoctrinated with dogmas will be satisfied with the standard answers and will neglect to undertake a highly individualized investigation of the patient's history. Like all other analytic procedures, such an investigation must be handled delicately and indirectly.

Earlier in this chapter the view of some behavioral scientists and assorted electricians asserting that dreams have no meaning and that psychotherapists can read anything they wish into a patient's dream was presented. The answer to those statements is, once more, that the first is not true and that the second is true only for inept therapists, such as those who doggedly and simplistically infuse their work with dogma. Expert psychotherapists using dreams do not read anything they wish into dreams; quite to the contrary, they accept the dream as guidance and instruction.

In lectures and writings psychotherapists often present their patients' statements or dreams as proof of progress in therapy. I have in front of me a brochure from a publisher of psychoanalytic books announcing the forthcoming appearance of a work on dreams. We are advised that it comprises 19 sequential dreams of a patient, "leading to the successful termination of his analysis." We are told that the work will help "predict more scientifically the approach of the termination phase" and offers "a new finesse in the art of dream interpretation."

Even though "positive" verbal statements or dreams of patients are obviously desirable, they alone are not convincing proof of solid progress. The experienced clinician knows he must consider many other factors. Frequent "good" dreams may occur when a patient is experiencing a satisfactory period, but they may vanish when the going gets tough. The proof will come when, years after the termination of therapy, and after the patient has experienced major vicissitudes of life, the therapeutic achievements remain undiminished.

I have seen many instances where authors, eager to prove their points, appear to have refashioned – or even constructed – the dreams they present. A telltale sign of such manipulation is that the dreams neatly fit the purpose for which they are cited. Most dreams, however, are not so accommodating and contain elements irrelevant to the argument one wants to make. A psychotherapist who has considerable expertise with dreams will be able to spot a dream that is, even partially, an artifact.

We have already mentioned the many psychodynamically oriented psychotherapists who, for one reason or another, do not attach any importance to the use of dreams in psychotherapy. They do, however, pay lip service to the primacy of the unconscious in an understanding of the human psyche. While they succeeded in making their lives more comfortable by embracing both those positions, a strong dose of rationalization is necessary to disregard the incongruity of such an attitude.

Thomas M. French and Erika Fromm

Now we turn to a widely acclaimed academic work as another example of what psychotherapists should not do with dreams. It is DREAM

INTERPRETATION, by Thomas M. French and Erika Fromm (1964). The authors state that their purpose is "to outline systematic methods of checking our intuitive art in order to make it an adequate tool for scientific investigation." The abstract "scientific" premises of these two authors, like many other authors in the academic field, show ignorance of even the simplest clinical facts. Their pretentious claim "to formulate explicitly, and examine consciously, the evidence for and against our intuitive insight" thus turns into a lamentable farce. Their microscopic examination of five of a patient's dreams results in an unbelievably neat, detailed, and complete explanation of every one of the many elements in the dreams by linking them specifically to a great number of factors operative in the patient's psyche. To accomplish such an unheard-of and colossal psychotherapeutic feat, and such an awesome demonstration of "intuitive art," one needs to have gained a complete understanding of one's patient over a long period of time. However, French and Fromm never saw the patient!

This "scientific" masterpiece of academic erudition, which claims to represent "a new theory of the dream work and of the nature of the thought processes underlying dreams" and professes unprecedented understanding of the patient's dreams and thought processes, was obtained entirely by proxy, being based exclusively on the notes of a third analyst, Dr. David Hamburg. It requires a great deal of talent and competent, patient work to obtain a reasonably fair picture of the psychic processes of a patient whom we know in the flesh. Asserting that they achieved full understanding of a patient whom they have never seen, and having given us a complete "explanation" of all his dreams, utterances, and associations with the help of their amazing "intuitive art," French and Fromm define themselves as academic superminds.

Judged in the light of psychodynamic reality, their enterprise starts out on the wrong foot and becomes more ludicrous as they go along. It is not possible to put one's psychotherapeutic intuition to use unless one is working directly with a patient. It is not possible to find a valid explanation for all the minute items in so many dreams, and it is even more unlikely if the person involved is not a patient of the therapist.

The constant designation by French and Fromm, and other academic authors on dreams, of their studies as being "scientific" is gratuitous. Just one simple argument out of many: A hallmark of the scientific enterprise is the possibility of testing the predictability of a hypothesis. But nobody can predict the next dream of a patient.

Once more, we have the example of academicians devising a pretentious project and claiming they have established a new theory of major impact. The fact is that their work lacks all credibility because of a dismal absence of clinical expertise and acumen. It is but one more example of how easy it is to construct scientific-sounding theories in psychotherapy if one does not choose to be confined by clinical reality. Moreover, it is an example of how meaningless academic degrees and prestigious academic positions are if talent and psychotherapeutic training are lacking. In far too many situations, the discrepancy between what is considered "officially acceptable" training and what constitutes solid clinical training is most disappointing.

Encountering such exceptional talent as French and Fromm imply they have is as easy as locating a unicorn. Nevertheless, the testimonials on the dust jacket of innumerable psychotherapy books assure us that such giftedness is plentiful in academia.

SOME COMMENTS ON THE NATURE OF DREAMS

Here again I will bring to the reader's attention some facts either seldom mentioned in the literature or commonly treated differently therein. I will limit myself to a few observations to clarify how dreams may be advantageously approached.

In this section we do not examine any theoretical considerations but restrict ourselves solely to clinical findings. Later in this chapter we will look at a number of working constructs that are not attempts at formulating generalized hypotheses but are simply useful tools for psychotherapeutic work with individuals.

We have touched, often critically, on a great number of writings on dream interpretation. As stated, we have done so as part of our attempt to ascertain the level of competence in psychotherapy, to define its problems, and to provide solutions to them.

EARLY CONCEPTS AND PRACTICES

Surely the last thing anyone wants to read is more "expert" remarks about Freud. The literature will be saturated with them for the next few hundred years. Yet the immense influence of Freud as the originator of many of the views and practices relating to dreams necessitates certain comments pertinent to our pragmatic endeavor. They will be held to a bare minimum.

More than likely, we would not be anywhere without Freud's contributions. We must always remember, however, that Freud had to start practically from scratch and had very little to compare with – certainly a formidable obstacle to his investigations. Nor could he benefit from what every analyst since him has experienced: analysis. If we believe in what we preach, then we know that no one, no matter how insightful, can fully bring light to his or her own blind spots. Thus self-analysis, and any analyzing of one's own dreams in particular, is necessarily incomplete.

Freud's fertile mind, his curiosity, and his experimenting coexisted with an overwhelming desire to discover and to impose order on apparent chaos. For that he paid a high price. A restricting framework and dogma at times obliterated the free view of clinical reality. Yet again and again Freud's thoughts, like wild horses, breached those barriers, often only to be caught again and brought under control. For that and other reasons, contradictions exist in many of his writings, often within just a few pages.

Here, of course, I am concerned only with the topic of dreams. I will look at a few instances where there are contradictions or statements that cannot be reconciled with clinical facts. In Freud's short paper "The Handling of Dream-Interpretation in Psychoanalysis" (1911) he writes:

> Even if a patient's first dream proves to be admirably suited for the introduction of the first explanations to be given, other dreams will promptly appear, so long and so obscure, that the full meaning cannot be extracted from them in the limited session of one day's work. If the doctor continues the work of interpretation in the following days, fresh dreams will be produced in the meantime, and these will have to be put aside *until he can regard the first dream as finally resolved.* (Italics added)

That implies that the psychotherapist can resolve the riddle of each dream if only he devotes enough time to the task. Of course, that is not so. Many dreams cannot be fully explained just by making a con-centrated effort within a matter of days or weeks. Therapy demands its time.

But a page later Freud states:

> In case of severe neurosis, any elaborate dream-productions must, from the nature of things, be regarded as incapable of complete solution. . . . The full interpretation of such a dream will coincide with the completion of the whole analy-sis; if a note is made of it at the beginning, it may be possible to understand it at the end, many months later.

Obviously, that statement is different from the first one. Here, too, a practical comment can be made. To understand a difficult dream, one may not need to wait until the conclusion of analysis. The dream may well belong to an area that, for practical purposes, has already been sufficiently clarified. Of course, there are analysts who feel that to understand each area fully, completion of analysis is necessary, because of the interrelationship of all parts of the psyche. Fortunate indeed, and rare, are the people who obtain a complete and success-ful analysis.

I bring up the apparent contradiction of the foregoing two state-ments by Freud not to nitpick but as simple examples. We can find such conflicting statements in all areas of Freud's writings. Many of his more rigid, and less endowed, followers have clung to one of the statements (usually the version easier to understand) while disregarding its amplification, or even negation, by another statement on the same mat-ter. Similarly, professionals attacking Freud's work will pick some state-ment by Freud, or some limited facet of his work, and present it out of context to justify their hatchet work. The ruminations of the "profes-sor" described earlier in this chapter are a prime example.

Even though I have selected two of Freud's statements to show their difference in viewpoint, they may provide another simple illus-tration. Only a few psychotherapists have noticed that the first state-ment was clinically incorrect. Most others do not mention it at all when reviewing Freud's writings on dreams. As mentioned earlier, Harold Blum holds that Freud's writings on dreams are practically the ultimate word on the subject, and that explains why the status quo has basically been maintained for so long. That is not true. Rather, it is clinical experience and aptitude, or the lack of it, that makes the difference in the understanding of dreams. Quite a number of therapists have been able to make considerable progress in the area of dreams.

Let us consider some of Freud's other statements on dreams that have caused confusion. On occasion, Freud speaks of dreams as hallucinations that fulfill wishes, or as abnormal psychological phenomena, or even as psychosis, whereas in other passages, such as the one cited earlier, he affirms that the rational and orderly desire of a dream is to solve problems and tasks that also occupy our waking mind. In THE INTERPRETATION OF DREAMS (1900) Freud states, "The dream-thoughts are never absurd — never at all events, in the dreams of sane people." Of course, that statement contradicts his assertions that there is no difference between the dreams of neurotic and non-neurotic persons.

To evaluate such statements and come to proper conclusions, clinical expertise is necessary. For instance, Freud's assertion that there is no difference between the dreams of "normal" people and neurotic people has no basis in fact. The vast majority of a normal person's dreams simply do not contain the unpleasantness, frustrations, and fears that are the marks of dreams of neurotic people. I have presented many such examples in this chapter.

Let us turn to different aspects that I have criticized when discussing other authors but that have their basis in Freud's work.

First I would like to mention the rigid, standard interpretation of symbols, which is often overemphasized by Freud and absurdly abused by many of his less talented followers. In many statements Freud (1916) confirmed his conviction that certain symbols have a fixed meaning. He even asserted that one may interpret a dream by relying solely on a fixed translation without asking the dreamer for his associations. He justified that claim by declaring that the dreamer cannot contribute anything as far as the meaning of the symbol is concerned.

In the "The Handling of Dream-Interpretation in Psychoanalysis" he states, "The question is to arise of whether many of these symbols do not occur with a permanently fixed meaning . . . and we shall feel tempted to draw up a new 'dream book' on the decoding principle." In practice, that happened. It became an open invitation for lesser minds to present themselves as instant, competent analysts. All one had to know were a few dozen symbol interpretations that could be hooked onto anything, even a refrigerator. No need to unearth laboriously the psychological history of a patient to determine his psychic structure and functioning or, as in the case of dreams, be bothered with the tedious work of investigating free associations. Thus the ever-growing influence of Freud's teachings over the years propagated not only positive knowledge on dreams but also misconceptions, which increasingly became manna for innumerable inadequate practitioners. More on that later.

True, a gifted therapist can often glean useful revelations from dreams without the aid of free association. But symbols are not a cut-and-dried affair, and free associations should be used whenever possible.

We must ascribe many of Freud's clinical misjudgments to the fact that he had to work in virgin territory and that while he was experimentally inclined and interested in exploring new territories, he also stubbornly held on to certain established concepts, in psychotherapeutic practice and, more often, in dogmatic theory. Ernest Jones saw that clearly when he wrote, "I feel sure that a good deal of Freud's more theoretical expositions were, as he certainly would have agreed, responses to his own intellectual needs rather than assertions of general validity."

I shall restrict myself to two more statements by Freud, both from "The Handling of Dream-Interpretation in Psychoanalysis."

The first one is this:

> Some psychoanalysts, even, in giving the patient instructions to write down every dream immediately upon waking, seem not to rely consistently enough upon their knowledge of the conditions of dream formation. In therapeutic work this rule is superfluous; patients are glad to make use of it . . . and to display great zeal where it can serve no useful purpose. For even if the text of a dream is in this way laboriously rescued from oblivion, it is easy enough to convince oneself that nothing has been achieved by the patient. Associations will not come to the text, and the result is the same as if the dream had not been kept.

That quote prompts three comments:

The reference to analysts not relying "consistently upon their knowledge of the conditions of dream formation" is one more example of the supposedly fixed-dictionary meaning. To apply that concept, one would learn psychoanalysis as one learns grammar – rigid rules for rigid minds. Of course, that is not the way to acquire this craft – and Freud knew better. It is one of the statements by Freud that in the light of other statements, one should wipe from the blackboard. It's a pity that the Concordance was not prepared during his time for his perusal, so he could avoid contradictions.

Freud suggests that to write down dreams is worthless. Not so. Clinical experience contradicts that sweeping statement. Freud must have arrived at that conclusion by reasoning that had no basis in observation. Dreams are valuable. True, we cannot analyze all dreams if too many are presented. Yet it is a pity to allow a dream to get lost, in the hope that the unconscious material will recur. How can we be sure such recurrence will happen? Isn't it possible that repression may work in such a way that some meaningful but painful dream content, which fortuitously slipped through and was recognizable, may be sealed off again for a long period? The last thing we can afford in psychotherapy is a cavalier attitude.

The statement "Associations will not come to the text" is simply not factual. How can Freud have arrived at that conclusion in so simple a clinical manner? One analyst advanced the opinion that Freud was so fed up with being inundated with dreams by his patients that he rejected any procedure that would result in receiving more dreams. Another possibility is that in this instance, as in others, Freud was simply rejecting as invalid the elements appearing in clinical practice that did not fit in with his basic theoretical assumptions.

The last quote of Freud's on dreams to be presented here is merely one more sample of the limiting influence of his credo: "One must be content if the attempt at interpretation brings a single, pathogenic, wishful impulse to light."

I will only make two more comments here to illustrate the serious misconception concerning certain dream categories to be found in Freud's writings.

To be able to include terrifying dreams in his wish-fulfillment theory, Freud postulated that they represent "wishes" of the superego to punish the dreamer. The formulation is unfortunate. Wishes should be considered solely as desires experienced by the dreamer, not by his superego. Of course, many people are subject to inner demands of self-punishment, consciously or not. Their dreams can clarify that matter. It is well to check those dreams for the following detail, astutely noted by Joseph Wilder: "Persons with strong guilt feelings may suffer additional injury if, in their dreams, they will resist punishment or deny their guilt." Cause and consequence here are similar to what occurs in court. The judge is more lenient with the criminal who admits his guilt.

However – and this is the important point here – many terrifying dreams are based not on guilt feelings but on other causes. Careful scrutiny of the dreams and thorough therapeutic work will lead an open-minded therapist to uncover the reasons for such an affliction.

Much nonsense has been written about examination dreams, particularly when the author insists that they all have identical meaning. That is just as blatantly untrue as the claim that all dreams of flying give us the same message. Each dream has to be carefully investigated in the light of the makeup and characteristics of the dreamer. The many poorly endowed mental health professionals, particularly among theoreticians and academicians, who tend to impose uniform explanations on those dreams are guilty of harming their trusting patients.

I hope that the next section, even though dealing not directly with dreams but with some fundamental questions on psychoanalysis and psychotherapy, will also help clarify comments made on the prior pages.

The inner realm

Some facts on the nature of dreams must be mentioned for two important reasons: First, these facts are intrinsically and fundamentally significant. Second, they ought to be widely known but are not.

Psychotherapists need to be aware of the many forms of mental activity present in both the waking state and the sleeping state. The emotional components, always present and inseparable from our being, may range from minimal to overpowering. It is necessary to distinguish between imagery and dreams. In the waking state, when one is relaxed and not concentrating, innumerable fleeting thoughts may run through one's mind. Concentrated, purposeful thought is totally different. That distinction is comparable to the distinction between imagery and true dreams in the sleeping state.

The therapist's ability to understand the dreams of his patients is linked to his capacity to perceive and visualize their inner psychic space and its dynamics. He can acquire that comprehension only by paying careful attention to the clinical material, which he must organize and constantly rearrange in his mind so that he can arrive at an optimal picture of the patient's psychodynamics. To do that work responsibly, the therapist needs time and will power. If he is a teacher, he must make sure that the students do their clinical homework. To engage in our craft properly, down-to-earth clinical labor and thinking about each individual are essential, and the therapist should express his findings in the simplest and clearest terms possible, for the sake of accuracy and to facilitate others' comprehension of the findings.

For that reason, I will describe procedures that force the therapist to clarify in his mind the clinical data he has obtained and to place them properly in a schema representing the patient's psyche. Doing so is far more constructive than engaging in a freewheeling flight of imagination, expressed in "profound" analytical and theoretical terms but having only a tenuous connection to the clinical data. It would be a great relief if some therapists were to master the ABCs of our craft before spouting forth on metapsychology. Later in this chapter I will describe a procedure that enables the concerned psychotherapist to visualize the inner universe of each of his patients solely on the basis of the data obtained. Only a thorough understanding of each patient's psychodynamics obtained by clinical work can bring about the hoped-for therapeutic improvement.

It cannot be stressed enough that dreams can be deceptive for those who do not have enough experience. The mechanics of dreams can be different from what we frequently find in analytic books and in teaching. In most cases, after sufficient treatment time, expert analysts eventually understand even the enigmatic dreams of a patient if they devote themselves to studying the patient as an individual and are not biased by a limiting dogma. A reminder: Some of the most deceptive dreams are those that appear unequivocal. Far too often I have heard analysts mention such dreams as proof of such-and-such. We looked at examples of such dreams in the section "Dreams in Psychotherapy."

There is an exceedingly rare type of dream in which the scenarios and interaction deal cogently with two major emotional problems of the dreamer at the same time. I cannot give examples because that would require a lengthy description of the psychodynamics of the patients. Such a dream would be a perfect representation of either of the two problems involved. I am not speaking here of what is commonly called condensation. The dreams I am referring to are often long and intricate. Yet each of the details and scenes is a meaningful representation of the two different problems. The fact that the unconscious can create such masterpieces is, even for a fervent believer in the unconscious, almost beyond comprehension. The most gifted analyst could not accomplish a credible construction of this kind.

It is easy even for the experienced analyst to forget how extensive the realm of our unconscious is, how independent its functioning, and how wondrous its manifestations. While we who are engaged in therapeutic work are mainly interested in the areas that are home to our emotions, there is much more in the unconscious than those domains. Artistic creativity has its roots in the unconscious. It would benefit the thinking of any mental health professional to seek out, and dwell on, any aspect of the unconscious that is unusual and can enlarge his view of the human mind.

Let us consider a phenomenon that, though minor, is puzzling enough to make us think about the capabilities of the unconscious. One of the analysts who contributed to our volumes can make himself wake up at precisely the time he wants to. Yet while awake, he needs to consult his watch to find out the time. Of course, there exist far more striking and unusual instances that require the open-minded and inquiring mental health professional to reevaluate the more traditional concepts of the unconscious.

Many psychotherapists treat manifest dreams as if they were of little value in therapy and only consider the unraveling of the latent content worthy of their time. As the samples in this book show, they frequently do that by using the simplistic dictionary translation of symbols. While the analyst proudly demonstrates his "skill," the true meaning of the dream is obfuscated beyond hope. The chief victim is the patient.

In fact, much can be learned from manifest dreams reported by patients. Just consider the dreams previously mentioned, such as the man lost in the streets, or the girl being told nasty things about herself.

A sensitive patient who tended to overreact to slights and unpleasant situations frequently dreamed that his apartment was invaded by dreadful or aggressive people and that he was helpless to remedy the situation. Another man starting therapy, appearing jovial and self-composed, told the following dream: "I am in a hotel room. I am calling the desk clerk on the house phone concerning some minor matter. He answers in a very insulting manner, calling me some name. I hear the other employees laughing loudly. I am quite upset and want to go down and hit him."

A lonely, middle-aged professor with a good position has repeated dreams in which he finds himself with groups of men "of standing." He finds them boring but feels intimidated by them and behaves ingratiatingly, almost submissively. When he wakes up, he feels depressed and empty. The dream shows not only his desire to come closer to men but also the fear underlying his inability to do so, all of which tie in with the childhood circumstances he has related.

An analyst to whom such dreams are available has important information about the patient's problems and patterns and will not need the uncertain crutch of Rorschach testing. Moreover, as treatment progresses, the vast separation between manifest and latent dreams frequently diminishes.

It is always surprising to find so many misconceptions about the nature of dreams and so much the confusion about the difference between images and dreams and the various types of dreams themselves. The most disconcerting view, as mentioned, is perhaps the one declaring that dreams have no meaning. As stated, one of the reasons for that misconception may be that dreams often have no recognizable meaning to the dreamers. Because of resistance, even analysts have more difficulty in fully understanding some of their own dreams than they do those of others.

What we in psychotherapy are likely to find are "cohesive" dreams, that is, dreams that show one or more scenes in meaningful sequence, even though on the surface the scenes may not appear connected by any logical thread. I refer here to the logic of the unconscious, not to what we commonly call logic. It is understandable that such dreams occur more frequently in psychotherapy, as it focuses on a fundamental area: the emotions and problems of the individual as they developed over his life span. Such dreams may also occur with people not in therapy, particularly if the dreamers are introspective or some event has aroused their emotions or thoughts.

Not all cohesive dreams are principally a reflection of the individual's pathology. Some people have cohesive dreams of long, satisfying walks in nature or in a city; others have dreams of concerts; and still others witness entire dramatic stories like movies. A creative man who had to spend almost half a year in a dull location reported an unusual number of such "entertainment" dreams. Many of the stories and plays, written and directed by the dreamer's unconscious, may seem surprisingly different from his surface personality as we know it. Of course, the same often holds true of writers and their works.

An obvious danger in dream interpretation is that an analyst, limited by dogma, will not recognize the essential facts in a dream. Open-mindedness is necessary in the search for the unpleasant, possibly dreadful situation that the patient has buried.

After a century of psychodynamic therapy, we know of the almost infinite number of problems that can harm a person of any age and afflict his psyche. To disregard such multiplicity, and to insist that the search for the causes of the injuries be restricted to the narrow confines of specific theoretical systems, is like forcing a square peg into a round hole.

Let us consider merely two kinds of emotional problems that can have disastrous effects: deep anxiety, even terror, not based primarily on conflict; and hatred of oneself, often unrecognized. Many circumstances can cause such afflictions. As dreams fit our personalities like a glove, they may guide the analyst toward the specific causes. Therapy can then be conducted, as it always should be, to address the unique emotional makeup of the patient.

An obstacle to satisfactory progress is that many patients cannot even attend two therapy sessions a week. Understandably, the more intensive the treatment, the more fruitfully the therapist will be able to use the dreams, not only through interpretation but, perhaps even more important, through well-timed, subtle questions referring to significant details in the dream.

Psychotherapists, whether or not they use dreams, should surely have as clear a picture as possible of the forces operating within the unconscious realm of their patients. Psychotherapists who do not use dream material in their work can construct models of their patients' psyche on the basis of the clinical material obtained, but their task is far more difficult. For the unconscious operates in terms of images, and images are shown in the dreams.

> Others apart sat on a hill retir'd,
> ... and reason'd high
> ...
> And found no end, in wandr'ing mazes lost.
>
> MILTON, *Paradise Lost*

I have repeatedly stated that we do need to create hypotheses to organize our thinking and that they must be based on expert clinical observation. The satisfactory understanding of individual patients is hardly possible without expertise in the comprehension of dreams. Furthermore, such understanding is greatly advanced if the psychotherapist has expertise and long-term experience not only in the practice of individual psychodynamic therapy but also in analytic group psychotherapy. The multiple transferences, and many other clinical factors, become more obvious in properly conducted analytic group therapy than in individual psychoanalysis and psychotherapy.

Surely, theories devised by practitioners who have talent for theoretical thought and who base their theories on expertise in the comprehension of dreams and in the practice of analytic group psychotherapy have a better chance of being realistic and useful than most of what is being offered now. The more expert the therapist, the more he understands specifically, on the basis of his clinical insight, what went wrong with the individual patient and how to remedy it. He will have only a minimal use for dogma and generalizing theories. It is the less endowed therapist who, lacking clinical expertise, tries to fill the gaps in his understanding of the patient with intellectual, generalizing theory.

I invite the reader to study the approaches to theory by clinicians such as Ralph R. Greenson, Paul H. Hoch, and Alexander Wolf, and then to compare them with the quality of many of the theoretical propositions and "innovations" that inundate "our-science" (we owe that term to Robert J. Stoller). Rarely can we find among the latter a cogent attempt at clinical justification or provision of related illustration, including expert reference to dreams. And when such reference to dreams is attempted, the results, as evidenced by the examples provided here, are almost invariably unconvincing, if not ludicrous.

Among the outstanding symptoms of a science writer, a man in his late 50s, was his inability to feel close to men and to relate to them appropriately. After eight months of psychodynamically oriented therapy on a once-a-week basis, the man recounted the following dream: "I am in a dean's office to discuss some work I am supposed to do for him. I am not explaining myself well and am acutely aware of it. A man enters the office. It is Senator F, whom I haven't seen for many years. An incredible surge of emotion overwhelms me. I embrace him, holding him tightly, and I cry uncontrollably."

The patient is puzzled by the dream. He comments that, while he feels depressed and empty much of the time, he never experiences such strong emotions. He cannot remember having cried since childhood. He adds that he had not seen, or even thought about, the senator since 25 years earlier, when he did some part-time work for him. The patient describes the senator as a fatherly, easygoing man but mentions that he did not have much personal contact with him. Nothing in the patient's previous clinical data pointed to the elements revealed in this dream.

Let us consider two questions: (1) Subsequent to this dream what would be the difference in the conduct of the therapy if this patient were in treatment with a therapist giving little importance to dreams and relying mostly on dogma and theory? (2) Would the patient prefer to be in treatment with a therapist who gave foremost attention to dreams such as that and the unique aspects of his psychic structure and dynamics, or would he rather be under the care of one of the many renowned and respected academic theoreticians who hold that dogma, in particular his own erudite generalizing theories, are the basis for understanding all patients?

The sensitivity and talent necessary to understand dreams, and to deal with them properly, is a subject that deserves far greater attention than it is receiving. Work at the American Mental Health Foundation has brought me into personal contact with a great number of therapists from different backgrounds. As stated, it became apparent that there are considerably more professionals well equipped to deal with dreams than one would assume from merely reading the literature on psychotherapy.

On the other hand, many therapists who could be beneficially engaged in working with dreams shy away from it. The territory appears alien to them, and they have not had the a proper guide to help them become familiar with it. But they should be encouraged; the enterprise is less forbidding than it may seem. Patients who come to psychotherapy, even those who are quite sick, have some motivation to improve. In most cases, that motivation will bring about relevant dreams, which will further the therapeutic enterprise.

When you travel in a foreign land, you fare better if you speak the language. The language of the unconscious is definite: the images it shows us, the feelings we feel. To reach the unconscious of our patients, we must seek to understand and use its language. If we do so, it will understand what we are trying to tell it, and it will respond – and so will the patients. Facile, purely intellectual theoretical abstractions that contradict clinical reality are worthless here. Uniform explanations that apply to all are the mark of sterile and uncomprehending minds, ignorant of this language where meaning abounds and illiterate in a land where diversity is the law.

> Now, Reader, I have told my dream to thee;
>   See if you canst interpret it to me,
> Or to thyself, or neighbor; but take heed
>   Of misinterpreting; for that, instead
> Of doing good, will but thyself abuse:
>   By misinterpreting, evil ensues.

JOHN BUNYAN
THE PILGRIM'S PROGRESS

2.   . . . AND OTHER NEGATIVES

So far, our study has presented us with a rather desolate picture of contemporary psychotherapy. It is understandable, then, that we want to examine alternative solutions.

> What shall we do with the drunken sailor,
> So early in the morning?
>
> SHANTY

> Give strong drink to him who is suffering,
> and wine to him whose life is bitter.
> Let him drink and forget his poverty,
> and remember his troubles no more.
>
> PROVERBS

> Do not forget that alcohol kept many more people out of mental institutions than put them in.
>
> LAWRENCE KOLB, PSYCHIATRIST AND
> FORMER COMMISSIONER OF
> MENTAL HYGIENE, STATE OF NEW YORK

> Medical science says all along,
> That drinking booze will do you wrong.
> But hark the voice from high above:
> Those who wrong you, you must love!
>
> AN AUSTRIAN REFLECTION ON CHARITY

And here is proof of the wisdom of the French. For many years the French government distributed large notices throughout the country saying "Alcohol kills slowly." Soon the answer of an informed citizenry appeared on the posters: "We are in no hurry!"

> Psychoanalysis and psychotherapy have kept me going for over 16 years. Still, it is only when I drink that I can be myself for a few hours. Then I feel free of my fears, my inferiority feelings, my inhibitions, and my depression.
>
> A BOSTON PHYSICIAN

Even drug use finds vigorous defenders: A congressman from New York City, whose electoral district includes an unusually large number of drug addicts and pushers, attended a meeting on how to stem ever-increasing sales. Suddenly a participant asked for the legalization of drugs and free distribution. Realizing that that would wipe out the livelihood of many of his constituents and arouse the ire of others, the congressman panicked. Not knowing what else to say, he screamed, "This would be a breach of our international treaties!" His outcry worked exceedingly well; rather than risk having foreign navies and planes pulverize New York, the proposal was dropped at once! An inconsequential fact: No treaties exist that have the slightest bearing on this matter.

The saddest solution of all is suggested by an Austrian saying: "Better an end with horror than a horror without end."

The sensitive and gifted Austrian writer Joseph Roth was a severe neurotic and an alcoholic. In his last novel, THE LEGEND OF THE SAINTLY DRINKER, he movingly recounts the final days and the death of a pious bum and alcoholic who believes himself in the presence of a merciful saint. Roth finishes the novel with this: "May the Lord give to all of us alcoholics such an easy and beautiful death!" Alas, no such divine mercy was extended to Roth. Due to the utter negligence and indifference of the physicians at the Necker Hospital in Paris, he spent his last days in indescribable agony and torture.

In view of the cost of psychotherapy, the solutions proposed in the previous two pages are the only options available for many people. Others choose them because of the immediacy of the results. To us, however, they are an incentive for further effort.

a. Through a Glass, Darkly

It is the customary fate of new truths to begin as heresies and to end up as superstitions.

THOMAS H. HUXLEY

Everyone is the farthest from himself.

NIETZSCHE

History is a distillation of rumor.

CARLYLE

The attempt to separate what is valuable from what is not requires that we return, briefly, to the origins of dynamic psychotherapy. Because of the immense influence of psychoanalysis on psychotherapy, we need to call special attention to some pertinent facts that were well known in their time but are no longer being focused upon. Thus what the reader finds here has been stated elsewhere.

Napoleon once commented, "History is the myth that men choose to believe." Each year in the United States and Europe, an incredible number of articles and books "authoritatively" discuss Freud and his work. In that ocean of paper, facts and realistic perspectives are submerged. One could fill an enormous library with writings about "the Freud who never was."

Ideally, psychotherapists would write only if they could, in one way or another, contribute something of value. But academicians are under immense pressure to write and publish. It is no wonder that many who are incapable of producing worthwhile original work instead produce an unending flow of writings on Freud. It is no favor to Freud. He would wish to be known and remembered for what he was, and not for what he was not.

Rarely is the present generation offered glimpses of the true Freud. The distortions, made to suit specific purposes, vary from the image of the all-knowing prophet to the images created by self-serving authors such as McCarley and Hobson and Yalom.

Compare such "historic" accounts with the sober portrait of Isaac Newton presented to us by the psychoanalysts, depicting him as the embodiment of scientific and mathematical thought, the idol of Freud, who modeled himself after him. Conveniently buried is the fact that Newton was convinced that astrology was the driving force behind our existence and the universe and that he wrote many works on that topic. Also erased from the records are his powerful mystical and spiritual convictions, which gave impetus to his work. No branch of human endeavor comes even close to using the words "science" and "scientific" as abundantly as psychoanalysis does. The pretense of analysts that they are true followers of the spirit of Newton is laughable. It is hard to visualize psychoanalytic organizations as temples of mystical quiet and meditation, where men may ponder the influence of the planets.

Many writers on Freud are not primarily interested in establishing the truth but instead seek their own benefit and enhancement. Gustav Bychofski indignantly called those who write pretentious and inconsequential papers on Freud and his work "parasites feasting on a corpse."

In a letter, Freud wrote: "Biographical truth is not to be had." An intelligent and perceptive person aware of the complexities of the human psyche realizes the difficulty of writing an accurate biography even of a close friend whom he has known for decades. What would these American writers think if 1,500 Viennese got it into their heads to describe in minute detail the formative years of former President George Bush, giving special consideration to the cultural, sociological, and economic conditions of Kennebunkport? No doubt it is a locality with which every Viennese schoolboy is familiar, as these authors are with Freud's Vienna. And how about 400 Bulgarians expounding on the differences in specific childhood influences affecting Baptists in Georgia and those in West Virginia in the early 1920s?

Quite a number of the writings about Freud are concerned with theory; others are intended to be historical. The latter are seldom more valid than those presented by Yalom of Stanford or McCarley and Hobson of Harvard, already examined in this chapter.

Many of the outpourings, despite their scholarly facade, show little concern for facts, clinical or otherwise. Even the writings that diligently attempt to digest and present available facts are hit-and-miss, and if the writer was not a contemporary of Freud, or at least of the next generation and close to people who knew him well, they are even worse. Presented here are two simple illustrations of how things can go wrong even when the author has researched Freud and his thinking. Each of the examples is meant to highlight a separate problem.

Alexander Grinstein's (1968) SIGMUND FREUD'S DREAMS and his (1990) FREUD AT THE CROSSROADS both attempt to reanalyze Freud's dreams. The attempts are based on the author's scrutiny of many books and events that Freud mentioned and considered pertinent. Grinstein describes in detail the effects that those books and situations had on Freud's unconscious. The impossibility of arriving at credible results by such a procedure has been pointed out before. What is offered can only be conjectures, most of them unconvincing. No psychotherapist of clinical acumen would claim to be able to establish such a consistent link between cause and effect, even with a patient whom he knows exceptionally well. Furthermore, it is impossible to evaluate, with the certainty that Grinstein claims, the specific influence of books and events so far removed in time and space.

The second example illustrates what happens when reality is pushed aside by an author eager to prove his point. I selected a misinterpretation by a well-known writer that strikes a disconcertingly wrong note. In his voluminous FREUD: A LIFE FOR OUR TIME, Peter Gay (1988) lends so much importance to a certain letter from Freud to his fiancée that he refers to it at length at the very beginning of the first page of his book. In the letter, written in April 1885, Freud advises her that he has destroyed numerous notes, drafts, and manuscripts. Alluding to future biographers, Freud describes his action as "an undertaking which a number of people, still unborn but fated to misfortune, will feel severely." Gay ponders that remark, takes it quite literally, and even links it to an unrelated comment about biographers that Freud made 25 years later.

Let us now look at the real situation. The Viennese are given to mixing, constantly and almost automatically, the jocular and the sarcastic into their speech and writings. It is part of the bon ton to show that one does not take life, or oneself, too seriously. It is not important whether or not the humor is witty, only that such remarks are made at all. One of the many results of such a bent is, for instance, the already-mentioned little Moritz, a household item of Viennese palaver in those days. In addition, Freud in his own right was known for his dry humor.

In 1885 Freud was a young man of 29, singularly unsuccessful and frustrated. His reference to "future biographers," when such seemed most improbable, is a typical Viennese joke. Otherwise his phrase "still unborn" would make no sense, and to say that they were "fated to misfortune" and would feel the loss "severely" would be an outrageously pretentious remark, completely out of character.

Let us now briefly go back in time.

Although at the seats of learning the experts in physics, biology, medicine, neurology, psychiatry, and psychology never even dreamed of an unconscious, the poets and philosophers did. It was Schopenhauer who wrote, "A man can determine what he wills to do, but he cannot determine what he wills." However, it is only thanks to Freud's exceptional talent that we have at hand the solid building stones on which psychodynamic theory is founded. Among them we find the all-important factors necessary to the understanding of the workings of the human mind, such as the existence of an unconscious; the significance of dreams, repression and resistance, and transference; and the need to elucidate the events of childhood.

Freud gave decisive impetus and much-needed dimension to the previous timid attempts at depth psychology. Psychoanalysis provided a fortunate change to the focus of psychiatry, which until then had been characterized mainly by description of emotional and mental illnesses.

Justifiably enthusiastic about the new insights into the human psyche, therapists in the early years had great expectations of significant clinical and theoretical improvements. The influence of psychodynamic thinking expanded within the mental health field. In the past few decades, however, we have witnessed growing disillusionment and fading hopes.

Yet from the very beginning a number of expert Viennese physicians, while appreciative of the valuable insights underlying psychoanalysis, were skeptical about the optimistic expectations. In spite of their good-will, they were also keenly aware of a number of serious shortcomings. Those deficiencies contributed greatly to the downslide of psychoanalysis. We need to focus on them for future correction.

Mentioned here are two of the internationally known clinicians representative of such a viewpoint. Both were among my teachers. One of them was Otto Kauders, who later became chief of the prestigious Wagner-Jauregg Clinic of the University of Vienna. As his friendship and coauthorship with Paul Schilder bear witness, Kauders was among the academicians in Europe who were well disposed toward psychoanalysis. The other, also an outstanding psychiatrist, was Joseph Wilder, for many years the director of Austria's most important mental hospital and later president of the Association for the Advancement of Psychotherapy in New York. Those two professionals and many others were convinced that the sought-after goal could be realized only if certain neglected fundamentals were vigorously pursued.

We have to touch on two divergent aspects of Freud, both of which influenced all his work. Because of his insights into the human psyche, made possible by exceptional talent, his fertile mind was unceasingly creative, impelled by curiosity and a willingness to experiment. Having to explore unknown territory, with practically nothing available for comparison, he knew that such experimentation was an absolute necessity. Later accusations against Freud for engaging in practices that do not correspond to present standards are unfair and uninformed.

On the other hand we encounter Freud's overwhelming desire to use his insights and theories as a basis for a general and all-encompassing psychological system. Let me repeat Ernest Jones's cogent statement: "I feel sure that Freud's more theoretical expositions were, as he most certainly would have agreed, responses to his own intellectual needs rather than assertions of general validity." It is understandable that Freud gave priority to the pursuit of developing a coherent underlying structure. In practice, however, the result was that many clinical factors and promising concepts that he would otherwise have considered were not taken into account or were forcibly modified to fit into the framework he had postulated. In short, dogmatic considerations frequently overruled clinical fact. In part, that was the cause of the many defections and deviations of some of his disciples, a number of whom later made similar errors.

Freud's emphasis on theoretical speculation leading to generalizing dogma became, quite naturally and automatically, the predominant modus operandi of many of his followers. Because few of them had Freud's talent, the trend of facile theorizing increased with time, at the expense of painstaking clinical observation and work.

Only clinicians with considerable expertise and acumen can fruitfully put order and meaning into data and observations. There is a world of difference between, on the one hand, working constructs and hypotheses arrived at on the basis of clinical effort and, on the other hand, general theoretical speculations, no matter how interesting. The latter are all too frequently based on intellectual considerations by those who lack adequate clinical experience and expertise. Broadly stated, it goes against the grain of clinicians to express themselves in terms of esoteric abstractions, whereas "theoreticians" simply have no alternative. It is not a question of whether or not one agrees with the clinical writers; the point is that one knows exactly what they have in mind. Let us consider only a very few examples of such clinical writers: Anna Freud, Karen Horney, Emil A. Gutheil, Paul H. Hoch, Ralph R. Greenson, Alexander Wolf, and Lewis R. Wolberg. Their writings are evidence of clinical talent and of their having engaged in extensive clinical work. The writings of abstract theoreticians often avoid any proof of such experience. In fact, in every case where investigation of that fact was possible, it was confirmed.

To be of value, concepts must be founded on solid clinical experience and facts. Starting with the intellectual, chesslike moving of abstract concepts only tenuously linked to reality has brought benefits solely to the "theoreticians," not to psychotherapeutic knowledge.

Stoller, in his introduction to this volume, states:

> Each time clear-cut observations are introduced into the argument, the effect is profound. To be sure, given observations will usually not resolve all arguments for which they are pertinent; multiple interpretations will still be possible. But these then call for further observations to

decide among them, and even if it is not immediately feasible to make them, orienting oneself on them confers a new quality on theory.

There is an additional problem to be considered: the inherent difficulty of effectively translating clinical observations into valid theory. Here is an illustration. For the longest time Freud tried in vain to reconcile the basic concepts underlying the topographical theory and the structural theory. Others also failed to find satisfactory solutions. It should be noted that those concepts are far more acceptable in the light of clinical experience than most of the abstractions that are the building blocks of present theoretical speculation.

However, and this is important, when the terms employed in the two theories are used not to arrive at a convincing theoretical solution but merely as useful working constructs in practical work, we find no such difficulties. As a matter of fact, many analysts, whether they realize it or not, use the terms of both theories side by side.

I want once more to stress that all too frequently such abstract theoretical thinking employs concepts that are only partially true or not true at all. Psychotherapists must use concepts that are clinically verifiable, for instance, transference. Using concepts that are merely flawed approximations of reality is an exercise detrimental to good patient care. Surely one would not entrust one's eyes to an ophthalmological surgeon whose instruments were badly damaged. It is imperative to question dubious theoretical concepts and formulations. The clinician should insist on credible information indicating that there are solid grounds to justify a concept.

We fully know how fragile and fallible clinical facts and clinical reality are. Yet we have nothing better to work with than the reports of gifted and experienced clinicians. And for them we should be grateful.

The conflict between two clashing priorities – namely, an expert, individualized clinical approach versus generalized theoretical thinking – is of immense importance to psychotherapeutic practice and teaching. Understandably, those who represent the latter approach deny that any such conflict exists, as they claim they are expert clinicians. However, convincing proof of such an assertion will not, and cannot, be forthcoming. The clinician is recognized by the way he expresses himself and approaches the problems of psychotherapy. As already quoted, Greenson writes:

> Only psychoanalysts with preconceived and rigid theoretical notions . . . have prefabricated interpretations for all types of patients, and disregard the fact that each individual human being is unique. . . . No clinical demonstration will change the opinions of those who are predominantly devoted to theory conservation or theoretical innovations. Their theories seem to be more real to them than the memories and reconstructions of their patient's life history.

Earlier I mentioned the Viennese psychiatrists who, while recognizing the great contribution made by psychoanalysis, also had grave concerns about a number of the serious shortcomings discussed here. Some 60 years later, Robert J. Stoller, an experienced clinician and expert critic of psychoanalysis, offered in his writing an impressive number of convincing and detailed complaints, many of them along similar lines. I have already spoken about Stoller's efforts. In his latest book (Colby & Stoller, 1988) he inveighs against generalizing theoretical abstractions: "Can you see how verbiage is used to make us (and the author) believe that precise enough measurements are in hand to support convincing generalizations on an aspect of human behavior?" (italics added). Next he questions the credibility of such unfounded assertions: "What pains me is how rarely we express the full measure of our unsureness, how gracelessly the unsureness appears, and how it can repeat and repeat and repeat, in sentence after sentence and paragraph after paragraph, and yet allow for a switchover into the most positive, declarative statements."

In the introduction Stoller contributed to this volume, he writes: "Unashamed theorizing is an occupational hazard of psychoanalysts. . . . And yet, as we create such theory in words of seeming clarity (which, however, are secretly known to be vague), our language will permit the infiltration of hidden wishes."

Stoller, like me, was a great believer in the potential of psychodynamic psychotherapy. But that potential will never be realized if the status quo, which is an abomination and largely a travesty of psychoanalytic therapy, is allowed to continue. I strongly urge those who are devoted to the cause of psychotherapy to study Stoller's cogent criticisms. They are an indispensable and scholarly complement to the criticisms advanced in this paper. Only by examining defects and abuses can we hope to eradicate them.

We need to determine the factors that have caused confusion and detrimental trends since the early days of psychoanalysis. Here it is impossible, and unnecessary, to examine all the tenets of psychoanalysis; it is sufficient to examine only one as a demonstration. Thus we shall look at the most important tenet, to establish which of its many aspects have positive value.

The Oedipus complex is considered the major organizing principle of psychoanalysis. The number of writings on the topic, representing an incredible variety of views, is immense. Here we will consider a few aspects relevant to our purpose.

The Oedipus complex is different things to different people. Freud's view, which by and large is also the one of orthodox analysis, is the starkest, close to the original myth. How strongly Freud felt about his view is shown by the following statements, from THE INTERPRETATION OF DREAMS (1900):

> Oedipus Rex is what is known as a tragedy of destiny. . . . The lesson which . . . the deeply moved spectator should learn from the tragedy is submission to the divine will. . . . Modern dramatists have accordingly tried to achieve a similar tragic effect by weaving (into their plays) a plot invented by themselves. But the spectators have looked on unmoved. . . . His [Oedipus's] destiny moved us only because it might have been ours – because the oracle laid the same curse upon us before our birth as upon him. It is the fate of all of us, perhaps, to direct our first sexual impulse towards our mother, and our first hatred and our first murderous wish against our father. Our dreams convince us that it is so. King Oedipus, who slew his father Laius and married his mother Jocasta, merely shows us the fulfillment of our childhood wishes.

Also in that work, he shows the same preoccupation when he refers to his "reaction to my father's death – that is to say, to the most important event, to the most important loss, of a man's life."

While paying lip service to dogma – here the Oedipus complex – many analysts, seemingly embarrassed by the original version, twist and shape it into something quite different. That was true even early on. In 1918 Smith Ely Jeliffe, one of the most prominent American analysts of his time and a founder of the American Mental Health Foundation, wrote:

> It [the Oedipus complex] can be used as a unit of measurement of all psychological situations. . . . It is the psychical elaboration of an enormously important part of a biological instinct. . . . Prostitution is not really sexual. . . . It is a satisfaction of unconscious hate rather than of love in terms of the Oedipus hypothesis. . . . The Oedipus hypothesis then attempts to establish some criterion . . . by which human contact may be valued as it looks forward to ultimate social and pragmatic truth, or goodness.

Thus, as can be plainly seen, Oedipus was really a precursor of Mother Teresa and his actions were for all to follow.

A few years ago a study, probably known to many American readers, claimed to establish scientific proof of the validity of the Oedipus complex. After we were given the benefit of much convoluted scholarly language and profound scientific reflections, the surprising findings established that boys liked girls and vice versa. While that was certainly a scientific discovery of the first order, the business of killing the father appears to have been lost in the shuffle. Rather, in view of the reported "oedipal" feelings, the youngsters probably preferred to engage in related scientific activity resulting in babies.

Many modern psychoanalysts, while maintaining the name "Oedipus complex," actually narrow the concept to mean the exploration of the triadic relationship of father, mother, and child. By maintaining the name "Oedipus," they identify themselves as faithful, card-carrying members of the psychoanalytic community. It would be far clearer to call a spade a spade. Precision is of major importance in psychotherapy, and those writers should merely refer to "the triadic relationship" when that is all they mean.

From among the thousands of writings on the Oedipus complex, let us select a recent one to illustrate further the ambiguity characteristic

of such handiworks: a review by Irwin Hirsch (1992) of Jay Greenberg's
OEDIPUS AND BEYOND: A CLINICAL THEORY.

Hirsch writes:

> The book is well organized into four major areas of discus-
> sion: triangulation and the Oedipus complex, drive concepts,
> structural concepts, and theory of therapy. . . . His [Green-
> berg's] primary effort is to maintain classical theory without
> depending on the explanatory principles of the biologically
> based, dual-instinct theory and the tripartite structure of the
> mind. He cogently argues for the existence of the oedipal sit-
> uation minus libido theory, the centrality of unconscious
> conflict and motivation in human psychology, and a psycho-
> analytic therapy which emphasizes the return of the repressed
> through developmental theory-based interpretations. . . . The
> title of the book and the introductory chapter emphasize the
> significance of the oedipal theme in human development and
> in the inevitability of conflict.

Hirsch then quotes Greenberg: "The Oedipus complex is the
greatest monument we have to the timeless power of childhood. . . .
Clinically, the Oedipus remains the most effective tool for talking to
adult patients about their archaic past."

And Hirsch again:

> Greenberg elaborates in his introduction that Oedipus is the
> best way to understand the coexistence of love and hate, child
> development from involvement to separation from the family,
> and the ubiquity of conflict. From the title and the introduc-
> tion, one would think that the oedipal theme is indeed still the
> shibboleth of psychoanalysis and would be prominently fea-
> tured throughout the volume. However, except for a number
> of references to the ever-present triangulation in the human
> psyche, it is decidedly not the main agenda of the author's the-
> orizing. Indeed, I do not think that Greenberg makes a strong
> case for Oedipus being quite so universal and central [the shib-
> boleth] in human development. Somewhat later in volume, he
> delineates the conflicting drives for safety within the family

and for the familiar versus the striving for separation, autonomy, and effectance, as the basic and central conflict and
theme on human development. This conflict need not be in an
oedipal frame, though Greenberg does expand Oedipus to
include this conflict. In his clinical illustrations, the classical
oedipal theme clearly is *not* emphasized. It remains *somewhat
ambiguous* whether he stills views the sexual rivalry dimension
of Oedipus as universal and primary or has shifted to a more
separation-striving version of Oedipus. (Italics added)

Hirsch describes Greenberg as being "obviously a very clear
thinker." I beg to differ. The need to prove oneself to be a flag-waving
member of the establishment and the desire to show off some "novel"
theorizing merely illustrate one more case of wanting to have one's cake
and eat it too.

Incidentally, one may wonder about the virulent antagonism of
many psychoanalysts to the advent of psychodynamic group therapy.
After all, this treatment modality allows for a clearer clinical crystallization of the original triad relationship than the dyad situation of individual analysis, where transferences toward father and mother are
projected onto a single person. The presence of both sexes in a group
greatly helps the emergence of the transferences toward father and
mother figures as well as toward siblings.

Let us now return to the original Oedipus complex and Freud. In
those days the number of physicians involved with emotional and
mental problems was extremely small. Those *Nervenärzte* knew of
each other and their special circumstances. A man like Freud aroused
considerable curiosity, and details about his personal affairs and family life were well known.

Freud, as a child, had an unusual situation to contend with. Not
only was he jealous of his father, but he was also envious of the closeness
of his young mother with his half brother, Philipp. We have spoken
about the physicians who were well disposed toward psychoanalysis but
had serious complaints regarding parts of it. One of their objections
concerned the Oedipus complex. Their position was that in view of the
fact that one's early childhood affects one's psychological development,

it was perfectly understandable that the Oedipus complex was an all-important component of Freud's psyche. They also agreed that the same forces were apparent in a number of other patients. What they did not agree with, and in fact strenuously objected to, was establishing the Oedipus complex as dogma and generalizing it to include all men and women. Doing so, they stated, would disregard the specific childhood circumstances of each individual that result in the formation of different psychological structures and problems. To work on the basis of a generalized, simple, and uniform theory is inadmissible, since it is not based on reality. Using such a theory as a basis for therapeutic work is counter to effective and diligent psychotherapy. Although their objections were drowned by the ever-increasing tide of psychoanalysis, there were at all times clinicians who continued an individual approach. Actually, some of them were psychoanalysts who simply followed their own wisdom.

Those who work with an unbiased clinical approach know, for instance, that many male patients who, for some reason, feared and hated their fathers can have severe neurotic problems without the slightest evidence of an oedipal complex appearing in clinical material. The same applies to many other patients, male and female, with the widest range of childhood constellations. The Oedipus complex, if you so wish to call it, is undoubtedly present in some patients, but much confusion is caused by an unclear definition of the term. If one is merely speaking of the triad constellation, then it is obviously a matter of common sense with general application. Describing it as dogma or scientific is pretentious.

The attachment to the mother, if it exists, can vary enormously in form and degree. Some patients occasionally experience overwhelming feelings of loneliness; others have those feelings chronically. In certain severe cases dreadful bouts of panic occur, and the very fear of such panic attacks is an additional curse. Quite a few of these people become alcoholics. In a number of cases prolonged therapy uncovers that the cause of the loneliness is indeed a deep longing for one or both parents but that no sexual element is involved.

In other cases where there is also a deep, underlying, but nonsexual attachment to the mother, the realization that she is a woman who engaged in sexual activity has never been integrated emotionally by the patient and may present difficulty in working through the problem. Owing to childhood circumstances and upbringing, these patients regard their mothers as "pure" and "motherly." To such patients, who were more prevalent a few generations ago than they are now, the thought of their mothers' having engaged in sexual activity is abhorrent. While it is only one facet of the patient's psyche, it requires special therapeutic scrutiny. Broadly speaking, there are two avenues available to the therapist. The first is to base his explanation on available clinical material. The second, more common, approach is to diagnose it, without further ado, from a dogmatic standpoint, as resulting from the oedipal situation. An unbiased investigator will, however, have a great deal of difficulty uncovering any convincing clinical evidence justifying such an unquestioning approach.

At any rate, it is untenable to generalize and to postulate that every child has had the same experiences and has responded to them in the same way – and thus has the same neurosis, namely, Freud's neurosis. If that were true, people would be far less different from each other emotionally than they are, and their individual psychodynamics far less diversified. The problem is that if the individual differences are not properly dealt with in treatment, and if they are merely addressed by an undiscerning therapist using a dogmatic approach, immense damage is done to the patient.

Once one has been indoctrinated to a definite conceptual system, it is difficult, almost impossible, to conceive that matters could be otherwise. The concept appears to be perfectly reasonable and has become a solid building block of the entire edifice. To illustrate: Freud claimed that infantile amnesia, that is, difficulty remembering what happened during the first two years of life, was due to repression of unpleasant and intolerable feelings related to infantile sexuality. Since the memories have merely been repressed and are not lost, he said, they can be recovered. None of that is correct. Recently reported, carefully conducted long-term studies show that the factors necessary for lasting remembrance are related to the development of language, thinking, and concentration, which usually occurs between ages three and four. However, Freud's followers considered their position in this instance, as in many others, the final, definite truth.

That example, however, shows that even tenets that are relatively undisputed can fall by the wayside. Despite analysts' rigidity in insisting on the universality of the Oedipus complex, it never enjoyed a safe status with all mental health professionals. No doubt, many analysts will argue that if a therapist fails to detect the "obvious" clues that confirm the oedipal theory in a patient's analysis, that is proof that the therapist did not receive sufficiently rigorous analytic training. They also affirm that the great number of analysts who subscribe to a fundamental system based on the Oedipus complex is proof of its validity. Numbers, however, do not constitute evidence of correctness (consider the beliefs of indoctrinated people, no matter how intelligent). The supposed proofs presented to us vary from subtle and sophisticated "clues" to those that show lack of competence, for instance, Palombo's interpretation of the refrigerator dream or Erikson's discussion of the Irma dream. Furthermore, can the analysts who do not find oedipal factors in the treatment of many of their patients be so incompetent, given that they are often able to discover meaningful facts that escaped the attention of singleminded oedipal doctrinairians?

Clinical evidence in many cases reveals how children, after initially experiencing strong aggressive feelings, will be subject to overwhelming fear of a brutal and frightening father. That results in an emotional cave-in and surrender: identification with the aggressive father and severe self-condemnation and self-punishment that result in the establishment of a cruel and unrelenting superego. In many of those cases there has not been evidence of oedipal tendencies, despite diligent search for such evidence.

Much valuable case material disproving the universality of the Oedipus complex is provided by instances where only one parent was present. I shall restrict my discussion here to what we consider available clinical facts based on observation. Alas, the observation is in the eye of the beholder.

The following case history, told to me by an analyst friend, is of interest: A young man had been referred to him by another analyst who had become chronically ill. The first analyst advised my friend that the patient was a textbook case of the oedipal problem but that he had not made much progress with him during two years of treatment. Briefly, the patient suffered from suffocation fears and became very anxious when in close confinement with people, such as in elevators and subways. He lived in a tough neighborhood in Brooklyn, and if a man came too close to him, the patient would attack him and beat him up. He did not attack women. The patient stated that he loved his father, a gentle person, as well as his mother, and had always done so. There was no indication in the clinical material, including dreams, to contradict his declarations.

In spite of his best efforts and an increase in the weekly number of sessions, my friend saw no progress. He finally resorted to hypnosis, a procedure he seldom used. It turned out that the young man was an exceptionally good subject who could rapidly be placed in a deep hypnotic trance. After a few sessions of age regression that took him back to a small village in Italy, the patient saw himself as a young child, possibly three or four years old. His parents had placed him on a bench surrounding a big oven used to heat the large, drafty room. The child found the heat insufferable, but his parents did not understand his crying, and they left him on the bench. From that point on, therapy – analysis no longer – brought gradual relief. "And that," my friend concluded, "is the story of Oedipus, the oven."

Surely, the universality of attraction between the two sexes, and the rivalry between members of the same sex, was known to the baboons long before the advent of man or Freud. But such strivings alone are not to be called the Oedipus complex.

We need to realize that Freud's unusual insight into matters of the human psyche was only selectively exercised. Concerning the universality of the Oedipus complex, the question arises: Did he actually not notice the many indications to the contrary, or did he merely brush them aside in his overriding quest for a streamlined theoretical system? One hopes that the self-appointed Freud scholars will spare us an answer to that question.

The same problem applies in other instances that are part of the fabric of psychoanalysis. The question of blind spots in Freud's perception brings up a significant fact, strenuously avoided by most analysts. One of the most important points psychoanalysis makes is that no one, no matter how insightful, fully knows himself. Resistance to looking at what has been repressed renders self-knowledge impossible. Long before Freud, Nietzsche stated: "Everyone is farthest from himself." And before that, in a different context, Jesus declared: "You see the speck in your neighbor's eye, but not the beam in your own." Freud, when confronted with the fact that he himself had not been analyzed, justifiably claimed special status. That, however, cannot be construed to mean that his own insights were not subject to the obvious limitations.

If one believes in the efficacy of psychodynamic theory, then one also will assume that if Freud himself had undergone analysis with a competent professional, his subsequent writings and theories would have been quite different. One may fantasize that he would have become more open to modifications of certain cherished dogmatic tenets, allowing his work with patients to give him further insights into their psychodynamics. In particular, his views on the Oedipus complex might have benefited from such newly acquired flexibility and open-mindedness.

We may therefore comprehend Freud's resistance, if such is the case, to noting the many clinical contraindications to the universality of the Oedipus complex. How is it, though, and what does it mean, that his followers did not note them either?

Generalizing theoreticians will be much chagrined when deprived of the notion of the universality of the Oedipus complex. However, not all is lost, and here are glad tidings. A certain type of yellow-spotted hyena gives birth once a year to two offspring. The second one is born an hour after the first one, which immediately attacks the newcomer. Papa and mama hyena, apparently following some expert psychological advice not to restrict a child, do not interfere. If the secondborn is of the same sex as the firstborn, the attacks are so savage that the secondborn dies. If it is of the opposite sex, the secondborn survives. Zoologists are puzzled by the fact, but the greater rivalry with a sibling of the same sex should explain it. Here, then, is rich material for a psychoanalytic innovator, born into a family of yellow-spotted hyenas, to develop the theoretical foundations of a new major organizing principle.

Here is another example, one of many, demonstrating how breakthroughs and improvements in generalizing psychoanalytic theories were not considered breakthroughs by those who did not work within the dogmatic confines of psychoanalytic concepts. Many years ago Heinz Hartmann was much acclaimed, particularly in the United States, as a foremost pioneer for postulating conflict-free areas. But the Viennese physicians who did not join the psychoanalysts never based their work on a generalizing theory that insisted that conflict underlies all psychodynamics; nor did many other psychodynamically oriented psychotherapists. So to them it was not a breakthrough. If the early analytic assumptions, discarded after Hartmann, were wrong, then how much damage to patients was done in those years?

In his introduction to this volume, Stoller estimates that Hartmann's proposal had more influence on psychoanalytic thought than any single work in the previous 50 years. He continues: "Yet even in 1939, psychologists might have shrugged at such an announcement, for, using a different language but the same observations, they had long known these . . . ideas. . . . One may complain that 70 or more years is a long time to wait for 'the ultimate conquest of the obvious.'"

We have complained that many psychoanalysts consider Freud's precepts unimpeachable dogma, even when clinical evidence shows otherwise. To accept dogma unquestioningly has many advantages, such as proving one's loyalty to one's fellow analysts or not having to rethink difficult psychological problems. But psychoanalytic dogma is accepted unquestionably only when doing so suits the interests of the analyst. When it does not, the much-vaunted loyalty to Freud vanishes. Here are two examples:

Freud, because of his convictions about the all-important role of dreams, considered THE INTERPRETATION OF DREAMS his most important work. But because considerable talent is necessary to work with dreams (talent that many analysts simply do not possess), is it any wonder that so many declare that dreams have no special place in analytic work – and that others neglect dreams altogether? Freud would not consider such therapists to be analysts. He would find psychoanalysis without emphasis on dreams inconceivable. He considered anyone who did not engage in dream interpretation but who called himself an analyst to be an incompetent interloper.

Freud viewed medical training as a drawback and bitterly opposed the decision of the American Psychoanalytic Association, largely motivated by economic interest, to mandate such a requirement. In his letter of July 3, 1938 (reprinted in the summer 1952 issue of Psychoanalysis), to Theodor Reik, who had complained about the hostile attitude of the American analysts and had been forbidden to practice, Freud referred to them as "colleagues for whom psycho-

analysis is nothing more than one of the hand-maidens of psychiatry."
When the American analysts opposed work by nonmedical professionals, they grounded their explanation on the noblest of motives – to
safeguard scientific values and to protect the patient. But what about
the many analysts who, simply by referrals of patients, made their
wives, relatives, and mistresses – nonmedical people all – into instant
practicing therapists?

The enormous difficulties besetting psychoanalysis and psychotherapy should not induce us to give up the struggle for improvement. The struggle would be hopeless indeed if we could not perceive a
way out of the wilderness. Fortunately, the solutions, difficult though
they may be, are tangible and clear-cut. We will approach them shortly.

b. Earnestly Talking Nonsense

You will be safest in the middle of the crowd.

Ovid

If we strip our etiologic knowledge from all the verbiage which covers our ignorance, it is quite clear that we do not know the etiology of most mental disorders and that practically none of the theories which have been put forth today – organic, psychodynamic, sociological – are really new. Most of these ideas have already been expressed in the past century.

Paul H. Hoch

The assignment of thousands of new recruits to the 31 imperial guard regiments by the Grand Duke Nikolai Nikolajewitch in the giant Michailowskij Manege in Saint Petersburg was a yearly social event of the greatest magnitude. All the young men present had to be tall, well built, and fit. They approached the Grand Duke one by one. Their selection by him for a particular guard regiment was speedily performed, following strict and well-established guidelines. For instance, all recruits referred to the Regiment Pawlowskij had to be straw-blond, snub-nosed, and pock-marked, in memory of Czar Paul I, murdered in 1801. Another regiment consisted only of men with blue eyes and black beards. And so it went.

As soon as His Imperial Highness had bellowed out his preference, an adjutant chalked the name of the regiment on the back of the recruit and directed him toward the sergeant representing the unit. The sergeant quickly turned him over to other noncommissioned officers standing in a line behind him, who moved the soldier rapidly out of the center.

Whereas you may feel dubious about that method of selection, rest assured that it was considerably superior, and far less harmful, than our present-day procedures of admitting individuals to the professions of psychoanalyst and psychotherapist.

And now let us start this section.

Some 40 years ago, even physicians and mental health professionals well acquainted with the wide incidence of mental and emotional illness were surprised at the magnitude of the problem as revealed by the Yorkville Study, an in-depth statistical survey of an entire section of New York City. Since then, a great number of research projects in the United States and abroad have confirmed the severity of the situation. The latest one, published in March 1992 in the JOURNAL OF THE AMERICAN MEDICAL ASSOCIATION, covered 18,571 adults and found that 23 percent suffered symptoms of major depression. The director of the study, Dr. Gerald Klerman of the New York Hospital, reported that the effects included a vast incidence of absenteeism, unemployment, dependence on public assistance, suicide attempts, and suicides. Klerman emphasized, "If you add them up, they are a large social burden. . . . There are so many of them, they have a major effect on the welfare of the country."

Certainly, those data are most saddening for all who have the welfare of the emotionally and mentally ill at heart.

One such research project was particularly poignant to those working at the American Mental Health Foundation. Early in 1950 we started to offer orientation sessions to people, seeking to determine whether they would benefit from therapy and, if they would benefit, what kind of therapy would be desirable. The project was under the direction of two psychodynamically oriented senior psychiatrists, Joseph Wilder and W. G. Eliasberg. Some of the interviews were conducted by them; others by experienced psychotherapists, also of a psychodynamic orientation. The patients were referred to us mostly by physicians, working in private practice or institutions and agencies throughout the New York metropolitan area. From 1950 to 1971 close to 6,000 such orientation sessions were conducted. Over 40 percent of the people interviewed had previously been in treatment.

The purpose of the orientation sessions was twofold. First, they offered a much-needed public service to individuals and their families, as well as to their physicians. Second, they provided the Foundation with a unique way of obtaining direct, in-depth information, thus adding considerably to our understanding of the mental health situation and practices and to our knowledge of the kinds of facilities and treatment modalities that were available. Most important, the orientation sessions helped us gain an impression of the quality of the services offered. Most of those who had previously been in therapy received two or more sessions so that we could obtain, as far as was feasible, detailed information on their treatment. Even though we tabulated some of the information, it was in no way intended to be a statistical study.

The people interviewed came from all walks of life, ranging from the well-to-do to the destitute. Many of those who had undergone prior therapy had discontinued it owing due to dissatisfaction with the treatment or for financial reasons. Others had discontinued their therapy elsewhere simply because they had moved to New York City. At any rate, it was always gratifying to hear some of those attending the orientation sessions say that they had been content with their previous therapy and that they had made considerable progress. For those whose work at mental health agencies and clinics necessarily brings them into contact with many disappointments, such comments are welcome encouragement.

Those who attended the orientation sessions were asked to call us after six months to let us know if they had secured treatment and, if they had, which type. In fact, most people did not call back, and our volunteers had to call them. Some could not be reached, even after considerable effort.

One notable factor stood out starkly: many of the people interviewed told life stories of genuine suffering due to severe depression and anxiety. Disappointingly, however, after six months less than one in seven had actually entered treatment appropriate to their problems.

The intake interviews at a small treatment center sponsored by the Foundation for special projects showed a similar picture. The center could accommodate only a limited number of applicants. Follow-up of those who had been referred elsewhere evidenced, once again, a disheartening situation.

There were, of course, people who did not come to our orientation sessions and about whom we would have liked to obtain in-depth knowledge: those who had discontinued therapy because they were disappointed with the results and were unwilling to return to treatment. Even though we made continuous efforts to obtain pertinent information on such cases from professional and nonprofessional sources, the results were limited.

The Foundation obtained other valuable information about the treatment of the emotionally ill by offering hourly consultant fees to people who were, or had been, employed in any kind of activity, governmental or private, in the domain of psychotherapy and mental health. The Foundation, being a long-established organization, received a great number of applications for employment, and the treatment center, sponsored for some 30 years by the Foundation, received even more. Most of the applicants were psychoanalysts and psychotherapists of varying background who were applying for positions as therapists. Many experienced professionals sought work as supervisors and teachers. The information we were able to gather from those applicants about their education and training was invaluable in helping us identify existing problems.

We all know of the problems that beset the mental health domain, such as the large number of people in need of treatment, the lack of qualified practitioners, and the time and effort it takes to help each person. In this volume we are concentrating on the emotionally disturbed people whose treatment should, to a considerable extent, consist of a psychotherapeutic approach. There is no doubt that the profession could and should do much more to alleviate the plight of those suffering from severe anxiety and depression. Indifference to, or acceptance of, the present situation is unconscionable. We could help many more people if only certain basic problems were squarely confronted and necessary changes instituted. Most of those engaged in mental health work would benefit greatly from the improvements we propose. The obstacle, however, is the inertia of the status quo.

Obviously, all those assertions need substantiation. In the foreword, preface, and introduction to this volume we focused on some major shortcomings pervading the psychotherapeutic profession. They afflict not only individual practitioners but the whole field and cover such vast areas as training and education, patient care, research, and mental health policy. We need to determine the specific causes of such an unacceptable situation.

Most assuredly, certain serious problems in the mental health field are not manmade. Foremost among them is the very nature of serious emotional and mental illness, which presents formidable obstacles to providing effective and lasting help. For that very reason, there is no room for professional mediocrity or incompetence.

b1 HONORED TEACHERS – MISLED STUDENTS

To theorize, perchance to be a Freud!

We will now look at the writings of four carefully selected professionals. In certain important respects, each falls into a different category. They have, however, three things in common: they are well known, they have received considerable professional acclaim, and they hold prestigious teaching positions. I chose them to demonstrate where the problems are and where they originated. We need to focus on the professionals who are representative of what is worst in the four categories under scrutiny. Unfortunately, these examples can be multiplied by hundreds. Add to them the people whose lack of acumen results in the employment of such incompetents and the people who uncritically, if not with admiration, accept their writing and teaching. What does all that say about the level of expertise of so many mental health professionals?

If those words seem unusually harsh, we must not forget that it is precisely the actions of such professionals, and their self-seeking pretense to expertise, that are a major cause of poor patient care and shoddy instruction of future practitioners.

Some circumstantial evidence is very strong, as when you find a trout in the milk.

THOREAU

It has never been easy to acquire valid psychotherapeutic knowledge. These days, because we are faced with a formidable information explosion and ill-informed teachers, the task is even more difficult. Yet during a century of psychodynamic exploration, we have accumulated a valuable body of knowledge. It is the responsibility of anyone who wants to become a psychotherapist to seek to acquire that knowledge and the indispensable clinical expertise to go along with it. Unfortunately, not many psychotherapists are willing to make the additional sacrifice, given their already strenuous "official" education and training. The resulting inadequacy is even more damaging when the practitioner succeeds in securing a position of importance and influence.

Even though I will only briefly discuss the four authors, the evidence presented is indisputable. It is based on their own words, which betray them. An experienced therapist scanning professional writings can often detect the telltale signs of incompetence, no matter how adroitly they are concealed behind grandiose assertions and scholarly presentation. Only the ill informed and those incapable of discernment are deceived. As Abraham Lincoln said, "You can't fool all of the people all the time." Each of the four authors cited has been severely criticized by colleagues whose sober judgment and seasoned expertise allow them to separate the wheat from the chaff.

It must be emphasized that the examples and quotes presented here were chosen because they are not only representative of the specific work but also illustrative of the whole approach and thinking of the author.

> They have a plentiful lack of wit.
>
> SHAKESPEARE

> Brother, thy tail hangs down!
>
> RUDYARD KIPLING

Leonard Shengold

Shengold is a clinical professor of psychiatry at the New York University School of Medicine and a training analyst. His articles appear in the traditional psychoanalytic journals.

In front of me is one of his books, entitled SOUL MURDER: THE EFFECT OF CHILDHOOD ABUSE AND DEPRIVATION (1989). The degree of Shengold's competence and the validity of his thinking are equally discernible whether one examines his clinical comments and case histories or his "analysis" of literary figures of the past. In the first half of the book are three core chapters: "Soul Murder, Rats and 1984," "Rat People," and "Clinical and Literary Examples of Rat People." Shengold asserts that rats are a frequent theme in associations, fantasies, and dreams of those who were abused and victimized in childhood.

The following quotes convey some of Shengold's thoughts on the matter:

Rat People

The compulsion to repeat dominates the lives of people who have been seduced or beaten by psychotic and psychopathic parents. I have stressed the importance for these people of fixation on the cannibalistic level of libido development and regression to it, with concomitant maldevelopment and regression of the ego and superego.

The clinical conditions I have been describing as the effects of soul murder sometimes appear in combination with a preoccupation with rats. In chapter 5, I characterize patient D. as a rat person. Obviously not all soul murder victims are rat people, and whether all people who are preoccupied with toothed creatures and rodents have suffered actual overstimulating experiences as children must also be subject to doubt. But such a preoccupation, evidenced by the frequent appearance of rats in analytic associations, should alert the observer to the possibility of soul murder. All the rat people I describe in this book were victims of soul murder, and my generalizations about them are applicable to other victims.

I view the image of the rat as a kind of hallmark indicating cannibalistic impulses and the presence of too-muchness (having had to bear the unbearable), and I will try to illustrate this in the clinical material of this chapter. . . .

The Rat as the Carrier of the Tooth

The rat imago appears as a leading motif in the study of oral sadistic and masochistic phenomena (tooth phenomena). The rat is a tooth carrier, endowed with the power to creep back and forth from level to level of libidinal development, from one erogenous zone to another, biting and being bitten. It is among the most common of many imagos that are first of all cannibalistic: carriers of the destructive tooth.

Anal Defense

It is necessary for the patient to get away from the torment of overstimulation and the rage and murderousness it brings forth by identifying with the tormentor and turning the rage on the self and on others. I conceive of what happens defensively as a regression to the so-called anal-sadistic period of development (between the ages of 18 months and 42 months), during which the child usually evolves defenses against a burgeoning aggressive drive; this regression may also be conceived of as an enhancement of the anal-sadistic period and eventually as a fixation on it. . . .

This implies that becoming able to control the anal sphincter (a momentous developmental achievement) has its psychic counterpart in the control of aggressively charged emotion (that is, murderous emotion).

Regarding patients' fears of rats, Shengold says: "These animals are endowed with the power of penetrating the body by eating through sphincters."

Shengold presents numerous case histories to substantiate his assertions regarding the omnipresent rat. It must be his outstanding craftsmanship that enables his patients to so clearly recall what happened to them during their earliest months of existence. Or does he get this material from nostalgic parents reminiscing about their joy in abusing the little ones?

The one notable exception to such alleged remembrance is Shengold's extensive preoccupation with the psychic life of the writer George Orwell. Orwell, who does mention his fear of rats in his writings, becomes Shengold's prime example of the abused child. Shengold discusses or refers to him on some 20 pages. There is only one minor problem: as Shengold himself admits, we do not have the slightest indication that Orwell was in fact abused in childhood! But not to worry – small matters like that are not an obstacle to this expert. Shengold asserts that Orwell's preoccupation with rats is a definite indication of his having been abused as a child, and if Orwell does not say so, it is merely because Orwell is a very private person and does not reveal his sentiments. But then Shengold gives us entire pages of material where Orwell describes, in detail, childhood events and emotions.

I have only one timid question: where do all these rats come from? They cannot be found in the reports of the analysts who see a phallic mother under each bed.

Just as the Jungians advise that mandalas are integral to the human psyche, Shengold devotes some 70 pages to the rat theme, which, he asserts, he discovered in so many abused patients. Speaking of a professional whom he criticizes, Shengold states: *"He has the certainty one seldom hears from the psychoanalyst.* For the most part the psychoanalyst learns from his patients how little he knows" (italics added).

After that insight, however, Shengold attempts to bolster his theories about the consequences of childhood deprivation by providing lengthy descriptions of the lives, personalities, and writings of some major literary figures, such as Dickens, Chekhov, and Kipling. The extensive, rather convoluted accounts are interspersed with innumerable statements of "fact," pinpointing the deepest forces and their interplay within the unconscious of the writers. He makes those assertions with a *certainty one seldom hears from a psychoanalyst.*

Two other examples of Shengold's modus operandi should be sufficient to illustrate the level, logic, and quality of his work and the depth of his thought.

Speaking of Chekhov, Shengold states: "I emphasize that Anton Chekhov was not psychotic. On the contrary, he appears to be singularly free of neurosis." Alas, our joy at having finally found a healthy writer of talent is short-lived. A page later we are advised: "Chekhov's neurosis cannot explain his artistic power." But don't worry; Shengold can clarify the contradiction. Even though there are no clinical data to support the analysis, he concludes by stating: "The longing for the Urfather [archaic father] reasserted itself. . . . One can see in his dream and creative fantasy . . . his negative oedipal striving for (sexual) union with his father." Surely, had he learned of Shengold's appraisal, Chekhov's father would have refused to share the bathroom with his son.

Describing Kipling's psychodynamics, Shengold quotes from one of Kipling's works: "My amazed and angry soul dropped gulf by gulf into that horror of great darkness which is spoken of in the Bible . . . despair upon despair, misery upon misery, fear after fear." To find the proper passage, Shengold consulted a Bible with a concordance. There one can find about two dozen references to "darkness." He selected the following passage from Job 24 as the one Kipling supposedly referred to: "The eye of the adulterer also waits for the twilight, saying 'No eye will see me'; and he disguises his face. In the dark they dig through houses; and by day they shut themselves up; they do not know light; for deep darkness is morning to all of them; for they are friends with the terror of deep darkness." Having found in that passage the magic key, the "open sesame" of Kipling's soul, Shengold proceeds to give us the ultimate revelation about Kipling:

> The passage shows the attraction of darkness, which is light to the murderers, thieves, adulterers, and those "who dig through houses." Kipling consciously rejected this identification with the criminals (soul murderers) yet he constantly sought the darkness. Note that the offending eye in the passage belongs to the adulterer, *evoking both the voyeur at the primal scene and the blindness of Oedipus.* (Italics added)

But before you start crying your eyes out about the terrible thing little Kipling had to see, relax; it did not happen! Shengold chose the passage because it allowed him to inject the primal scene, as well as Oedipus and other analytic bargains. But he definitely presented the wrong passage. His elaborate explanation of Kipling's psyche along the lines of Shengoldian reasoning and associations collapses when one studies the passage Kipling referred to.

The passage from Job that Shengold selected definitely and unmistakably speaks of the evildoers who truly *enjoy* darkness as if it were the beauty of the morning and who are *friends* with the "terror of deep darkness." Kipling, quite to the contrary, speaks about "the horror of great darkness . . . despair upon despair, misery upon misery, fear after fear."

What, then, is the correct biblical quote to match Kipling's horror, fear, and despair? It is Matthew 22:13 (and corresponding passages): "Bind him hand and foot, and cast him into the outer darkness; in that place there shall be weeping and gnashing of teeth." Alas, there is no voyeuristic eye here to enjoy the primal scene.

We would not be overly concerned if this were merely another literary essay by one of the many overintellectual and underendowed analysts. But it is presented to us as a pioneering psychotherapeutic work that, according to the dust jacket, "will open up new horizons for colleagues and students alike."

This book is representative of innumerable writings. The true "horror of outer darkness" is that professionals, incapable of clear thinking, without enough sensitivity and acumen to be aware of emotional connections and without responsible restraint in their writings, are treating patients and indoctrinating students. Occupying positions of leadership and influence, they constitute a formidable obstacle to obtaining quality in patient care and teaching.

> The learning and blundering people
> will live on.
> They will be tricked and sold
> and sold again.
>
> CARL SANDBURG

Martin Grotjahn

Having glanced at the productions of a teacher of individual analysis, let us now turn to the achievements of an analyst who foisted himself on group psychotherapy.

Authors who are engaged in teaching often use the notes for their courses as a partial basis for their books and articles. We thus can divide the content of their writings into what could be called the common ground, that is, what others have said, and their own contribution. The selection of items in the "common ground" depends on each author's orientation, bias, and acumen.

I have repeatedly said that I deplore the activities of the simplifiers of psychotherapy who bank on the mass appeal of easy-to-learn treatment approaches. Understandably, there is much mutual support among those practitioners, as they need to justify and rationalize their basically untenable positions.

Grotjahn is an outstanding example; he uses two of the tactics in their armamentarium. One is to assert that the approach used is psychodynamic or psychoanalytic when actually it is not. The other is to boldly rewrite history. I have discussed those tactics elsewhere; for instance, when speaking about Yalom's writings.

At the end of his ART AND TECHNIQUE OF ANALYTIC GROUP THERAPY, Grotjahn (1977) lists a few books as "especially recommended reading." As can be expected, Yalom and S. H. Foulkes are the foremost recipients of Grotjahn's kudos. Grotjahn's comment about a work by the latter is as follows: "The founder of group analysis develops his basic concepts and technologies." Whereas Foulkes indeed labeled his writings analytic, he is definitely not the founder of group analysis; instead he was responsible for introducing the concept of the "group mind" in group psychotherapy. The catch is that if one accepts the idea of a group mind, one is definitely nonanalytic. Psychoanalysis is the careful, indepth investigation of the individual. It has no use for a superficial mass approach. Since Foulkes started to advocate this concept, I have maintained that "those trends in a particular group that give the appearance of a so-called group mind are actually resistance. As the transferences are examined, the resistive motivations of each group member causing such conformity become apparent. Any neurotic submergence of the individual in the group must be dealt with by the analyst until it is dissolved" (de Schill & LaHullier, 1956).

Freud stated that the two absolutely essential ingredients of psychoanalysis are the examination of transference and of resistance. Thus the advocates of a group mind, by failing to scrutinize transferences and resistances *of the individual*, have no justification whatsoever to claim that their procedures are analytic. Grotjahn, however, is an obsessive attention-getter; he will say almost anything to obtain the desired result. He has to go Foulkes one better by creating the term "group unconscious." Here is a quote from Grotjahn (1977):

> It has been claimed that the therapeutic task in psychoanalysis and group analysis is the same. I doubt the correctness of such a statement. In psychoanalysis the analyst's foremost assignment is to interpret the resistance of the individual against insight into his unconscious. In group therapy the therapist's assignment is to remove roadblocks in communication. The "unconscious" of the group is represented by that which is not shared communication.

Caveat emptor, or let the sucker beware. Obviously, too many psychotherapists and academicians in this field fall for such high-sounding but hollow verbiage. Will the "unconscious of the group" be followed by the "group dream" and the "group childhood"?

The analyst's foremost assignment in individual and group therapy is to use his expertise to bring about the emotional improvement of the individual. To succeed, he must properly master a large number of sophisticated and delicate approaches. To say that the analyst's assignment in group therapy is solely to remove roadblocks in communication is to reduce psychotherapy to the level of kindergarten.

The following is Grotjahn's (1978) advice on how to conduct the psychoanalysis of elderly men:

> The most favorable transference situation in analytic treatment of the elderly is one which I call the "Reversed Oedipus Constellation." In my opinion it is necessary to allow the development of such transference situation, to experience it fully, to utilize it, to interpret it, and finally to dissolve it again and integrate the entire experience. It is possible, however, that the experience of this transference neurosis has to be much stronger and much more intensive than in the psychoanalysis of neurotics of younger age. This may constitute a principal difference between the psychoanalysis of a psychoneurosis and of an old age psychosis. Differently expressed, it could be considered an essential difference between working through and living through.
>
> The patient is allowed to see in the therapist the younger person. He may later accept in his therapist the representative of the younger generation and perhaps of the future. It was once the task of the son to work out his conscious and unconscious relations to his parents. It is now time for the father to go once more through his unconscious relation to another man in reversed order. In relation to the therapist, he has once more the chance and task to analyze in the transference relationship the Oedipus complex, but this time in reverse. The father should not submit to the son, nor should he kill him like the father

of Oedipus tried to do. The father should realize that his life may be continued in his son.

As usual, Grotjahn's facile and grandiose assertions could be the basis for innumerable questions and comments. Here are just a few:

—   What psychoanalysis of the elderly? Where did that ever take place? As if that were not enough, Grotjahn speaks of the "psychoanalysis . . . of old age psychosis"!

—   Grotjahn's assertion that in his psychoanalysis of the elderly, he allows "the development of such transference situation, to experience it fully, to utilize it, to interpret it, and finally to dissolve it again and integrate the entire experience" deserves our utmost admiration. He is able to accomplish a trick no other analyst has ever claimed to have done.

—   Grotjahn also defines what the outcome of the analysis of an elderly man ought to be: the realization that "his life may be continued in his son." Such a generalizing platitude, however, is in stark contrast to the highly individual emotional resolution that a capable therapist strives for.

Equally noteworthy are Grotjahn's statements concerning patients' dreams about the dead. He states that the dead appear as "haggard and greyish." That claim is completely without basis in fact. One would expect such a description from an eleven-year-old working on a school play. It may come as a surprise to Grotjahn, but the unconscious of each individual is different. Therefore representations of the deceased vary according to the individual's emotional factors and circumstances.

I do not want to imply that Grotjahn never states anything correctly. I did, indeed, find one statement that should be accepted. His enormous feeling of self-love and conviction of self-importance are apparent in the title of his autobiography, MY FAVORITE PATIENT. An entire section is devoted to an event he considers to be of worldwide interest: "I Pass a Stone."

Thus enriched by the wisdom only a double emeritus could produce, we next turn to a man whose profound understanding of the workings of psychotherapy is matched only by his selfless sacrifice in giving much-needed time to his severely emotionally ill patients – that is, a full 50 seconds of it.

It is sad testimony to the status of psychotherapy that professionals who are far from having mastered our craft and who lack clinical expertise to a large extent dominate our field, occupy positions of influence, and are widely published and accepted as authorities.

I wish I could reprint on each page of this volume two statements I have mentioned before:

> There is something fascinating about science. One gets such wholesale returns of conjecture out of such a trifling investment of fact.
>
> MARK TWAIN

> *If you talk enough, you will become a leader, even if you do not know what you are talking about.* An extensive study conducted by Dr. Cabott L. Jaffee at the University of Tennessee's Department of Psychology demonstrated that female students who monopolized discussion but who were hardly ever correct in their statements, were selected as leaders of their groups far more often than were the quiet girls, who were frequently correct.

It certainly denotes a lack of the specific intelligence required for our work when a professional brazenly and constantly spouts forth statements and writings of little merit. However, as we can well see, such a lack is no obstacle to success. The success is even more pronounced when the professional is a shrewd politician and has marked writing and speaking abilities. Frequently such men present to each of their audiences what is appealing to that particular group, rather than address harsh facts and the need for the arduous task of acquiring clinical expertise. Politicians do not ask for tax increases.

Earlier in this chapter, when discussing Yalom, surely one of the master politicians in our field, I first cited his assertion that he is an expert practitioner of state-of-the-art psychotherapy. His expertise appears to be mere book knowledge. We must never forget that mere book knowledge is pseudoknowledge. Would we submit ourselves to a surgeon whose only knowledge is derived from texts? In Yalom's case, we were able to juxtapose his deceptive and self-laudatory pronouncements with the simplistic approaches he actually practices.

Later in this section we will encounter a pertinent evaluation of such professionals by Stanley Lesse, one of the most competent and intelligent critics of the field of psychiatry and psychotherapy. Lesse remarks on the fact that many of the men who occupy positions of importance in our field have had little clinical experience or insufficient intensive training.

> Some people sell their soul, and live with a good conscience on the proceeds.
>
> LOGAN PEARSALL SMITH

Toksoz B. Karasu

We are going to look now at a professional of outstanding political shrewdness. We will first scrutinize the primitive and unnerving "psychotherapeutic" practices and policies that he stands for and manufactures. Then we will present his lofty and noble statements professing his deep concern for achieving quality psychotherapy. Once more, I want to remind the reader of the immense damage to patient care and student training and the misinformation such men cause. The bargain-basement discount hawkers have been eminently successful in using simplistic methods and mouthing scholarly-sounding pseudotruths in the place of arduous clinical work and experience.

Toksoz B. Karasu is the author of numerous books and articles. He is a professor of psychiatry at the Einstein Medical College and the director of psychiatry at the Bronx Hospital Municipal Center in New York City. Karasu's "accomplishments" notwithstanding, I suspect that it is he who gave the Bronx a bad reputation.

In this section the focus is on the many professionals considered representative of the worst in psychotherapy and mental health. Unfortunately, this is not the place to speak about the psychotherapists and psychiatrists whom I regard highly for their dedication and wisdom. They all have one goal: to improve the lives of the emotionally ill by means of more effective treatment methods and more available treatment time.

In many instances the damage caused by unfortunate childhood circumstances cannot be undone by the brief and infrequent therapy sessions that Karasu proposes. Quite to the contrary, responsible psychotherapists consider adequate treatment time to be of outstanding importance. Even the most skilled professional can do little if a patient can come only occasionally or for only a limited period.

No such humane concerns carry any weight with the populist simplifiers. Realistic approaches requiring knowledge and extensive labor are of no interest to them. Only facile promises of easy-to-learn and easy-to-apply treatment methods seem to be their concern. Those methods, hardly taking account of the characteristics and requirements of the individual patient, are a bonanza for such practitioners.

Many years ago knowledgeable and dedicated colleagues began to mention the telltale signs that indicated Karasu's advocacy of easy approaches at the expense of responsible patient care. Ordinarily one would not pay special attention to one more professional supporting deplorable methods. Karasu's tactics, however, were eminently successful. By discrediting intensive psychotherapy and emphasizing the use of drugs as the principal mode of treatment, he was able to acquire a large and loyal group of followers. Eventually he succeeded in getting himself appointed chairman of the American Psychiatric Association's Commission on Psychiatric Therapy, and with that as a stepping-stone, he became chairman of the task force determining the advisable treatment of psychiatric disorders. In the latter capacity Karasu directed the work of more than 200 participating psychiatrists.

Having met with such success, Karasu has dropped his former caution. He no longer tries to disguise his populistic ambitions and his methods of advancing himself. When it is opportune, he openly presses his mass-appeal efforts, embellishing them with supposedly "scientific" arguments.

Let us take a look at Karasu's "credo," or rather his sales pitch, which holds out the promise of an easy life and good fortune for his enthusiastic followers. He generously includes, gratis, ready-made rationalizations in his package. This particular version, similar to the others, is taken from the journal PSYCHOSOMATICS (Karasu, 1987).

The article is entitled "The Psychotherapy of the Future." The first subhead is "The 50-Second Hour." It should be explained that it was mere serendipity that brought to Karasu the find of his life, the idea that was to become the basis for his populistic evangelism. Like innumerable other professionals, Karasu had to face the problem of limitation in governmental and private insurance payments, a cause of added suffering to many emotionally ill people. Thus in the paper we are considering, Karasu starts out, as he frequently does, with a discussion of the plight of the most destitute patients. He asserts that drug treatment combined with occasional brief psychotherapy sessions is the only workable approach for them. But then – and this is the product he is peddling – he states that the same approach should be applied to the treatment of all the emotionally ill, since "a protracted course of therapy is neither practical in today's economically pressured era nor experientially desirable." He calls favorable attention to therapies that "abbreviate duration and/or decrease frequency and length of sessions." He explains that

> the basic time focus of psychotherapy has also evolved – from that of the past (i.e., repressed memories of early childhood) to that of the present (i.e., current realities of living) to that of the immediate moment (i.e., spontaneous interactions in the here and now). The latter is expressed, for example, in the existential philosophy of how therapeutic change occurs:
>
> Beyond all considerations of unconscious determination – which are true in their partial context – the only thing that will grasp the patient, and in the long run make it possible [for him or her] to change, is to experience fully and deeply that [he or she] is doing precisely this to a real person . . . in this "real moment."
>
> Regardless of ideology, however, shortened treatment, like time per se, is both an objective and a subjective experience.

Trying to justify the sharply reduced treatment time he advocates, Karasu continues:

> Lacan presumably based his ten-minute therapy sessions on the clinical experience that the most important material tended to emerge as the sessions were coming to a close. This interesting phenomenon has recently been

confirmed by Gabbard, who expressly examined the "exit lines" of his patients. There were dramatic end-of-the-hour utterances, which represented heightened transference-countertransference manifestations. The author concluded that *the exit line may be the most important communication of the hour*," offering the patient the final fantasy that he has triumphed over the finite limits of the session. (Italics added)

Karasu goes on:

Also, the "50-second" hour addresses the pivot of psychotherapy – therapeutic communication. It suggests that what is said (and not said) at every moment is significant, and that no interaction between therapist and patient, however brief, be regarded as unimportant. It means that both partners are participating at all times consciously and unconsciously, verbally and nonverbally, cognitively as well as behaviorally, or, as the philosopher Wittgenstein so aptly put it: "Words are also deeds." In effect, self-knowledge and actions are one, and drawn-out, attenuated forms of insight are no more or less significant than the "eureka-type" tidal waves of illumination or enlightenment. Each microinsight and every microinternalization becomes a foundation for the next, yet is itself therapeutic. In the "50-second" hour *No time is lost*. Thus, the "50-second" hour represents a microcosm of treatment in all its richness and complexity – an expression of its infinite possibilities in finite form.

In his conclusion Karasu states: "Special theoretical and practical challenges confront the future psychotherapist who will be increasingly called upon to be eclectic, to treat symptoms primarily with pharmacologic agents, to deliver psychotherapy within less than 50 minutes in each session, and to see patients infrequently and for a limited duration overall."

It is most appropriate for Karasu always to quote his idol, Lacan. It takes considerable psychotherapeutic inexperience and ineptitude, however, to insist that it is the ending of the session that produces the patient's most relevant material. The ending is merely the result of the preceding therapeutic effort, which opens up access to the patient's emotions and unconscious. With patients who can come only for one therapy session a week, we can clearly see how frequently the "opening" has closed again and how therapeutic work is once more required to obtain significant psychological material.

To provide some scientific-sounding background music, Karasu expresses, in the vaguest of terms, his hopes for a pragmatic era of "pharmacopsychotherapy": "The end of gurus and psychotherapeutic romanticism is thus a portent of the future, of pluralism or enlightened eclecticism in practice. It symbolizes the trend toward ultimate integration – the rich array of therapeutic ingredients transformed and condensed into a unified amalgam or essence."

Karasu fails, however, to explain how the amalgamated therapeutic fruit salad he proposes can possibly be "manufactured" in practice, nor how it can bring results when the patient is not allowed the time to swallow the hodgepodge.

When Karasu asserts that present-day protracted therapies are not "experientially desirable," it is a case of the pot calling the kettle black. All therapies fail at the hands of incompetent, poorly trained practitioners. The therapies so severely criticized by Karasu, however, when administered by expert professionals, have brought about satisfactory results where all other approaches failed. Karasu must know that. In spite of his constant affirmations, there is no such thing as instant psychotherapy, and there never will be. Ineptly disguised by transparent rationalizations, his is a cruel attempt to deprive patients of indispensable expert treatment in order to bring facile benefits to unknowledgeable or self-seeking professionals.

Karasu bases his sales pitch on a myth. He indicates that pills are the pillar of treatment for all who are emotionally ill. Reluctantly, to silence inconvenient voices, he adds a touch of a still-to-be-concocted mimicry of psychotherapy. But even optimistic estimates indicate that medication can help, and often to a very limited degree, only 40 to 60 percent of patients, and then only if they are treated with concomitant psychotherapy. Such a combined procedure may stabilize the patient and keep him going, but if the psychotherapy component is inadequate, there will be no structural progress. Without any psychotherapy, the percentage is estimated to be about half those figures.

Karasu's campaign brings to mind a similar effort by Nathan Kline, who achieved national status and acclaim, and considerable personal gain, by such policies. Kline's pronouncements had much in common with those of Karasu; they were aimed at a broad audience and never failed to relegate psychotherapy to a place of minimal importance or necessity. In the end, Kline was able to avoid indictment only because of his old age, but the government forced him to desist from continuing his practices and to sign a binding agreement to that effect.

Understandably, it was not the protectors of the interests of the emotionally ill who were Kline's doom. There are hardly any such protectors, and those who exist lack influence. It was another powerful group of mental health practitioners that brought about his downfall. The group felt that their financial interest, namely, the practice of analysis or some form of psychotherapy, was being hurt by Kline's aggressive "advertising" of his own pill-popping clinic.

One wonders what Karasu's reaction would be if, requiring extensive lifesaving surgical intervention, he were informed that all he would receive was 50 seconds of surgery, and that this treatment was in his best interest.

Since I joined the American Mental Health Foundation in 1948, the goal of better and more intensive treatment of the emotionally ill has been our priority. Consequently, we oppose any approaches and policies that have the opposite effect. Most professionals to whom I showed Karasu's article were not surprised. A few, though, were shocked. They had believed him to be a stout advocate of quality in psychotherapy. Indeed, Karasu has always been eager to present himself as a dedicated man of outstanding expertise.

Alas, that image dissipates in no time when one scrutinizes Karasu's actions, maneuvers, speeches, and writings. Ever the crafty politician, he speaks without the slightest hesitation or embarrassment out of both sides of his mouth. He is willing to say anything as long as it will promote him or win an audience. He does not hesitate to cover up, or even contradict, his basic psychotherapeutic approach, the only one that he can handle and feels comfortable with; namely, "psy-chotherapy" in the framework of the shortest possible session.

"Psychotherapy is like a slow-cooking process that has no microwave substitute." How true! But where is that from?

Believe it or not, it is from Karasu's recent WISDOM IN THE PRAC-TICE OF PSYCHOTHERAPY. In spite of his ardent advocacy of the "50-sec-ond" session, Karasu, as an accomplished politician, always changes his tune to accommodate different audiences, no matter how contradictory his assertions end up being. According to the August 1993 catalog of the Psychotherapy Book Club, which is distributing the book, Karasu is the author, coauthor, and editor of eight books and over 100 articles. His new book is representative of Karasu's manner of proceeding and political craftiness, and there is no need to further discuss any of his other writings. A brief examination of this work will reveal all the points worth making.

The dust jacket of this book, like Yalom's books, has numerous enthusiastic endorsements expressed in superlatives by other well-known academic authors. It also has a description of the book that is grandiose and enthusiastic. It should be mentioned that according to the written policy of the publishing house that owns the book club, it is the author himself who is asked to write the description.

This fact should enlighten us on the profound "wisdom" of this self-designated wise man: In the whole book Karasu does not say a single word about dreams. It is obvious that he ignores their important role in psychotherapy, that he does not understand them, and that he does not know how to handle them. That lack alone should alert the reader to the pretense and fallacy of Karasu's entrepreneurial enterprises.

In the catalog we find the following description of the book, pre-sumably written by the author himself: "Offers wisdom of experience: While the work is grounded in the overriding theoretical concepts of various major psychologies – drive theory, ego psychology, object rela-tions theory, and self-psychology, in juxtaposition with language and communication theory and existential philosophy – its emphasis is on the synthesis of diverse schools." Here again we find Karasu offering us a hodgepodge of present-day theoretical positions. By using a maxi-mum of ingredients, he feels he is onto a winner.

The content of the book consists of some 50 "axioms of wisdom," each followed by a brief explanation. Let me quote a few examples:

The therapist must establish a psychologically safe environment, wherein anything can be said and any feeling experienced [no. 6].

The careful interpretation meets four criteria: optimum timing, minimum dosage, concrete detail, and individual focus [no. 36].

I have one question about the second exhortation from Karasu's pulpit. Assuming the four criteria are valid, how can a psychotherapist apply them in his practice unless he possesses clinical expertise far superior to that evidenced by Karasu?

Quite a number of the so-called axioms sound as if they are intended to demonstrate the "brilliance" of the author. Unfortunately, to an experienced clinician they sound more like trite truisms.

In the section about axiom no. 25 – "The therapist must develop a latency of response, then work further to shorten the time" – Karasu cites his mentor, Lacan, as follows:

Lacan suggests that the decisive function of the therapist's reply to any single verbalization of the patient is not, as some believe, "simply to be received by the subject as acceptance or rejection of his discourse, but really to recognize him or to abolish him as subject. Such is the nature of the [therapist's] responsibility whenever he intervenes by means of speech."

Karasu continues by giving us an illustration from his own experiences:

Three years after termination, a patient came for a single session to give the therapist [Karasu] a progress report on her life. She said, retrospectively, that the most important change occurred to her after something the therapist had said. The therapist, alas, could not figure out what that might have been. . . . She said, 'When I was going out with one charming man after another . . . you simply suggested that I should look for less charming people. Now I am married to one and am very happy.'

I am not quite sure how all that ties together. But this is Karasu's most expert psychotherapeutic comment, and I guess we must consider ourselves fortunate that he has shared it with us. Let me repeat. As explained by him, it is "grounded in the overriding theoretical concepts of various major psychologies – drive theory, ego psychology, object relations theory, and self-psychology, in juxtaposition with language and communication theory – its emphasis is on the synthesis of diverse schools." Who am I to question such a learned pronouncement? At any rate, the comment is a fine example of the synthesis Karasu advocates and the expertise and sophistication he has achieved by prolonged and intensive studies of matters psychotherapeutic.

The reference list of the book is six pages long. Quite a number of additional authors are listed in the index. We thus can safely assume that Karasu owns at least a few hundred books. I am not claiming that Karasu has never seen a patient, but I do want to state that any person who has read enough about psychotherapy, even if he has never seen a single patient, can easily, just by going over the passages he marked as interesting, create a volume of a couple of hundred such axioms. All it takes is writing ability, and Karasu, like Yalom, possesses that talent.

It is hard to understand how Karasu could have been selected for the delicate, complex, and sophisticated work necessary to guide the American Psychiatric Association's Task Force on Treatment of Psychiatric Disorders.

Recently Karasu became the editor in chief of the AMERICAN JOURNAL OF PSYCHOTHERAPY, a post for many years occupied by the late Stanley Lesse, who was also a coeditor of our companion volume. Lesse was an outstanding expert in the matters of psychiatry, psychotherapy, and mental health, a highly original thinker, and a most intelligent and outspoken advocate of necessary improvements and reforms. The change in editorship is a sad reflection on the deterioration of the level of knowledge and competence in our field.

My statements about Karasu's emphasis on the use of medication should in no way be construed as implying that medication is not important in the treatment of the emotionally and mentally ill. We need only remember how desperate the situation was before the advent of helpful medication. A further improvement of the medications is surely a major hope for the future.

At the same time, attempts to cut down on necessary psychotherapy should be resisted. Most patients, even those who benefit from insurance, do not receive sufficient therapy. To a large extent, the intrusion of managed care into psychotherapy has worsened an already unsatisfactory situation.

Taking into consideration inflation, the cost of outpatient psychotherapy to the patient for the two decades before the advent of managed care did not substantially change. Now, however, much of the money that was once spent on patient treatment is used to cover the considerable costs of managed care.

If there were some abuses by psychotherapists hitherto, the new "cure" is far worse than the malady. It severely impedes a psychotherapist's ability to devise an optimal treatment plan for each patient and to provide adequate and appropriate therapy. Treatment quality is greatly impaired by the insurance industry's insistence on short-term therapy and treatment plans that favor medication over psychotherapy. Harmful, often insurmountable obstacles to the application of the treatment best suited to the needs of the individual patient are created by the trend of removing decision making from the psychotherapist and allowing decisions to be governed by the desire to minimize expense.

When payments depend on the insurance industry or government agencies or on arrangements with health maintenance organizations, the treatment offered is in many instances a shoddy palliative. Obviously, such a situation is unconscionable. Even in the cases where medication reduces anxiety and depression, the underlying psychological pathology is not addressed. Frequently, symptoms return when medication is discontinued. Furthermore, the additional bureaucratic demands, including paperwork, placed on the psychotherapist infringe on valuable time previously available for patient care. Worse yet, as the therapist grows older and, it is hoped, wiser, the more difficult and time consuming the bureaucratic requirements become.

Robert S. Wallerstein, in his article "The Future of Psychotherapy," which appears in this book's companion volume (THE CHALLENGE FOR PSYCHOANALYSIS AND PSYCHOTHERAPY: SOLUTIONS FOR THE FUTURE), declares:

> We certainly all know that the varieties of depressed people, in all life stages and subject to all varying circumstances, have myriads of psychological problems, traumatic happenings and losses, conflicted interpersonal relationships, and inner and outer disequilibrating pressures that will not be resolved just by mood-altering medications that take them out of dysfunctional despondency and render them more able to try to face and deal with life's difficulties.

One needs to oppose vigorously all those who sacrifice patients and psychotherapists alike by an unsophisticated and blind insistence that treatment time can be reduced. For the last 45 years the American Mental Health Foundation has devoted its efforts to developing intensive methods that offer patients greatly increased treatment time at lower cost. As a result, the need to consider third-party payments is greatly reduced, or even eliminated, and there is no financial sacrifice for the competent therapist. More about that later.

The ever-increasing volume of psychotherapy writings renders it impossible to keep abreast of the literature, even in one's own country. Thus when it comes to publications in foreign languages, I greatly depend on the advice of experienced colleagues who are aware of the kind of material the Foundation needs for its examination of the mental health situation in the United States and abroad: (1) the best in terms of improved treatment approaches and (2) the worst in terms of therapy abuses and harmful procedures engaged in by influential professionals. On the basis of such information, both positive and negative, the work of a number of professionals in various countries for many years, including the one who is the subject of our next discussion, has been followed.

The folly of taking a metaphor for a proof, a torrent of verbiage for a spring of capital truths, and oneself for an oracle!

PAUL VALÉRY

That fellow seems to me to possess but one idea, and that is a wrong one.

SAMUEL JOHNSON

Peter Fürstenau

In our present examination of different categories of professionals representative of the most undesirable trends in psychotherapy, we have focused on an analyst who considers himself a clinician engaged in individual analysis, another who describes his "clinical" approach in group psychotherapy, and a third who favors methods based on short, occasional treatment sessions. We now turn our attention to a "theoretician" who claims to be bringing considerable improvement and progress to clinical practice.

Fürstenau is the originator of numerous psychoanalytic writings, has been the editor of several journals, and is currently the director of the Institute for Applied Psychoanalysis, in Düsseldorf, as well as a professor at the University of Giessen, in Germany. We have been scrutinizing his writings since the late 1970s.

Most of Fürstenau's works are concerned with his improvement of psychoanalytic "praxeology," a term he obviously considers to be more scientific than the usual one, "clinical practice." At other times, he uses the term to denote "theory of clinical praxis." We will encounter yet another definition shortly. We will focus on the means by which he is achieving, he claims, remarkable "improvement."

Professionals of little expertise who nevertheless have considerable influence on their colleagues and students are causing considerable damage to psychotherapy and mental health. We often hear the complaint that too many in the world of business and finance fail to devote themselves to constructive efforts. Instead they seek large and facile gains merely by moving money around. The many people responsible for destructive takeovers, and the currency speculators successful in pilfering the financial reserves of entire nations, are just a few examples. One finds a parallel situation in psychotherapy. All too often considerable prestige and outstanding positions are obtained by "theoreticians" who lack psychotherapeutic experience and expertise but are adroit movers of scientific-sounding words and manipulators of purely intellectual concepts whose clinical foundations are shaky. It is particularly insidious because such facile theorizing has substituted for, and displaced, clinical know-how and acumen in psychotherapy and its instruction.

It suffices to refer to only two of Fürstenau's writings. Both deal with his so-called praxeology. I will merely touch on his paper "Die beiden Dimensionen des psychoanalytischen Umgangs mit strukturell ich-gestörten Patienten" (the two dimensions of psychoanalytic treatment of patients with structural ego-disturbance) (Fürstenau, 1977). It is followed in the same issue of PSYCHE by a critique by another analyst, Professor Hermann Argelander of Frankfurt am Main.

The French have an excellent term: "*un dialogue de sourds*," which means "a dialogue of the deaf." Even though Argelander can agree with Fürstenau on some points, their exchange is typical of many such discussions; abstract concepts, pretending to reflect clinical realities, are countered by abstract concepts. Of course, because we are dealing not with clinical facts but with mere abstractions, no resolution, no proof or disproof, is possible.

Many authors have discussed basic approaches in psychoanalysis and psychodynamic therapy – in particular, traditional analysis, which involves a more passive approach by the analyst and allows the transference to develop, and more active, psychoanalytically oriented psychotherapies. Fürstenau does not use the latter term; he calls everything psychoanalysis. Of course, he is not the only one to use the term in that way. Fürstenau affirms that today most patients under the care of psychoanalysts are suffering not from neurotic disturbances but from structural ego deficits. He claims that he can bring about marked improvement in patients with structural ego defects by the "praxeological" integration of those two approaches and that such integration, originated by him, is indispensable for the proper development of the psychoanalytic process.

Actually, the problem of modifying traditional psychoanalysis has been approached by innumerable authors, including Ferenczi some 80 years ago. Fürstenau does indeed follow many authors in stressing the need to ascertain not only the degree but also the specific form of the structural ego deficits in these patients. We therefore expect him to offer clearly described, specific theoretical foundations for each clearly described, specific clinical approach for each of the forms of structural deficit. To the contrary, as the reader will shortly verify for himself, Fürstenau's supposedly pioneering "improvement" of psychoanalysis comprises his usual avalanche of convoluted generalizations. He consistently transforms matters that are discussed far more understandably by other authors into an imprecise, poorly defined, and pretentious academic stew. Under such circumstances, even the simplest matters are difficult to pin down.

In trying to work one's way through his maze of words, one is frequently confused about what Fürstenau is actually referring to at any given time. The previously mentioned difference between the two approaches, when discussed by knowledgeable writers, is a relatively clear and simple matter. Not so when Fürstenau addresses it. The reader can imagine how impossible understanding is when Fürstenau tries to tackle complex and delicate issues merely by tossing off a multitude of grandiosely conceptual terms. His fantasies of theoretical grandeur cannot be translated into anything that even approaches clinical reality. Shortly I will present extensive quotes from Fürstenau's book, proof of the pattern of chronic obfuscation.

What, then, are Fürstenau's much-vaunted "improvements"? As far as can be ascertained, they comprise the recommendations from his article and the "theoretical" model described in his book. We will be able to admire the recommendations and the model shortly.

Fürstenau speaking: "An enlargement of our concepts of our treatment methods with the analysands is absolutely indispensable if psychoanalysis should remain a treatment method of relevance. Psychoanalysis disposes of a *theoretical-conceptual* base of unique universality" (italics added). He goes on to say: "In addition, psychoanalysis, in the last decades, has accumulated a large and differentiated clinical experience. However, the views on the methodology of psychoanalytic treatment, and in connection with this, the analyst's understanding of his own role functions, have not been able to keep in step with clinical progress."

Fürstenau then affirms that it is the primary task of psychoanalytic praxeology, "the science of the art of analyzing," and of the analyst "to advance the psychoanalytic process by insuring that the conditions which optimally allow the start of the analytic process, would be maintained and further developed until the goal *prescribed by the model* has been accomplished" (italics added). When we examine the core thesis of Fürstenau's book, we will gain an impression of how he goes about that task, and how adequately he does it.

Fürstenau's penetrating thought represents, indeed, a pioneering breakthrough for psychoanalysis. Only he could devise the clear-cut, simple-to-follow solution he proposes at the end of his paper: to integrate the psychoanalytic traditions "in a coherent, multidimensional, complex, strategically conceptualized, psychoanalytic praxeology." For a master of verbositology, that should be easy.

To conclude our discussion of this paper, let us look at some comments by its reviewer, Professor Hermann Argelander. He has enough perspicacity to declare, with clear understatement, that Fürstenau's "scheme is not commensurate with the complexity of clinical experience." Indeed, in his paper Fürstenau attempts to achieve his goal, namely, the "enlargement of treatment methodology," exclusively by a purely intellectual convoluted exercise: the freewheeling moving around of the abstract concepts that are part of the contemporary literature. One cannot find in his elaborations a trace of clinical understanding; nor is he able to give us even the faintest clinical justification for his assertions.

> It is the dull man who is always sure, and the sure man who is always dull.
>
> H. L. MENCKEN

Our impression crystallizes when we turn to Fürstenau's book, ZUR THEORIE PSYCHOANALYTISCHER PRAXIS (on the theory of psychoanalytic practice) (1979). Its basic thesis is the same as that of the 1977 article. That bring us to the point I want to make.

Fürstenau consistently describes himself as a clinician par excellence and an avant-garde reformer of psychoanalytic practice and theory. Indeed, a number of professionals and students acknowledge him as such, and his writings have received considerable acclaim. In his introduction he speaks about himself and refers to the "interests and convictions [that] have determined and guided my scientific work." We are thereby informed that we are dealing with a scientist.

He then describes the first of the fundamental convictions that move him: "a strong need to seriously search for the truth in science and research." We are thus informed that we are dealing with a sincere and noble searcher for truth. Modestly Fürstenau continues: "By this I mean a critical attitude regarding all tendencies which separate scientific activity and its productions from the truth by stereotyping, adherence to tradition, isolation or loss of what experience has brought us." We are thus also notified that we are dealing with a man of acumen who knows what the truth is and how to defend it against all negative influences. But there is more: "My critical search for knowledge, fired by studies of philosophy, of the theory of science, of the history of science, and of sociological science, did not leave me after turning from my exclusive preoccupation with philosophical problems toward psychoanalysis and psychoanalytic social science." And a little later we read: "My writings intend to open up new perspectives, or reinforce same in the battle against untruth." Clearly, we are dealing here with the stuff Nobel Prize winners are made of.

The following demonstrates the procedure by which Fürstenau will bring about the considerable improvement of clinical work and theory and the establishment of truth. After criticizing traditional psychoanalytic therapy, he refers to recent psychoanalytic developmental and etiologic research. He then affirms, "These for the clinical practice relevant psychoanalytic studies can, however, only be adequately used in praxeology *after* the conceptual frame of reference for psychoanalytic practice has been widely enlarged" (italics added).

In short, Fürstenau asserts that no useful extension of clinical work could be engaged in until he created the heretofore nonexisting theoretical foundation for such an enlargement. Obviously, such an expert design by a master clinician-theoretician can only result in outstanding improvements of clinical practice, which he baptizes praxeology. Let us look at Fürstenau praxeology in action.

The core of the book is concentrated in two chapters: "The Constituting Factors of the Psychoanalytic Situation" and "The Structure of the Sequence of Proceeding in the Non-focused Individual Psychoanalysis."

In the first of those chapters Fürstenau begins with the statement that "at present times the analytic patients suffer, more or less, from structural ego-disturbance." He then refers to authors who have dealt with that topic. It is striking to see how, in this chapter and throughout the book, he manages by means of a bombastic vocabulary and by "superscientific" academic ruminations, to turn topics that have been clearly expressed by other authors into a foggy scholastic labyrinth. My correspondent in Germany, a well-known analyst of outstanding acumen who had called my attention to Fürstenau productions, appropriately termed them *Kochlöffeltheorie* (cooking-spoon theory), meaning that a maximum of abstract theoretical terms are thrown into a cauldron and stirred around at great length, and the resulting brew is presented as a pioneering breakthrough in theory. At all times Fürstenau plays it extremely safe by expressing himself in abstract concepts that pretend to be practical clinical realities. The fact is that his assertions, employing terms gleaned from theoreticians, are twice and thrice removed from any verifiable psychological and clinical facts.

Fortunately, there is at least one subject, the one apparently of most concern to him, on which he is crystal clear and not abstract at all. As we have noted when looking at Karasu and other authors, it is a proposition that, probably owing to its scientific interest, never fails to result in a considerable following for the pioneer scientist who proposes it. I already mentioned that Fürstenau likes to play it safe, and he does so here as well. Understandably, this particular matter leaves no room for his usual ambiguous abstractions. It requires utmost clarity to ensure that things not go wrong. And to make even more sure, he insists on it three times in a row. Here are the three quotes:

> This domain includes all activities of the analyst devoted to realization of the treatment relationship with his patient . . . , including the patient's obligations concerning . . . *finances, as well as all activities of the analyst concerning the maintenance, protection or modification of such obligations.* (Italics added)
> Foremost, these activities must concentrate on three points: that the agreement with the patient . . . must take into account the material interests of the analyst.

Regarding the functioning of the analysand within the psychoanalytic situation we mention his willingness to devote himself to the fulfillment and maintenance of the material (realistic) premises of the analytic relationship, including those of the agreed upon arrangement.

Thus he establishes for the patient the principal *conditio sine qua non* for successful analysis. Those quotes should put to rest the many voices maintaining that Fürstenau is not capable of clear and realistic thinking – unless it turns out that the sentences were formulated by his accountant.

We now turn to the chapter that describes the focus required of the analyst to ensure that the proper course of the "nonfocused psychoanalysis" is being strictly followed. Fürstenau states: "A typical model of the structure of the course of the psychoanalytic process in treatment, based on present day knowledge, must be valued because the analyst cannot pursue long-term treatment in a professionally justifiable form without being oriented by a conceptual model of an optimal treatment sequence." He proceeds by giving us what he considers his creative masterpiece: the specific conceptual model for the necessary optimal treatment procedure. He emphasizes that without that theoretical foundation, no valid and serious clinical work can be engaged in.

Fürstenau describes the theoretical aspects of each treatment phase. The first is the initial phase. The second phase deals with the clarification of symptoms and the building up of the patient's relationship with the analyst. The third phase represents the "the analytic effort required to work through the negative aspects of the patient's early relationship with his mother." The fourth phase is "a turning of the patient toward himself." And there are other phases.

Let us now look at some samples of Fürstenau's praxeological theoretical construct, paying particular attention to the fact that Fürstenau, throughout, gives the impression that (1) the patient, like a college student following a strict course curriculum leading to an academic degree, passes through definite, circumscribed analytic phases that follow each other neatly, in lockstep, and are separated by clear demarcation lines, and (2) the work of the analyst and the psychodynamic pattern of each patient are precisely the same.

A few excerpts from Fürstenau's detailed descriptions of phases four and five (translated by H. De Rothermann) are sufficient to illustrate the depth of his thinking and of his praxeological methodology.

> *Fourth Phase: An Inward-Turning*
> *Working-through of the carry-over relational pattern*
> The treatment of the thematics of the injuries and aggressive urges carried over from the early relationship with the mother, now hidden behind the presently apparent symptom complex, leads, together with an improvement of the more or less diffuse depressive-schizoid symptoms (including their physical manifestations), to a stronger cathexis of the self. There now appear a number of narcissistic fantasies and daydreams, some of these carefully shielded from the view of others, in addition to mostly mental preoccupations and frequently also to an obsessively ritualized means of instinctual satisfaction, either affectively unrelated or experienced in guilt-ridden torment: Masturbatory practices, or perverted dissocial or compulsive behavior patterns.
>
> This narcissistic world of the self has a more or less clearly defined significance of omnipotence, but at the same time bears an anti-instinctual and ascetic trait; this brings about both a distancing from the shared societal reality and an impulse of diffusely helpless protest and defiance.
>
> This is the – pathological – form which has adopted the urge towards self-realization and self-assertion under the terms of the patient's childhood. The unfolding of this narcissistic world implies a certain withdrawal from the analyst, which, however, is compensated by the fact that the patient, in the shared analytical situation, for the first time *talks to someone* of this world of his very own self, which sooner or later also leads to the revelation of the attitudes, influences and reactions of the patient's parents in the face of the attempts at self-assertion, independence and autonomy on the part of the analysand during childhood. . . .

Fifth Phase: Definition of Gender Identity

In this treatment phase the difference between the genders asserts itself so overwhelmingly that it is recommended to differentiate any treatment description according to the gender of the patient.

Male Patients
Working-through of the carry-over relational pattern

The treatment of the narcissistic world of the self, evolved in compensatory reaction, leads to a certain liberation of hitherto strongly suppressed or, respectively, of obsessively ritualized, partner-related sexual tendencies, specifically and in this phase primarily in the form of a libidinous dependence on the sex-identical parent and his present-day representative, accompanied by the wish for identification by way of incorporation. This involves a scenic unfolding of all the related memory material with special emphasis on all disappointing experiences and on those typifying rejection, incomprehension and intimidation, together with the refusal of incorporative identification, developed reactively by the analysand in his childhood.

In the course and to the extent of this working-through of those memories and attitudes, a conscious dialogue with representatives of the same gender is being initiated which ultimately leads to an overcoming of the strongly ambivalent psychological position and of the rejection of identification. The libidinous shift towards the sex-identical parent is centered on sexual fantasies and impulses, at times also on acts of anal incorporation and penetration. This kind of sexual thematic embroidery is to be differentiated from an out-right passive-feminine homosexuality, since it is marked by both an unequivocally male instinctual drive and by an equally male identifying intent. It nevertheless is possible that such a singular narcissistic development may have been connected with a re-enforced passive-feminine sexual position which, in that treatment phase, may bring about the apparition of outright feminine fantasies and behavioral attitudes, in which case the afore-described 'male' imagery of anal incorporation and penetration in relation with the father image only will show up subsequent to the working-through of the feminine imagery phase.

Associated with this father-related position is a certain libidinous distancing from the mother (and her representatives) which will show in differentiated affective shades of symptoms (shame, guilt, triumph, contempt, indifference), in accordance with the early antecedents of patient and the extent to which it already was possible to work through his maternal relationship.

If – in this firstly discussed case of male patients – the analyst also is a male, then the image scenery of this treatment phase unfolds directly within the transference and can be treated primarily within that dimension. If, on the other hand, the analysand is treated by a female analyst, then the thematic tapestry will be developed and acted out primarily within the memory material associated with the father and the father representatives in childhood, as well as with paternal authority figures in the present, extra-analytical area of the patient. Instead, the female analyst is being vested (apart from her general qualities of an adult life style and her professionalism) with the maternal aspects of the phase-specific libidinous constellation: the patient distances himself somewhat from his female analyst by verbalizing those above-described affects and fantasies.

On the other hand and in accordance with the mechanics of countertransference, the male analyst soon will become intensely conscious of the libidinous shift on the part of the analysand – at first in a somewhat anxiety-ridden, critically aggressive and yet demurely hesitant form, but, with time, in an openly sexual manner. The patient now shows a clear interest and sharp powers of observation with regard to his analyst, while earlier he perceived him merely as a diffuse, undetermined schematic projection or in a selectively partial manner.

The analyst shall have to work through the patient's fear in relation to penetration on the basis of material provided by analysand, since this fear hitherto had prevented the patient to win for himself a clear-cut gender identity through a personal affective and incorporating interlocution with the sex-identical parent. At the same time the analyst will elaborate together with the analysand those aspects of his relation with his mother, which had served to brace the defensive structure developed by the analysand regarding this gender identity.

If the patient has a female analyst, the latter will not let herself be distracted by the mother transference, enacted by the patient in the afore-described manner, from assisting him in the elucidation of a father identification towards which his impulses are urging him. She will endeavor to achieve this by means of a working-through of the impeding bonds from the subsisting maternal relationship, including the anxieties, conflicts and obstacles which, for the patient, are associated with the homosexual libidinous thematic imagery. The thought associations revealed by the patient pointing to relations with sex-identical partners, for the female analyst will be an indication of the fact that the analysand – in the sense of entering this particular phase of his treatment – is thrusting out of his early maternal bond and towards more complex libidinous relational constellations – as a first step towards the identification with the father and the concomitant release from the maternal bond.

It is only when the patient has reached, by way of the incorporative identification with his male instinctual modality, the acceptance of the penetration of the female body, that he will have assumed that position which is the essential precondition of his further development on the oedipal (triangular) level.

Let us take a close look at what Fürstenau has been saying. According to him, this was the first time that we were offered the indispensable theoretical basis for an expertly conducted psychoanalysis along the lines of his praxeology. It purports to describe the consecutive phases of such a treatment as well as the task of the analyst and the psychodynamics and the reactions of the patient in each of the phases. It was presented as a fundamental model, an X ray of praxeology.

But what did we get instead? In spite of the innumerable analytic and "scientific" terms, it is nothing but a naive, unknowledgeable fantasy of what little Moritz imagined psychoanalysis should be and how it functions. Even the most meaningful psychodynamic terms become utter nonsense when mixed up and misused in this manner. Fürstenau lists in his index of authors some 200 professionals, many of them well-known contemporary theoreticians. He generously uses their terms and thoughts. His specific pioneering contribution appears to be the following: With the discernment only little Moritz could muster, he sorts those items neatly into separate drawers, labeled first phase, second phase, and so forth.

Of course, none of what he says corresponds to reality. The content of the inner psychic universe of each patient is completely different from that of every other patient. It is not rigidly arranged in the same identical layers for each person. Thus an experienced clinician proceeds on the basis of the highly individual reality of each patient's unconscious; he does not dogmatically and clumsily superimpose, as Fürstenau does, the same artificially constructed, rigid pattern on each patient. In view of the enormous variety of psychological structures, no facile, simplistic procedure can be ethically defended. While such a procedure makes the analyst's work much easier, as he does not need to discover the circumstances of each patient's psyche, it also crucifies the patient.

Once again, the proper way to advance clinical practice is to explore improved techniques, carefully developed on the basis of long-term expert clinical observation. I do not know of a single instance where the intellectual fabrications of the self-important "theoreticians" have produced anything except superfluous academic papers. Fürstenau criticizes traditional psychoanalysis and calls himself an innovator of "praxeology." But in important aspects, the ingredients of his proposition are parts of an ultraconservative analytic approach that many modern practitioners have discarded. Examine, for instance, his uniform approach to the postulated potent omnipresence of a negative mother and of homosexual components.

Fürstenau asserts that his book deals with clinical practice. But there is not a single specific clinical reference nor any indication that would allow us to evaluate his clinical work – if it even exists. For instance, one may want to find out how he handles dreams. But there is no subject index. One has to scan the entire book to find that it contains nothing on the topic. Also, to understand his manner of clinical work in the session, one would need to study his work with transference. Fürstenau renders that impossible.

In any professional book one simply checks the index for the respective references and links them into a meaningful context. But as there is no index, that simple procedure is impossible here. All we get are freestanding, grandiose, scientific-sounding generalizations that are claimed to be valid for every patient! Even Fürstenau's favorite invention, the term "praxeology," is marked by his usual dense nebulosity. As I said earlier, in certain places it refers to clinical practice, and in others to the theory of clinical practice. He also defines it as "the science of the art of interpretation." We are thus informed that we are dealing here not only with an academic scientist but also with an outstanding artist. I wish the dean of his university would call the professor in, explain to him that it won't do to have three different definitions of the same thing, and make him enroll in Logic 101.

Even the newspaper astrologers, who are severely criticized by their colleagues who prepare highly detailed individual charts, allow for 12 personality types and thus for the same number of approaches. Fürstenau, as we have seen, has only one approach for everyone; thus he postulates that all people have basically the same psyche. Of course, he applies the same facile, unthinking, mass approach to group psychotherapy. In a dismal article on a number of groups he has conducted, Fürstenau (1970) stresses that they were based entirely on psychoanalytic concepts. After inundating us, as usual, with grandiose statements to impress us with the outstanding sophistication of the treatment plan and the high quality of the treatment offered, Fürstenau naively trips himself. He states that his groups show great improvement after one or two weeks and that thereafter a period of depressive regression sets in, followed by more improvement. And so forth. The fact, however, is that no such global uniform reactions occur. Even a novice group psychotherapist who pays due attention to the individual members and their transference reactions, and proceeds accordingly, is keenly aware of major differences in their attitudes and reactions at any given time.

The expert psychotherapist bases his clinical work on careful observation. He detects certain facts, and as treatment proceeds, he uncovers additional facts. Simply put, hypotheses enter the picture in two ways: (1) If, in the case of a particular patient, the accumulated facts are insufficient for the necessary understanding, hypotheses may have to be formulated to temporarily fill the gaps and to be used in devising steps in treatment. (2) If one has accumulated a wealth of significant clinical data from a number of patients, one may cautiously proceed to formulate hypotheses about common denominators. Formulating hypotheses is a task that should be the domain only of clinicians of outstanding expertise and talent. Unfortunately, that is rarely the case, and most certainly it is not the case here. Much theory, old and new, comes from professionals of little clinical ability. The high-sounding academic terms indeed seduce many mental health practitioners and students incapable of discernment.

In Fürstenau's case the situation is even more disastrous. Here is an academician who, as can be easily seen in his writings, lacks clinical expertise and relies solely on theoretical book knowledge. *His thesis is that purely intellectual theoretical considerations and stratagems are the proper basis for, and thus must precede, whatever is done clinically!* In many instances he expresses that credo and justifies it with a tidal wave of references to the ideas and analytic terminology of modern writers. Although Fürstenau severely attacks traditional metapsychology as being far removed from clinical experience, the grandiose, "up-to-date," theoretical concoctions with which he attempts to establish himself as a pioneer are surely no closer to clinical reality. I urge readers to acquaint themselves with his work. By studying what is incompetent and undesirable, we are forced into awareness of the problems in psychotherapy that must be overcome.

Some may wonder why more pages were given here to Fürstenau than to any of the preceding three authors. One reason is simply that the other three authors wrote in more concrete terms. Reading Fürstenau's work, on the other hand, is like turning over a big stone and seeing thousands of insects and worms crawling around. To describe them requires space. The other reason is that Fürstenau's writings are an excellent illustration of the weaknesses inherent in the purely theoretical edifices of many authors. These authors, less incognizant and more subtle than Fürstenau, may manage to hide their deficiencies. Fürstenau is, therefore, a more suitable demonstration object for our purposes.

Of interest is the startling similarity among the methods many of these theoreticians use. We have mentioned Fürstenau's lack of responsible discrimination in his use of scholarly terms and psychoanalytic abstractions and his cavalier disregard of clinical facts and cohesion when he links those terms and moves them around. His entire approach forcefully brings to mind other authors who also claim to be eminent innovators of psychotherapy. Here are some of the common denominators: their abundant use and manipulation of psychoanalytic terms and concepts; their justification of what they are doing on valueless "theoretical" grounds, frequently advertised by them as a pioneering achievement; their grandiose and grandiloquent style and presentation; their advocacy of facile, much-simplified therapy methods, again masked by scholarly and "scientific" language; their claim that their findings are the fruit of an unrelenting search — and the considerable success each of them achieved by those means.

We consider a woman who ostentatiously covers herself with an abundance of fake jewelry to be vulgar. The same applies to a considerable number of our theoreticians and "scientific" writers.

It may be impossible to determine to what extent the creators of praxeology and other purely theoretical edifices are inebriated by their own "scientific" jargon. After all, there are no limits to rationalization where self-interest is involved. Lacan once remarked that his thinking was so profound that on occasion he himself was unable to understand what he said! What concerns us here is that these allegedly therapeutic approaches have been eminently successful in seducing unwary patients and students, as well as pleasing money-minded or unknowledgeable professionals, and thus in supplanting responsible and competent patient care and the study of it.

I have referred to some of the professionals whose work we have reviewed as self-seeking or self-aggrandizing at the expense of the public interest. The rewards they seek include publicity, publications, recognition, positions, and so forth. The damage they cause to psychotherapeutic practice and training is a major and direct source of untold suffering for the emotionally ill. Unfortunately, in this domain, as in others, it is frequently the aggressive, not the knowledgeable, who acquire positions of influence.

b2   THE USURPERS

> Kings walk like beggars
> and beggars ride like kings.
>
> ECCLESIASTES

Psychoanalysis and psychodynamic therapy have steadily lost ground in professional and public appeal and esteem. Yet I am convinced that in the hands of gifted and expert professionals, they are already, without any further breakthroughs, the therapy of choice for a wide number of emotional afflictions.

Before we can present our solutions, we must further examine the afflictions that permeate our craft.

Thus we will now attempt to determine, on the basis of such an examination, the nature and extent of the problems that afflict psychoanalysis and psychotherapy, how those problems can be eradicated, and which constructive approaches would bring major improvements in psychotherapy and mental health. To identify and elucidate the problems, we have, throughout this chapter, touched on numerous writings. For the purpose of further discussion of the difficulties in our field and to enable the reader to locate comments made previously, I list below the writers whose work, or some aspects of it, were criticized. (The authors appear in the order in which they were discussed.) Their shortcomings range from serious deficiencies in clinical knowledge to complete incompetence. With only a few exceptions, pretense and pretentiousness are common denominators. When I speak critically of academicians and theoreticians, these are the kinds of people to whom I am referring.

A. FROM THE CLINICAL VIEWPOINT
SHORTCOMINGS IN PSYCHOTHERAPY

1. FALLOW FIELDS – SPREADING DESERTS
a. The Voice of the Experts

Francis Crick and Graeme Mitchison

Christopher Evans

Robert McCarley and Allan Hobson

Leon L. Altman

b. The Bookish Theoric
b1 Dr. Faust and Little Moritz

"The professor"

Donald P. Spence

J. W. Reeves

b2 Curiouser and Curiouser

Charles Fisher

Alfred Winterstein

Stanley R. Palombo

Erik H. Erikson

Kris Study Group

Ernest Hartmann

Helen B. Lewis

Heinz Kohut

J. O. Wisdom

James L. Fosshage and Clements A. Loew

Angel Garma

John H. Padel

b3 The New Majority: Academic Populism

Irving D. Yalom

.

c. Heaping Stones and Rolling Eyeballs

Jean Michel Gaillard

Robert McCarley and Allan Hobson

Steven LaBerge

Ramon Greenberg and Chester Pearlman Jr.

David M. Berger

Morton F. Reiser

d. Dreams and the Feeling for Feelings
Talent versus the Imitation of Science

Calvin S. Hall

Thomas M. French and Erika Fromm

2. . . . AND OTHER NEGATIVES

a. Through a Glass, Darkly

Alexander Grinstein   Irwin Hirsch

Peter Gay   Jay Greenberg

Smith Ely Jeliffe

b. Earnestly Talking Nonsense

b1 Honored Teachers – Misled Students

Leonard Shengold   Toksoz B. Karasu

Martin Grotjahn   Peter Fürstenau

The foregoing list was intended to remind the reader of the territory covered so far. It is part of the basis for our forthcoming conclusions and proposed solutions.

The reader is reminded, once more, that the present commentary is based on work done during the course of more than 45 years at a foundation devoted to the defense and advancement of the public interest. Reporting the findings, no matter how critical, requires utter frankness. Fortunately, the public interest and the interest of discerning psychotherapists converge in striving for the same goal: the improvement of psychotherapy.

"SCIENCE" BUT NOT KNOWLEDGE
KNOWLEDGE BUT NOT SCIENCE

Among the many fruitless and extended discussions in our field, the defensive arguments that analysis and psychotherapy, or, at least parts of them, are scientific are possibly the most tedious. Stoller has stated that "psychoanalysis need not claim to be a science to legitimate both its process of discovery and the discoveries that resulted." I would gladly have sidestepped the issue as irrelevant. Unfortunately, I could not. Considerable harm is caused, not so much by attacks by professionals from other disciplines as by the negative influences on our work that are created by our own profession's desire to appear scientific. Valueless projects and research that seemingly fit into the scientific framework receive favorable attention, whereas many endeavors of vital importance are ignored, or even attacked as unscientific. As we have seen, the trend also plays into the hands of those who address our tasks by means of desiccated, intellectual, theoretical, and academic speculation, in some cases engaging in a purely mechanical approach. In short, much of the focus and the perspectives in psychoanalysis and psychotherapy are out of kilter, and the literature mirrors that state of affairs.

If we listen to some behavioral scientists, and in particular to a number of psychoanalysts, we hear that ours is "the noblest science of them all," for it combines science with something the other sciences cannot offer; it is the science of man. To them, mathematics is a poor and distant second best. And how does one join this elite circle of superscientists? One needs, first, to have some kind of degree in one of the many areas of behavioral sciences and, second, to repeat incessantly, without blinking, that one is a scientist.

Before offering my own comments and conclusions in the matter, I cede the floor to Robert J. Stoller (Colby & Stoller, 1988):

> What pains me is how rarely we express the full measure of our unsureness, how gracelessly the unsureness appears, and how it can repeat and repeat and repeat, in sentence after sentence and paragraph after paragraph, and yet allow for a switchover into the most positive, declarative statements. I think we use oracular thundering to drown out the soft sounds of uncertainty that show us and our audiences how little we know. What is the function of this junk language if not to make an unsupported claim for knowledge, truth, accuracy, reality? That really is a shame, for it puts in doubt what we do know and makes it seem to everyone but us that we yell "science" to dismiss our own doubts of the value of what we do. We bewitch ourselves.
>
> Over and over, and over and over appear words like "our science" in the papers and books of analysts. I have not counted how often, but the phrase occurs over and over. Does any other profession or intellectual discipline say "science" so much? Here are building-blocks, from the writings of psychoanalysts, for "the edifice of science." In a six months' period, using only the four psychoanalytic journals to which I subscribe, association newsletters, and a dozen or so books, I found hundreds of examples. (In many of the

sentences, if "science," "scientific," and "scientifically" is removed, the meaning of the sentence is the same): the science of analysis, scientific laws, scientific method, scientific activity, scientific accuracy, this new and unique science, human science, the science of Man, the Science of man, the scientific awakening, investigative science, realm of science, scientific paper, the usual scientific paper, scientific presentation, valuable scientific contribution, our scientific ranks, an explanatory science [as opposed to non-explanatory sciences?], an explanatory science which could prove things, the philosophy of the science of psychoanalysis, for scientific use/usage, natural scientific psychology, scientific tradition, scientific discourse, scientific needs of our field, scientific knowledge in our field, scientific publication, scientific enterprise, scientifically conscientious, experimental science, scientific research, valid scientific research in psychoanalysis, scientific problems, acceptable scientific framework, scientific theory, scientific explanation, scientific understanding, scientific sophistication, high-level scientific abstractions, scientific discovery, scientificity, scientific understanding, scientific opinion, scientific attitude, scientific exchange, scientific loci, scientifically warranted, scientific justification, scientific outlook, creative science, scientific life, scientific doctrine, scientific correlation, scientific endeavors, scientific work, scientific progress, scientific verification, scientific argument [process of logic], a scientific study of the case, quite scientific, very scientific, scientific program [three usages: meeting, overall research plan, political activity], an interpretive and an objective scientific discipline, psychoanalysis as a scientific discipline, a scientific type of theory, scientific congress, scientific standards, scientific values, scientific conceptual framework, the usual [?] scientific framework, within the framework of what is currently known scientifically, scientific psychoanalytic contributions, a contribution to the science of psychoanalysis, scientific foundations, scientific manner, scientific ethos, scientific ethical standards, scientific status, substantiated (and agreed upon) scientific status, scientific metapsychology, scientific argument, scientific truths, scientific approach, scientific ideology, scientific scrutiny, scientific study, scientific stand [position], scientific means [nonfinancial resources], scientific liabilities, scientific objectivity, scientific paradigm, scientific field, this field of science, our field of scientific work, scientific utility, scientific commitment, scientific form, scientific symbolization, scientific terms, scientific purposes, scientific responsibility, a scientific psychoanalysis, the heart of science, the mold of science, hermeneutics, the art or science of interpretation, a science of meanings, cultural sciences, scientific clarity, scientific background, scientific grounding, modern scientific basis, scientific spirit, scientific spirit of inquiry, scientific thinking, scientific thought, meaningful scientific research, scientific gains, simultaneously clinically and scientifically relevant, natural scientific psychology, scientific view of the world, the science of the mind, scientific edifice, scientific debate, scientific career, scientific task, applied science, scientific conclusions, scientific conceptualizations, scientific character [i.e., quality], our traditional science and road to science as bequeathed to us by Freud, the study and advancement of psychoanalytic science as founded and developed by Sigmund Freud, our current and ongoing scientific march, the scientific use of the 'peculiar', our science *qua* science, respectable and appropriate science, a descriptive science, in a state of 'normal science' (Kuhn), scientific world-view carried on by a scientific community, our ordained future course as a science, our crucial scientific tasks ahead, our domain as science, the serious stamp of science, that stamp of science, the science of the inner world, a structural science, a comprehensive scientific theory of the mind, an evolved, explicit scientific theory, our psychoanalytic scientific task, the kind of science that the psychoanalytic endeavor creates for us, our peculiar science, an objective and scientific attitude, scientific predilections, scientific rigor, scientific purview and prestige, scientific validation, metapsychology may be a branch of natural science, a branch of science, the new science, our new science, further scientific advance, further development of the science, a specialist science, a clinical science, one unified science, a developing science, poetic science, a sound scientific basis, systematic scientific scrutiny, sound and scientific clinical theory, a unified science of human behavior, scientific journals, scientific content of journals, the scientificity of psychoanalysis, scientific forums, scientific media, scientific nature, the scientific function of Freud's hypotheses, vigorous scientific thinking, scientific methods of thinking, psychoanalysis as the science of man, this process of scientific assessment, scientific aims, scientific system, scientific potential, scientific growth, scientific insight, scientific findings, scientific complexity, scientific simplicity, scientific inference, scientific difficulties, scientific comprehensiveness, scientific work in analysis, a firmer scientific footing, interpretation as a valid scientific procedure, scientific value of an interpretation, scientific reconstructions, scientific productivity, scientific production [two usages: a product such as a paper; a process or capacity that massively bears fruit], scientific implications, implications for science, scientifically serviceable, scientifically fertile, scientifically validated, scientifically speaking, scientific objectivication, scientific discipline [two usages: field, rigor], scientific labour, scientific controls [as in isolating factors for an experiment], psychoanalytic scientific activities, scientific observations, adequate scientific observation, scientific empathy, the science of introspection, depth psychology and the other sciences, the science of the study of metapsychology, psychological (psychoanalytic) science, psychological science (in its own right) and in its place among the array of sciences, psychoanalytic scientific research.

Who would deny that the analytic literature is full of that vocabulary? In the space of an 11-page paper (on empathy, not on analysis as science), Kohut gives us the following, all in reference to analysis: "The essential simple and clear scientific message," "scientific pursuits," "scientific sobriety," "scientific rigour," "scientific hypothesis," "the scientific 'high road,'" "decisive scientific action," "substantial intrinsically scientific grounds," "less of a science and more of a moral system," "less of a scientific procedure . . . and more an educational procedure," "the depth-psychological scientist's perception," "all my scientific colleagues," "a phase of scientific working through," "the scientific road I have been following," "spurred me toward scientific action," "falling within the domain of the natural sciences," "scientific system," "its scientific results," "nonscientific, perhaps," "the two universes accessible to science . . . the sciences which explore the fields that are accessible via extrospection: the physical and biological sciences. And the sciences which explore the field that are accessible via introspection: psychoanalysis *par excellence*." He uses "science" and "scientific" nine more times.

Is there any other subject, discipline, practice or art that keeps nattering on about being a science? Certainly none of the fields the rest of the world considers sciences. I hardly ever see "science" in the scientific reports of the journal SCIENCE, even though it is published by an association that wants to advance science.

After having expressed so much criticism in this chapter, it is a tremendous relief to let Stoller do some of the work. His outstanding intelligence and exceptional expertise are a light that shineth in the darkness. Here I will repeat some statements from his introduction to this volume.

A field becomes a science when it develops techniques that have feedback mechanisms in them to guarantee an ever-increasing accuracy. Those well-known thoughts apply to the ideal of the analysts – but not to the performance so far. What troubles me is that, while analysts idealize precise observation, predictability, control of variables, sharing of data with others to rule out misperceptions and misinterpretations, laboratories for the creation of models, and methods for correcting defects, none of these exists in psychoanalysis. More than that, the analyst not only seems to miss them but, when an attempt is made to introduce them, he is apt to feel they are unnecessary – or even harmful – to his "science."

And later:

No field accepted as a science
1. has such a high amount of reference to authority to bolster an argument
2. can demonstrate so little of its data to others
3. has a higher ratio of theory to observation
4. prefers as much to refine concepts by reference to other concepts rather than by observations
5. uses metaphor and analogy so profusely
6. has such disagreement among peers about so many key words
7. strings together to such an extent one unproved statement after another, using devices such as "it seems," "probably," and the like to arrive at a conclusion worded with the same assurance one would use if one had strung together a series of demonstrable facts to arrive at a new conclusion.

The psychoanalytic writer is an essayist, not a scientist; there are few scientific papers in the literature, but many, many essays.

We all agree that at the beginning of the process called science is precise observation; yet we also agree that observation must be refined and synthesized, for it is blind without concepts that unify and focus. Conceptualization has power to improve observation and prediction, but it fatally attracts intellects to exalt their concepts and so distorts their vision, that is, to propagandize. This is too often true of some analysts, who, with only minimal data, attempt to soar, powered by theory alone. The speed with which some leave observations behind and begin theorizing can be so fast that one suspects that, with an extreme of efficiency, facts would become completely superfluous.

The temptation to theorize without data is increased by the privacy and trust without which analytic treatment cannot proceed. As a result, no analyst has ever reported what he observed, nor has anyone else seen it. What science can make *that* claim? This is not our fault. What is our fault is that so many of us do not admit to regretting it. Some have argued cutely that in astronomy and theoretical physics one also cannot observe or experiment directly; but that is about all that psychoanalysis and such fields have in common, for the latter have been much more intent on precision about *whatever* evidence is required in any given case than analysis has been. To act in science is to be implacably oriented to returning to events, perhaps not right away but after a measured span of indirection. There is no such adamant drive in the psychoanalytic credo.

And further on:

But as galling as is the habit of generalizing from the single case, it hurts even more to realize that once a psychoanalyst has learned his theory well, he need never see another patient and yet will hardly be at a disadvantage with his colleagues in using the theory or in creating new theory. Theory is now a perpetual motion machine.

The Russians have a proverb: "You should beat your wife every day. You don't know why, but she knows." However, as Stoller points out, the offenses that analysts have committed are known. One can well imagine the damage caused by such freewheeling theorizing as Stoller describes when it is actually applied in daily practice with patients. It would bring a glimmer of hope into "our science" to have practitioners and students read Stoller's writings once a day.

Alas, wishful thinking will not help, and we had better return to reality with some additional realistic remarks by Stoller (Colby & Stoller, 1988):

An author writes of "tender object cathexis." Why does he choose that phrase rather than "tenderness"? How does "cathectic constancy" differ from "constancy"? I feel manipulated when "castration anxiety" becomes a synonymy for "fear." Think on the following epigrams:

Most of the fundamental ideas of science are essentially simple, and may, as a rule, be expressed in a language comprehensible to everyone.

EINSTEIN AND INFELD

Even for the physicist the description in plain language will be a criterion of the degree of understanding that has been reached.

HEISENBERG

If you cannot – in the long run – tell everyone what you have been doing, your doing has been worthless.

SCHRODINGER

We are trying to get a free ride when we blather about our science.

What other science, respected by analysts, does not use some or all of the following interventions as part of its scientific method: testable hypotheses, theory models, the challenging of parts of theory by formal experiments, calibrating the instruments, measurements, organizing data with statistics, using observable/confirmable data, presenting repeatable data, producing new facts, and prediction? What kind of a science is it that has no trusted way to move from guess to validation?

Analysts beg dispensation from the rules others accept for defining science.

It is indeed a pleasure to read how a professional of outstanding integrity and intelligence such as Stoller cuts the Gordian knot of unashamed pretense, blatant rationalization, and second-rate reasoning that imbue this field. My intention is in no way to diminish the value of psychodynamic therapy, but it is difficult to imagine how analysis could be considered a science. Of course, one has to be careful. For instance, in German one can speak about the exact sciences, but the word for science, *Wissenschaft,* is also used in a broad sense, as in *Musikwissenschaft* (knowledge and history of music) and *Kunstwissenschaft* (knowledge and history of art). However, when analysts refer to analysis as a science, they insist the term be interpreted in the stricter sense.

We cannot spend much more space on this issue. Interested readers will find Colby and Stoller's exhaustive examination to be most thoughtful, fascinating, and of great value in clarifying the matter.

Both Stoller and I are firm believers in the potential of psychoanalytic therapy. Our criticisms are intended to create solid and realistic foundations for our endeavors by eliminating spurious and self-serving claims. The worth of psychotherapy is not nullified by its not being a science. To qualify as a science, a discipline must possess a number of prerequisites. If even one is absent, it is not a science. In the case of psychodynamic therapy and analysis, a multitude of essential factors are missing. Analysts, motivated by self-interest or by protective affection for their craft, have advanced fancy and spurious arguments to justify their clamor to be admitted to what they consider to be an elite club.

The hundreds of writings trying to establish the fact that psychoanalysis, or at least part of it, is indeed science are an insult to the knowledgeable reader's intelligence.

Let us look briefly at a paper that is a notch more reasonable than most, by Cecilio Paniagua (1987), a professor of psychiatry at Georgetown University.

After deriding the idea that psychoanalysis is a "hermeneutic science," Paniagua argues that it should be considered a science nevertheless, as it has the characteristics of a natural and experimental science. As particularly salient arguments, he cites that the analytic "process takes place in a controlled atmosphere . . . and the great reduction of external variables through the analyst's anonymity, neutrality and abstinence, makes it experimental, or, at least laboratory-like." In another section he asserts that predictions in analysis are entirely feasible.

Sadly missing is the realization that in this "laboratory" the observations of the recording instrument, that is, the analyst, are highly subjective, that the "instrument" cannot be measured or controlled, and that the observed "facts," changing from moment to moment and unique for each instant, will never be repeated. As for Paniagua's descriptions and explanatory comments regarding the predictions an analyst can provide, they are somewhat less satisfactory than those a farmer can offer regarding his pigs. Thus, while he fails to make a convincing case on behalf of analysts, he does succeed in laying the groundwork for pig farmers to be recognized as scientists.

On the whole, Paniagua presents a thoughtful description of the psychoanalytic panorama. One of his paragraphs is quoted here, as it deals with the influence of insurance companies on our efforts, a subject to which we already gave some consideration:

> Pressure mounts for analysts to prove theory is scientific. . . . The issue is not a new one, but time has made it more pressing for psychoanalysts as the insurance companies have become progressively reluctant to reimburse for medical services of a specialty that seems to have failed to adhere to such time-honored yardsticks of science as precise definition of terminology, clear correlation between theoretical concepts and observables, reliable predictions, criteria for confirmation of hypotheses, use of independent observers, statistical studies, etc.

We now return to the reason we need to discuss pathetic attempts to dress up analysis and therapy as science. I would like to repeat a statement that I wrote in 1954:

> We would have been far better off to limit the use of the term "science" *only* to the basic sciences, thus avoiding interminable and fruitless discussion.
>
> Many areas of inquiry do not lend themselves to the constraints of the scientific method. The use of some "scientific" procedures and criteria alone does not transform such realms into "science." The eagerness of professionals to bestow the badge of science upon their special areas of endeavor is unfortunate. It imposes inappropriate requirements that hamper and distort their work. On the other hand, to belittle as "nonscientific" any area in which science is *not* equipped to operate is also unconscionable.
>
> What we should really care about is that the methods employed are intelligent, relevant, pertinent to, and evolved from the specific field investigated.

The quest by analysts to be recognized as scientists has damaged our field immensely by altering the perspectives, the focus of thinking, and the procedures of far too many analysts and psychotherapists. Ours is a unique field of unique value. Trying to crash a party in a house where we do not belong is both demeaning and fruitless. Rather than presenting spurious arguments that we are members of a group "high" in the hierarchy and trying to sneak across the color line by painting our faces, we should finally concentrate on and cultivate our own backyards. No apologies will ever be necessary.

We must determine what is valid and solid in psychotherapy. We must not claim as truths that our observations or other procedures are objective and scientific when they are not. We can do our work better when we admit our limitations rather than cover them with makeup and sophistry. We must concentrate on our strong points without constant soul searching and hand wringing about whether or not they fit scientific requirements. An area of human endeavor as important as ours deserves humility and responsibility from those who are equipped to give it.

We can now move closer, at long last, to the core of our study. But we are not quite there yet; we need to do a little more house cleaning.

> The chief danger (to psychoanalysis), apart from laziness and woolliness, is scholasticism, . . . which is treating what is vague as if it were precise.
>
> I. RAMSEY

> He, cleaving to shallow things,
> Eternally feasts on empty terms,
> This worm, claiming mighty wings,
> Finds happiness unearthing worms!
>
> GOETHE

PHARISEES AND APPARATCHIKS

We have discussed the craving of analysts to be accepted as scientists and their endeavor to squeeze themselves into that mold. There is a second advantage for them in doing so. When they imitate and paraphrase the language of science, they can sound important without really saying anything of substance, particularly when they wax theoretical. Such posturing is common in psychodynamic therapy and in all other areas of psychotherapy, psychology, and mental health.

To remind the reader that I am not alone in holding such blasphemous views, I quote some experts on the matter, some of whom have appeared before in this volume. I reiterate that we are engaging in this effort not to destroy psychotherapy but to help it. It is precisely the abuses and shortcomings of which I speak that have brought about the deterioration, and even disrepute, of our craft. Even worse, they are the cause of much suffering among patients who are subjected to incompetent therapy. The solutions that would eliminate those shortcomings are clear, but there are tremendous obstacles within our profession.

I will quote three competent therapists who speak about those problems.

> When complaining is a crime, hope becomes despair.
>
> BENJAMIN FRANKLIN

Ralph R. Greenson

As a dedicated and exceptionally endowed clinician, Ralph R. Greenson always insisted on the absolute need to explore meticulously the specific inner universe of each patient. One of the chief instruments of that exploration was his remarkable sensitivity, allowing him to understand the emotions and dreams of his patients. He felt that the presence of ungifted and incompetent therapists was a scourge to patients and a disgrace to our profession. His scornful remarks were numerous. Two samples should suffice:

> I find the concept of an "overall strategy of the conduct of the analysis" an impressive, high-sounding phrase but, in reality, with the present state of knowledge, this overall strategy is at best loose, subject to frequent changes and revisions, and full of unknowns. Only psychoanalysts with preconceived and rigid theoretical notions are sure of an "overall strategy." And they also have prefabricated interpretations for all types of patients, and disregard the fact that each individual human being is unique.

I realize that no clinical demonstration of the value of dream interpretation will change the opinions of those who are predominantly devoted to theory conservation or theoretical innovations. Their theories seem to be more real to them than the memories and reconstructions of their patient's life history. Working with dreams is not only an enlightening experience for the patient, but it may be a source of new clinical and theoretical insights for the analyst, if he has an open mind. Furthermore, there are some analysts who have no ear or eye for dreams, like people who find it hard to hear and visualize the beauty of poetry, or like the tone-deaf who cannot appreciate the special imagery and language of music, or those who have no faculty for wit and humor. Such analysts will lower the importance of dream interpretation, no matter what evidence you present. Finally, there are analysts who, for some other reason, have never had the opportunity to learn how to listen to, understand, and work with dreams.

Let me call the reader's attention to Greenson's severe condemnation of psychoanalysts "with preconceived and rigid theoretical notions" who "have prefabricated interpretations for all types of patients" and "those who are predominantly devoted to theory conservation or theoretical innovations." Because of the importance of the matter, I invite the reader to contrast Greenson with writers such as Fürstenau who are representative of the dogmatic, prefabricated approach.

So are they all, all honourable men!

SHAKESPEARE

Robert J. Stoller

Let us hear more of the views of Stoller (Colby & Stoller, 1988):

Most people, including analysts, read less of the analytic literature than they would if it were written more simply. Second, the reader may suspect that the murky writing hides murky thinking, with the nasty possibility that the writer knows he is covering up his murky mind.

One can see how verbiage is used to make us (and the author) believe that precise enough measurements are in hand to support convincing generalizations on an aspect of human behavior. Since this style is the ordinary manner of communication among analysts, we really should be more diffident in accusing nonanalysts of unjustly accusing us of being unscientific.

When an analyst, in a clinical description that is to confirm a theory, uses words such as the following, do we know what is meant? Are we not expected to believe that they strengthen the argument, add weight to the evidence, make the premise scientific? *When no data are given* – no numbers, no measurements on any scale – what do these otherwise useful words mean: more, less, many, some, most, immense, significant, highly significant, very, few, discernible, considerable, numerous, inordinate, persistent, recurring, almost, rare, rather rare, by no means rare, not infrequently rare, it is more than likely that, severe, intense, extraordinary, truly extraordinary, and so on. (Let me briefly undertake to essay a try at attempting, in a rather small yet not totally insignificant way, a perhaps not completely exaggerated example: ". . . not at all infrequently rare, in fact, perhaps, often possibly not at all infrequently rare, even bordering on common.") In this way, supposedly, the demand to honor the economic viewpoint in metapsychology is met.

On and on. And never the data that could let the audience also judge whether an occurrence is, as the author says, massive, extraordinary, usual, normal, influential, mitigating, contributory, or significant. Arguments are won by means of sentence structure.

Words drawn from the natural sciences are the best; though they start humbly as metaphors, they soon transmute our ideas into true science. We use odd locutions, such as "It came to be understood," so that we do not have to make clear in our report that *we* made the interpretation to the patient, who never really understood it but just acquiesced and in that way made us almost aware we did not really understand either. To admit that the proofs of our treasured theories are so precarious would ruin the our-science we have built in us.

Fustian; bombast (perhaps even fustianistically bombastical, if not vice versa); orotundity, platitudinous ponderosity, polysyllabic profundity, pompous prolixity, rodomontade.

Certainly this may be possible. It is of no small significance, after all, that there may arise the possibility that . . .

Does anyone consciously record these devices? We absorb them "unthinkingly" as we read, and so did the referees for the journals and books that accepted these writings. This gabbling is our model, our disguise, an illness. Analysts are so forgiving (of ourselves, at any rate). Surely, you say, these rhetorical devices are only stylistic or metaphoric. Surely they are, not to say, in addition: without doubt, indeed, of course, unquestionably, positively, absolutely. And also obviously, assuredly, definitely, decidedly, clearly, unequivocally, unmistakably, undoubtedly (if not indubitably), undeniably, indisputably, incontestably, incontrovertibly, irrefutably, doubtlessly, by all means (perhaps even by all manner of means), in all events, make no mistake about it, and beyond the shadow of a doubt. For, when all is said and done, it goes without saying.

Freud, by his example, gives those who follow, permission to rattle like that. Freud: "No doubt it is conceivable that there may also be . . ."

If I concentrate on my concern with the definitions of our psychoanalytic vocabulary, sentences turn to gas.

Being mostly a clinician, I am of course forever dissatisfied at not understanding well enough and not being a good enough therapist. So I want help: tell me what actually occurs in the treatment whence you drew your ideas so that words such as these come to life: persistence, primitive, ego, component, deprives, remaining, considerable, amount, energy, interferes, full, development. I cannot translate these words into precise, tangible clinical data; that, doctor, is your responsibility. And it is not just that one sentence, for that sentence is embedded in a whole paper written in the same style. And the paper is part of an issue of a journal that is part of a volume that is part of a series that is part of the literature, a literature swollen with that kind of communicating. Phallic prostheses. "She always took something (a corsage, a napkin, a book of matches) from each boy to put into her file. It must be something concrete, like the hair, which analysis had shown represented her mother's pubic hair and hidden penis, her father's penis, and her little brother's penis." Maybe analysis showed that, but the author did not.

In real sciences when a rule or finding has been tested and repeatedly confirmed, there is no need – except in a historical study – to credit the discoverer; the discovery has become common knowledge. In analysis, we cite back for generations with only a few of our ideas so acceptable that we do not need "Freud said." Psychoanalysts act as if a field becomes a science by promise and proclamation rather than demonstration.

If, as some say, certain analytic propositions can only be tested on the couch, then analysis is not much of a science. We cannot (at least we have not done so yet) validate any of our theories in the clinical situation. And if not there, then where? How can our field be a science if no concept, word, theory, or idea is definitely ruled out except by being shouted down or anathematized? Why the tendency to splits and cults? Because there is no accepted technique, in the way there is in true sciences, for practitioners to agree on "yes" or "no." (Though consensus is no proof, either, of course.) Nagel's point is pretty well known by now to analysts: "A theory must not be formulated in such a manner that it can always be construed and manipulated so as to explain whatever the actual facts are, no matter whether controlled observation shows one state of affairs to obtain or its opposite." Collins reminds us of "the . . . problem of psychoanalysis as a scientific method in which interpretations had the status of experimental hypotheses that had somehow to be tested without contamination by an experimenter whose prestige was intimately involved in their credibility."

In analytic treatment, we can never say something one way, observe the effects, and then go back to the same situation and give a different response, thereby creating an experiment. To report what happened to colleagues and then ask their opinion of what should have happened next is also no experiment. To record what happened and then replay it to get their opinions would only demonstrate that each colleague interprets the clinical moment differently. Even the consensus we believe we have built among ourselves in regard to clinical concepts (such as transference, repression, unconscious forces) has not carried us much beyond that early stage of scientific method: naturalistic observation illuminated by, at best, a brilliant observer.

Yet, the following exemplifies a common belief: "From one point of view, every psychoanalysis represents [why 'represents'; why not 'is'?] a validating, replicating experiment of previously existing findings and theories. To the degree that psychoanalysts have been able to report their findings, there is a high level of *consensual validation* of findings and general agreement upon the nature of certain phenomena occurring within this dyad experiment. There is the reservation in scientific validation of this nature, that each psychoanalytic worker may carry a bias toward discovering only those findings that have already been reported, and may have overlooked or not 'seen' other data that may exist."

One – analyst or patient – can be quoted almost accurately. Perhaps only a word is changed, or an inflection, or the context, and yet the whole thing is now somehow all wrong. (This must be one reason why most public figures fear and hate most reporters. Though even worse can be the accurate, in-context quote.) The meanings and communications in a process as intimate as an analysis do not occur through words alone, but, as everyone knows, in nonverbal expressions, most of which are subliminal or deeper. (If a transcript shows me saying "Oh, yeah," how can you know what I meant: comfort, kindness, sarcasm, boredom, comprehension?)

We ought not to equate science and psychoanalysis. At the least, the stupefying use of quotes from authorities indicates that psychoanalytic (like canonical and talmudic) scholars operate from a different meaning of "evidence" than is fitting for a scientist.

Analysts never reach the point in their descriptions at which the question of reliability arises, for their descriptions are vague, the terms badly defined, and the data at the mercy of the fierce editing processes (e.g. countertransference, the restrictions of language) that transform experience into communication. It is monstrous of analysts to claim that analysis is a science. We do not even report what *we* do – experience – and how that has influenced what the patient experiences. ("Following my interpretation, the patient understood that . . .") Let Freud's statement that he never in his practice abused suggestion exemplify the endless times when we must accept a declaration because, as different from genuine science, the data are not available. Instead of observations, there is a fight in which one side argues that, for instance, Freud can be taken at his word because he is Freud while the other argues that he cannot. But all the reasons mobilized cannot tell us what happened in his office. [Lustman says:] "Psychoanalytic treatment is the basic method of psychoanalytic research. As clinical research, at bedrock it is the method of the expert observer and judge. *The reliability of the research depends upon the reliability of the analysis* . . . The controls on this are better within psychoanalysis than any other treatment method, because of the extensive personal analysis of the analyst, the rigor of his training, and his continuing self-analysis. In addition, the method of supervisory consultations can be used as a control if uncertainty exists."

Who believes this?

Can an accurate report of an analytic treatment be presented? Of course not. Analysis is a process. Yet it must appear in the literature as if it were mostly episodes of understood dreams, salient interpretations, obstacles overcome, accurate reconstructions, and resulting moments of insight and relief, softened by understandings that such reports cannot reproduce the realities of the treatment. The actualities, such as the working through that keeps us at it for years, are beyond the reach of even the best writers!

In the play about the Caine mutiny, there is a remarkable line: "We all have to earn a living, but it makes a great difference how we do it."

Is there any cause in nature that makes these hearts hard?

SHAKESPEARE

John E. Gedo

Continuing to review problems that blight our profession, let us now look at some meaningful statements by Gedo. They are from his introduction to this book and are repeated here for the convenience of the reader.

As American psychiatry has increasingly espoused a reductionistic biological orientation, it has attracted a shrinking number of medical graduates, and those who do choose this specialty tend to be among the less able students. (Statistics about those matters are regularly compiled and published in periodicals devoted to medical education.) . . . In every institute there are many "problem candidates" who have no hope of mastering the skills required to perform adequate clinical work.

Many of those individuals, Gedo continues, should have been turned away as unqualified in the first place, and "in fairness to them, they should be advised to drop out" as their deficiencies become apparent to the faculty. Instead, they are allowed to continue and are finally granted a "compassionate graduation."

> The minimal criteria [for graduation] are now periodically breached by allowing the analyses, either those of the analysts-to-be or those of their analysands, to be conducted in fewer than four visits per week; by providing less supervision than is necessary to ensure competent management of cases; or by graduating candidates who have not achieved a successful termination with any of their patients – presumably because the delay in reaching the goal is not attributable to any deficiency in the student. . . .
>
> Although [the] certification procedure seems quite lax in comparison with the procedures in other disciplines, voices for egalitarianism and a larger membership have succeeded in eliminating certification as a criterion of eligibility for membership in the American [Psychoanalytic Association]. In other words, membership no longer implies anything beyond graduation from a local institute. About a decade ago, approximately half of such graduates were certified when they applied for membership in the American, although some who failed initially were subsequently approved if they submitted better case reports. (I am certain that that possibility led to the creation of a great deal of low-quality fiction.) At any rate, the ranks of the American have been considerably expanded by the ingathering of graduates who could not be certified. . . .
>
> Over the past generation . . . the increasingly biological orientation of most psychiatry departments has contracted such opportunities for psychoanalysts, whether they have a background in psychiatry or in clinical psychology. . . .
>
> Of course, psychoanalytic educators can always follow Candide and cultivate their private gardens – or private practices. But academicians are understandably reluctant to fall back to the position of mere providers of services. Moreover, the very fact of being members of the

faculty of a psychoanalytic institute gives analysts an opportunity to develop private practices of an advantageous type – practices more focused on the performance of analytic work proper than on other forms of psychological therapy. . . .

Achieving training analyst status is the easiest way to obtain a steady supply of analytic referrals. In certain communities it may well be the only way. Of course, many observers feel that training analyses do not provide the conditions required for optimal analytic work. But that problem may be diminishing as a result of general acceptance of the rule that the analyst provides no information about his work to the institute.

All in all, then, we expect psychoanalytic institutes to provide instruction to most applicants *willing to pay*, in preference to persevering in self-defeating efforts to uphold the training standards proclaimed in their bulletins. . . .

Patients ready to undertake psychoanalysis are very rare. Analysands are not born; they are created through careful preparation. To accomplish that task, the therapist who has been consulted must be convinced that he can do a better job for the patient if they jointly choose the method of psychoanalysis. . . .

I am convinced that the presence in a community of a significant number of effective analysts will actually increase the number of patients who will seek analytic assistance. The most effective advertising for any method of treatment is word-of-mouth – the recommendation of a satisfied patient, particularly one whose improved adaptation is easily observable. We may also put the matter conversely: If the pragmatically oriented American consumer has turned away from psychoanalysis as a preferred method of therapy for personality disorders, the most important reason for that disaffection may well be that as actually performed by its practitioners today, *that form of treatment has not been sufficiently effective.*

The activities of graduate analysts cannot be monitored, but the unsatisfactory results of analyses performed
by trainees have been widely reported. . . . The damaging
effects of poor work by trainees on the public reputation of
psychoanalysis should not be underestimated.

Former patients who are bitter or discouraged or outraged about their analytic experiences often share their
grievances with anyone willing to listen. Institutes are often
more concerned with giving candidates every opportunity
to "make it," whatever that may mean, *than they are with
protecting the patients whose analyses are botched by marginal
students*. It is by no means unusual to encounter candidates
in good standing who have provoked more than a half-
dozen patients into flight shortly after starting analysis with
them. My experience as a visitor to various institutes where
I have personally observed a score of ongoing supervisory
sessions has led me to conclude *that no more than 15 to 20
percent of the ongoing analyses about which I heard were conducted in a manner that had any chance of success. The supervisors were almost always aware of the candidates'
unsatisfactory performance but seldom expressed skepticism
about their suitability for the profession*.

In the present context, however, I raise this matter not
to argue for more stringent criteria of candidate selection and
progression – although such policy changes are certainly
desirable. I do so to examine the implications of *the all-but-
universal lack of concern on the part of all participants for the lamentable outcome of most analyses conducted under institute
auspices. I should, in fact, put the issue more strongly, for lack of
concern is the more benign form of official reaction to such failures. It is actually just as common to hear contemptuous statements about various qualities or behaviors of the patients who did
not achieve a satisfactory analytic result – as if every analysand
always got his just deserts*. (Italics added)

Referring to frequently encountered views of analysts regarding their
profession:

It is characteristic of such belief systems that they are unaltered by the outcome of the performance of the prescribed ritual. The happy results attributable to chance alone suffice to confirm believers in their faith. Failures are invariably attributed either to insufficient attention to liturgical purity or to the unworthiness of the petitioner. Psychoanalyses carried out in that spirit are equivalent to medieval trials by ordeal; poor results mean either that the analyst did not carry out the task with the requisite sacred fervor or that the patient was irredeemably wicked.

Unfortunately, that spirit of esoteric ritual is widely prevalent within psychoanalysis, and indifference about the outcome of analyses conducted by less-than-competent candidates (or graduates, for that matter) is by no means the only evidence pointing to the corruption of its scientific essence. To cite one further indication of the presence of such regression to magical ideation, witness the widespread tolerance of the use of ready-made interpretive schemata — a tolerance of inadmissible dogmatism that is thrown into bold relief by the contrasting attitude or moralistic outrage that even minor proposals for technical innovation, however well-reasoned they may be, are likely to evoke. In other words, the outward *forms* of psychoanalytic therapy are viewed as sacrosanct by our cultists; at the same time, those subverters of scientific methodology silently lay claim to the esoteric wisdom of the guru or the Zen master. . . .

Kohut rightly emphasized that training analysis may serve the function of perpetuating such a priestly conception of the analytic role.

One often hears calls for restricting the application of the psychoanalytic treatment method to the narrow segment of the patient population consisting of those who can allegedly profit from the use of a "classical" technique – that is, from an exclusive resort to interpretation of intrapsychic conflicts that manifest themselves in the analysis in the form of transference and resistance. Even if we granted the dubious claim that patients actually exist who require nothing more in the way of analytic intervention, adopting such a policy would amount to reducing psychoanalysis to a role of insignificance and relegating the vast majority of patients to nonanalytic therapeutic methods.

Of course, Gedo's complaint is just one out of many that have been raised over the years by open-minded analysts. They have felt that the claim of analysis to be the foremost cultural and intellectual beacon is incompatible with the verbose scholasticism and narrow-minded dogmatism so widely prevalent.

Most assuredly, after all those necessary but depressing verities, the reader needs some fun. I found these clever comments by Jay Haley in a book review in the quarterly journal PSYCHOANALYTIC BOOKS:

> Skill in oneupmanship has raised extraordinary problems when analysts compete with one another at meetings of psychoanalytic associations. No other gathering of people exhibits so many complicated ways of gaining the upper hand. Most of the struggle at an analytic meeting takes place at a rather personal level, but the manifest content involves attempts to (1) demonstrate who was closest to Freud or can quote him most voluminously, and (2) who can confuse the most people by his daring extension of Freud's terminology. . . . The manipulation of language is the most startling phenomenon at an analytic meeting. Obscure terms are defined and redefined by even more obscure terms as analysts engage in furious theoretical discussions . . . the area for debate becomes the process within the dark and dank interior of the patient. Attempting to outdo one another in explanations of the bizarre insides of patients, each speaker is constantly interrupted by shouts from the back of the hall as, "Not at all! You're confusing an id impulse with a weak ego boundary!" or "heaven help your patients if you call *that* cathexis!" Even the most alert analyst soon develops an oceanic feeling as he gets lost in flurries of energy theories, libidinal drives, instinctual forces, and superego barriers. The analyst who can most

thoroughly confuse the group leaves his colleagues feeling frustrated and envious (one-down emotions). The losers return to their studies to search their minds, dictionaries, science fiction journals, and Freud for even more elaborate metaphorical flights in preparation for the next meeting.

The professionals cited here are but a few of many who refer to fundamental shortcomings that pervade the many areas of the "behavioral sciences" – psychotherapy, psychoanalysis, psychology, sociology, and others – and related educational activities. We are dealing with a vast array of diversified professional activities within a wide and loosely defined framework. The reader will remember the great number of professionals whose work we critically discussed and who are active in such varied areas as neurobiology, psychology, and the sleep laboratory. As a curiosity, we have cited Reiser, who affirms that a huge number of disciplines and subdisciplines have direct impact on our work and thus need to be mastered.

To attempt to determine the causes of those shortcomings, we will have to use the phrase "system of systems" (for lack of a better term) to refer to the many professional groupings and subgroupings in our field, as well as those in related educational endeavors. As those entities are often in conflict with each other or barely related, it is fortunate that we will use the phrase only briefly. However unsatisfactory the term "system" is, I hope my use of it will become more understandable as we proceed. Here one runs into a similar problem to that encountered when one refers to the "financial establishment": it can be plausibly argued that there is no such "establishment," and one can point to the fierce, often ruinous, competition in that area of activity. Of course, one could avoid all those complications and potential confusion by using a simple, honest, and realistic term, namely, "our industry," even though that may run counter to the rationalizations of a multitude of colleagues.

For our purposes, we need to determine the major factors that are the common denominators in the "system of systems" that underlie our activities and bind them together. John E. Mack, a professor of psychiatry at the Harvard Medical School and a man of social concern, has coined a phrase that is applicable here: "malignant professionalism." It refers to the fact that the great diversification and specialization in the professions lead to a "fragmentation of responsibility" and, in consequence, to an actual abrogation and denial of responsibility for the consequences of one's actions. For those of us who are deeply concerned about the quality of patient care, it is a crucial issue. Few complain about the status quo of psychotherapy; no one assumes responsibility for it! I will elaborate shortly.

The statements by Greenson and Stoller quoted earlier follow closely along the lines of our findings in this chapter, as do many of Gedo's comments. Where there are differences of opinion, they are partly due to dissimilar life experiences. Gedo arrived in the United States as a preadolescent. I am considerably older, and I remained in Europe until the end of my studies. My mentors and friends were renowned psychiatrists during the early years of the psychoanalytic movement, and I benefited from their comments and criticisms regarding the events in those years.

To understand the causes for the deficiencies in our field, we need to consider the problems related to the selection, training, and competence of practitioners. In that area Gedo's experiences and mine converge. Earlier in this chapter I spoke of the invaluable information we were able to gather from the many interviews conducted with former patients and people who had been active in the mental health field, quite a number of them in teaching and training. Gedo's estimate that only about 15 percent of the candidates are adequate seems near the mark. Consider this, however: There are a great many other training institutes that do not count themselves among the limited number of institutes accredited by the American Psychoanalytic Association. For example, in the greater New York area alone, there are some 60 to 70 training facilities for analysts and psychotherapists, all struggling to attract candidates for training. For most practitioners, finding patients for analysis and psychotherapy is not easy. By forming institutes, they hope to secure a steadier source of revenue. Much of the income of the faculty members of those institutes is derived from the training, supervision, and analysis of their candidates, most of whom have degrees in medicine, psychology, or social work. Thus any person who has such a degree has access to psychotherapy training and can end up with a certificate.

Let us stay with the 15 percent figure suggested by Gedo and consider the following: It is not likely that these adequate candidates will have the good fortune to have as their teachers, supervisors, and training analysts precisely those 15 percent of the faculty members who are competent and who would provide adequate training. Thus most of the talented students will definitely not obtain satisfactory training. That creates major difficulties for them in their subsequent professional work and reduces their satisfaction; obviously, the more solid the know-how of a practitioner, the easier it is for him to tackle the problems of his patients.

It is no secret that many analysts and therapists were dissatisfied with their training analysts and supervisors. Once one is in a training program, requesting a change may be impossible. I am less optimistic than Gedo regarding training analysis. Even though the candidate is assured that the training analyst will not share his impressions with institute colleagues, that assurance does not soothe the apprehensions of the candidate, particularly if his fears are unconscious. Furthermore, the candidate knows that no words are necessary; the analyst's subtle facial expression, or a simple gesture, can communicate his opinion of the candidate to the other faculty members. All that, as discussed in many places, creates psychological impediments to a genuine analysis. Yet there are fierce advocates of the training analysis who nevertheless critically point out the obstacles inherent in Freud's attempt to analyze his daughter; she too would be reluctant to speak with complete frankness to her father.

Of course, there are many therapists who are not caught in the rigid situation existing within the training institutes. But for them, also, it is most difficult to find teachers, supervisors, and analysts of excellence.

None of that is a revelation. It is as trite as it is sad. I repeat it here only to remind the reader.

Gedo is right to complain about the deterioration of psychotherapeutic training and professional standards. Looking back, one remembers much excitement, enthusiasm, and hope among students and teachers who devoted themselves to psychodynamic therapy. In retrospect, it seems that times were easier then, less stressful. The cities were not crowded and were more pleasant, the restaurants less expensive and far better, and even if one was poor, as most students were, life did not have to be miserable. Yet one can also remember the many decades when psychoanalytic institutes were fortresses of dogmatic rigidity and intolerance, reminding us of the long, dark night that enveloped medicine when Galen's doctrines prevailed. Gifted young people desirous of becoming psychotherapists but too intelligent to accept dogmas unquestioningly ran into insurmountable obstacles and were lost to our profession. The open-minded and talented analysts who chose not to abandon their institutes simply could not assert themselves.

> Learning will be cast into the mire,
> And trodden down under the hoofs of a swinish pack.
>
> BURKE

> The mental health field is akin to politics. The best realize our limited understanding while those who know least often claim great knowledge and push their way to the top.
>
> STANLEY LESSE

Stanley Lesse

Let us review other obstacles to adequate psychotherapeutic training. Obviously, psychiatrists do need extended medical training. For those who follow up with additional analytic or psychotherapy training, however, the road is more than arduous.

Here too we find many regrettable shortcomings. In my introductory chapter I briefly quoted Stanley Lesse's opinions regarding this matter as he presented them in the AMERICAN JOURNAL OF PSYCHOTHERAPY. Lesse, the late coeditor of our companion volume, offered these comments, about "the training of incompetent clinicians," for this chapter:

> In many editorials, we have called to the reader's attention various factors that have served as polluting effects inhibiting an orderly transition from a past oriented, anachronistic university, medical school and hospital system to a unified health sciences structure that will be optimally applicable and beneficial to our future society as it is likely to be. We

feel that the pathetic and even dangerous trends that have developed in our medical training programs must be exposed, re-evaluated, and radically changed. We must face the unfortunate reality that the massive, propagandistic pyrotechnics that have increasingly characterized our medical schools, research institutes, and teaching hospitals conceal the unfortunate fact that the quality of medical clinicians currently being trained has deteriorated and is decidedly less than it should and could be.

Despite the "pretty" window dressing in the medical school curriculum in the form of additional hours allotted to psychiatry, psychodynamic medicine, and medical sociology, in reality our current crop of medical students and young staff physicians too often view patients as so many biologic-psychologic-sociologic fragmentations. While some of them lament with justification the inequities in the medical services available to various groups and regions, many of those who pontifically expound upon their concepts of social righteousness evidence very little empathy or positive feeling tone for the anxious physio-psycho-social being that is the individual patient. Their concern about man as a social group is to be applauded. However, their relative lack of concern and apparent insensitivity to man as an individual is lamentable and leads one to hold their broad social attitudes suspect. This seeming depreciation of the individual patient is a threat to meaningful progress in the mental health sciences.

Those who currently dominate our teaching hospitals and medical schools must bear the blame for these tragic trends. This group includes (1) hospital administrators, (2) medical school deans, (3) the chairmen of the clinical departments, and (4) the full-time, tenured, laboratory oriented faculty members who increasingly have monopolized clinical teaching.

We emphasized that the medical administrator (whether he is a hospital director or medical school dean), has become the dominant voice in organized medicine. His central interests and awareness are group oriented. He is the medical version of the corporate head of a large, hierarchically ordered industrial organization, and in harmony with his industrial brother he commonly professes love for mankind as a whole, but often appears to harbor distrust or even dislike for man considered as an individual.

We also emphasized that the medical administrator introduced Madison Avenue huckster techniques to the medical scene, for he is at his best as a public relations man appealing to the N.I.H. [National Institutes of Health] money dispensers or to politicians' medical patriotism.

His contact with the individual patient, medical student or resident physician is at best circuitous and often nonexistent, for authority is exercised through committees that all too frequently serve no better purpose than the investigation of the work of other committees. It is a ponderous, expensive, inefficient, impersonal system better suited to the production of automobiles or television sets than for the humanistic treatment of individual patients or the training of humanistic physicians. In the main, the administrators surround themselves with men and women of limited vision whose allegiance too often is directed primarily toward preserving their carefully nurtured niches in the organizational structure.

The administrator in his selection of department heads commonly appoints men who are cast in his own image, good organization men, men chosen for their ability as administrators and fund raisers rather than for proven worth as clinicians and teachers. The day is fast disappearing when a department head is appointed because he is the most knowledgeable clinician or a scintillating and inspiring instructor. With increasing frequency he delegates all teaching responsibilities to assistants, until finally he often becomes defensive about his fading clinical capacities. Unfortunately, very few of these men have the capacities to impart an appreciation of the sensitivity and finesse that go into the making of an expert clinician.

The inadequacies of full-time, tenured clinical faculty are often striking. Lamentably, from a clinical standpoint, many of the clinical staff members garner their clinical experience, in the main, from limited exposure in the outpatient clinic or from periodic assignments on hospital wards. This type of exposure is inadequate to develop clinical expertise. This type of physician-teacher is a clinical dilettante. His experience is inadequate to permit the detection and illustration of the nuances of clinical diagnosis and treatment that only intense contact with patients can develop.

Too often this type of man is a "nine-to-fiver" who literally does not comprehend the concept of true and total responsibility for a sick individual. To this type of pseudo-clinician the patient is seemingly born upon entering the hospital, and for all practical purposes does not exist after being discharged. His comprehension of the adaptive problems that await the discharged hospital patient is woefully inadequate.

Finally, this type of physician is too often cast in the role of a marionette being controlled directly and indirectly by strings maneuvered by administrators. The "clever" young physician learns to dance to the tune of the administratively controlled cash register. Independent, free-thinking clinicians and clinical researchers have been effectively and thoroughly eliminated from positions of authority or combed out of many institutions altogether.

Since psychiatric and psychological specialty clinics are of much interest, I am presenting here some quotes on the subject from Lesse's editorial in the July 1983 issue of the AMERICAN JOURNAL OF PSYCHOTHERAPY.

The Growing Abundance of Psychiatric
and Psychologic Specialty Clinics
As the industrial era fades and is superseded by a rapidly developing postindustrial society, traditional role playing

becomes dramatically altered. An all-pervading trend toward superspecialization characterizes this current sociotechnologic revolution. Our culture pays a bonus to those individuals who develop increasingly finite expertise, who know more and more about less and less. This observation represents a general truth; it has both positive and negative implications. These superspecialists have become more often than not our heroes and heroines. They command the highest salaries; they are in the public eye; they are the men and women on horseback in this, the last quarter of the twentieth century.

Superspecialization dominates all aspects of the health sciences, including psychiatry and psychology. A seemingly limitless variety of new titles adorns the doors along university or hospital or clinic corridors.

A plethora of specialty clinics run by psychiatrists, psychologists, or social workers is an outgrowth of this phenomenon. Specialty clinics have literally exploded onto the clinical scene during the past ten years, but especially during the last five years. Many are extensions of university departments of psychiatry, psychology, or social work; others are offshoots of hospital services. An ever-increasing number of specialty clinics are franchised spin-offs of private organizations that have facilities over much of the country.

In general, these clinics are of two types. One group is organized to emphasize a specific technical procedure. For example, there are approximately two hundred types of psychotherapy and there are clinics extolling the virtues of each. In these clinics it is a rarity that the treatment is designed specifically for the patient; rather the patient is commonly molded to fit the therapy. In similar fashion, clinics designed for the dispensing of various psychotropic drugs have become increasingly common. It is extremely infrequent that any of these clinics will combine organic with appropriately designed psychotherapeutic procedures in a planned, organized fashion.

Very recently we have become deluged by a rash of clinics specializing in different symptoms, syndromes, or illnesses. In brief summation, we now have a myriad of clinics espousing expertise in anxiety, phobia, depression, schizophrenia, borderline states, behavior disorders, alcoholism, sexual dysfunction, gambling, drug addiction, hereditary disorders, and so forth and so forth.

We want to give recognition where recognition is due. Many specialty clinics serve a major purpose either in terms of their clinical roles or as research organizations. Some are well-conceived, well-run, humanistically oriented facilities staffed by competent clinicians and researchers. A few have made meaningful contributions to our understanding of various psychotropic drugs or psychotherapeutic disorders; a few have broadened our understanding and treatment of some clinical symptoms and syndromes.

However, there are awesome psychiatric and psychological specialty clinics that are far less than they should be. Some are set up to attract attention to the clinic chief, a type of ego trip; others are vehicles whose main purpose is to attract funding; some are set up primarily to give legitimacy to surplus staff personnel; many are out-and-out gimmicks to make big bucks. The last point pertains most particularly to some of those franchised clinics that are beginning to dot the landscape like so many fast-food outlets.

Too often, specialty clinics are promoted in tasteless fashion by the press or mass media bent on sensationalism. At times the interviewers or broadcasters remind one of so many shills recommending this or that clinic with an aura of dogmatic certainty.

The quality of care varies broadly from clinic to clinic. They often are staffed with relatively inexperienced transient personnel in the form of students, residents or junior staff members. More often than not, experienced senior staff members are not intimately or directly involved in patient care or patient investigation. The franchised clinics could be staffed by a crew of inadequately trained, naive personnel.

Superspecialization at times results in patients being viewed in a fragmented fashion, like an organ inappropriately detached from the body — specific symptoms or syndromes defined in splendid isolation from the broad, integrated psycho-bio-social whole that is the patient. Patients are literally rushed through some clinics. Specialty clinics may narrowly focus on this or that symptom or syndrome, while failing to recognize a broader, more serious clinical matrix. For example, severe underlying depression is too often missed or inadequately weighed in patients attending phobia clinics.

Certainly Lesse's comments are merely samples of a vast spectrum of serious, often outrageous, shortcomings.

Robert S. Wallerstein

As bad as all that is, the future looks even bleaker. What follows is quoted from "The Future of Psychoanalysis," a chapter by Robert S. Wallerstein that appears in THE CHALLENGE FOR PSYCHOANALYSIS AND PSYCHOTHERAPY: SOLUTIONS FOR THE FUTURE, this book's companion volume.

After describing the situation prevailing during his student years, which allowed for more intensive training in psychotherapy, Wallerstein continues:

Presenting the picture of the nature and conditions of psychiatric training and practice at the point at which I came into the field in 1949, just over 40 years ago, highlights clearly I think the vast changes that have taken place when we compare all this with the nature and conditions of training and practice today, especially as we hold to the guiding thread of concern for the transformation undergone by the psychotherapy enterprise — its place in the overall psychiatric scheme of things — over this time. I won't try to trace all these kaleidoscopic changes in the nature, the scope, and the content of psychiatry over these four decades stepwise and sequentially over time. I have spelled those out at length elsewhere and will merely state them here in very condensed form.

First, of course, is the literal explosion of knowledge in neuroscience and neurobiology, especially in its molecular biological and molecular genetic dimension with the spectacular growth of intelligence of brain-behavior interrelations in the domain of mental and emotional disorder, with specific scientific focus on the elucidation of genetic markers of mental dysfunctions and on the multiplicity of interlocking and interacting neurotransmitters and cell receptors. Biological psychiatry has rapidly become a most significant and exciting scientific arena and is now the research and clinical focus of many academic psychiatric careers and major psychiatric space and money resources.

The second and related major development, also in the biological realm, is the modern era of psychoactive drugs as a central therapeutic modality in the management and treatment of the psychiatrically ill, especially the sicker, psychotic patients whom we psychodynamically trained psychiatrists have tended anyway to avoid and who have been historically such a heavy, collective, undischarged social responsibility of our profession – for long warehoused in large public mental hospitals, often neglected at best, and badly abused at worst. I do not need to recount the great proliferation of psychoactive drugs and of classes of such drugs since the inauguration of the modern psychoactive drug era in 1954 – the major tranquilizers or neuroleptics, the antipsychotic drugs; the minor tranquilizers, the so-called antianxiety drugs, the several classes of antidepressants, or the very special drug lithium with its so poorly understood effects in relation to manic and depressive disorders. Suffice it to say that the existence of all these drugs has vitally changed the practice characteristics of psychiatrists (not to speak of the ministrations to emotionally and behaviorally troubled individuals by nonpsychiatric physicians) and has forced accommodations in the psychotherapeutic arena where adjuvant or concomitant use of psychoactive drugs has become commonplace, especially with the less well-integrated patients, for the most part those outside the normal-neurotic range, and where understanding of drug-behavior interactions and of the psychological meanings of such chemically induced mood and behavior changes has become part of what we must know and teach in our psychotherapeutic working.

The third major dimension of change in the field of psychiatry is in the psychological arena. Here I need only point out that psychoanalysis is no longer the unquestioned prevailing psychological theory guiding and illuminating our understanding of the human mind and its aberrations. It has now been challenged by the astonishing growth of two fundamentally different and competing psychological paradigms, the one the learning-theory and stimulus-response conditioning model (partly classical, partly operant) with the behavior modification technology derived from it; and the other, attacking both psychoanalysis and behavior modification as being mechanistic and stripped of essential subjectivism and humanism, the so-called existentialist-phenomenological tradition of European philosophy and letters brought to America as humanistic psychology and leading to the whole encounter and human growth and potential movement, to some extent within our profession, and to a far larger extent, outside it. Of more practical consequence to those of us practicing and teaching dynamic psychotherapy is the encroachment of the behavioral technologies into our clinics and training programs, for example in the sex therapies, or the eating disorder clinics, both now popular arenas of subspecialization.

The fourth major dimension of change is in the social science (and social policy) arena. Here I want to mention another influence, as potent as the psychoactive drug revolution in transforming the character of modern American psychiatric and mental health practice, and that is the community mental health center movement, inaugurated by the

Kennedy legislation of 1963. This community mental health movement is clearly a new center of gravity in political power and in access to funding in the whole field of mental health and illness; it is also a succession of linked conceptualizations and ideologies, not necessarily all politically inspired, and many of them developed both before and outside the official community mental health movement. I refer to the concepts of the open hospital and the therapeutic community pioneered by Maxwell Jones in England, and of milieu therapy as designed by D. Ewen Cameron in Canada and further developed with psychoanalytic sophistication by Will Menninger and his colleagues at the Menninger Clinic in Topeka, Kansas, as well as the current and dominant concept of deinstitutionalization that has already carried us from the era when most of our sicker patients were kept, or rather, incarcerated, in our large public mental hospitals for very long periods of time, even for their whole lifetimes, to the current time when hospitalization is by and large very short and mainly for acute and unmanageable life crises and psychological decompensations and when most of even the very sick, chronically psychotic patients are managing (or not managing) in outpatient lives in the outside world – and where we now see the new untoward consequences of the deinstitutionalized life, the patients once neglected and abused in state hospitals, now often neglected and abused in board and care homes and cheap inner-city hotels, or worse yet, swelling the ranks of the homeless living on our streets. In any case, a host of major problems and issues that stamp the whole face of current mental health practice and that are necessarily a major concern of academic psychiatry in preparing its student for their professional life ahead.

Fifth, and last in this cataloging of the major dimensions of impact upon psychiatry over the last four decades, are the correlated developments of theory that relate to the changes in emphasis from the therapeutic to the preventive ameliorative models and from the idiosyncratically individual to the socially controlled family and group and social system concerns that characterize the philosophic thrust of the community mental health movement. Some of this theory was developed within psychoanalysis, such as crisis theory as innovated originally by Lindemann; most of it has been developed outside psychoanalysis, in academic sociology and social psychology, such as role theory, theories of deviance, theories of social group behavior, and social systems theory. Again, the main point is that there are other bodies of knowledge, social science knowledge, which are being brought to bear as explanatory frameworks upon many of the phenomena that are within the purview of psychiatry, and that in terms of the issues surfaced by the emphases on our crisis clinics and community mental health centers, are presumably better, in the sense of being more broadly encompassing or more directly relevant, or perhaps just more easily understandable or commonsensical as explanatory frameworks.

So much for the tabulation of some of the major developments within and around psychiatry in these four very fast-moving decades. All of them have found their way into the seminar sequences and the clinical rotations of the psychiatric residency training program. Though the typical residency is now a four year sequence, at least a half-year and up to a year in many of the programs is given back to what used to be in the separate internship year, rotations in general medicine, in neurology, and/or for those who look to futures as child psychiatrists, in pediatrics. In three to three and a half years of specifically psychiatric training experience, major rotations exist through inpatient services, which are no longer psychotherapy focused but rather are drug-management focused since lengths of stay are rarely, except in some very specialized clinical centers, longer than 30 days; through outpatient emergency rooms and crisis clinics and acute inpatient emergency units with their lengths of stay usually a week, or less if forced by the pressure of new admissions; through substance abuse wards and outpatient detoxification and methadone maintenance units; through consultation-liaison services; through specialized inpatient and/or outpatient geriatric units. Significant amounts of the so-called outpatient years are devoted to community mental health centers with their brief therapy and group therapy focus and often to specialty clinics like affective disorder clinics, all with their drug treatment and/or behavior treatment focus. All of these significant time allocations and major teaching and learning foci, it goes without saying, have been carved from the time once given to the teaching and learning of psychopathology, and psychodynamics, and psychotherapy, since these were the activities that once consumed almost the entire residency training and since they are anyway presumably more flexible in the more-or-less time that needs to be devoted to them.

And, of course, I should add to the many pressures that conduce to the diminution of the time and effort devoted to the teaching and the practice of psychotherapy, the pressures of the insurance carriers and the various governmental sources of third-party reimbursement whose concerns for cost-benefit balances and for demonstrated therapeutic efficacy of the reimbursed service have led inexorably to the progressive shortening of the coverage afforded to long-term individual psychotherapy in favor of brief therapy models, group therapy, and psychoactive drug management. *This of course has had an inevitably chilling effect upon the readiness of mental health care providers, whether institutional or individual, to offer intensive psychotherapy to the extent that it is truly indicated and clearly socially and individually useful.*

It would be a digression here to elaborate on *the conceptual and technical complexities of the process and outcome research* that would be necessary to establish the comparative efficacy of intensive psychotherapy vis-à-vis briefer or drug-centered approaches to the array of disorders in the psychopathological spectrum but suffice it to say that in terms of the criteria central to governmental and insurance carriers, concern for the relief and amelioration of presenting symptoms and disturbed or disturbing manifest behaviors, it is unlikely that intensive psychotherapy will be (or can be) established to be indubitably superior. Its putative benefits lie rather in the subtler and less measurable realms of enhanced life satisfaction and more effective and adaptive life functioning consequent to inner character and personality shifts and alterations. And beyond this, much of what we treat people for in intensive individual psychotherapy, gross dissatisfactions with the course of their lives, difficulties in the areas of interpersonal relationships or work adjustment, school or work inhibitions, etc., are not considered formal diseases by the third party payers for which they should expectably carry the treatment costs. After all, the inability of a graduate student to complete a doctoral thesis in comparative languages or in anthropology which will result in one less doctoral degree holder and one less academic career, is hardly considered a disease state for which an insurance program should provide treatment, no matter how tragic the career and life consequences for the disappointed and frustrated individual. And certainly the casting of disease criteria, reimbursable disease criteria, into DSM-III terms with its specific symptom criteria for illness has further compounded this problem. Again, all factors that will chill even further the ardor of the potential long-term psychotherapy provider.

Given all this as the context of changes that have occurred in psychiatry and in psychiatric practice since the time period of my own training into our discipline with which I began this presentation, where does that leave us today in relation to our concern for the well-being and the vitality of the psychotherapy enterprise, both the education for it and the continuing practice of it? It is clear from everything that I have recounted to this point of the major new components of contemporary psychiatric education that the teaching of the theory and the techniques of psychotherapy has been progressively and severely eroded in our training program curricula, even in those programs that have tried to resist the current tides and to maintain time-honored commitments to psychodynamic thinking and practice. Typically, in today's psychiatric residency programs, the third year of the four year sequence is designated as the "psychotherapy year." What this means in actual practice is that, given the other time demands, even in that year, even in the so-called committed programs, the expectation will be at most for 12 hours per week of individual psychotherapy, which for a maximum of 50 weeks, though almost nowhere are residents' vacations plus time away for educational leaves limited to but two weeks a year, would come to something a good deal less than 600 hours of logged time, i.e. the very maximum 12 hours for 50 weeks. Though there may be a patient or two seen in psychotherapy prior to that psychotherapy year, and some continuing of some of those third year patients into the fourth year (depending on other program pressures), except for that minority of residents within that minority of programs that have specialized psychotherapy tracks available for fourth year electives, the basic less than 600 hours of third year psychotherapy experience supplemented a little – often very little – in the second and fourth years becomes the totality of psychotherapy teaching in today's residency programs at their very most. Compare that with the 3,000 hours of psychotherapy experience typically logged by the residents in just about every program in the immediate post–World War II era in which I was trained and which was regarded then as what was minimally necessary for the residency training programs to feel satisfied that they were graduating residents qualified and competent to enter into independent practice with requisite skill and experience, individuals to whom they would be willing to refer private patients.

Lest you feel that this is too stark and exaggerated a contrast, let me quote from two articles which appeared just this year, 1990, in the AMERICAN JOURNAL OF PSYCHIATRY. The first is by Paul Mohl and six collaborators, the lead article in the January issue entitled, "Psychotherapy Training for the Psychiatrist of the Future." The article was the product of a joint task force of the Association for Academic Psychiatry and the American Association of Directors of Psychiatry Residency Training. It endeavored to lay out an *optimal* psychotherapy training program within the context of present-day psychiatry and its various parameters and constraints. In the first, PGY-I year, the program emphasis would be on clinical care, i.e., "diagnosis, crisis intervention, pharmacotherapy, and extensive history taking and treatment planning." And the "residents follow hospitalized patients with a primary focus on understanding the natural course and resolution with treatment [meaning psychoactive drug treatment] of major psychiatric illness, rather than the provision of psychotherapeutic treatment." This, incidentally, by way of contrast with my own initiation into psychiatry where I was thrown into 20 hours a week of scheduled psychotherapy from my very first day on a psychiatric service, buffered as best as possible against all my anxieties, by very intensive and very high-grade supervision by a senior psychoanalytic supervisor.

But to go on with this recounting. In the PGY-II year, "clinical care in the second postgraduate year largely involves hospitalized patients [meaning again, brief treatment via drugs and ward management, not psychotherapy], but assignments should also include at least two patients for whom psychotherapy is the predominant or exclusive form of treatment." Translated, this turns out to mean once-a-week psychotherapy, a maximum of two hours each week over the whole year or 100 hours in the hypothetical 50 week working year, but in most cases it would work out to half of that, one hour a week, or up to only 50 hours. PGY-III is of course the presumed big psychotherapy teaching year. Here the disappointing recommendation is "Clinical care during PGY-III consists of 4–7 psychotherapy hours per week and at least one patient who is seen more than once a week." Let's call that an average of six hours per week or up to 300 hours per year in the big psychotherapy teaching year, an official statement of optimal intent that is only half of the 600 hours that I had built into my word-picture of where we have come from the 3,000 hours of my own psychiatric residency training experience.

And then for the final residency year, the authors propose, "In PGY-IV, most residents will not add new long-term cases but will add cases that provide the opportunity to use a subspecialty form of psychotherapy." And these they had specified earlier in the article – brief psychotherapy, hypnosis, cognitive therapy, sexual therapy, etc. – all laudable perhaps, but not the same thing. They also say, "There should be some unsupervised cases during this year." Do those of us who have devoted many years to psychotherapy training and experience, both as students and as teachers, really feel that our residents are ready to do unsupervised work after so minimal an exposure to psychotherapy under supervision? I would submit that this is not an issue of mature adulthood and autonomy vs. infantilization as some would have it, but the kind of message it conveys of what we think constitutes adequate enough psychotherapy training and experience. Contrast that with the comment made to me recently by a senior psychoanalytic colleague who told me *that now after some 40 years of full-time clinical practice he has at last attained to the comfortable feeling that he really knows what he is doing when he treats his patients and feels that he can be of maximal help to them.*

What is to me the dismaying capstone to this article comes then towards the end when the authors ruefully acknowledge that only some residency training programs will have the resources (let alone the will) to meet even these, to me, extremely meager, training demands. They therefore state that for all the rest there is also a "model curriculum for minimum training in psychodynamic psychotherapy." To meet these objectives, each resident must spend a minimum of 200 hours treating patients with psychodynamic psychotherapy. These sessions must be at least weekly and last at least 45 minutes, and the purpose of each session must be to engage in psychodynamic, expressive, exploratory psychotherapy. Preferably these 200 or more hours of experience will extend over the entire training period of the general psychiatrist. Each resident should see at least four different patients, at least one for more than 50 sessions and at least one, preferably more than one, who is treated until termination. Given that the total four year residency program constitutes up to 8,000 scheduled hours, and the 200 psychotherapy experience hours constitute only 2-1/2 percent of that, one can well ask what other branch of medicine would consider as adequate *specialty* training, the devotion of 2-1/2 percent of its total training time to the treatment of but four patients, only one to completion, by the most characteristic, distinctive, and widely used treatment modality at its disposal?

What can be seen as a codicil to the article by this task force is one appearing three months later, in the April 1990 issue of the AMERICAN JOURNAL OF PSYCHIATRY, by Kenneth Altshuler entitled, "Whatever Happened to Intensive Psychotherapy?" Altshuler's article is based on a questionnaire survey of 212 psychiatric residency programs to which he secured 163 responses. To introduce just one of his dismaying findings, less than 40 percent of the respondent programs required any patients to be seen more than once a week within the total residency training period. This means that more than 60 percent of our programs graduate residents, into careers of psychiatric practice, who will never in their training period have seen any patient more than once a week. And of the 59 programs out of the 163 that do require some patients to be seen at least twice weekly, only 10 across the country require that there be at least three such twice weekly patients – the others divide into 21 programs that require one such and 28 program that require two.

This in sum total is the picture of psychotherapy training, 1990 style, across our nation's psychiatric residency programs. In this context it should be no surprise then that the American Association of Directors of Psychiatric Residency Training can have panel discussions at their annual meetings, not on how much psychodynamic psychotherapy experience and teaching there should be in a contemporary psychiatric residency, but on *whether* psychotherapy training should still be required or be only optional – optional for those who want to pursue that, now-called subspecialty within psychiatry as their career choice. Those who believe that psychotherapy training should be optional argue that there are so many knowledge areas in contemporary psychiatry that require full medical training for their proper understanding and utilization like neuroscience and its clinical applications in the psychopharmacological treatment of severe psychiatric disorders, and further that dynamic psychotherapy is the one area of psychiatric expertise that can be shared with, and learned equally well, by non-medical practitioners, who can then also practice it equally well and presumably less expensively, and that therefore the psychiatrist's relationship to psychotherapy can properly be confined to understanding the range of its indications and contraindications and the appropriate prescription for it by referral to the non-physicians, in a manner similar to referrals by orthopedic physicians of physiotherapy to be carried out by allied disciplines. Of course, ultimate medical control should be maintained and the psychiatrist must assume administrative and supervisory responsibilities for this prescribed psychotherapy carried out by other mental health professionals. Quite aside from the inevitable political turf battles with our fellow mental health practitioners in other disciplines over this no longer acknowledged assumption of medical-psychiatric hegemony in the mental illness treatment area, there is also the irony – which seems to have escaped the proponents of this position — *that the psychiatrist could be presumed to be in the position to supervise psychotherapy without ever having had the requisite training to himself or herself carry it out properly.* (Italics added)

There can be no doubt that in spite of such utterly insufficient training in psychotherapy, some of those psychiatrists will eventually engage in the part-time or full-time practice of psychotherapy and in the teaching of that discipline. The resulting deterioration of the already dismal standards in patient care and student instruction is beyond imagination.

I have presented many illustrations explaining my pessimistic evaluation of the status quo. Some more need to be added, however. The American Mental Health Foundation, like most mental health agencies, receives a huge number of letters from patients who have complaints. Of course, it is natural that we would receive mostly negative letters. Satisfied patients have no reason to write unless, owing to geographical dislocation or another reason, they request our assistance in finding suitable professional help. I will not select examples of dismal patient care from this ocean of complaints, since their objectivity and basis in fact is difficult to establish without further investigation. Rather, I will describe three situations of which I have direct personal knowledge. Since we have discussed problems connected with teaching hospitals and clinics, I have selected pertinent examples that occurred in those settings.

In this chapter we concern ourselves with the quality of psychotherapy. Without question, the subject of patient care, both in psychiatric outpatient facilities and in hospitals, requires intensive scrutiny and extensive discussion. Unfortunately, notwithstanding all the material we have gathered in the United States and in Europe and the urgency of the problem, it is impossible to examine the matter here beyond the few pages we are giving it. It would require a huge volume with hundreds of reports and the testimony of concerned and knowledgeable people to sufficiently describe the situations encountered. Many of the situations evidence dismal and cruel lack of concern for even the minimal well-being of the patients and failure to provide them with a minimum of valid psychotherapeutic assistance. Even though the facilities may be physically clean, many of them must be considered snake pits, causing additional suffering in the patients. Incredibly, many of the facilities are under the direct responsibility of professionals who have written extensively on psychoanalysis and psychotherapy, who claim special competence in it, and who propose "improved" theoretical models.

Many professionals claim that psychotherapeutic care for both hospitalized patients and outpatients has greatly deteriorated. Others assert the opposite. All I can do is briefly describe three situations out of many that I have witnessed over a period of some 50 years. Disconcerting though they are, they pale in comparison with the situations described in the letters we receive. A total disregard for the feelings and needs of the individual is evident in innumerable cases, both in the United States and in Europe.

Some 50 years ago there was a most prestigious private clinic located in Connecticut. It had beautiful grounds and catered mostly to the wealthy. In brochures it claimed to offer exceptional psychiatric and psychotherapeutic care. The fact is that the psychotherapy offered not only was minimal but was administered by inexperienced practitioners. Moreover, before visits by relatives, the patients were routinely given heavy doses of electric shock treatment. Naturally, when the relatives arrived, they found the patients confused and disoriented, a plausible reason for prolonging their stay at the sanatorium.

The following incident took place in a well-known hospital in the capital of a Western European country some 20 years ago. The chief psychiatrist, a frequent author on psychotherapy, was offering a "psychotherapy" session to a recently married farmer who had complained about impotency and the resulting feelings of despair and hopelessness. A local clinic had advised him to travel to this renowned hospital. The one-way trip required six hours.

The session, which took place in a large room with some 20 residents attending, consisted of the psychiatrist's asking the "patient" to report in intimate detail his sexual failures. The farmer, a sensitive man mortified by his experience, answered politely. But the pain of having to speak of his ordeal, particularly in front of so many people, was obvious.

When the psychiatrist asked the residents to pose questions to the man, they tactfully refrained from doing so.

After the meeting was over, I inquired what the treatment plan for the man would consist of. The answer was that this was the only "treatment session" the man would get for at least 10 months.

Another situation, which occurred in 1992, involved two hospitals of the highest rating, both located in New York City. Owing to tragic occurrences in her life, a retired and artistic woman in her 50s had become an alcoholic. To overcome the problem, she had entered psychotherapy and, by the time of the events I am about to relate, had made tangible progress. Because of recurring neck pains, her physician referred her for brief testing by a neurologist whose office was located in one of the hospitals referred to. Contrary to what he had arranged with her physician, and even before he gave her the test, the neurologist, noticing that the woman was shy and could be manipulated, told her that he would give her a second, more prolonged test that the referring physician had not requested. The test required that she spend the night in the hospital. The woman and her companion, a professor of nursing, told the neurologist that she would like to go home first to get the necessities for spending the night and the next morning in the hospital. The neurologist would have none of it.

The next morning the woman was upset at being in the hospital without even the simplest amenities. Even though the tests did not indicate anything abnormal, the neurologist declared that she was too upset to return home. Of course, the abrupt cutoff from alcohol, even though her intake was much reduced by this point, added to her distress. To make a long story short, the neurologist kept her in the hospital, accumulating an astronomical bill for his "services," although on most days he showed up in her room for merely a minute or two. No psychotherapeutic assistance was given to the woman. Obviously, even the most balanced person would have been angry and despondent if thus imprisoned without recourse and forced to spend 24 hours a day isolated with nurse's aides who, at that hospital, were simple women from the Middle East who spoke no English.

After three weeks, when the scandalous situation had became impossible to prolong, the neurologist, though continuing to insist that the woman was unable to return home, finally agreed to have her transferred to the alcoholic unit of the famous psychiatric division of a renowned hospital. The psychiatric facility was headed by two psychoanalysts widely known for their writings. In its brochures, the alcoholic unit and the therapeutic services offered were described in glowing terms. In spite of an incredibly high daily cost, however, the facility offered hardly more than custodial care, under conditions that cannot be viewed as beneficial. The "treatment," even though called group therapy, consisted merely of lectures by caseworkers. There was one recreation room with one television set. The patients, mostly men, selected baseball programs, which were of no interest to the woman. Besides the corridors, there was no place to go. The patients were not allowed to walk in the beautiful park outside. The woman sat all day long alone in her room. For reasons that were never explained, she, a music lover, was not allowed to have a radio in her room.

One day, however, a female staff psychologist visited with her, and they went for a walk in the park. The psychologist asked the patient numerous questions and took notes. The woman was overjoyed that at long last, a staff member was giving her some attention. She hoped that things would improve. It turned out, though, that the conversation was merely a one-time routine interview, a part of the established policy of the clinic. A few days later the woman was glad to notice the psychologist in the corridor, approached her, and greeted her with warmth. The psychologist merely walked past her, without making any response.

The woman and her friends asked repeatedly that she be permitted to return home. Again she was told that it was not possible. She was a prisoner, and her depression became even more severe.

Then, all of a sudden, a miracle happened, and she was a free person. No, it was not because they considered her cured. It was merely that her insurance money had run out! The expenses for six weeks of misery totaled $73,000, and much of the cost was not covered by insurance. It took months of psychotherapy to undo the damage inflicted on her. One more thing: According to her psychiatrist, who obtained a copy of her file from the alcoholic unit, both her diagnosis and her prognosis were wrong.

Many psychiatrists who devote themselves exclusively to psychotherapeutic practice regret that they could not gain the all-important experience of working with patients at a much earlier stage in their career.
The same opinion has been expressed by gifted professionals who
entered the study of psychology to become psychotherapists but found
out that there is little correlation between the two disciplines.

Much has been written about that subject, and I do not want to
belabor the obvious; namely, that a special training program for psychotherapists must be created, eliminating today's superfluous preliminary study courses and concentrating on the essentials from the very
beginning. Even though I would have designed the program differently,
Robert S. Wallerstein's proposed doctorate in mental health was
definitely a step in the right direction. His valiant efforts in the 1970s
and 1980s to institute a doctorate in mental health program at the University of California branches in Berkeley and San Francisco are to be
admired. Alas, the powerful forces of those who benefited from the status quo soon squelched that promising beginning (see Wallerstein,
1991). If any psychotherapist deserves the Congressional Medal of
Honor, or even the Nobel Prize, it is Wallerstein, for his long and dedicated effort. It is an outrage, and a reflection on our profession and on
academia, that the program failed as a result of indifference and opposing forces motivated by self-interest.

I repeat for emphasis: We can never hope for even a minimal
number of competent psychotherapists if we do not institute a highly
specialized study different from that which is offered in medical, psychology, and social work training. Such a program would allow the
trainees to start supervised work with patients much earlier than they
do now. Only with more expert psychotherapists, unencumbered by
nonpertinent academic ballast, can we advance our knowledge and
offer better patient care. However, the current unavailability of such
training, disastrous though that lack is, is not the worst of the
afflictions besetting our profession. That we will approach shortly.

We saw Lesse complain about the trend favoring specialty clinics. Anyone who picks up psychiatric and psychological writings published during the last century becomes aware of the enormous number of trends,
fashions, beliefs, practices, and theories that arose, dominated our field

and academia for a time or found a considerable following, and then vanished. (Some of the trends did, however, reemerge in later periods.) Quite a number of the trends we can look at with wonderment that they were ever possible. One could fill volumes just listing such past trends and fashions. Here are a few examples:

Starting with the early days of analysis, approaches that postulated a single major cause for neurosis found many followers. Adler, Rank, and others each presented a different cause underlying neurosis. From time to time other proposals would turn up, often quite strange, such as the "primal scream." In the early 1960s I heard an analyst assert that all neurosis is caused by "the baby's blindness in the first few days of life." Over the years, various techniques were hailed as the best approach to achieve therapeutic success; one of them was to provoke and disagree with the patient. Nondirective schools flourished also.

A frequent occurrence in the early days of analysis was that analysts, on the basis of one or two cases that fell into a specific clinical category, would present generalizing theories and claim that their "conclusions" regarding those specific patients applied to all people who belonged in that category. There was a period when there was a cornucopia of psychoanalytic case descriptions wherein the analysts expounded how they, by "expert" analysis, had brought about a sudden recollection of a traumatic event. As a result, an instant cure of the patient's terrible affliction occurred. Tests too are matters of fashion. For a long time the Szondi test was considered a valuable tool by many practitioners and academicians, but years later, nobody was using that test. And so it goes.

Here are comments by the writer Jay Neugeboren on the changing diagnosis and recommended treatment of his brother over a period of some 30 years, corresponding to the changing fashions and trends in psychiatry and psychotherapy:

> He was schizophrenic when enormous doses of Thorazine and Stelazine calmed him; he was manic-depressive (bipolar) when lithium worked; he was manic-depressive-with-psychotic-symptoms or hypomanic when Tegretol or Depakote (anticonvulsants) or some new antipsychotic or antidepressant

promised to make him cooperative; and he was schizophrenic (again) when various doctors promised cures through insulin coma therapy or megadose vitamin therapy or gas therapy.

During these years, Robert also participated in a long menu of therapies: group therapy, family therapy, multi-group family therapy, Marxist therapy, Gestalt therapy, psychoanalytically oriented psychotherapy, goal-oriented therapy, art therapy, milieu therapy, et al.

Surely, all that bears testimony to the flimsiness of the foundations of most practitioners' knowledge. They view the hapless patient through the spectacles of transient fashions or rigid dogma rather than base their treatment on the solid grounds of clinical expertise. These years we are inundated by numbing and repetitious articles by self-appointed experts on borderline cases and narcissism.

How does all that affect those who are in dire need of competent intensive treatment?

> And behold I saw the tears of the oppressed
> and that they had no one to turn to.
>
> ECCLESIASTES

b3   THE CONVENIENCE OF CONVENIENT ASSUMPTIONS*

> Now this is the law of the jungle –
> as old and as true as the sky;
> And the wolf that shall keep it may prosper,
> but the wolf that shall break it must die.
>
> RUDYARD KIPLING

> The worst enemy of truth . . . is the solid majority.
>
> HENRIK IBSEN

> The world's great men have not commonly been great scholars, nor its great scholars great men.
>
> OLIVER WENDELL HOLMES

Who are the great men and women in psychotherapy? In my mind, they are the many psychotherapists who have both the sensitivity and the desire truly to understand their patients on an individual and personal basis and who try to increase their knowledge and skills to render better and more complete service. They are the men and women who refuse to use the damaging shortcuts of generalizing dogmatic approaches and the time- and labor-saving gimmicks advocated by the likes of Yalom and Karasu.

No other field in public health is in as much need of separating the wheat from the chaff and of stringent reforms as psychotherapy and, particularly in the United States, nursing homes for the elderly. It is often much easier to spot dismal conditions in the latter. In psychotherapy, even more than in politics, a brazen pretense of competency brings far greater success than possession of actual knowledge. Even among those who are aware of that calamity, hardly anyone has the stamina and the spirit of sacrifice to speak up. Some of the few who do are noted in this volume.

---

* This chapter is not identical with the chapter of the same name in our companion volume CHALLENGE FOR PSYCHOANALYSIS AND PSYCHOTHERAPY: SOLUTIONS FOR THE FUTURE.

Our profession is imbued with rationalizations that frequently take the form of convenient assumptions and, without being questioned by most, become part of our professional culture, the vast and complex system of systems I have mentioned before. Let us glance at a few of the more commonly held assumptions.

THE PSYCHOANALYST IS A NEUTRAL SCIENTIFIC OBSERVER AND INSTRUMENT

It is unnecessary here to describe the various meanings of neutrality in the psychotherapeutic context. The "distant" emotional attitude of the analyst toward the analysand was held, for a long time, as a sine qua non of the therapeutic process. That position, even though lately abandoned by many, is still defended by some. The assumption is of utmost importance to those who maintain that psychoanalysis is a science and uses scientific methodology.

Of course, there have always been psychotherapists who considered the proposition spurious and without merit. The arguments that brought that long-lasting belief to an end existed all along. No new proofs, no new ideas, have been added since then. Yet as long as the establishment remained tightly knit and strong, the fiction could be maintained, and adherence to the credo enforced.

Some 35 years ago I demonstrated in a lecture how three well-known analysts, addressing a simple situation occurring in a therapy session, could not possibly respond in an identical manner, as a registering apparatus would. I based my assertions on the positions they took in their writings, which were at variance with each other, and on their divergent personalities. The response of many in the audience was derision of my views and outright hostility.

Now, of course, as evidenced by the extensive literature on the matter, the relationship between analyst and patient is viewed from various perspectives that are quite different from the traditional stance. A number of knowledgeable colleagues who deal with younger professionals have noted, however, that many of the latter, in spite of the change in the "official" climate, feel more comfortable maintaining a distant and neutral attitude.

The widespread abandonment of the "neutral" attitude has not markedly discouraged those who continue to view psychoanalysis as a science and the analyst as a "scientist-observer." We have looked at Stoller's incisive arguments that psychoanalysis can never meet the criteria of a science. He also comments that Wallerstein never doubted that psychoanalysis is a science. It is interesting to note what Wallerstein and Sampson have to say in their chapter in our companion volume: "The [psychoanalyst's] notes provide a permanent and 'public' record of a systematic series of observations by a *highly trained participant observer*. They constitute a record that therefore does allow for independent and concurrent observation" (italics added). Elsewhere, however, in the same paper they state, "Psychoanalysis has indeed profited enormously from the natural (and the fortuitous) observations of *gifted individual* observers" (italics added). And here we have a most important point: A gifted analyst will come up with observations and interpretations completely different from those of a less talented one; and each analyst, gifted or not, being an individual with his own history, cannot help but have different impressions, associations, and reactions.

The following may help illustrate the wide array of positions and perceptions in psychotherapy. Merely by going through several professional journals spanning about two years and checking the indexes of several books, one of our staff members, for a purpose not related to this chapter, selected the names of the more recognizable theoreticians, authors, and schools. Of course, a list thus assembled is far from complete and has no organic structure. It does not need to. Its sole purpose is to bolster my argument, which, as the reader knows, is identical to the one held by Stoller. Here are the names:

Adler, Alfred

Anzieu, Didier

Arlow, J. A.

Balint groups

Behavior therapy

Brenner, C.

Ego psychology (Hartmann et al.)

English object relations school

Erikson, Erik H.

Fairbairn, W. R. D.

Federn, Paul

Ferenczi, Sándor

Freud, Sigmund

Fromm, Erich

Gedo, John E.

General systems theory

Gill, Merton M.

Giovacchini, P.

Hermeneutics

Holt, Robert R.

Horney, Karen

Jung, Carl

Kernberg, Otto F.

Klein, George S.

Klein, Melanie

Kohut, Heinz (self psychology)

Kubie, Lawrence	Racker, H.	Stekel, Daniel
Lacan, Jacques	Radó, Sándor	Stern, Daniel
LaPlanche, J.	Rank, Otto	Stolorow, Robert
Lichtenstein, H.	Rapaport, David	Sullivan, H. S.
Loewald, Hans	Reich, Wilhelm	Szasz, Thomas
Mahler, Margaret M.	Reik, Theodor	Waelder, Robert
Masterson, James F.	Rogers, Carl R.	White, William Alanson
Mitchell, Stephen A.	Schafer, Roy	
Peterfreund, Emanuel	Searles, Harold F.	Winnicott, D. W.
Psychodrama	Spitz, R. A.	Wolf, Alexander

We have here over 50 names, and a widely known textbook, LEHRBUCH DER PSYCHOANALYTISCHEN THERAPIE, by Herbert Thomä and Horst Kächele, lists, in the first volume alone, well over 500 authors. A "neutral scientific instrument," however, looking at the same object, namely, the human psyche, could not possibly present us with such vastly different results as these "neutral scientific observers" do.

We are dealing with individual observations, judgments, and misjudgments, the furthest thing from an objective instrument. The "highly trained observer" aspect (which is a basis for the "science" claim) focuses, in practice, on demanding that the therapist be able to "detect" in the patient what dogma dictates he look for. One of the most visible consequences is the inept cliché interpretations of dreams and dream symbols that we criticized previously in this chapter. Various new definitions of science have been manufactured in an attempt to create loopholes through which psychoanalysis can be squeezed into the coveted category of "science." Those intellectual acrobatics show more sophistry than sophistication.

Considering the calamitous condition psychotherapy and mental health find themselves in, it is unconscionable to give priority to pretentious trivia and sterile speculation. For psychoanalysis and psychodynamic therapy to move closer to their potential, and for those who are suffering to receive more effective help, the priorities described in this chapter are indispensable. We must discard many of the present ineffective policies and approaches that avoid the necessary but laborious tasks and that avoid focusing on the essentials.

ALL PSYCHOTHERAPISTS ARE COMPETENT

To a large extent, the literature implies that mental health professionals are competent at what they are doing. For instance, when we look at statistics on emotional disorders, it is assumed that all diagnostic assessments are correct. When Wallerstein describes the more desirable training conditions prevalent when he was a student himself, the implication is that those trainees eventually became competent psychotherapists.

It is rare to hear a critical assessment like Gedo's. Because of the importance of the subject, let us dwell on it for a moment. Gedo estimates – and Lesse and other experts agree – that at present only about 15 percent of the graduates of training institutes can be considered adequate. But what about the days when both selection and training were supposedly better? We must keep in mind that the deterioration he speaks of did not occur abruptly from one generation to another; it was a gradual process. We also need to consider that these "lesser" candidates will become the teachers and analysts of the next generation.

Gedo does not tell us what percentage of the trainees he considered to be adequate in the "good old days." It is the estimate of some analysts and therapists that in those "better" times 25 to 30 percent of the graduates of training institutes were truly adequate. My own estimate and the estimates of other senior therapists are more pessimistic.

There are other factors to be considered as well. Not every competent trainee becomes a competent therapist. It depends, to a large extent, on the quality of teaching he receives and the quality of his own psychoanalysis. It is here that we encounter a major problem, which I have discussed with many knowledgeable professionals. Many analysts have expressed dissatisfaction with, and doubts about, the ability of their former training analysts. Most did not express those concerns to their analysts; others did not dare to make any negative comments to them. It is difficult for a competent candidate hampered by such unfavorable conditions to become a competent therapist.

Connected to the problem of professional adequacy, we run into another assumption:

BY MEANS OF HIS PERSONAL ANALYSIS, EACH ANALYST HAS "WORKED THROUGH" HIS OWN EMOTIONAL PROBLEMS

He has? Not if you listen to his colleagues! Of course, I am being face-tious now, but I daresay that frequently analysts, good-naturedly or not, say something negative about the emotional status of their colleagues that will contradict the "worked through" assumption. Let us consider a few examples of emotional problems. In some analysts neurotic traits are obvious. Others who appear to have been reasonably well balanced at the outset, with no major problem to work through, have only limited com-prehension of emotional problems. Still others have character disorders and a limited capacity for emotional warmth. It is strange to find those analysts writing about the importance of empathy. In all those instances it is hard to know to what extent, if any, "working through" occurred. I have yet to meet a person, even among his admirers, who would declare that Lacan had ever "worked through" his emotional problems.

There are analysts whose expectations of the results of the train-ing analysis are more modest. They declare that its chief purpose is to acquaint the future analyst with the procedure as well as to bring him to the point where his own emotional problems will not interfere with the proper treatment of his patients. In fact, that alone would be no mean accomplishment.

Let us hear another opinion about the extent to which estab-lished analysts have worked through their problems. In a report on a vicious power struggle within the New York Psychoanalytic Insti-tute, which we will return to later in this chapter, we find an inter-view with Dr. Jay Schorr, a senior member of the Institute and chairman of one of its more important committees. He is described as an affable man and a chain-smoker. And that is what he considers to be the reason for the infighting and the antagonism between mem-bers of the Institute, "unanalyzed transferences." He goes on to say, "Hopefully, if somebody is well analyzed, they wouldn't experience another person as scary." True – nor would he be a chain-smoker.

ALL PATIENTS RECEIVE THE NECESSARY NUMBER OF WEEKLY SESSIONS

That assumption makes experienced clinicians uneasy when reading certain "clinical" studies and case reports. If the greatest problem in psychotherapy is the quality of the treatment dispensed, the second greatest problem is that many patients cannot afford enough weekly sessions, particularly over an extended period.

The realities of clinical practice, therefore, more often than not present the following difficulty: The therapist, in consideration of the pathology of the patient, would ideally see the patient for a certain number of weekly sessions. Financial limitations force him to attempt to reach the desired therapeutic goal with insufficient tools, that is, fewer sessions. That, of course, involves a change of strategy, which entails clinical considerations. But how often have you seen that major problem addressed by the professionals in their case studies? Where is this never-never land where patients come as often as necessary and thus the number of weekly sessions is never an issue? Do they all practice in a world where patients have unlimited resources, or do they practice at all?

We will later return to the problem of clinical practice with patients of limited means.

One can think of many more assumptions that belie the realities of professional practice, but let this be the last one:

ONE CAN TREAT SEVEN OR EIGHT PEOPLE
SUCCESSFULLY IN A GROUP BY GIVING THEM
AN HOUR AND A HALF ONCE A WEEK

On the basis of decades of experience, I am convinced of the value of group psychotherapy for many people who fall into a variety of clinical categories. However, it is valuable only if the groups are conducted by an expert therapist. Also, we must be very specific: what kind of group psychotherapy? Basically, we have to distinguish between analytic group psychotherapists, who focus on the individual, and group processors, who deal with the group as a whole. The reader will find the necessary details in the group therapy chapter in this volume. Unfortunately, most of the practitioners using those two modalities give their groups merely an hour and a half a week.

It would be desirable for each patient in individual treatment to receive at least two sessions a week; that would constitute almost two hours a week. Alas, that is often not possible! Where in the world do all these geniuses come from who can perform the incredible feat of "curing" seven to nine people in group therapy in so little time; namely, one and a half hours a week? Some of those therapists are my friends – but they have never told me their secret!

A PAUSE

At this point it might be desirable to address the reader on a number of points. Some of them I have mentioned before, but in view of the long and tortuous road we have been traveling, they may have lapsed from memory or been overlooked before.

First, I would like to remind the reader that I was requested to write not a scholarly paper but a personal commentary, based on my many years at the American Mental Health Foundation, on what I consider the major problems in the field of psychotherapy and mental health and what remedies I consider the most urgent and promising.

I would also like to state again that when I speak negatively of academicians and theoreticians, I refer strictly to those whose freewheeling productions are in blatant contradiction to the psychological realities observed by expert clinicians. The criticism is not restricted to analysts and psychodynamic therapists; it also very much applies to all the social "scientists" in various disciplines whose lack of acumen is matched only by their audacity in making nonfactual statements regarding matters psychotherapeutic. They are included in the 40 some examples offered in this chapter. My criticisms must not be construed as applying to any who do not engage in the practices I criticize.

I also mentioned before that the material of this chapter could not be arranged as writings on subjects in the realm of psychotherapy usually are. Here the sequence of the material was dictated by a different rationale; namely, to present to the reader, step by step, the serious problems afflicting psychotherapy and mental health.

And a last remark: Because of my extended criticism of so many professionals in our field, some have assumed that I enjoy such an enterprise. The contrary is true. Who wants to listen to music he intensely dislikes? It was necessary that I dig through writings I consider pretentious, nonfactual, and indigestible; I would much rather have read articles that I deemed relevant and constructive and – what I most seek – that teach something of value.

b4 Generalizing, Theorizing, Metapsychology, Metadentistry

A great deal of what passes as attested theory in psychoanalysis is little more than speculation, varying widely in plausibility.

EDWARD GLOVER

We know that the tail must wag the dog,
for the horse is drawn by the cart;
But the devil whoops, as he whooped of old:
"It's clever, but is it art?"

RUDYARD KIPLING

I have mentioned a list of factors that caused psychoanalysis and psychoanalytic psychotherapy to fall into disfavor with the public and the teaching establishment. However, the single most important factor is that far too many people have been disappointed by a failure of the procedures in the hands of "professionals" who view patients through the generalizing spectacles of dogma and theory. They have neither the sensitivity nor the talent to engage in this work. We are faced with the problem of a massive "negative selection" of those who engage in psychotherapy and its teaching, orally and in writing. Although psychotherapists who engage in full-time clinical practice but lack the necessary qualifications cause damage to their patients, they do not cause massive misinformation that comes of an important teaching position and widely distributed writings. Furthermore, there are many people who would make good therapists but who, owing to the present climate in our field and the poor training, can never obtain the knowledge they hope for. They may not even know that such knowledge exists. In the words of the Bible, they asked for bread, but we gave them stones.

Robert S. Wallerstein thinks that in due time the pendulum will automatically swing back, and interest in psychoanalysis and analytic therapy will revive. I am convinced that this will not happen until the glaring shortcomings are wiped out.

We will soon draw conclusions from our findings and propose steps to remedy the deficiencies and bring about improvements. I have repeatedly discussed various negative forces that have influenced the present "climate" and "culture" in psychotherapy. To complete the picture, however, we need to focus on some facts.

It took some 13 centuries before a Vesalius dared to investigate the truth about the human anatomy. And only in 1992, after 359 years had passed, did the Vatican admit that it was in error and that Galileo had been right. In spite of the ever-darkening shadows, let us hope that it won't take that long for psychotherapy to rid itself of the causes that underlie its problems and the consequent suffering of so many.

The light at the end of the tunnel is not yet in sight. On one hand, a number of dogmas considered sacrosanct by the analytic profession are being discarded; on the other hand, the ever-growing number of psychotherapists coming from the ranks of medicine, psychology, and social work, but having insufficient training in psychotherapy, has contributed to the increasing shoddiness of psychotherapeutic instruction and wide acceptance of facile treatment methods. The result is that the widely used, less effective treatment methods have greatly limited the range of those who can be treated with success. People who suffer from serious disturbances, such as phobias, deep anxiety, and depression, are thrown to the wolves. Fortunately, some have found that their pain can be alleviated by drugs. However, drugs do not change the underlying psychological problems, and there are still a great many who cannot obtain significant relief through medication.

According to all available information, the number of psychodynamic therapists who are expert enough to treat the more serious cases successfully is decreasing to a disquieting extent. Lack of knowledge is being masked by academic-sounding jargon, which impresses many of the poorly informed. Even sadder, the trend to use such language is followed by some therapists who should know better and should resist such pretense.

The scholarly language we encounter is so far removed from the language used by the unconscious that it is utterly inadequate to describe the structure and operation of the unconscious. Such a delicate and sensitive subject requires of the writer the utmost clarity and precision. As we have amply shown in this volume, scholarly language lends itself admirably to obfuscation while making the hollow sound important. It has the further advantage of making it difficult to pin down its false assertions, since it expresses itself in diffuse abstractions and concepts twice, thrice, or light years removed from concrete psychological fact.

Compare scholarly language with the clarity of honest writers in our field. With them one knows exactly where one stands, and it is extremely easy to respond, to agree or to disagree. In psychotherapy we need people of such sincerity, because the damage caused by the others is immense. We will come back to that later.

A simple illustration of what I have in mind follows. Anna Freud (1965), in "Normality and Pathology in Childhood: Assessments of Development," makes a number of clear and categoric statements, for example: "When a child complains about excessive boredom, we can be certain that he has forcibly repressed his masturbation fantasies or masturbatory activities." No academic ambiguities there. The straightforwardness of her assertions makes it simple for us to declare that we believe otherwise.

We have already declared that we have to be suspicious of all generalizations and submit them to scrutiny. I said that I would not get involved in any theoretical arguments. Thus I am mentioning here only simple psychological facts. Also speaking about childhood, Kohut asserts that wanting to be admired and recognized is a top priority for children. Of course, that assertion supports his theoretical position regarding grandiosity and narcissism. But if the reader replaces "wanting to be admired" with any phrase of his choice, such as "wanting to be loved," it may still make a lot of sense, but it would not bolster Kohut's hypothesis. Overemphasizing one fact, no matter how true, will make for a one-sided theoretical structure.

Turning to a different aspect: I believe we have the right to demand that those who wax so eloquent about the theories that should govern psychotherapy should have a solid basic knowledge themselves and do everything possible to enrich that knowledge, particularly where vital areas are concerned. There is much evidence, however, that many do not. As stated, many writers, staying safely in the realm of theoretical speculation, do not betray evidence of actual clinical expertise.

To turn out book after book about therapy, those theorists should certainly have a measure of expertise in its basics. Again let us choose a simple example: transference. I assert categorically that individual therapy is insufficient for a full understanding of transference in all its dimensions. Analytic group therapy has been around for many decades. There is a vast literature concerning the multiple transferences in such groups and the crystallization of the transferences that allows for far more understanding than individual therapy, where all transferences are projected on one analyst. For instance, claims by the theorizers notwithstanding, an individual male analyst cannot evoke sexual female transferences to the same degree as can an attractive woman in the group.

No therapist has a complete understanding of transference phenomena unless he has spent considerable time in a group as one of its members and then conducted psychodynamic groups himself. One would imagine that the theorists who ooze therapeutic pontification would, in their eagerness to help mankind, rush to acquire such indispensable know-how so that they could better understand transference and thus psychotherapy. Alas, to the best of my knowledge, none of them wishes to be thus inconvenienced. That, of course, does not stop them from writing further "fundamental treatises." Shrewd avoidance of clinical subjects that could become telltale signs of ignorance, and a measure of writing ability, can successfully mask the lack of clinical knowledge.

The reader will find considerable discussion of outcome research in our companion volume, THE CHALLENGE FOR PSYCHO-ANALYSIS AND PSYCHOTHERAPY: SOLUTIONS FOR THE FUTURE. However, the question of professional competency is one that bedevils such research, and I would like to inject a few remarks here. Outcome research attempts to evaluate the results of certain forms of psychotherapy and to compare them. Later in this chapter I will discuss one of the most widely acclaimed studies of outcome research. Constituting a mountainous accumulation of valueless "data," it is a museum piece of pretense and inanity.

As the reader knows, many well-publicized studies have claimed to show that the success of various forms of psychotherapy is about equal. The premises of the research contain, however, a number of fallacies. By far the most important fallacy is as follows: Although it was stated that, for example, psychodynamic therapy showed such and such results, there is no way to evaluate the results of psychoanalysis and analytic therapy, or any other sophisticated form of therapy. Not all therapists are equally competent, and not all therapists practice a similar method. Using previously mentioned figures, let us assume that about 15 percent of analytic therapists are truly competent and that what they practice can, without doubt, be called analysis and analytic therapy. On the basis of my own experience, I would separate the remaining 85 percent into two categories: the 50 percent or so who constitute a "beneficial therapeutic" presence, and the remainder, whose presence is "nonproductive" or even "damaging." Neither of those two categories can be considered to represent analysis and analytic therapy for the purpose of research studies. We can assume that the percentage figures are similar for other therapeutic approaches.

We, however, are concerned with the 15 percent of the therapists who are sufficiently expert. It is here that we run into trouble. Even though they come under the heading of analysts and analytic therapists, their work and their personalities are far from uniform. To the contrary, they are highly individualistic. To compare: We cannot say that Leonardo da Vinci and Monet produced the same kinds of paintings, nor Mozart and Gershwin the same kind of music. The reader may be convinced, as I am on the basis of many decades of observing the work of gifted colleagues, that psychodynamic therapy can be of utmost value. Such personal observations are perfectly valid, but we cannot call them outcome research. Outcome research is a different matter, and its premises have been shown to be grossly wanting.

Outcome research studies are only a minuscule part of the innumerable projects and writings in the mental health field that, by aping the methods and format of science, often with graphs and statistics, claim credibility. Yet, of the practitioners in all the disciplines that are part of the mental health endeavor, it is the expert psychotherapist – a rare specimen – who comes closest to understanding the human psyche and is thus capable of recognizing the faulty premises in research studies and theories.

Take introjected images, for example. When we speak of them, we are speaking of verifiable psychological realities. But most concepts used freely in outcome research studies and in analytic writings are abstractions that do not represent facts. Once such concepts and abstractions are used, we find ourselves in a different dimension not related to reality. Creating those artifacts, and moving them around so adroitly, may have an intellectual appeal and may be indicative of a special talent. But that talent is not the one that a psychotherapist should possess if he is to pursue his craft diligently. His hypotheses are vastly different from those we have criticized. We shall refer to them shortly.

We have examined the shortcomings and obstacles in psychotherapy. Doing so was necessary before undertaking the task of eradicating them. As I have said, we are repairmen. When you bring your shoes in for repair, the repairman examines them and states what they need, new soles or heels or what have you. The dogmatic therapist and the theoretician, however, know what is wrong beforehand, without even having seen the patient. The patient is made to fit into the theory. If those "professionals" had the necessary acuity and talent, they would not be writing what they are writing, and their priorities would be vastly different.

I have spoken of our calamitous system of systems and of our Pharisees and apparatchiks, all formidable obstacles to improvement. Am I the only one to complain? No, I am not. Let me quote from an article in the SCIENCE TIMES of September 30, 1986. It discussed a report of the American Council of Learned Societies that examined the quality of articles published in scholarly journals. The Council asked whether those articles represent scholarship exploring new intellectual ground. More than 5,000 scholars were polled, of whom 71 percent responded. Most of them answered in the negative, stating that "pioneering voices were often overlooked in favor of conservative opinions sanctioned by the academic establishment or trendy views already approved by powerful intellectual in-groups." Moreover, "a frequent complaint was that when younger scholars seek university tenure their writings are often weighted for quantity rather than quality." And further: "There is pressure to publish, though there is virtually no interest in content." It is far easier to be published, the survey found, if the research or scholar is on a prestigious campus or uses "currently fashionable" ideas that do not upset the establishment elders. About a third of the respondents said that they rarely found articles of interest, even in leading journals. Finally: "The fact that three out of four respondents considered the procedure biased in favor of certain groups leaves little question about the need for reform."

That report was published almost 10 years ago. Has there been any reform? Far from it! The dinosaurs are more entrenched than ever. Of course, what the American Council of Learned Societies found applies most emphatically to the hierarchies in the mental health professions, their teaching, and the publishers of books and journals in our field.

Of the innumerable illustrations we find in literature of the almost unsurmountable, pernicious power of the established systems, let me offer one of the briefest (from THE LEOPARD, by Giuseppe di Tomasi Lampedusa):

> The Cardinal of Palermo was a truly holy man; and even now that he has been dead for a long time his charity and his faith are still remembered. While he was alive, though, things were different: he was not a Sicilian, he was not even a Southerner or a Roman, and many years before he had tried to leaven with Northern activity the inert and heavy dough of the island's spiritual life in general and the clergy's in particular. Flanked by two or three secretaries from his own parts, he had deluded himself, those first years, that he could remove abuses and clear the soil of its more obvious stumbling blocks. But soon he had to realize that he was, as it were, firing into cotton wool; the little hole made at the moment was covered after a few seconds by thousands of tiny fibers, and all remained as before, the only additions being cost of powder, ridicule at useless effort, and deterioration of material. Like everyone who, in those days, wanted to change anything in the Sicilian character, he had soon acquired the reputation of being a fool (which in the circumstances was exact) and had to content himself with works of charity.
>
> These, however, diminished his popularity still further since the beneficiaries of such charity, previously accustomed to receive it without the slightest effort on their part, now had to come themselves to the Archepiscopal palace.

Even in a field far better defined than psychotherapy, we find bitter complaints against obfuscation and the exploitation by a system of systems that is detrimental to students and to the public interest. As reported in the NEW YORK TIMES of February 4, 1994, the Massachusetts School of Law in Andover has started an antitrust suit against the American Bar Association, complaining "that a select group of association insiders acts as a kind of cartel by imposing costly and unnecessary standards that protect the financial interests of professors, law librarians and standardized test-systems. The cost of this protection is shouldered largely by students, because they are frequently denied a solid legal education *placing emphasis on practice – rather than on theory* – that they could acquire from innovative law schools" (italics added).

The suit contends that within the ABA's legal education section, a group of law school deans, professors, law librarians, and practitioners has controlled accreditation for the last 20 years, rotating among formal positions on committees, councils, and boards that deal with law school practices.

The system of law school accreditation is only one of the innumerable microsystems that operates within a larger, but equally stagnant, detrimental, and parochial "culture," its own system of systems. In psychotherapy, a far more amorphous field than law, the damage done by the prevailing system to the public interest, and specifically to the emotionally ill, is far greater.

The ubiquity of interlocking systems is obvious; they are as immovable as a range of mountains, formidable obstacles to intelligent improvement, no matter how badly needed.

George Bernard Shaw stated: "The reasonable man adapts himself to the world. The unreasonable one persists in trying to adapt the world to himself. Therefore, all progress depends on the unreasonable man."

Once the professional has become part of any of those systems by virtue of his education, training, and need for gainful occupation, he will most likely conform to its confines, willingly or resignedly. The victim becomes the victimizer.

Our goal should be to ensure that psychotherapy is conducted by professionals who have the necessary talent for the task and who have been able to acquire the necessary expertise. The trend of the last few decades has been to move further and further from that goal. One can read a hundred pages in books and journals and not find one line that proves to us that the author is qualified. Instead, the literature abounds with writings that are full of theoretical assumptions and abstract concepts and with writings that claim to be scientific studies, complete with graphs and tables to impress us but lacking the necessary solid premises. In both kinds of writing, the experienced clinician, a breed that is becoming rarer and rarer, has no difficulty finding the inherent fallacies.

It has never been easy to acquire valid psychotherapeutic knowledge, and these days, in the face of a formidable information explosion and ill-informed teachers, the task is even more difficult. The ever-growing quantity of psychotherapeutic writings notwithstanding, that knowledge may well disappear. Many therapists do not even realize that it ever existed.

Still, during a century of psychodynamic exploration, we have accumulated a valuable body of knowledge. It is the responsibility of everyone who wants to become a psychotherapist to seek that knowledge and the clinical expertise to go along with it. Unfortunately, few psychotherapists are willing, or are in a position, to make the extended sacrifice that needs to be made over and above their already strenuous "official" education and training. The resulting inadequacy is even more damaging when such a person is ambitious and self-seeking and succeeds in securing a position of importance and influence. If our criticisms seem harsh, we must not forget that it is precisely the actions of such professionals that are a major cause of poor patient care and shoddy instruction of future practitioners.

The evidence presented in this chapter is indisputable; each author's own words betrayed him. Scanning professional writings, one can often detect the telltale signs of incompetence, no matter how adroitly they are concealed behind grandiose assertions and scholarly presentation. Each of the authors cited has been severely criticized by colleagues whose sober judgment and seasoned expertise render them capable of separating the wheat from the chaff.

When we inveigh against those using facile treatment approaches, we have in mind all those who try to avoid the difficult therapeutic work by giving less and less time to the patient or by eliminating the difficult tasks that are part of serious and valid psychotherapy. We have examined many examples.

How can we extricate ourselves from the quagmire? It will not be easy. The system is self-perpetuating. Robert S. Wallerstein, in his first chapter in our companion volume, describes a small aspect of it. The other aspects are equally dismal. As a first step, we need to define the areas of the psychotherapeutic endeavor that must be strengthened and those that we must try to eradicate. For that purpose I will separate the areas of psychotherapeutic writing and teaching into three dimensions.

DIMENSION I

The shoddy approaches I complained about must be contrasted with the work of the expert psychodynamic psychotherapist, who, having the necessary talent and sensitivity, is able to demonstrate his understanding of the workings of the unconscious, by properly handling feelings and dreams, using transferences, understanding repressions and defenses, working through resistances, obtaining relief for the patient from an overly strict superego, exploring childhood events and their links to the psychic structure and its functioning within the patient, reconstructing capably in his own mind a realistic and detailed three-dimensional picture of each patient's inner universe, and, having done all that, formulating highly individualized temporary hypotheses for the patient, rejecting the influence of generalized dogma that is unsuited to explaining and dealing with the specific constellations and needs of the individual patient. The clinician should also, in his communications to the patient, stay as close as possible to the language used by the unconscious itself by referring to the feelings expressed and the images manifested in dreams.

The work needed to accomplish those tasks, if done conscientiously, is formidable, and no one can do it perfectly. That is why many professionals try to circumvent it. The rationalization for using facile shortcuts frequently takes the form of generalizing dogma and theorizing. By unashamedly superimposing dogma and theory on the hapless patient, one can avoid the arduous task of investigating and trying to understand that patient's unique psyche. Grandiose assertions couched in scholarly language substitute for the laborious repair work of the serious clinician.

Each person is born different. The psychotherapist needs to arrive at an understanding, not easy to obtain, of the specific ways each unique individual was affected by events in his childhood and later.

In 45 years of extensive exploration of many forms of psychotherapy at the American Mental Health Foundation, we have arrived at the firm conviction that all psychotherapists must acquire the knowledge and skills just listed. They are indispensable, even if the therapist wants eventually to engage in behavior modification, marriage counseling, child therapy, group psychotherapy, or any other modality of psychotherapy. The more adept the therapist is in using the skills and in reconstructing in his mind the patient's unique inner world, the less he will be tempted to substitute ready-made pseudoanswers. Understanding the structure and the dynamics of the patient's psyche, he will be able to detect the causes of his patient's problems and work toward their resolution.

The knowledge we refer to should constitute the basic knowledge of psychotherapists, to which they would add the specific skills in which they are interested. Like a surgeon, each would have different instruments at his disposal. But how can we ever achieve that aim as long as aspiring psychotherapists are forced to spend many years taking mostly irrelevant courses before being permitted to enter the study of their choice?

Few therapists have the talent and the knowledge to operate with expertise. One of the psychotherapists I consider most knowledgeable has spent 13 years in psychoanalysis and psychotherapy with several therapists and some 20 years in various forms of supervision. It will take people like that, imbued with a driving thirst for knowledge and guided by a definite talent, to bring psychotherapy back to its essence.

The sensitivity and psychotherapeutic talent that make possible an understanding of feelings and dreams of necessity result in a better understanding of the self and its functioning. Applying that comprehension to the development of additional effective psychotherapeutic techniques would open up a promising avenue for psychotherapy. However, that requires another book. I plan to call it DREAMS AND THE MODIFICATION OF THE SELF.

DIMENSION II

In Dimension II we will find the root of all evil. It is the area in which most professionals, teachers, and writers in our field operate. Even though they may claim that their thinking and activities are based on clinical realities or scientific exploration, there is actually little overlap with Dimension I, the dimension of clinical expertise.

A powerful force in Dimension II is what I have called academic populism. It is the glib answers and easy solutions, the avoidance of dealing squarely with issues of psychotherapy. In the mental health professions such populism is manifested by one or more of the following:

- advocacy of facile treatment approaches, as contrasted with the required work discussed in the section on Dimension I
- intellectual speculation resulting in generalizing theory and dogma, which, all claims to the contrary, is not anchored to the reality that governs an individual psyche
- the use of readily available precepts, theoretical references to dictums by "authorities" (often Freud), and other devices showing lack of independent thinking (the indiscriminate and routine use of cliché analytic interpretations of dream symbols, with disregard for the psyche of the particular patient, is a simple example).

All those practices severely damage patient care, whether carried out in the name of psychoanalysis, psychotherapy, psychology, or science.

Despite the academic and "scientific" language, general theorizing is easy; it applies to all. It can be engaged in by people with little or no psychotherapeutic expertise. Actually, many of the academic writings in our field are by professionals with little or no competence who make innumerable references to other writers of little or no competence. As stated, much of the time the concepts employed are distinct from clinical facts and demonstrate a lack of psychological and clinical acumen. Their abstractness permits endless discussion. Because they remain in the abstract realm, proof and disproof are impossible.

We are facing a situation where a great number of "professionals" who never properly learned even the fundamentals of psychotherapy, and who do not understand its essence, have usurped roles as experts, teachers, and leaders.

Those shortcomings necessarily affect the quality of the theories presented to us. For the theories advanced to be valid, the psychological structure and dynamics of the human psyche, and consequently all forms of emotional illness, would be far more uniform than they are. Stoller cogently remarked that many of the theories that are taken seriously are actually based on poor observation or are merely the product of naive and pretentious speculation. Moreover, few of those who boldly make generalizations about psychoanalysis actually have enough psychoanalytic patients to back them up. For instance, how can one discuss regression when the number of weekly sessions is so limited that it cannot even be brought about? Gedo, among others, remarks on the paucity of cases where psychoanalysis is actually performed. Of the many who write about psychoanalysis, surprisingly few actually practice it. According to the best available information, and not counting training analysis, the figure is estimated to be around 5 percent.

We do invite theory. But it must evolve from the vast body of clinical psychotherapeutic experience and be formulated by expert clinicians. The fact is, however, that clinical talent is not common, clinical expertise is hard to come by, and clinical work is difficult to perform. When, in this chapter, I inveigh against theoreticians, I am referring to the many who indulge in theorizing without having the necessary clinical expertise to build upon.

To emphasize: When we allow course work rather than ability to be the deciding criterion, the result is negative selection among those who practice, write about, and teach psychotherapy. We facilitate admission of the unsuitable.

For almost a hundred years now, we have attempted to repair, rearrange, and reinvent faulty theories – and the patchwork still does not work. The denizens of Dimension II, with their endless intellectual discussions and disputes based on faulty premises and abstract concepts, have created special cultures of their own – psychodynamic, psychological, and psychiatric jungles, each with its own jargon, in which even the untalented and least knowing can operate comfortably. It is a safe haven, free of the realities, concerns, and priorities of Dimension I and blithely unconcerned with human suffering.

Creating these artifacts, that is, these abstract concepts, and moving them around may have an intellectual appeal for some and may indicate certain propensities in them. These people may join a chess club and develop chess theories. But, alas, there they will have to apply their theories to the game, something they need not fear when writing about psychotherapy.

In contrast, the temporary hypotheses of the clinician who works within the confines of Dimension I are based on his understanding of the individual patient. They take into account the experience he has gained from other patients and what he has learned from other clinicians. He bears in mind, and may tentatively apply, theoretical positions developed by himself or by clinicians whose observations and thinking he considers to be of merit.

I would like to offer an illustration. Eighteen years ago a young woman sought assistance and advice at our Foundation. She suffered from an eating phobia and had been in treatment, without improvement, for almost three years with an analyst internationally known as an author and outstanding theoretician. He was, and still is, in a leading position as a teacher and administrator in the psychiatric branch of a prestigious hospital. In no way am I implying that a therapist, no matter how accomplished, cannot have failures. Yet all we hear about from this man is the outstanding value of his generalizing theoretical position and the benefits to be derived from its application to one and all. Maybe so. However, rather than his theories, I would prefer to have a detailed clinical report on his treatment of the woman, what he thinks went wrong, and what new approach, if any, he would take were he to continue treating her. And all that, please, for a change, in clear language that does not require prolonged meditation on what the precise meaning of what he says could possibly be.

One more point: The woman mentioned that the doctor seemed to have few patients. How could it be otherwise? With all the administrative, teaching, and supervising duties, the lectures both in the United States and abroad, attendance at national and international conferences, and the preparation of so many books and articles, he has little opportunity for regularly scheduled psychotherapeutic work. Why is it, as Stanley Lesse also asked, that those who have little exposure to clinical work with patients are the very ones who pontificate abundantly and claim to know the workings of the human psyche? On the other hand, few psychotherapists who devote themselves to a full-time practice with patients inundate us with lectures and writings. Of course, they have a much smaller chance of having their works accepted by journals and book publishers than do those with prominent academic positions, no matter how ignorant the latter are.

> I have invented an invaluable permanent invalid called Bunbury, in order that I may be able to go down into the country whenever I choose.
>
> OSCAR WILDE

DIMENSION III

For a brief paper W. W. Meissner created a title so apt that it is bound to go down in history. I have no intention of following the cogent line of thinking he developed in his paper, but I will use his title for my own purposes. He asks, "Metapsychology, who needs it?" My answer is simple: the academic theoreticians who would otherwise have no way to muscle their way into psychotherapy.

As is frequently the case in matters psychoanalytic, J. LaPlanche and J. B. Pontalis (1967) offer the best definition: "Metapsychology constructs an ensemble of conceptual models that are more or less far removed from empirical reality."

The Swiss psychoanalyst and theoretician Oliver Flournoy (1994) correctly points out that metapsychology leads to the possibility of "viewing the psychical apparatus as identical in all people" and to the possibility that "anyone could declare himself a psychoanalyst since it does not require experience."

Even though the following statement usually provokes indignant outcries, it is certain that while there is little overlap between Dimensions I and II, the boundaries between Dimensions II and III are practically nonexistent. As expert clinicians know, too many psychotherapy and psychology studies and writings are far removed from clinical reality and lack the proper premises. What may seem an acceptable statement to the psychotherapist of little knowledge and the freewheeling theorizer is an abomination to the clinically experienced expert.

Rather than revel in grandiose speculations about childhood development, the theorizers should have first learned the ABCs of psychotherapy and become acquainted with its tangible realities, that is, obtain the clearest possible picture of the patient's inner world and understand the forces operating in it. And they should do that not by using the terms of high-sounding theoretical abstractions but by using the language of the unconscious, as found in the feelings and dreams of the patient. When we use the language of the unconscious, we are dealing with emotional forces and images found in the dreams – some helpful, some frustrating, some terrifying. Some are seen, and some are only sensed, as they are lurking in yet unexplored regions. If the therapist consistently employs the language used by the patient's unconscious, then, as treatment progresses, what has been hidden gradually emerges. Injecting prefabricated theory into the dealings with the patient will obscure and vitiate the process.

The proposed correct proceeding, however, can only be engaged in by a psychotherapist with talent and sensitivity. It is no wonder that so much of our literature is in effect an immense warehouse of ready-made crutches for those of little talent: theoretical fabrications that are trapped within the confines of their own limited systems. Even when the theories try to break away from the problems and postulations of prior dogmas, they remain deeply enmeshed with the past constructs and mostly do not represent any noteworthy new insight in regard to the real psychological apparatus. Some of the theorists who are eliminating parts of the old dogmas are now being hailed for their great achievements. We must not forget, however, that at all times and without any fanfare, competent psychotherapists have worked successfully without subscribing to the theoretical components now being shed with so much self-congratulation.

The scholarly disputes have created cultures and cults of their own. Just because the discussions may appear intellectual, that does not mean that they are intelligent. They can be profoundly unintelligent. The exploration and understanding of the unconscious, however, takes place in a different dimension, not accessible to the theorizers who are blind to its very existence. Gustav Bychofski used to paraphrase G. B. Shaw: "He who can, does. He who cannot, theorizes." As stated, many of the theoreticians are incapable of dealing clinically with the most important elements of the unconscious, and thus of psychotherapy. They assiduously avoid them, shrewdly building their constructions in safe, distant, and facile areas. Of course, they do find enthusiastic admirers among the therapists who feel secure in "intellectual" realms but are deaf and dumb about matters of the unconscious.

In an interesting volume, BEYOND FREUD: A STUDY OF MODERN PSYCHOANALYTIC THEORISTS, the editor, Joseph Reppen, has assembled exhaustive essays examining the work and the positions of 14 well-known theoreticians. Eleven, among them the more "important" ones, have nothing to say about dreams, nor about their link to feelings. The other three refer to dreams only tangentially, in connection with some major themes being discussed. The same phenomenon is evident in practically all theoretical treatises. The scholastically inclined of all ages ignore the essential and relish in masquerading their trivial intellectual artifacts as issues of importance. We could easily use 10,000 wise men like Nathan Leites to cut through the verbiage and expose the fuzziness of language and thinking. Leites, greatly admired by Greenson, Stoller, Klineberg, me, and others, had the outstanding intelligence and infinite patience to dissect and expose the vacuousness of the writings of many well-known theoreticians. Boileau has stated, "The man who thinks clearly, writes clearly."

Freud emphasized the prime importance of dreams in analysis. Harold P. Blum has expressed the opinion that patients who cannot provide dreams cannot be analyzed; when there is no dream to interpret, there is no analysis. Those positions mean that the analysts who cannot properly deal with dreams – and that includes the practitioners who merely use prefabricated interpretations – cannot be considered true therapists. Where does that leave the theoreticians? And where does that leave their patients?

The practice of far-fetched speculation and pretentious "scientific" claims is by no means reserved for metapsychologists. We find such abuse in all areas of psychotherapy, psychology, and mental health. Likewise, uncritical acceptance of valueless and misleading academic studies can be found among professionals everywhere. Such credulity sadly reflects on the lack of expertise of those professionals. Let us look at one example out of innumerable instances.

A work of close to 900 pages by three psychologists who also practice behavior modification, Klaus Grawe, Ruth Donati, and Friederike Bernauer (1994), recently caused a sensation and found much acclaim in Germany. It would easily take ten times as many pages to refute, one by one, the innumerable grave misconceptions, errors, and ludicrous conclusions of the work. It is an outstanding example of the disaster that is bound to happen when "professionals" who have a purely academic orientation but lack the necessary psychodynamic background, as well as comprehension of and sensitivity for any form of meaningful psychotherapy, set themselves up as arbiters.

The book starts out on the wrong foot and goes downhill from there. Let us look at its title and first sentence. The title, translated into English, reads PSYCHOTHERAPY IN CHANGE: FROM CONFESSION TO PROFESSION. The desire for sensationalism and the simpleminded framework of the authors can be detected right there; to claim that an intelligent, sophisticated method such as psychotherapy started out as a mere "confession" is a blatant untruth. The first sentence reads, "Who loves psychology, has often reason to be ashamed of psychotherapy." Why, one must ask, would a psychologist be ashamed of psychotherapy? Psychotherapy is not an offspring, or a relative, of psychology! Psychotherapy owes nothing to psychology. On the contrary, psychotherapy, when and where it has been incorporated by psychology, has given it life and enriched its barren regions.

The book is based on some 40 outcome research studies. The authors conveniently accept the validity of such projects. We have devoted considerable time to the scrutiny of process studies and outcome research studies. They pretend to measure what cannot be measured. We have shown that such studies are invariably based on faulty premises and misleading oversimplification. Those defects can be readily seen by looking at their approach to the three basic areas they are concerned with: emotional illnesses, the various forms of therapy, and the evaluation and classification of therapists.

For instance, I have already stated that only about 15 percent of the therapists engaging in psychodynamic psychotherapy have sufficient expertise to do so; the remainder can merely be classified as having a beneficial presence or a nonbeneficial presence. However, the authors do not hesitate to bolster their "scientific research" by including all the therapists who claim to be psychodynamic psychotherapists, no matter how unqualified they are. A similar situation exists for all other treatment forms. For any evaluation, we should include only the therapists who have mastered the specific therapy method being examined.

Outcome studies can only be produced by disregarding essential factors. Let us consider a few of the oversimplifications.

Many of the outcome studies use control groups of people who do not receive treatment. However, such a procedure is useless. Let us look at a simple example, without the detailed descriptions that would ordinarily be included. Let us assume that the study is examining the effect of psychodynamic therapy with a group of 20 depressed people. The control group would be 20 depressed people who do not receive treatment.

First of all, it is impossible to match the first group in any meaningful way. Even keeping matters simple, using only the simplest determiners, one would have to consider the following factors in regard to each of the depressed people: Is the depression chronic? Is the depression cyclic and independent of tangible outside circumstances? Is the depression reactive, that is, triggered by outside circumstances, and if so, how severe do the circumstances have to be to trigger it? How deeply anchored (tenacious) is the depression? Has the person been treated with medication; if so, which medications were helpful and which were not? What psychotherapeutic help has the person received, and was it helpful?

As explained, those are only superficial questions. More meaningful questions would attempt at least a minimal exploration of the psychodynamic structure of the person. In many instances, only prolonged expert treatment can reveal the true nature of the condition. However, even those simplistic questions should show that it is impossible to create two groups of matching people.

Therefore some might forgo the use of a control group and merely focus on a certain number of depressed people who would receive treatment. So let us continue with the 20 depressed people and postulate that they will be treated by 20 psychodynamically oriented psychotherapists. Where are we now? Exactly nowhere! The problem mentioned above applies here too; the variables are far too many. For such a study to work, one would need 20 identical people treated by 20 identical therapists.

Second, only a small percentage of therapists can be considered competent in their psychotherapeutic specialty, and incompetent therapists cannot be used to test the treatment method. Moreover, as stated, the therapists who are competent in the treatment form under investigation would have major variations in treatment approaches and personalities. Thus even if the 20 people they treated were identical, which is an impossibility, the results would be meaningless, since the method applied would not be uniform.

The best we can do is carefully study the clinical history of each patient, ask the previously mentioned questions and many more, and entrust the patient for two or more years to a competent therapist whose procedures should be described as well as possible. One should thus end up with a meaningful case history. But one must beware of calling it outcome research. By merely applying the simple criteria above, one is forced to conclude that the outcome studies presented to us with such fanfare are undertaken either by professionals who are ignorant of even the rudiments of clinical knowledge or by those who believe they can pass pretentious sophistry off as a scientific masterpiece. Unfortunately, the latter are often right in that belief.

How about group therapy? Grawe, Donati, and Bernauer devote a few pages to encounter groups – the most rudimentary and primitive form of group methods and not recognized as an acceptable form of therapy by expert group therapists. From then on, the authors speak only about group therapy without giving any details, lumping together all the forms of group psychotherapy, even though the methods are utterly different from each other and are based on completely different theoretical and methodological approaches. For instance, the group processors who "treat" the group as a whole and the therapists engaging in intensive analytical therapy of the individual in an interactive group setting are worlds apart.

The authors show the same irresponsibility and absence of basic knowledge throughout the volume. Another example is the chapter devoted to "eclectic therapy," which they define as any treatment wherein the therapist combines at least two different treatment forms. They do not care what the two or more ingredients are but blithely make statements about their positive achievements. It makes as much sense as a cook's declaring that any combination of two or three foods will make a delicious meal, no matter whether it's prime steak with baked potato or dogfood with whipped cream.

If those who engage in outcome research studies had even a minimal understanding of psychotherapy, that understanding would be reflected in the design of their studies. However, I have never seen outcome research that had even halfway acceptable premises. A study of psychodynamic psychotherapy should, for example, attempt to compare treatment in which dreams are used intensively with treatment that does not use dreams at all. Dreams are one of the most important components of psychotherapy. Their proper use greatly influences the efficacy of treatment. Thus a work claiming to evaluate treatment methods should devote much space to the question of whether or not dreams are used. But check the index; there is not a word about dreams.

The authors seem to believe that by listing a great number of therapies, valid or not, they can extract from the mountainous hodgepodge some conclusions of value. But the most important factor in the success of treatment is the expertise and talent of the therapist. Outcome studies conveniently disregard that fact, since otherwise the projects would be impossible. Similarly, all other essential factors have been oversimplified to the point of being meaningless. Only such mutilation allows for producing "data" that can be fed into a huge number of statistics. Abundant statistics and jargon become a substitute for psychotherapeutic expertise, and pretentious, pseudoscientific language is used to bestow the appearance of importance on a meaningless academic artifact.

It is obvious, however, that when most premises are false, and most details wrong, the result, constant referrals to "science" notwithstanding, can only be a lamentable, confusing, and confused intellectual construction, far removed from the realities of psychotherapy. Poincaré has correctly stated that "a collection of facts is no more a science than a heap of stones is a house." What makes it even worse is that what is presented by the authors as "facts" are not facts at all.

Since we are speaking about treatment effectiveness with nonpsychotic patients, we might as well consider the following: For treatment to be effective, adequate treatment time is essential, and only a patient who is well-to-do or benefits from a generous insurance policy can afford that. Under present conditions, what are the prospects for a patient who suffers from a medium to several emotional disturbance and who, like many others, has not benefited in any major way from the new mood-altering drugs? Estimates, shared by a number of expert colleagues, are that his chances of encountering a competent therapist who might bring about slow, basic, lasting improvement are 5 to 15 percent; the Foundation's survey indicated an even smaller number. His chances of meeting a well-meaning but not too knowledgeable therapist who might bring about some improvement or at least may keep him going are about 40 to 60 percent. The remainder of the patients receiving help from professionals, well-meaning or not, are in harm's way.

Before arriving at metadentistry, I would like to offer three vignettes about matters I have complained about previously: pretentious discussion of Freud's life and work, and pretentious use of stilted "scientific" language. Such abuses, always frequent in psychoanalytic and psychotherapeutic writings, seem to be on the increase. Because of the amorphous nature of that domain, malfeasance can mushroom easily. However, I will present examples from other areas in order to highlight the absurdity of what is common fare in our field.

> Nobody can write the life of a man, but those who have eat and drunk and lived in social intercourse with him.
>
> SAMUEL JOHNSON

There is a great affinity between good literature and psychotherapy. No wonder both manifest similar ills. As with psychotherapists, there are academic writers who are gifted, sensitive, inspired, and inspiring. On the other hand, alas, we also find hordes of scholarly termites, who, lacking talent and understanding, thrive on applying their dull minds to nibbling away on works of beauty and value. Subjecting us to their shabby perspective, they reduce magnificence to their own lowly level.

Earlier in this chapter I complained about the many mental health professionals who present themselves as authoritative biographers of Freud and commentators on his work. They may be writing only a few paragraphs, an article, or an entire book. It is the mark of pseudointellectuals, aiming to present us with what they believe to be a dazzling display of scholarly profundity, to make a sorry mess even messier. There is a simple trick to writing a "successful" biography, whether about Martin Luther as a young man or about Freud. The "biographer" accumulates a large amount of data and then, *with absolute certainty*, writes his story describing actions, feelings, and motivations of the main character and other people. There is never a doubt why any person performed any action. The "biographer," whether an analyst or not, is omniscient. For instance, he always knows which person and which book had what influence on the person he is writing about.

In our field we find widespread ignorance manifested in the reviews appearing in professional journals and in the general acceptance of "scholarly" writings about the history of our craft, writings that have no psychotherapeutic validity. I have given many examples in this chapter of widely acclaimed incompetents.

Like many valuable works in psychotherapy, the finest works in literature are frequently subjected to destruction by little minds. I am reprinting here, in part, an editorial on Shakespeare that appeared in the NEW YORK TIMES on September 4, 1993. It was entitled "That Heavenly Rhetoric."

> Is Shakespeare truly the ruling genius of English literature, or was he just another writer? Is the insistence on teaching Shakespeare to schoolchildren merely a sinister plot to bolster the agenda of the right? Was Shakespeare a misogynist? A bourgeois hegemonist? An apologist for imperialism?
>
> If you, gentle reader, don't have an opinion on any of these questions, never fear: Academics, a whole raft of them, have plenty. Together they have created a publishing mini-industry that has lately been labeled the Bardbiz.
>
> Did you think "King Lear" was about a relationship between father and daughters? Please. It is really about "new forms of social organization and affective relationships." In your naïveté, did you believe the sonnets to be a great fistful of small gems, to be taken out and examined from different angles over the course of a lifetime? No, no, no. They merely "articulate the frustration of language's indeterminacy." And of course "The Tempest" is merely an allegory about colonialism. We all know that.
>
> Will the pinched pronunciations of these critics trickle down to their students and eventually into school curriculums – with the result that Shakespeare will be taught or not as an optional extra – just another writer?
>
> It is a privileged but shrinking group who had at least one play, at least one sonnet, drummed into their heads as adolescents. They still go forth and find magic from that

source. . . . Let the academics prattle. They're a bunch of
myopic spoilsports who miss the point entirely. Shakespeare
. . . needs no further defense.

And now: how to prove that one is a true scientist? Reported in
the INTERNATIONAL HERALD TRIBUNE of November 28, 1992, I found
quoted the following term, employed in an erudite scholarly paper by a
"social scientist": "immediate permanent incapacitation." For the
admiring but possibly confused reader: The author wanted to create an
improved, scientific definition of death.

With appropriate piety, one can only respond with a prayer: "May
he and his ilk never rest in peace!"

As long as one uses high-sounding "scientific" language and bombastic
terms in one's writing, many people will assume that it has a deep meaning. Such an article, written by Prof. Alan Sokal, a New York University
physicist, was published in May 1996 by the scholarly social science journal SOCIAL TEXT. The article was entitled "Toward a Transformative
Hermeneutics of Quantum Gravity." Here are two quotes from it:

> The π of Euclid and the G of Newton, formerly thought to
> be constant and universal, are now perceived in their
> ineluctable historicity; and the putative observer becomes
> fatally de-centered, disconnected from any epistemic link to
> a space-time point.

> Here my aim is to carry these deep analyses one step further,
> by taking account of recent developments in quantum grav-
> ity: the emerging branch of physics in which Heisenberg's
> quantum mechanics and Einstein's general relativity are at
> once synthesized and superseded. In quantum gravity, as we
> shall see, the space-time manifold ceases to exist as an objec-
> tive physical reality; geometry becomes relational and con-
> textual; and the foundational conceptual categories of prior
> science – among them, existence itself – become problema-
> tized and relativized. This conceptual revolution, I will
> argue, has profound implications for the content of a future
> postmodern and liberatory science.

But then came a big surprise: Professor Sokal, writing shortly thereafter in the magazine Lingua Franca, revealed that the paper was nothing but a parody, intended to ridicule the positions taken by Social Text and the obscure jargon that seriously damages the sciences.

The New York Times (May 18, 1996), rejoicing in Professor Sokal's satire, describes his clever construct as "coiled gibberish in a thicket of prose" and "an impenetrable hodge-podge of jargon, buzz-words, footnotes and other references." I wonder how the Times would feel about the "erudite" camouflage of ignorance and incompetence in our field. The misuse of language in academia and education, demonstrated and criticized by Sokal, does damage mostly to the cause of intelligence and honesty. In our field, however, unknowledgeable professionals benefit from the wide acceptance of pseudoscientific pretense at the expense of the untold suffering of human beings.

What about metadentistry, mentioned in the title of this section? Dear reader, here is a rhetorical question: Would you rather go to a dentist who is spouting forth scholarly, "scientific," generalizing dogmas about teeth and their proper place in the universe, and who, if one tooth has problems, will pull all of them and replace them with ill-fitting dentures, or to a dentist who limits himself to giving his best attention, competently and patiently, to the one tooth that is affected?

During the last century we have witnessed the appearance, transmutation, and disappearance of many theoretical positions, often contradicting each other in their emphasis on what is important about the structure and the dynamics of the human psyche. Certainly, many of them were interesting, and some of them enticingly convincing. But just because a hypothesis appeals to the intellect, that does not prove it to be psychologically valid. In this realm, the improbable is often reality. What could be more improbable than the existence of consciousness? And the existence of the unconscious adds insult to injury!

Psychological validity can be ascertained only by humble and expert clinical observation. In the final analysis, an overview of the multitude of theoretical assertions is no more conclusive than the statement by a cab driver I was privileged to hear: "It does not help me; it does not hurt me. Quite to the contrary!"

B. FOLLOWING A DIFFERENT DRUMMER: QUALITY IN PSYCHOTHERAPY

So far we have looked at the tenets and practices in psychotherapy that are the result of insufficient competence and the desire to avoid effort. In many instances, I have also indicated which positive approaches are required instead.

In the following three sections we will continue to focus on constructive solutions.

1. SLASHING THROUGH THE GORDIAN KNOT

The Saxon is not like us Normans. His manners
are not so polite.
But he never means anything serious till he talks
about justice and right.
When he stands like an ox in the furrow with his
sullen set eyes on your own,
And grumbles, "This isn't fair dealing,"
my son,
leave the Saxon alone.

KIPLING

Let the reader transpose and modify the above
quote so that it will apply to the matters at hand.

All theory, dear friend, is grey.

GOETHE

If you can look into the seeds of time,
And say which grain will grow and which will not,
Speak. . . .

SHAKESPEARE

WHAT PSYCHOTHERAPISTS NEED TO LEARN

No, I am unable to foretell the future of psychotherapy, and for the sake of my peace of mind, I may be better off for it. My past work at the Foundation, however, enables me to describe what is necessary to arrest the decline of psychotherapy and head it in a positive direction.

Contrary to what the peddlers of superficial methods and the theoretical generalizers may claim, when years of damage have left deep scars on a person, it takes much expertise and treatment time to discover his unique drama. When we read about the "great" successes, we would do well to remember the rarely mentioned "law of initial value" enunciated by the brilliant psychiatrist Joseph Wilder. It is as important as it is simple. When describing the treatment of a patient, we must report, as accurately as possible, his emotional level in terms of the negative and positive factors present at the beginning of treatment. We must also estimate and report (1) how deeply the patient's disturbance is anchored and (2) how firmly it is entrenched. That is a difficult task, and errors are often made. The best in-depth diagnosis can be made only after a prolonged time of observation and treatment by a professional of considerable clinical expertise.

We may also recall Gustav Bychofski's astute remark that the patients "successfully" treated by psychoanalysis are never the sickest ones, because psychoanalysis cannot treat those who do not show sufficient motivation and because the sickest patients are so despondent that they do not believe help is possible and therefore do not come for therapy. Of course, that still leaves a large number of quite disturbed patients who will seek out treatment – and stay with it.

In both individual and group therapy the assured presence of a person, or people, one can be with, and even talk to about one's pain, often fills an important emotional need and is thus a positive factor. And being in therapy provides an element of hope, the hope that one will become stronger and happier. Whether, however, true psychotherapy actually takes place in many of those situations is another question.

Based on our present knowledge, painfully acquired over the course of a century, we do know something about what good psychotherapy requires. The indispensable prerequisites are the sensitivity and talent of the therapist.

As stated, psychotherapists worthy of the name should be able to demonstrate their understanding of the workings of the unconscious, by properly handling feelings and dreams, using the transferences, understanding repressions and defenses, working through resistances, obtaining relief for the patient from an overly strict superego, exploring childhood events and their links to the psychic structure and its functioning within the patient, reconstructing capably in their own minds a realistic and detailed three-dimensional picture of each patient's inner universe, and, having done all that, formulating highly individualized temporary hypotheses for the patient, rejecting the influence of generalized dogma that is unsuited to explaining and dealing with the specific constellations and needs of the individual patient.

The work needed to accomplish those tasks, if done conscientiously, is formidable, and no one can do it perfectly. That is why many professionals try to circumvent it. The rationalization for using facile shortcuts frequently takes the form of generalizing dogma and theorizing.

However, all the skills are useless unless the therapist is capable of creating in his mind a three-dimensional representation of the forces extant and the specific ways in which they operate in each individual. That is no mean task; later we will discuss how to achieve it. Without such a representation, the therapist cannot establish a link between cause and effect; that is, discover the roots of the patient's problems. To use theory as a substitute for that labor is to fail in one's responsibility to the patient.

Later on, we will also elaborate on how the clinician should, in his communications with the patient, stay as close as possible to the language used by the patient's unconscious by referring to the feelings expressed and, most particularly, the images manifested in dreams.

The task of the clinician is far more difficult than the generalizing theoreticians suggest. Each of us is born different. The psychotherapist needs to understand the specific ways in which each individual has been affected by childhood and subsequent events.

After 45 years of extensive exploration of many forms of psychotherapy at the American Mental Health Foundation, we have concluded that all psychotherapists should acquire the knowledge and skills just listed. They are indispensable, even for a therapist who wants eventually to engage in behavior modification, marriage counseling, child therapy, group psychotherapy, or any other modality of psychotherapy.

That knowledge is, in fact, indispensable to anyone who wants to understand the human mind and its myriad psychological manifestations. Yet theorizers who have not obtained the necessary basic knowledge inundate us with their teachings and writings. Without having learned their ABCs, they venture into far higher regions, with pretentious productions and disastrous results. Sadly, those theorizers are often accepted and even acclaimed by the milling crowds. It is true that "the higher the monkey climbs, the more you see his rear," but only the relatively small number of clinical experts can see it for what it is.

We have looked at many examples of ignorance and absence of talent in so-called teachers and authorities. We have seen the negative effects on students and psychotherapists in search of knowledge and on patient care. Let us stop and think about the latter for a moment. For the longest time, invalid dogma and lack of clinical knowledge have caused immense damage to patients. Remember, for instance, the damage done in the psychoanalysis of women. Dismal results were and are commonplace.

Let me give you a few examples, outside psychotherapy proper, of how professional shortcomings cause problems in the mental health field.

We have already shown how incompetents in the sleep laboratories, pretending to be knowledgeable investigators of dreams, have completely bungled the task and have failed to engage in any projects of validity in that area. We have demonstrated a similar lack of understanding of the basic essentials in the equally pretentious and spurious claims of the neurobiologists.

The psychologists who foist on us pretentious theories and equations, such as learning theory based on experiments with rats, pigeons, and college students, would be able to formulate their projections more sagaciously and base them on far better premises if they had first acquired the basic knowledge about human beings that we advocate.

Let me give you another example: the application of lie detector tests. I know of two sociopaths who beat the test even though they were guilty, and as they reported with glee, they did not have to engage in any special effort; it occurred naturally. On the other hand, I am convinced that extremely self-destructive neurotics can register guilty responses even when they are innocent. Let us take as an example a young man, constantly plagued by nightmares, who in school would burst out in laughter whenever someone told him not to laugh. He laughed not because he thought the request was funny but because his action would be damaging to him. He also laughed when he was told that someone had died. His self-destruction manifested itself in many other situations, particularly in his attempts to come closer to women. If such a person were subjected to a lie detector test, his self-destructive unconscious would have a heyday.

Much damage has also been done in the area of intelligence tests, although quite a number of thoughtful studies have pointed out serious shortcomings. If those designing the tests had more of the basic knowledge I advocate, there could be great improvements in all kinds of testing. Many people are highly intelligent in one or more areas but, because of lack of interest, emotional reasons, or other reasons, test as "unintelligent" in other areas. There are still too many misconceptions in this area, and they can have deplorable consequences. Whenever the late Albert Shanker, the president of the American Federation of Teachers, writes about how to raise the skills and develop the intelligence of students, he focuses merely on mathematics. But he forgets that some people are highly intelligent in some areas but do poorly in others.

Here is a little anecdote on the matter of testing: A very intelligent man I know, in his 50s, wanted to acquire a second doctorate at one of the foremost universities in the United States. The admissions exam lasted over five hours. He scored extremely high. The graduate students in charge of the tests gave an unofficial handicap to those whose mother tongue was not English, so they could compare the foreign-born applicants with the others. With that figure included, the man's score was above the maximum. My friend told me, however, that if the test had included mathematics, as many such tests do, he would not even have passed it.

We are now going to tackle a crucial problem. Many therapists in the United States and in Europe are acquiring their know-how in psychoanalytic training institutes. Some of the institutes are affiliated with the International Psychoanalytic Association, and some are not.

I want to remind the reader of the estimate by knowledgeable professionals that only about 15 percent of trainees have the necessary capabilities. The chances that those candidates will be taught by competent teachers, also estimated to be about 15 percent, are therefore quite small. Without expert teachers, however, their training will be grossly inadequate.

Elsewhere we have discussed at some length that the number of patients who actually receive psychoanalysis is very small. For reasons already carefully explained, we cannot include the students who receive training analysis. Nor can we include institute patients who receive "psychoanalysis" by those students; John Gedo cogently explains the shortcomings of such treatment in his introduction to this volume. Among the reasons that so few people are in analysis are the high cost and the time commitment required – four or five sessions a week. Many therapists themselves shy away from accepting patients for psychoanalysis, for reasons mentioned earlier: the frequent necessity of reducing the fee per session, the large gap if a patient leaves, and for some the monotony of seeing the same patient five times a week. Most important, however, may be the fact that too many patients have been disappointed.

The situation, then, is that the future psychotherapist sacrifices much time and effort to learn a treatment procedure that he will only rarely practice. His practice will probably be filled with psychotherapy patients. The crux of the matter, however, is that he has never learned psychotherapy.

In principle, the psychoanalyst's task is much simpler than the psychotherapist's. The psychoanalyst accepts only those whom he considers suitable for the procedure and sufficiently motivated. He proceeds according to the instructions and dogma given to him in his training. The psychotherapist has no such restrictions and excuses. He has to deal with the patients as they come and is obliged to apply a much wider range of techniques. Whereas psychoanalysis is a relatively passive approach, in which the transference is allowed to develop, the psychotherapist needs to master that procedure as well as the more active ones. He uses the procedures he deems most appropriate, given his evaluation of the patient and certain outside circumstances, such as the number of sessions per week the patient can afford and is willing to come. The less frequently a patient can come, the more active the stance the therapist may have to take. The professional trained in psychoanalysis does not know how to proceed. He never learned the more active techniques in his training.

What would be a better course of training? We have already looked at the weaknesses of training analysis. A far better procedure would be to acquaint the trainee with the wide range of methods of psychotherapy, which would include both the passive procedures of the more traditional approach and the more active procedures. Most important, after completing his training in individual therapy, he would be trained in intensive psychodynamic group therapy. That will require his undergoing individual therapy and then intensive group therapy. It may also be valuable for him to receive individual therapy from more than one therapist, to acquaint himself with various treatment styles. The supervision of the trainee should be far more intensive than it commonly is today. I am aware of the practical obstacles, but the present training procedures are unacceptable. I refer the reader to Robert S. Wallerstein's chapter, "The Future of Psychotherapy," in our companion volume.

Can an unpleasant truth defeat a pleasing lie?

IBSEN

A CRUCIAL MATTER:
THE SELECTION OF PSYCHOTHERAPY TRAINEES

As we have already seen, unsuitable candidates are accepted as psychotherapy trainees, and we have no procedures for determining who is qualified. It is like freely admitting the tone-deaf and the ungifted as musicians as long as they have book knowledge about music. Incompetent musicians would become the majority and would rule the world of music. They would also publish papers in which they abundantly quoted other incompetents to reinforce their positions. As in politics, the belief of the many is strengthened by the reassurance that multitudes follow in the same track. Fortunately, there are too many knowledgeable musicians around to allow the unencumbered admission of incompetents. That is not the case in psychotherapy. Paraphrasing the words of the philosopher, rare indeed is the professional who has enough expertise and sincerity to say what he means and mean what he says.

The present system of selecting trainees for careers in psychotherapy is comfortable and advantageous for the academic institutions and the training institutes, as well as for the educators and professionals involved. It is disastrous, however, for the gifted student and for the quality of patient care. We need to consider the selection practices of the training institutes from the viewpoint of the training institute, the applicant, and the public interest.

The literature about admission to training is not abundant, and what there is ranges from the shallow to the mediocre. Even though the issue is of primary importance, the pervasive attitude is that the present system, comprising a series of interviews by institute members, is acceptable. A few of the papers suggest procedures that could be followed in addition to the interviews. Among those suggestions are psychological tests, trial analyses, and looking at the applicant's work with patients. The latter is the most interesting, but of course it could not be done until the candidate had already engaged in enough preliminary studies to allow him to start supervised work. As far as one can determine, the only one of those suggestions that has ever been followed is the use of psychological tests, which a few training centers use as a minor adjunct to the basic interviews.

The various papers present a shopping list of the noble qualities the candidate should possess plus another list of the shortcomings that would exclude him. Among the latter we find a number of neurotic traits. Now, one would expect that those traits would eventually be worked through in the candidate's personal analysis. It is bizarre to

expect the candidate to be free of the neurotic traits that are the very
material of his analysis.

The institutes claim that both the positive and the negative factors can be satisfactorily established by the interviews and the study
of the candidate's life history, as related by him. Can the institutes
actually accomplish that feat, or do they advance those naive claims
for their own self-interest? Let us consider a simple example. Honesty and a sterling character appear frequently on the list of desirable
traits. Their presence in the candidate is established by his answers to
questions intended to discover his true motivation. Does he want to
explore the truth about the human psyche, or does he want to have a
comfortable income and livelihood? Unless the interviewing faculty
members are clairvoyants with unheard-of capacities – in fact, omniscient – they must take the candidate's answers at face value. Most
applicants are clever, though not necessarily in ways that would qualify them for the profession of psychotherapist. They have a fair
understanding of the orientation and policies of the institute in question and what the interviewers are looking for and will phrase their
answers accordingly. If they have sociopathic tendencies, they will
even do better.

Robert Wallerstein (1991), speaking from his own experience,
states, "The psychiatric residents devoted considerable time and energy
to learning from, and also to impressing, their psychoanalyst teachers,
hoping that all this would eventually facilitate their acceptance by the
[Psychoanalytic] Institute."

Phyllis Greenacre (1961), in one of the better papers dealing with
the selection of psychotherapists, pointedly states: "We frequently hear
expressed as a positive recommendation of an applicant that he has a
'psychological gift' or 'access to the unconscious' or 'a high degree of
intuitive understanding.' Is it feasible to determine in preliminary
admissions interviews how this psychological gift has been used and has
seemed to influence the applicant's life?" In short, Greenacre doubts
that such a gift can be detected in the interviews.

That position is held by many sincere analysts. For example,
Grete Bibring (1954), as mentioned by Greenacre, decries the preponderance of career seekers in applicants as well as the preponderance of
character problems, rather than neuroses. We need only look at the

professionals populating the field of psychotherapy to know that that is true. Are they really the people we want to see in this profession?

Thus, as we can see, nothing has substantially changed in all these years, except, as Gedo has pointed out, the admissions criteria, which have become even more relaxed. The institutes continue to employ interviews to the exclusion of better procedures. The faculty members consistently claim that this method of selection is not merely adequate but erudite and sophisticated. Their descriptions of the interview procedures are masterpieces of scholarly language and thought. The reader will have to decide how much rationalization is involved here, but this we know is true: Interviews are the easiest procedure for the faculty members to use. They are also the worst.

It is not easy to establish which applicants possess the necessary sensitivity and talent to eventually become qualified psychotherapists. There are three methods, and I shall discuss them in order of their efficacy.

The best procedure is to place the candidate for training into an intensive psychotherapy group. He should be the only psychotherapy trainee in the group; otherwise, undesirable disturbing elements will make their appearance. Although the method would be cumbersome, it is feasible nevertheless. Here is one of the many examples of how talent can become evident: One of the most gifted people I ever encountered for the profession of psychotherapy was a young commercial artist who attended one of my groups. He was unassuming and reserved. He had no psychological education or prior psychotherapeutic experience. He did not speak up frequently, but when he did, his comments showed unusual understanding of other members' psychodynamics, dreams, and feelings. He did not use that ability to avoid looking at his own psychological problems. By the way, despite my encouragement, he would not consider training for professional work as a psychotherapist because he would have had to acquire the necessary academic degrees in medicine or psychology. He is not the only gifted person who has expressed the same hesitations. Unfortunately, many training institutes do not have a group therapy division, and those that do have one conduct group therapy in a manner I consider quite inadequate. That is a major obstacle to the placement of candidates into intensive psychotherapy groups.

Another effective procedure would be for the candidate who has been admitted on a conditional basis to bring in the dreams of his patients together with the notes recording all the associations, feelings, and comments of the patients regarding those dreams and the comments and thoughts of the candidate himself. It would allow his supervisors to gain a fair picture of the candidate's aptitudes.

The supervision of the candidate must be on a far more intensive level than is now customary.

The above procedures would be, however, perfectly useless unless the group therapist or supervisor in question was himself a sensitive and talented clinical expert. A denizen of Dimension II – that is, an intellectually and theoretically focused professional – will select only candidates who are in his likeness.

> Gratuitous theorizing in teaching has all too often replaced clinical expertise. While the number of academic courses demanded of the psychotherapy student has increased considerably, overall clinical expertise is markedly in decline.
>
> STANLEY LESSE

> I am not bound to please thee with my answer.
>
> SHAKESPEARE

THE ROOT OF MOST EVIL

How did the current disastrous situation in psychotherapy come about, and why is it permitted to continue? Why do so many of our professionals in leading positions and practicing psychotherapists have so little clinical expertise and simply rely on what they have learned from courses and the professional literature?

Nothing of what I will say here is new. Other authors and other concerned psychiatrists and psychotherapists have voiced similar criticisms.

There is a tendency in the mental health professions, probably more than in any other sector of public health, to overlook even the most glaring shortcomings and abuses. Efforts to eliminate them and to eliminate the problems resulting from them are practically nonexistent. We hear objections only when the material interest of the professionals is involved.

It is easy to avoid trying to improve the quality of our profession, because the practice of psychotherapy is only vaguely defined, allowing wide interpretations of what can be involved and including unqualified practitioners.

The fundamentals of our present system of systems – from the preliminary academic studies in medicine, psychology, social work, and other areas to the subsequent psychotherapy training – are practically unmovable. The present requirements are unnecessarily cumbersome and do not lead to the desired goal. Once a student has begun this unfortunate curriculum, however, he becomes increasingly enmeshed in the vast, insidious spiderweb, the system of systems. He may rationalize that fact or just accept the situation, not allowing himself to be bothered by unpleasant considerations of its cruel consequences for patients. Thus it is always moving to discover notable exceptions, such as the objections against the crucifixion of patients voiced by John Gedo in his introduction to this volume.

Let us return to the system of systems. Tip O'Neill, the knowledgeable former speaker of the U.S. House of Representatives, once shrewdly commented, "There are no national politics; there are only local politics." That is, both the elected politicians and the voters are guided by their own self-interest, at the expense of the common good. Similarly, the mental health field is made up of several influential professional unions with large memberships; governmental and nongovernmental agencies; associations and organizations; faculties, hospitals, clinics, and halfway houses; training institutes; journals and publishers; national and international conferences; and what have you. All those are special-interest groups, each fiercely defending its turf. The professional organizations see their main task as playing the role of unions for the professionals they represent. Each professional group unfailingly cites the public interest as the reason for its crusade, but that is, in fact, the least of its concerns. Except for a small number of dedicated and knowledgeable professionals, parochial interests hold sway at the expense of the public interest.

The policies of those groups cannot influence the work and examinations of the American Mental Health Foundation, which has the public interest in mind. One must not politely look the other way when so much suffering is involved. Everyone is disgusted to hear about unnecessary operations performed by surgeons for their financial benefit, and horrified to hear about a physician blinding scores of patients for the same reason. But just as much harm is done to the emotionally ill by maintaining the present systems that are the result of professional policies dictated mostly by self-interest.

We need, however, to complete the picture. There do exist a number of mental health professionals who possess fine minds, unusual expertise, and considerable goodwill. Yet those dedicated men and women have proved unable to translate their good intentions into a change of policies that would benefit a majority of the emotionally ill, and they cannot stem the decline in the profession. That raises questions for which we must find answers.

Think of all the money being spent by the federal, state, and local governments, by the universities and hospitals, and by private donors and all the money that goes into publishing professional books and journals and holding conferences. All of it is supposedly spent to improve mental health professionals. Where are those improved professionals? The fact is that the vast majority of severely depressed and anxious people and those who suffer from deeply rooted phobias have nowhere to go for help. They are being thrown to the wolves. Even the well-to-do may never find treatment resulting in lasting improvement.

> Undergraduates owe their happiness chiefly to the fact that they are no longer at school. The nonsense which was knocked out of them at school, is all put back at Oxford or Cambridge.
>
> MAX BEHRBOHM

Why are we at such a stage? The most important factor, as I have pointed out again and again, is the lack of competence of too many mental health professionals. And the most important cause of that lack is the appalling fact that anyone, even those who have no ability whatsoever for this profession, can become a psychotherapist as long as he is willing to do the necessary course work to obtain an academic degree in one of the disciplines in mental health, or even in a tangential area such as education. He can then enter a training institute, many of which are quite anxious to attract students. Here, too, years of course work are the essential part of the training. As Gedo stated, in the last few decades the institutes have graduated virtually all candidates, no matter how unsuitable they are for the profession. It must be pointed out, however, that even in previous times the training institutes graduated most of the trainees. Only the discovery that the student is a serial murderer or, worse, that he consistently questions dogma would be an obstacle to graduation.

It is advantageous for the schools and institutes to increase the course work under the pretext of improving the education. Courses are easy to give and are an easy source of revenue. The happy result is a larger faculty and more prestige.

Courses are, however, an inadequate and shoddy substitute for intensive, prolonged individual instruction and painstaking personal supervision. Such teaching and supervision are admittedly cumbersome. Moreover, they require expert clinicians.

It was once the case, conveniently forgotten now, that many of the older psychoanalysts would train gifted candidates privately, outside the institute setting. I have met quite a number of therapists trained in that way who are far more competent than the average institute graduate. On the other hand, the sad truth is that many of the writers whom we have severely criticized in this volume are well-known, respected teachers in the institutes and the universities. Supervision and instruction by them could cause only harm, even to a gifted and discerning student. At present, qualified teachers are rare, and only dramatic changes in our system will gradually increase their number.

There is an unfortunate permissiveness in psychotherapy, an anything-goes and live-and-let-live attitude as long as the professional has some kind of degree in the behavioral sciences. There is also a careful avoidance of the issues that really matter, such as improving the selection and training procedures, increasing clinical knowledge, and developing better and less expensive treatment methods. All those are priorities of the American Mental Health Foundation.

The sincere and gifted student who wants to acquire valid psychotherapeutic know-how will be confronted with some bewildering choices. One choice is which path to follow. Robert S. Wallerstein, in his first chapter in our companion volume, condemns the ever-increasing deterioration of the psychotherapy teaching that psychiatry students receive. If the student chooses a different road, namely, acquiring a psychology degree, he must enter years of study that have little to do with his goal.

Furthermore, the gifted student may run into obstacles; doctoral and postdoctoral programs at some of the better-known schools pride themselves on being most selective and accepting few students. A careful study of the writings of the faculty members responsible for the selection of students and their subsequent education will clearly establish their mind-sets. And when one studies the writings of the students they graduate, some of them having acquired teaching positions of their own, one uncovers the same mind-set. The teachers and the students they so carefully select are cut of the same cloth; they are almost invariably academically oriented denizens of Dimension II. However, as we have seen, what we need are the sensitive and talented people in Dimension I.

The situation concerning training institutes in psychoanalysis and psychotherapy is aptly described by Gedo. The requirements in the other institutes vary greatly, but extensive course work is the backbone of all their programs. Some of the smaller institutes, mostly run by psychologists and some now affiliated with the International Psychoanalytic Association, declare that their admission criteria are extremely selective. Admissions, however, are based merely on interviews and academic achievements. The trainees may have to spend seven years before they can graduate, and their only practical experience may be having carried two patients in psychoanalysis under supervision. We can gain a picture of the dimension in which they operate by scrutinizing their writings and attending the conferences they organize. The picture is similar to the one related above.

At any rate, a student who has a halfway acceptable degree, and many allowances are made here, will be able to find a training school.

We have looked at a list of the basic skills and areas of expertise the psychotherapist must have. Without them, all theorizing is without merit, but the psychotherapy student cannot necessarily distinguish between the essential and the valueless. Unfortunately, the student may not even realize that valid knowledge does exist, difficult though it may be to find.

The talent for taking courses is in no way related to the talent for psychotherapy. I have known a considerable number of gifted psychotherapists who intensely disliked many of the courses they had to take, finding them boring and not pertinent to the knowledge they longed for. And we all know intellectuals who are simply not too bright but who thrived on course work.

In his introduction to this volume, Gedo rightly complains that trainees receive considerably less supervision than is necessary to ensure competent management of cases, and he contends that the institutes graduate candidates who have not achieved a successful termination with any of their patients.

The clinical inadequacy of psychotherapists who were supposedly fully trained was a constant problem during the many years that the American Mental Health Foundation sponsored a treatment center. We informed the candidates for positions as supervisors and therapists that we insisted on extensive clinical knowledge and experience. We asked them to describe and document their experience. A great many of the applicants presented letters from senior psychotherapists, frequently their former teachers and supervisors. Often the letters would praise the candidate as being "theoretically strong." Unfortunately, their clinical background and capabilities proved to be insufficient.

The reader would be shocked to learn how many of the candidates, from various professional backgrounds, surprised by our requirements of prior personal psychotherapy and supervised work, would exaggerate or even fake their experience. One such case was an applicant for a group therapist position who had a doctorate in clinical psychology from a prestigious university. He indicated in his curriculum vitae that he had undergone five years of group psychotherapy with a well-known group therapist, who happened to be a friend of mine. When I mentioned to my friend that he was named as the therapist for this man for a period of five years, he exclaimed: "The time period is correct, but it was not he who was my patient. It was his sister."

To obtain the cogent and expert information necessary for the work of the American Mental Health Foundation and the International

Institute for Mental Health Research, in Switzerland, I maintain contact with a number of friends who are open-minded, are interested in the improvement of psychotherapy, and have unusual clinical wisdom. I rely on them to bring to my attention desirable and undesirable elements in our field and its literature.

From time to time I ask the following question: Let us assume that we present to academicians in the field of the behavioral sciences, or to teachers and supervisors in training facilities, some 20 or so meaningful dreams of a patient, all his associations to and feelings about the various portions of each dream, and an extensive description of his childhood. What are the names of the academicians or teachers who could give us a tentative but clinically acceptable presentation of the psychodynamics of the patient? The answer is that there are hardly any such academicians or teachers. I encourage the reader to pose the same question to knowledgeable colleagues.

Thus neither in his university studies, which are supposed to be the foundation for his future work as a capable psychotherapist, nor in his psychotherapeutic training, does the student get the instruction he needs. Many students never realize that the years and years of course work will produce only meager results and will include mostly disinformation. No matter how impressive their credentials, most of the teachers the student has to face are dilettantes. They have no clinical expertise, and of course, they cannot teach what they do not know. They are therefore restricted to theorizing and book knowledge. They glorify the inconsequential, since only there are they on safe ground. The reader need not take my word for those assertions. He can instead look to the wisdom of such outstanding clinicians as Ralph R. Greenson, Paul H. Hoch, John E. Gedo, Stanley Lesse, and Robert J. Stoller, all quoted in our volumes.

"Intellectual" is not the same thing as "intelligent." Goethe illustrated that magnificently in his portrayal of Wagner, Faust's assistant. Let us once more quote Goethe, speaking in Faust's voice:

> He cleaving to shallow things,
> Eternally feasts on empty terms,
> This worm, claiming mighty wings,
> Finds happiness unearthing worms!

Does that seem harsh? We must never forget that the obstacles these people present are the reason that innumerable people with deep-rooted emotional problems will not receive the help they desperately need. Moreover, these teachers and professionals stand in the way of improvements that are well within our reach.

Once again, we can safely say that the overriding emphasis on course work, at the expense of clinical expertise, allows the unrestricted admission of incompetents into psychotherapeutic work and does not provide suitable students with even a fraction of the needed instruction.

I have pointed out that one of the major reasons that psychoanalysis, and to some extent analytic psychotherapy, have suffered such a decline in their appeal to students, particularly in the medical field, and to the patients seeking help is that so many of its practitioners were not sufficiently competent to deliver the hoped-for improvements. And that despite the almost complete stranglehold those particular treatment procedures had over the field for many decades. Gedo, speaking most tactfully in consideration of the sensitivities of his colleagues, expresses a similar view: "If the pragmatically oriented American consumer has turned away from psychoanalysis as a professed method of therapy for personality disorders, the most important reason for this dissatisfaction may well be that that form of treatment has not been sufficiently effective."

For the sake of the patients, we must attack the obstacles to improvement wherever we find them. We must not forget that the older generation of psychologists were quite adamant about keeping their discipline apart from all psychotherapeutic endeavors. It is not that they were trying to keep psychologists out of the practice of psychotherapy but that they thought it to be only honest to point out the vast gap between the two areas. Some psychologists still feel that way. Here is an example, one of many, of such a gap: Freud pointed out that to understand the unconscious, and thus the human mind, one must study and understand dreams. Surely, that approach is vastly different from the one that psychology takes. However, self-interest won out; an ever-increasing number of psychologists demanded easier access to the interesting – and, they hoped, financially rewarding – field of psychotherapy.

Thus we now have a considerable number of qualified psychotherapists who have psychology degrees.

But the fact that some psychologists have sought the additional knowledge that would enable them to practice psychotherapy in no way justifies the gratuitous claims that psychology studies and degrees are the necessary first academic step for a psychotherapist. If that were the case, all psychiatrists would be barred from practicing psychotherapy. Even worse is the claim that psychological studies themselves bestow the know-how to practice psychotherapy. Any such claim is fraudulent, as is the claim that physicians with no psychotherapy training are capable of practicing psychotherapy.

We demand that politicians seeking public office disclose their finances and inform us of the activities they have engaged in. No such disclosure of matters of true importance is required of psychotherapists. Most directories of psychiatric and psychological associations list academic background and teaching and other positions that have been held. The bibliographical directory of the American Psychiatric Association also mentions training at any of the psychoanalytic institutes. Gedo and I have already discussed the frequent weaknesses of training in such institutes.

However, the most important elements of training are not listed. They are his personal psychotherapy – how long, how many sessions a week, the names of the psychotherapists, and the periods when he was seen by them – and the complete details regarding the supervision of his work. While such annotations would not guarantee the quality of his personal therapy or of the supervision he underwent, they would be a step in the right direction. Since the so-called therapists can usually show the rather meaningless academic credentials but are lacking in psychotherapeutic experience, we can expect indignant opposition to that proposal from the psychotherapists who are psychotherapeutically weak.

In the directories of the American Psychiatric Association and, to a lesser degree, of the American Psychological Association we find a number of professionals who do not even offer any details on their academic background. While that may be owing to laziness, writer's block, or the burdens of home cooking, it can also have nefarious reasons.

Let us take the sad example of a psychiatrist with whom I am quite familiar. Although he is from my hometown in Austria, I did not know him there, since he is older than I am. However, once he had become established in New York, psychiatric friends warned me about him. They stated that he was a clever opportunist without any conscience and an inveterate liar. In my hometown he was active in the city's ghetto, apparently not to help but to exploit. In New York he obtained a desirable position as a psychiatric consultant to an important community-oriented organization. As one would expect, after some years the assignment terminated in unpleasant circumstances. The point, however, is this: In the APA directory all that is listed for this person is his name, city, state, and zip code. If he had been obliged to list complete information, the organization in question could have obtained pertinent information from the entities listed, and considerable suffering to patients could have been avoided. Obviously, the directories are designed to protect the interest of the union member, not the consumer.

Since I am trying here to point out the shortcomings of psychotherapy and its practitioners, I have to dwell on the negatives. Over the years, however, I have had the good fortune of making the acquaintance of colleagues of diverse backgrounds, both in the United States and in Europe, whose expertise, decency, and concern for their patients are admirable. I have only one complaint, a matter that saddens me greatly: why do these brilliant people, some of whom are in positions of responsibility and are fine writers and speakers, not come forward and insist on the reforms so urgently needed?

> A craft for the humble,
> A task for the wise.
>
> PIERRE JANET

> Nothing will ever be attempted, if all possible objections must be first overcome.
>
> SAMUEL JOHNSON

TO TAKE ARMS AGAINST A SEA OF TROUBLES: THE STRUGGLE TO ESTABLISH A NEW PROFESSION

The first line of that title, a quote from Shakespeare, appears for the second time in this volume, and for good reason. Powerful professionalinterest groups are fighting, and so far defeating, a change that common sense tells us is indispensable for the public interest. The writer Isaac Asimov has stated: "No decent human being would allow an animal to suffer without putting it out of its misery. It is only to human beings that human beings are so cruel as to allow them to live on in pain, in helplessness, in living death, without moving a muscle to help them. It is against such attitudes that this book fights."

No, it is not to this volume that Asimov refers, but to the Hemlock Society's FINAL EXIT. However, his statement applies here perfectly. Our volume deals with the suffering of the nonpsychotic emotionally ill and the lack of available help.

All the evidence in this volume points to the need for a new profession, the competent clinical psychotherapist. Is that a new idea? Not at all. Some 50 years ago the psychiatrist Lawrence Kubie, a man concerned with patient welfare and devoted to improving psychotherapy and making it available to far more people, again and again made that point. We have also spoken of the laudable efforts of Robert S. Wallerstein in that direction. Any professional interested in the idea should read THE DOCTORATE IN MENTAL HEALTH: AN EXPERIMENT IN MENTAL HEALTH PROFESSIONAL EDUCATION (Wallerstein, 1991). Additional information about Kubie's outstanding efforts and a number of the quotes that the reader will encounter further on in this volume are to be found in Robert R. Holt's chapter in that book. Another volume of much interest, edited by Holt, is NEW HORIZON FOR PSYCHOTHERAPY: AUTONOMY AS A PROFESSION. In that book Holt also briefly mentions the American Mental Health Foundation's efforts in this matter.

Since early 1948 the Foundation has made the establishment of the new profession one of its priorities. Our focus is considerably less on academic course work than Kubie's and Wallerstein's focus. It is instead on intensive clinical experience and supervision. In 1957 and 1958 I met with Kubie three times regarding those matters. Since then, the situation has worsened considerably. The present emphasis on short-term treatment and superficial methods, as well as the many other factors mentioned in this volume, have rendered effective treatment for serious emotional illness practically impossible to obtain.

People are aware of the existence of the homeless, since they are visible. Despite that, indifference to their misery has become generalized, and hardly anything of consequence is being done. How much worse is the fate of the seriously emotionally ill, who suffer their agony unseen and mostly alone! As dreadful as it seems, those who can commit suicide may well be the lucky ones. And we should not hesitate to point the finger at those who are largely responsible.

The only remedy for the present intolerable situation is to create a new profession entirely devoted to psychotherapy and mental health. In an age of specialization among physicians and psychologists, it is absurd that a discipline that requires specific knowledge and extensive training has not been allowed to come into existence. The major reason is the opposition of the professions that now provide the teaching of the studies that precede psychotherapeutic training and those that offer the training itself. Robert Holt asks, "Can we continue to urge the continuance of our disciplinary self-interest and the unnecessary brake it puts on progress?" Because of the dearth of professionals of vision, moral integrity, and dedication to improved patient care, such as Kubie, Wallerstein, and Holt, the reactionary professional forces have prevailed. One of the consequences was the downfall of Wallerstein's meritorious project. As Thoreau aptly wrote, "Any man more right than his neighbors constitutes a majority of one."

Change can come about only when those who sincerely want to acquire valid psychotherapeutic knowledge and those who suffer from the present professional inadequacies persistently clamor for quality training and quality care. So far, there is mostly silence.

How should the education and training of the profession of psychotherapist be structured? We have in this volume described what is positive and what is negative in psychotherapy. We have pointed out which knowledge and which skills are essential, and we do not need to repeat that information.

Obviously, the conditions and facilities necessary to establish a special education for this profession will vary enormously from place to place, resulting in considerable differences in the initial curriculum. It will be difficult to find the kind of professional one would really like to fill the faculty positions and supervise the students' psychotherapeutic work. However, it is important that the first steps be taken, while insisting on certain fundamentals. Difficult though it will be, the selection of students should be on the basis we outlined.

Courses must be carefully established and kept to a minimum. The whole enterprise would be destroyed if self-interest were allowed to turn it into another academic behemoth. All the courses should be selected with one goal: to become the building stones that will allow the student to acquire clinical expertise. We are therefore emphasizing the studies and activities that fall into the domain of Dimension I and excluding to the greatest possible extent the subject matter in Dimensions II and III. That focus alone will create an educational endeavor infinitely more useful than the pseudointellectual and pseudoscientific waste offered to students today. Robert Holt succinctly asks, "Can we seriously propose to waste the time of so many urgently needed therapists in years of irrelevant and marginally useful training along traditional lines?" Holt envisions the new professionals as knowing "all that they need to know in order to be excellent psychotherapists, without being loaded down by unnecessary intellectual baggage."

Holt carefully and cogently discusses the academic work required of the psychiatric, psychological, and social work students, something we cannot do here. Nevertheless, let me quote a few of his comments on the formation of clinical psychologists, because they contradict the spurious claims frequently made that psychology studies bestow competence in psychotherapy.

> Like psychiatry, clinical psychology only gradually became differentiated from its mother profession. When I got my Ph.D. in 1944 it was simply in psychology; there were no specialized graduate programs for particular kinds of psychologists. Graduate training expressly and exclusively for *clinical* psychologists began after the second World War, helped along by the rapid expansion of the Veterans Administration's efforts to meet the mental health needs of returning veterans. Despite this practical impetus, the design and control of the new graduate programs remained firmly in the hands of conservative, elder, academic psychologists with little knowledge of clinical practice, but with a firm conviction that anyone calling him/herself a psychologist of any kind had to have a sound scientific education and research apprenticeship culminating in a Ph.D.

dissertation. (That was known as "maintaining standards.")
Consequently, generations of clinical psychologists went
through programs in which their first year or so of graduate
work was identical with that of peers who were headed for
academic careers of teaching and experimentation in general, social, child, or physiological psychology. A large part
of what they studied and mastered for their qualifying
examinations, even in generations when psychotherapy had
become the dominant theme of their future practice, had as
little relevance to clinical work as most of the psychiatrist's
post-graduate studies. It generally took from four to six
years to get the Ph.D. if all went swimmingly, plus a year of
internship – direct practice under supervision, but often
with a strong emphasis on diagnostic testing. Even after
about 1960, when clinical doctoral programs were giving
both theoretical and practical instruction in psychotherapy,
which was also stressed in the internship, many clinical psychologists sought further postdoctoral training in psychotherapy (most of it being mainly practice under supervision).
Since large numbers of them experienced years of delay in
completing their dissertation research, the psychologist's
postgraduate training years were generally no fewer than
those of the psychiatrist.

As far as Holt's comments on social work studies, I will only
excerpt the following: "Because psychotherapy was a late addition to the
skills of case workers, a high percentage of the two graduate years is
spent on learning content and skills of little eventual applicability in a
therapeutic career."

Holt also points out: "Whether in an institution or in private practice, what actually transpires between the provider and the recipient of
the service differs remarkably little according to the diploma on the
therapist's office wall." That is true. And the quality of that professional
activity would be considerably higher were it not for our inane system
of selection and education.

The supervision of the student's work with patients and his personal psychotherapy experience form the core of his training. The

supervisor will need to be able to teach the student how to build a three-dimensional representation of each patient's unconscious, based only on the clinical data he has patiently gathered. Unfortunately, few supervisors currently have the necessary expertise. We will show in the last section of this chapter how to create such a representation. The student must do so without using any of the terms of accepted dogma. No use of "anal," "pre-oedipal," "oedipal," and "phallic mother" when describing the clinical data. Theoretical and dogmatic considerations can be brought in later, when the student can discriminate what he does and does not need for his understanding of the psychodynamics of the patient and to form the necessary temporary hypothesis. The more gifted he is, having the necessary sensitivity to understand feelings and their linkage to dreams, the more he will be able to build those hypotheses without the crutches of generalizing dogma. The student will modify the hypotheses he has constructed as he proceeds in the treatment of the patient. Dreams will become more revealing, reaching deeper and more meaningful levels, and guide him to the proper course of action.

Once more: the more gifted a therapist is, the less he will use the crutch of dogma. Frankly, those who are capable only of a simple approach, applied indiscriminately with every patient, have no place in this profession. If they insist on engaging in academic work, their capabilities might qualify them for work in statistics or administration. But why should they, when they can secure far more remunerative and prestigious employment in the faculties of our universities, as supervisors and analysts of the trainees in the institutes, and as the supposed "healers" of patients?

Of course, no matter how accomplished a therapist is, the treatment of the seriously emotionally ill is difficult. The clinicians who deal with difficult cases are unsung heroes who deserve our admiration. But their labor, dedication, and continuous striving to acquire additional knowledge that can help their patients are not enough to stop the deterioration of psychotherapy.

During all the decades that were marked by the hegemony of intellectual and dogmatic institutions, there have been men and women who, without fanfare, strove to do the right thing. It is their valuable knowledge that we are trying to unearth and revive. We need teachers and supervisors who have such clinical expertise. They will form the core of the program.

We are trying to have this volume published in many languages and distributed in many countries. The obstacles to creating the new profession will vary greatly from country to country. In some places third-party payers will make insurance payments only to psychiatrists and psychologists. However, that is not a hindrance in many situations, because the average wage earner will be able to pay the relatively moderate cost of the intensive, extended group psychotherapy out of his own pocket. If the teaching and training programs are properly set up and dedicated professionals of quality are involved, recognition of the new profession will expand.

Those willing to set up such a program would do well to study the pioneering work and experience of Robert Wallerstein and modify it according to their own judgment. Speaking about men of courage and goodwill, such as Wallerstein, Samuel Butler wrote these memorable words: "The first undertakers in all great attempts commonly miscarry and leave the advantages of their losses to those who come after them."

2. THE TOUCHSTONE BY WHICH WE TRY: THE TWO TALENTS

By different methods different men excel:
But where is he who can do all things well?

Charles Churchill

A special kind of sensitivity is necessary to
understand the vast spectrum of colors unique to the
psyche of each individual. This distinguishes the
psychotherapist from the generalizing theorist.

S.deS.

The therapist variables most frequently selected by researchers for study are, unfortunately, such simplistic global concepts as to cause this field to suffer from possibly terminal vagueness.

PARLOFF, WASKOW, AND WOLFE

There is no substitute for talent. In its absence, industry and good will are of no avail.

ALDOUS HUXLEY

For understandable reasons, one of the rarest words in psychoanalytic and psychotherapeutic literature is "talent." In a system where even the least gifted and most sterile pseudointellectual can, without difficulty, enter the profession, and even achieve prominence, the word is taboo. Insist on talent, and the whole profitable system of professional education in our field collapses. Rare indeed are those who, like Jerome D. Frank, have the courage to assert that giftedness is an essential requisite for the exercise of this craft, just as it is necessary for a musician to have special innate qualification.

What possibly should have been a long section will be a brief one. The reasons will shortly become apparent to the reader.

Why do I touch on this topic at all? It is because I want to make a point that has not been made elsewhere and yet is of importance to the matter of psychotherapeutic talent. The point is that it is both advantageous and realistic to speak of two talents.

The first talent is simply an analytic talent. A person who has such a talent can sense, based on the therapy sessions with a patient, the psychodynamics of the patient, understand to a great extent his feelings, fantasies, and dreams, and realize where his problems lie and how they are tied in with childhood events.

The second talent is the capability of bringing about psychotherapeutic improvement of the patient.

The ideal therapist possesses both talents to a major degree.

Alas, such therapists are rare. I have known quite a number who had considerable analytic talent but had less success in working through the patient's problems than one would hope for. They see the problems correctly but seem unable to bring about sufficient improvement. There are many possible reasons for that. In some instances, the therapist's neurosis, his insecurity, or his personality is an obstacle. For example, a brilliant analyst may be too impatient to work successfully with patients who need long-term treatment. He may have too short an attention span. A group psychotherapist who has a fine analytic understanding of his patients may use the wrong approaches. Talented psychotherapists do fail. Although each case has its own reasons for failure and has to be looked into individually, all such cases indicate a deficiency in the second talent.

On the other hand, there are therapists who are not too strongly endowed with the first talent but do achieve, to varying degrees, therapeutic improvements with a considerable number of their patients. As I have mentioned, quite a few expert clinicians have estimated that only about 15 percent of psychodynamic psychotherapists can be considered accomplished professionals. The remaining 85 percent can be divided into those whose presence is beneficial and those whose presence is nonbeneficial.

One can postulate that a professional who is rather weak in the first talent but has given evidence of the second talent would be among those whose presence is beneficial. If that is true, then those who possess the second talent, which we may call a psychotherapeutic personality, can fall either in the top category of accomplished psychotherapist or in the category of beneficial presence.

How can we define the psychotherapeutic personality? It is enormously difficult to give an adequate and realistic answer rather than an abundance of scholarly words that amount to nothing. We do not want a glib intellectual "explanation." The only people who can help us are the experts capable of evaluating the therapeutic results of experienced colleagues. In fact, such situations are rare in professional life. It is far easier to obtain such information about the psychotherapeutic work of trainees, but even there the knowledge may be tainted by their inexperience and their not having sufficiently worked though any interfering personality problems of their own.

Experience shows that the second talent can be found in people of the most diverse personality types and dispositions. That is why I am forced to keep this section short. Over the years, I have given much thought to this matter and have searched for common factors.

As mentioned, in the American Mental Health Foundation we had the opportunity to collect much data on the effectiveness of the work of many practicing psychotherapists, some of them well-known writers and teachers. Anyone attempting to tackle an explanation of the second talent in a book would have to start by providing all available details about the personality and formation of each of the therapists in question and relate his successes and failures – an almost impossible task. Despite the amount of data the Foundation collected, the information available is far from sufficient.

Even though not profound, I want to make only one cautionary comment based on experience: we must be careful not to make premature judgments, either about who has the second talent or about what the common factors are among those who do have that talent. I have known some self-assured therapists who spoke beautifully and cogently about psychotherapy but who turned out to have serious shortcomings in their aptitudes.

Such experience negates the assertions of the seemingly omniscient faculty members of the training institutes who claim that it is perfectly all right for them to select candidates merely on the basis of their interviews – and damn the patients. How can they justify that? With more concern and mental effort, much human suffering could be avoided. Obviously, the method of screening applicants merely by interview can be evaluated by considering its results. Take a good look at those who are analysts and psychotherapists. How many of them would you select as your own analyst? I explained in the previous section how to select candidates who show definite promise.

In psychotherapy much of what is said and written is, in basic attitude, still on the same level of gratuitous intellectualizing that the scholastics practiced hundreds of years ago. Only the topics are different, not the level of comprehension. Too many of the people we allow to intrude and dominate our craft do not have the special intelligence, the necessary talent.

We know that to become an accomplished tennis player, one needs to have the necessary ability; without the talent, merely reading books about tennis will be of no help. It is only in the mental health profession that even the most basic requirements of talent are waived. Instead of talented people, we have people who can do well in course work. Those people are the ones who will later be selecting candidates just like themselves. It is a vicious circle, a self-perpetuating system of learned ignorance.

The talents of the tennis player, the musician, the artist, and other gifted individuals are recognized by kindred people, though perhaps not immediately. In psychotherapy, however, the situation is quite different. To be sure, many of the acclaimed teachers and authors speak and write beautifully and convincingly and attract followers and admirers among students and psychotherapists. But that is not the talent we are looking for. Our system, now and in the past, produces only a small number of true experts. It is only they who have the talent and the acumen to distinguish the valid from the valueless, to detect the many teachers and writers who lack the fundamental knowledge on which psychotherapeutic work must be based and who are therefore unable to see what is important. We will clarify that in the next section. Because the experts are a small minority, their public criticism of the unqualified is subdued or even nonexistent. Only in private do they voice their true evaluation.

The situation is unacceptable. We must insist that psychotherapy become a competent study in depth of each individual it is dealing with and that therapeutic work be done only on that basis. We must direct our efforts to that end. If improvement gradually takes place and progress ensues, in a few hundred years knowledgeable people will look back at our present beliefs and procedures in the "behavioral sciences" with as much dismay and derision as we have for the beliefs of a few centuries ago.

3. WHAT HAS VALUE?

In nature's infinite book of secrecy
A little I can read.

SHAKESPEARE

> Understanding man is written in this great book – I mean our life – which stands continually open to our gaze, but it cannot be understood unless one first learns to comprehend the language and interpret the characters in which it is written. It is written in the language of the human heart, and its characters are feelings, dreams, and thoughts, struggling to be expressed in words or rushing to disappear forever. Without being able to read them, any understanding is impossible, and one wanders in the darkest labyrinth.
>
> PARAPHRASE OF GALILEO

There is no doubt that a considerable number of students have set out with a genuine desire to acquire the skills and knowledge necessary for the practice of psychotherapy, and surely many of the teachers in the various disciplines who are attempting to guide them toward that goal are making an honorable effort. Nevertheless, psychotherapy, and the entire mental health endeavor, are in a lamentable state.

We have looked at the vast self-perpetuating system of systems that affects all aspects of psychotherapy. It is an intricate network of forces and factors that could be described as immovable, except for the fact that it is sliding downhill.

However, if one complains about the state of affairs to mental health professionals, only the rare experts in psychotherapy understand what one is talking about. The rest assume that things are fine. Laymen, of course, are completely ignorant of the facts.

How has the unfortunate situation become so widespread and endured for such a long time?

To understand, we may profitably look at an analogous situation in a different domain, a situation that may be the most calamitous financial abuse of recent times: the "lost" $500 billion plus of the American savings and loan industry. How could such a huge malfeasance continue for so many years without an outcry from the public – an outcry that even now has not been forthcoming?

First, many members, prominent or not, of both political parties benefited from this source. Prudently, those who did not benefit kept quiet, to avoid creating problems for themselves.

Second, such matters are too complex to allow for understanding by the general public. Because of the magnitude of the situation, the public mistakenly assumes that proper control is maintained by governmental agencies and by responsible participants, their organizations, and the industry as a whole.

The same two answers apply to the status quo condoned by the various professions that constitute the "behavioral sciences," an area that is even more complex and esoteric than the savings and loan industry. The public is able to form an opinion, right or wrong, only about matters that it believes to be within its comprehension, such as taxes, employment, unions, retirement, cars, health insurance, social security, crime, the death penalty, ecology, abortion, and so on. Thus the "behavioral sciences" need not fear exposure and scrutiny.

In the savings and loan situation immense amounts disappeared into the pockets of corporations and individuals. There was no conspiracy, no coordinated intent, just innumerable individuals working within a financial system of systems, a spiderweb covering the entire country and resulting in immense damage to it. Yet the average citizen, even after disclosure, is not aware of the effects and is therefore unconcerned.

It is nearsighted to assume that just because a system is in place and operative, it has proven its worth.

This illustration demonstrates that even in matters that profoundly affect each citizen, ignorance and apathy are common. Such noninterference is infinitely more prevalent in matters of emotional illness and mental health, matters that most people hardly think about. To realize how disastrous the present decline is, the reader should acquaint himself with the chapter "The Future of Psychotherapy," by Robert S. Wallerstein, in our companion volume.

In our present system of psychotherapeutic endeavors, the patient, the aspiring student, and the practitioner attempting to acquire valid knowledge are the unfortunate victims. How can we extricate ourselves from this quagmire? The first step is to refuse to accept our present system of systems as the best of all possible worlds.

Let us now turn away from the problem of the odious system and focus on the positive, wherein we place our hope: the respect good therapists have for the uniqueness of each individual and their willingness to explore that uniqueness for the patient's betterment. Such a quest is in stark contrast to the facile generalizations of the many practitioners who reduce the individual to a psychological mass product, so that one dogma fits all, and provide a few convenient subcategories to add a touch of separating coloration to the herds.

For the remainder of this chapter we will concentrate on how to gain the optimum picture of the unconscious, a picture that is unique for each individual. The representation should enable us to better pursue our therapeutic endeavor. Let me repeat the list of the basic skills required. The psychotherapist should be able to demonstrate his understanding of the workings of the unconscious by properly handling feelings and dreams, using transferences, understanding repressions and defenses, working through resistances, obtaining relief for the patient from the consequences of an overly strict superego, exploring childhood events and their links to the psychic structure and its functioning within the patient, reconstructing capably in his own mind a realistic and detailed three-dimensional picture of each patient's inner universe, and, having done all that, formulating highly individualized temporary hypotheses for the patient. The therapist must reject the interference of generalized dogma that is unsuited to explaining and dealing with the specific constellations and needs of the individual patient. The work needed to accomplish those tasks, if done conscientiously, is formidable, and no one can do it perfectly.

The American Mental Health Foundation was the pioneer of many improved treatment forms. Among them was extended, intensive group psychotherapy, described elsewhere in this volume. Because of the great number of requests, our publications describing that treatment form went through six editions in the 1950s and early 1960s, and we received a considerable number of inquiries from those wanting to obtain training in the specialty. Owing to the unavailability of qualified instructors, we could not offer such a training course. We did, however, have a need for psychotherapists to conduct both individual psychotherapy and the specialty groups at our affiliated treatment center.

Over the years, many therapists sought positions at the treatment center. The applicants were all psychotherapists, some with medical training but most of them psychologists. All those professionals had completed their psychotherapy training elsewhere. To evaluate their clinical expertise and aptitude, we asked them to undergo a series of interviews. Unfortunately, there was no practical way to apply the selection method we suggest for candidates for psychotherapy training; namely, to place the applicants into extended psychodynamic groups for observation. Part of our evaluation procedure was to have each candidate present a brief case history of a patient he had treated. The results were rarely satisfactory and often disconcerting. Theoretical language, such as that criticized by Stoller and Leites, was frequent, and the description of the patient's psychodynamics often followed dogmatic lines. In this respect, the nonmedical therapists tended to be more dogmatic than the medical ones. Some of the more talented applicants were able to present an adequate childhood history of their patients. When it came, however, to a discussion of the patients' dreams, interpretations within the framework of dogma were again frequent, and the recognition of obvious links between childhood events and dream content were sadly lacking. Few candidates could offer an even halfway acceptable description of the psychodynamics of a patient.

Let us return to our current topic: how can the psychotherapist gain a true picture of each patient's psychological structure and psychodynamics so that he can map out a tentative treatment plan?

There are a number of tools necessary for that formidable task. After all, even the best of surgeons needs adequate instruments. I will keep the description of the tools as simple as possible, to facilitate understanding.

DREAMS

I have already committed many pages in this chapter to the fundamental importance of dreams. There is a great variation in the degree to which psychotherapists are able to understand, interpret, and use dreams in their therapeutic work. As long as the psychotherapist understands the importance of dreams, even if he falls short in his ability to handle them, some good may result, particularly if he studies the patterns of the manifest dreams. But we should beware of those who falsely claim an expertise in dreams, based merely on dogmatic dictionary-type interpretation, and those who ignore the matter of dreams altogether. We have looked at a considerable number of such professionals in this chapter. Here I fully agree with Ralph Greenson and many of the other clinical experts mentioned: when so much human suffering is at stake, there is no place for blatant ignorance. Psychotherapy needs psychotherapists!

Let me repeat a warning I made earlier. It is important to distinguish between dreams and imagery. Imagery, as opposed to true dreams, is far more common in people who are not in psychotherapy. The difference between dreams and imagery in the sleeping state is like the difference between concentrated thinking and drifting thoughts when one is awake.

A true dream may consist of a single word or picture, or it may extend into a drama. Regardless of its length, it is meaningful to the person's emotional pattern and personality. Fortunately for the psychotherapeutic endeavor, dreams of patients in psychotherapy tend to be of this nature. Otherwise, the attempt to treat the seriously ill would frequently be doomed. In view of that fact, it is a sad indication of ignorance that so many of our well-known authors and theoreticians simply sidestep the subject of dreams.

I should also repeat my warning that dreams can be tricky. Some simple dreams are quite "deep." Other dreams may be intricate and baffling, and many months of psychotherapeutic work may pass before still other dreams bring in clarification. A patient may have innumerable dreams of the same pattern, and then, after months or even years, a dream that occurs only once may show something completely different and incongruous. The therapist has to take all the dreams into account.

One of the most important things about dreams, ignored by most therapists and in the literature, is that they provide us with a formidable tool for communicating with the patient: the special language that the unconscious of that particular patient uses to express itself. That is the language we must employ to reach the unconscious and to influence it. This will be explained later.

We will now look at a number of additional tools that will help the dedicated psychotherapist construct an adequate model of each patient's inner world.

THE ARCS

An arc is simply a semicircle, like a rainbow. The psychotherapist can use arcs to help him visualize certain essential factors in his patients' psychic structure. Doing so forces him to evaluate those factors, which he might otherwise ignore or might not take into account sufficiently. We will first discuss one of the most important arcs – namely, the arc of guilt – to see, in a simple manner, how to use such arcs for improved understanding.

At the extreme left of the arc we place people who have the most guilt, people who are seriously disturbed, anxious, or depressed. At the extreme right we place those without any trace of guilt, severe sociopaths. Thus the degree of guilt diminishes as we move from left to right. At the zenith, the top midpoint of the semicircle, we locate people who have "normal guilt feelings." Since that phrase confuses some people, I will give a simple illustration. If a person injures a child through his negligence in driving, he should experience guilt; his guilt feelings are "normal."

Although the zenith divides the arc into equal sections, that does not mean that the same number of people will be found on the left half as on the right half. Merely for the purpose of our working concept, we can place neurotic people on the left half and those with character disorders on the right half. Phyllis Greenacre opined that most professional people are in the latter category.

Two or more arcs of guilt may have to be constructed for the same individual. A mafioso, for example, may feel no guilt about torturing and killing a stranger but may feel some guilt about injuring a family member. Furthermore, one must be careful to distinguish between genuine guilt and fear of punishment and also between guilt and shame. Shame requires a separate arc.

Another important arc shows the degree of dependency of the patient. Others show compliance or rebelliousness, shyness or self-assertion, ego strength, self-discipline, fear and courage, practical abilities, capacity for love, compassion, social concern, presence or absence of religious or spiritual feeling, health, physical abilities, and so on. On each page showing such an arc the therapist needs to write clarifying comments, such as whom the patient is dependent on, rebelliousness against, afraid of, and so forth. The comments on each page should also show how important the trait or activity is to the patient himself.

It would be desirable for the therapist to have a standard set of 15 basic arcs and some 10 to 20 additional arcs tailored to the particular patient. They will remind him to think of the corresponding character traits of his patient. The psychotherapist may also want to create a separate set of arcs for dreams, with arcs for anxiety dreams, nightmares, tedious dreams, repetitious dreams, pleasant dreams, dreams that show representations of his father, and dreams that include other family members or important childhood figures. Here, however, the arcs indicate the frequency of such dreams. The zero point can be placed on the extreme left, the starting point of the arc. Again, each sheet needs explanatory comments.

The therapist has to estimate at which point on each arc to place the mark indicating the status of a particular patient and should revise them from time to time, as more information becomes available. It is likely that even a conscientious therapist who has established a set of some 30 or more arcs for each patient will have to leave many of them unmarked, as he will not have an answer for the question each arc poses. But using arcs will force him to create a more thorough representation of the patient's personality traits than he would otherwise do.

Some psychotherapists who have heard me talking about arcs have advised me that they use scales, for similar reasons. In most instances I was able to obtain a list of the topics their scales cover, and to a large extent, those topics are quite different from the ones I have mentioned here.

The practice of using arcs is far less cumbersome than it may appear here and will enable the psychotherapist to engage in the all-important next step, which I am now going to describe.

THE REPRESENTATION OF THE UNCONSCIOUS

Here let us discuss two necessities in psychotherapy: creating a three-dimensional representation of the unconscious and using the language of the unconscious.

The procedure we will now look at enables the concerned psychotherapist to envisage the inner universe of each of his patients solely on the basis of the clinical data he has obtained. Prefabricated dogmatic notions must not be permitted to color the clinical construct. Some therapists may prefer other methods of achieving the same goal. However, I know of no procedure that is as close to the structure and the language of the unconscious as this one.

The work that the therapist does when following this procedure is the basis for his psychotherapeutic work with each patient. Without that basis, without a tentative optimal concept of the psychological entities and their dynamics within the psyche of the patient, his further work will lack the necessary substance.

These suggestions have also proved helpful, over a number of decades, in the teaching of students, who benefit greatly from acquiring the habit of constructing in their minds a model of the patient's psyche.

It is essential that the model of the patient's psyche be simple and that the language used in it be as clear as possible. The therapist should stick closely to what is manifest in the patient's dreams and other clinical data. He should avoid the temptation of demonstrating his analytic perspicacity and knowledge of scholarly theories.

The "scientific" academic language used in psychotherapy, psychology, and sociology lends itself well to high-sounding but clinically imprecise, and even valueless, formulations. Although the contents of the inner psychic space are not as clearly visible as the drawings of a draftsman, the clinician must express what he sees in the most unequivocal language possible. Anything else reflects poorly on his integrity.

To illustrate how to use a patient's dream images and clinical data to construct the three-dimensional representation of the psyche of a specific patient, let us consider a patient with a powerful and fearsome father image. Please note that I speak here of a father image rather than a father. It is the image of the father that has actually appeared in the patient's dreams, either as the father himself or in disguise. If the father image was in disguise, the therapist may only refer to the image as a father image if the patient himself recognized it as such.

When we speak of a father image, a mother image, or any other image that is relevant to the patient, there are many factors to be considered. While those images belong to the all-important childhood and adolescence, they obviously affect current relationships. The psychotherapist's task is to establish the degree to which they do so and their effect on sexual feelings, attitudes toward other men, tender feelings toward women, and an infinite number of other feelings. As there are many spheres in each person's life, the influence of each basic dream image and its association with the other images need to be established. The task requires a great deal of sensitivity and work.

The nature of the father and mother images, among others, can be quite different from the characteristics of the real father and mother. For instance, the images can be more benevolent or more malevolent than the actual parents. It is also possible that a patient has more than one father and mother image, and we must try to know each of them. Most of the writers who expound in general, theoretical terms shy away from such highly individualized labor and do not have the wherewithal to undertake it adequately. In most cases they avoid discussing the clinical aspects of treatment altogether. If they do discuss those aspects, their inadequacies become apparent.

Before I continue with the much abbreviated case history of the patient and demonstrate how to construct the model of the patient's psyche, I want to make some suggestions.

It helps to envisage oneself as an onlooker standing in front of a large three-dimensional space, like a big aquarium. Let us imagine that the elements in the upper half of the space are visible. Descending from the midpoint, one finds the lower area increasingly cloudy. At the bottom it is impenetrable darkness. The upper part is populated by images like those we see in our dreams. The same images, however, extend into the lower half of the space, and those are the parts of the images that we habitually repress and of which we are not readily aware. Furthermore, for practical reasons we postulate another important element, the "forces." While in reality they are linked to specific images, owing to inhibitory factors, they may take on forms that disguise the original image. They may appear, for example, as a dangerous animal or a truck bearing down on the dreamer. They may manifest themselves in a strong feeling permeating a situation or in repetitious situations, such as being on top of a high ledge and in danger of falling or being in depressing surroundings; or in frustrating events, such as being unable to find one's home.

The forces, which originate from powerful positive or negative situations in childhood and adolescence, may have been caused by one image or by a combination of images. While it is easy to visualize images, we have to improvise how to place the forces into three-dimensional space. It is necessary that we obtain optimal visualization of the inner world of each specific patient and that we remember it when we think about him. Since it is impossible to keep the complete picture in mind, we must make detailed sketches and notes. To actually build a three-dimensional model would be too cumbersome. Making three sketches, each on a large piece of paper, allows us to keep in mind the many details we must remember. First, we need to prepare the sketches.

The first sketch presents the foreground of the three-dimensional space and shows the figures that we know to be emotionally most important for the patient. We use an ellipse to indicate a figure and a rectangle to indicate a force. The size of the ellipse or the rectangle should show the impact on the patient – the larger the shape, the stronger the impact. In our example the ellipse representing the father image is the largest.

Each shape needs to be identified; abbreviations like *F, M, Br,* and so on, are sufficient. We must also write in the number of the subfile that deals with the particular image. Needless to say, each subfile may have many pages about the childhood history as reported by the patient and pertinent clinical data, including meaningful fantasies and dreams about the particular image. Cross-references are necessary.

In each rectangle indicating a force must be written the name of the force – for example, fear, despondency, or inferiority – and the subfile number. If the patient or the therapist feels that there is a link between certain of the elements in the sketch, lines should be drawn linking those elements on the sketch, and the notes should also mention the connection.

The second sketch shows the images and forces located behind the foreground elements. They are the ones considered to be of secondary importance to the patient. The third sketch shows those of even less importance.

As treatment progresses, and the nature and origins of the forces become clearer and crystallize into definite images, their strength, if negative, will gradually diminish. The therapist will then need to revise the sketches and make the necessary additions to his notes.

The sketches show, of course, a "frozen" picture of how the therapist views the inner world of the patient. The therapist's notes must describe the links between and the "movements" of the various images and forces; that is, how an image may interfere with another image. An example of such interference would be a father image stopping an aggressive or self-assertive move on the part of the dreamer.

Here is an example of a movement, an interference, caused by a force whose identity is, at least at the outset, unknown: In this chapter I spoke of a woman who has been the patient of a well-known psychoanalyst, a head of an important psychiatric hospital. The patient suffered from a phobia; she was not able to eat in public places. The treatment did not result in improvement. According to her, she had never had a dream that indicated why the impediment existed, perhaps because her therapist did not intensively pursue dreams and never made their importance clear to her. Obviously, there is a force operative in her that prevents her eating in public. The clinician will have, of course, a tentative hypothesis, and chances are that he will be right. However, as in many situations in which a strict superego has a damaging interference in the patient's life, little progress may be achieved unless the therapist finds clarification. In many cases, such clarification can be found in the patient's dreams, particularly if the therapist uses the language of the unconscious as expressed in the dreams.

Some therapists may look down their noses at the "elementary" tasks I describe here. However, these tasks take considerable clinical talent and sensitivity. Even for a therapist who has that talent, preparing the sketches and notes will be challenging, though well worth the effort. Every time he consults those papers, the resulting clarification of the patient's inner world will aid him in his clinical thinking and work.

To elucidate how to visualize the forces within the psyche of a patient, I will now present a brief description of the significant images in the dreams of a male patient in his early 40s who had been in therapy for three months on a twice-weekly basis. Shortly after the third month, the patient had to discontinue therapy, as his company transferred him to another city. I mention that because it means that my comments on his dreams are based on that three-month period; they are not influenced by any information subsequently obtained. I selected for my illustration the initial treatment phase of a patient, because during that period the facts that can be reported are still limited in number. A year later such a clinical report would require many more pages.

Of course, dreams do not come in the form of clear-cut diagrams. For this report I eliminated many of the secondary details of the dreams and concentrated on the more meaningful characteristics of the entities most frequently present. I should mention that the images I speak of have nothing to do with the archetypal images postulated by the Jungians. I never had the pleasure of meeting such an image in a dream. I refer instead to the highly individualized dream creations of a single patient.

The more important and dominant an image is to the patient, the more centrally it is located in the representation of the patient's psyche. By studying dream after dream, we can estimate the strength of each image and begin to determine which parts of his psyche they affect, whether those parts overlap, and what the relationship of the images to each other is.

In the dreams of the patient under consideration, I quickly became aware of a threatening father image. However, by the end of the third month of therapy, much of the father image, in spite of its evident size and strength, was still unknown to me, hidden in darkness. The unknown parts of an image are (1) the parts that the patient does not focus on, as his attention dwells on other aspects of the image, and, more important, (2) the parts that are repressed because of the unpleasant or painful memories tied to them.

Most often the father appeared not as himself but in the guise of other dangerous, unsavory people. On two occasions he was represented by situations. In the first, the patient was walking at night on an empty street bordered by towering, ominous buildings. He felt lost and scared and was unable to find his way back home. In the second, the patient was in a government office, desperately but unsuccessfully trying to fill in a questionnaire necessary to obtain some vital document.

Sometimes in the patient's dreams, when he felt fearful, a protective but weak and ineffective influence appeared, which the patient pinpointed as his mother. She was never seen but was represented, once by a melody she used to play on the piano and another time by some flowers she liked.

We try to understand the forces acting in the inner space in terms of their strength. In some dreams the dreamer is the principle actor; in others he may not be visually present. The patient in our example, anxious and depressed, never showed strength in his dreams, whatever the situation.

In dreams that were less threatening, because the father image was more quiescent and temporarily receding, images of young, attractive women took precedence. It must be explained that the patient's parents paid great attention to the looks and beauty of both males and females. They made frequent comments about looks, and looks came to have great importance for the patient. Even though the parents, critical in many other matters, did not criticize the patient's appearance, he felt that he was ugly and weak. He developed idealized images of beautiful young women who, in his mind, would be attracted only to good-looking young men. The patient thus suffered from a severe inferiority complex. He was extremely shy when an adolescent and had hardly any contact with girls of his age. He adored them from a distance. Whenever he spoke to an attractive girl, he would blush, break into a cold sweat, and be so nervous that he acted ridiculous. It is no wonder that he had no girlfriend as an adolescent and even in his 20s. Images of attractive girls appeared frequently in his dreams, but even there, he could not approach them. They remained unavailable to him, as if on a pedestal; he was weakly and unhappily on the periphery.

Now we can formulate a tentative hypothesis, which only further psychotherapy would have proved or disproved. The patient's mother was frequently sick and had only the patient to look after her. Whenever the patient, as a child or an adolescent, would go out to try to enjoy himself, he would feel guilty, even though his mother always encouraged him to go out and also to meet girls. It might have been because of his guilt that the two images – the mother image and the idealized girl image – never showed up simultaneously in the dreams. However, the patient never alluded to that fact, and it would have been premature to comment on it at that stage. As a matter of fact, the girl image would not show up when the father image, causing anxiety, was present.

Another image of some importance was that of an aunt who lived outside town in a villa and whom the patient visited occasionally. She was a quiet, somewhat retiring, but friendly person. Her residence and garden were of exquisite beauty and elegance. The patient, who had a pronounced sense of beauty, often thought about his aunt's home. Contrast that with his frequent dreams, arising when he felt his existence endangered, in which he found himself in dismal abodes and surroundings.

There were, of course, many other areas within the emotional realm of the patient. Here we can only glance at a few of the images. By scrutinizing many dreams, one can determine the habitual location and strength of the images; whether they interrelate, and if so, how; and, most important, how the patient experiences himself in each situation. Looking at the dreams of this patient, we note the link between the father image and the mother image and the fact that the girl image could only emerge when neither the father image nor the mother image was activated, that is, when the patient's anxiety and guilt were somewhat abated. One could not detect any oedipal representation of the mother image in the girl image, a statement that many psychoanalysts may scoff at.

We must remember that we have seen only a few parts of each image; other aspects and dimensions would have been obtained had therapy continued. Moreover, the above description is merely an outline, reduced to a minimum for the purpose of illustration. A much fuller picture was gleaned.

Having presented that rudimentary report on the patient's images, let us see how we should proceed in making the sketches.

I would tentatively place four images, two forces, and the patient himself in the first sketch. The center would be occupied by the ellipse representing the overwhelming father image, and next to it would be the rectangle representing anxiety. On the other side of the father image I would place a smaller ellipse for the mother image. Separately we would have a large ellipse for the idealized girl image and, linked to it, an ellipse for the idealized male image. The latter two ellipses would be linked to a rectangle for inferiority. On the far right is a small circle representing the dreamer, who experiences himself as minor and weak, compared with the other images and forces. Because this is a greatly simplified case history, on the second sketch I would place only the aunt. In practice, however, there would be quite a number of images on the second and third sketches. As I have mentioned, all the entries carry numbers referring to the subfiles that supply the necessary details.

Even if the patient dreams of himself as being weak, and other images in his dreams are far stronger, and even if he is on the periphery of the action or not present at all, it must be made clear that he is at all times, just as in his waking life, the main figure in the story. It is around his consciousness and awareness that the drama revolves. It is crucial, however, to recognize this important point: a person with a strong and healthy ego is the strongest entity in his inner kingdom and thus in his dreams. No other image is stronger than he is, frightens him, hurts him, or humiliates him. In the dreams of our patient, alas, that was not the case. He was weak and scared.

The psychotherapist, in addition to visualizing the different images in various sizes, according to their strength, should visualize them on higher or lower levels, determined by the feelings of the patient. That simply means that an image that the patient fears or looks up to is situated on a higher level in the sketch than the patient himself. On the other hand, an image that the patient does not hold in esteem and does not fear is placed lower than the patient. Of course, those levels have no relationship to the level on which a dream takes place. We will look at that shortly.

Properly defining the images requires far more clinical acumen than creating theoretical concepts unencumbered by reality, and following this procedure entails a considerable amount of work. What if the psychotherapist is engaged in group psychotherapy and has many patients to consider? I maintain that a psychotherapist needs to know as much about the history and psychodynamics of each of his group therapy patients as he would if they were in individual psychotherapy. Yet I have heard group therapists assert that one does not need to know everything about a patient. Translation: a little is enough. And even more outrageous is the rationalization that the group processors offer, that one can deal with the group as a whole and simply ignore the specifics and needs of the individual. Ministers, priests, and rabbis may deal with the congregation as a whole, but taking that approach in psychotherapy is unconscionable.

Experienced therapists frequently state that trainees, although they use an abundance of analytic terms, do not have a clear clinical picture of their patients. The same is true of many fully trained therapists. However, a simple graphic conceptualization of the images in the inner space, as outlined above, can be of considerable help. By keeping elementary matters clear, one can easily view basic factors that have become evident during therapy. The procedure outlined forces the student and the therapist to understand each patient in a concrete manner. It is interesting to note that many therapists and teachers who express intellectual, theoretical concepts with ease have great difficulty with the detailed perception of the individual factors within their patients' psyches. A trainee who has such a teacher will never develop clinical expertise. In fact, many students and therapists have great difficulty in productively translating even valid theoretical concepts into clinical application.

At any rate, following this procedure will help a therapist visualize the inner structure of a patient's psyche. What matters is that therapists and students make a sincere effort to gain the clearest possible picture of the unique psyche of each patient and be aware of the inner events as therapy progresses. To do that properly is a formidable task, even for the best.

Whether psychotherapists use dreams or not, they surely should have as clear a picture as possible of the forces in the unconscious realm of their patients. Psychotherapists who do not use dream material in their work must also construct models of their patients' psyches based on the clinical material obtained, but their task is far more difficult, for the unconscious operates mostly in terms of images, and they are shown in the dreams.

DREAM LEVELS

Does the dream emanate from a level close to consciousness or deeper in the realm of the unconscious? When we speak of dream levels, we cannot compare them to the clear-cut separation of floors in a building. We are dealing with a continuum. A dream on the highest level is near consciousness and may include logical thought. A dream on the lowest level is in the realm of hidden emotional depths, completely veiled by the unconscious forces. It is necessary to estimate the level of the dream, and even the level of each part of the dream. As a dream's action proceeds, the dream may move from one level to another, sometimes in a split second. For instance, a dream dealing with a difficult emotional situation may move, owing to resistance, from a deeper level to a much more superficial level, closer to cerebral consciousness. Or for the same reason it may move to a different scenario in a less threatening area. There are other forces, positive or negative, that can draw the dreamer into deeper, less accessible, more repressed, or archaic, levels. The positive force may be that the patient, overcoming resistance, is seeking to understand and deal with what has been hidden. The negative force may be a whirlpool of anxiety that overwhelms the patient's feeble ego and immerses him in terror and helplessness.

Various emotional forces are operative within the individual at all times, but to varying degrees on different occasions. It is in the shallower dream stages that pronounced cerebral activity, such as an elaborate intellectual discussion, may be found. Dreams on a deeper level have a different tone and quality. The drama of the dream may be intelligently conceived, but not by the dreamer's cerebral activity. Instead, it is written by the unconscious. The people who appear in the dream are actors in the play. The less ego strength the dreamer has, the more he is a puppet in the dream, a powerless victim or just a witness of the drama.

In 1910 Ferenczi stated that on a shallower level of sleep, the dreamer can actually guide his dreams. What is known today as lucid dreaming also takes place on the shallower sleep level. That use of dreams by an insular Pacific tribe, the Senois, was studied in the 1920s by Kilton Stewart, whose reports were much praised by Margaret Mead. Incidentally, I am dismayed that some of the academic psychotherapists who have written on the topic, copying the many procedures that Stewart described, do not even mention his name.

Dreams on a high cerebral level often show little distortion, as they are relatively unaffected by threatening emotional forces. If the dreamer sees himself giving a complex lecture and is aware of his words and thoughts, the dream is obviously close to consciousness. However, the presence of words in a dream does not necessarily mean that it is close to the surface. There are dreams in which meaningful words, often startling or inspiring fear, are suddenly heard. Such dreams are on a deeper level. The same may be true of dreams that picture a frightening event, such as the danger of falling into an abyss or actually falling. If, however, the dreamer does not experience the expected feeling of fear, the psychotherapist should refrain from jumping to conclusions; he should rely on subsequent work to reveal the causes for such an absence of feeling.

One must be wary in evaluating the level of a dream. Only empirical work with a patient can provide enough information to allow such an evaluation. Facts and events that one might expect to be deeply repressed may not be; other events, seemingly innocuous, might be buried. All those considerations are necessary in creating valid sketches.

While we are on the subject of depth, let me say that the Irma dream, though interesting, did not take place on a particularly deep level. Parts of it were on a more cerebral level. If the dream had been one of many that a particular patient had, it would not be considered especially memorable, except possibly through the marvel of misinterpretation by Erikson.

To understand the specific inner emotional universe in which a patient is living, the therapist must also pay attention to the various scenarios that appear in the patient's dreams. We may compare dreams to a drama in which the main characters remain the same but the scenes change.

The patient we have been discussing had many dreams that took place in unattractive and depressing surroundings. For years he had been threatened by a ruthless landlord who wanted to evict the tenants and sell the building. The dreams that had as their settings dismal apartments reflected his fear of being forced to live in such a place.

The patient also had many dreams in which other people were in his apartment against his will, and he felt helpless. The patient was a sensitive person, easily upset by other people's offensive behavior and damaging acts against him. Often his emotional reactions, such as fear, were more painful to him than the actual slight. When threatened, he simply could not brush it aside; he remained disturbed for long periods. It may be that the dreams about the invasion of his apartment represented the injuries and threats caused by others that so easily inundated his inner realm. I did not mention that possibility to him, however, as it would have been premature.

A few times the patient, a man of pronounced aesthetic sense, saw himself in elegant hotels. But nothing positive ever happened to him there. He was not in pleasant company, and he did not have a meal; he just wandered around, an awkward outsider. The only relatively agreeable dreams he had, and they were rare, were those in which he found himself in a beautiful landscape. However, he was always alone, despite the fact that he deeply longed for love and friendship.

The patient's anxiety, inhibitions, and depression were frequently evident during his waking hours. In the passivity of the sleep state the unconscious overtakes consciousness, and fearful events and threats experienced during the day stimulate the patient's basic and original fears. It is then that the resulting dreams and nightmares lead us to the causes we are looking for. Like so many others who suffer from deep anxieties, the patient hardly ever woke up refreshed; he felt worn out and depressed, and he dreaded the coming day.

The conflicts within the human psyche are shown by the interaction of the dream images and forces, though in certain cases it may take some time in therapy before they become crystallized and clarified. The procedure I have described results in a representation of a person's unconscious based entirely on the images and forces found in the patient, complemented by the other clinical data obtained from the patient. It provides a solid clinical base on which to build the three-dimensional model, unadulterated by theory and dogma. It can thus be used to formulate valid temporary hypotheses.

THE LANGUAGE OF THE UNCONSCIOUS

Paying close attention to dream images has another benefit of utmost importance to psychotherapy. Dreams are the main language in which the unconscious expresses itself. As therapists, we try to reach the unconscious, to have it reveal itself to us, and, we hope, to influence it. In our communications with the patient we should use, as far as feasible, the language given to us by the unconscious.

It is now several decades since I started to refer to the "father image" and "mother image" rather than to the father and mother and to focus on those images and others that appear in dreams. I would discuss the material the patient brought up in relation to the images and events in significant dreams. We would frequently focus on the intertwining of the dream content with his feelings and actions and would pay attention to any rivers running deep in his unconscious and emerging in his dreams that were not related to his daily life. The unconscious, particularly when stirred up by proper psychotherapeutic intervention, works on deeply buried emotional forces that have a life of their own. The therapist not using dreams has little access to those hidden realms.

I am convinced that when we keep in mind the content of a patient's dreams and refer to the images in them, his dreams become clearer and reach deeper levels earlier and more often than would otherwise happen. The benefits to the patient are evident. The communications with the patient become more meaningful, easier, and more harmonious. We know that Freud, starting practically from scratch and having to try out a multitude of approaches, would attempt to convince his patients that his interpretations of their dreams were correct. Such a procedure had to result in many failures. In the procedure outlined here, such difficulties cannot arise.

The intensive use of dreams in treatment appears to be unfamiliar to most therapists; it is alien to their habitual thinking. No wonder every time I speak about such matters, I am inundated with questions about dreams and images. Even though I addressed the subject previously in this chapter, I would like to make some comments that should answer some frequently asked questions.

As psychotherapy proceeds, the therapist may note two factors: (1) repressed traits, often unpleasant and threatening, of the father and mother images and of other images will become apparent, and (2) those images will undergo some changes. The changes should be cautiously and carefully examined. Only later in treatment should the therapist tactfully attempt to explore any discrepancies that the patient notices between the father and mother images and the actual father and mother as he remembers them. This, of course, holds true as well for other images of relevance.

If the patient frequently has unpleasant or even frightening dreams, the possibility of self-hate and the nature of the superego forces operating within the patient have to be examined. Recurring anxiety dreams, such as getting lost in the streets, being unprepared for an examination, and being unable to turn on the lights in an apartment, need the most careful and patient scrutiny. We are dealing here with fundamental problems.

The benefits of the procedure are not served to us on a silver platter. To reap the benefits, the therapist must be sensitive and thoughtful, and he must refer frequently to the images and the content of dreams. As stated, if he does so, the dreams will become less repressed, free associations will become clearer, cause and effect within the psychodynamic system will be clarified, and the patient will have true insights.

Even when those improvements have occurred, and the therapist can more clearly see the connections between cause and effect, he still has to perform the major portion of a formidable task: bringing about lasting change. The task is even more formidable if the emotional damage is severe and deep rooted. For example, Marilyn Monroe was intelligent and sensitive. She could afford intensive analysis over many years by some of the best-known and experienced analysts. Yet her destructive inner forces inexorably drew her deeper and deeper into annihilation. The procedures applied were simply not good enough. The search for better tools is imperative.

We are flooded with literature on short-term therapy, with proposals for therapies giving less time to the patient, and with facile and superficial treatment methods. Who are these authors treating? The healthy?

The power of the negative forces in the unconscious and the difficulty of overcoming them are well illustrated in a male patient of mine who, like the other patient I have talked about, had a terrifyingly brutal father. In one form or other, the father frequently appeared in his dreams. One night before he fell asleep, the patient told himself that he would fight the father image. That night he had a dream in which he saw himself in a medieval or renaissance setting. There were several aristocrats there, but outstanding among them was an obnoxious, loud, large man who bullied all those present. The dreamer, without any feeling of rebellion, subserviently kissed his hand. The patient woke up disgusted with himself. The dream shows the power of the negative forces in his unconscious. Not only did they wipe out the dreamer's feelings of opposition, but adding insult to injury, they made him a willing slave of the hated enemy.

Of course, an analyst will find additional material of importance in that dream. However, this is not the place to discuss it. The important fact for us is that only the analyst using dreams has access to the relevant material demonstrating the enormous power of the inner forces that vigorously and relentlessly oppose change. To clarify the patient's psychodynamics and, more important, to help the patient achieve change for the better, the therapist must refer to the positive and negative forces, as represented by the dream images.

A serious obstacle to improvement is the hesitancy, or even inability, of many patients to express hostile feelings toward their therapists. Many therapists fail to encourage the patient to express such feelings if they occur. Therapists who use dreams, however, find them a valuable tool in discovering such unexpressed feelings and overcoming the impasse. More about that later.

Another procedure that can help facilitate change is probing into why the patient imbues the negative images with so much power. Such probing is done principally to weaken the negative images and the forces they represent. Thus the therapist allies himself with the positive self-sustaining forces of the patient by questioning the validity and power of the negative ones.

Even the valid procedures in psychotherapy are painfully slow and difficult, particularly in the case of the seriously ill. Faster and more effective procedures would be a gift from heaven. It may be that eventually techniques that go beyond the procedures involving images, as explained in this chapter, may bring about effective results. Perhaps such a technique would be the actual manipulation of the specific images of a patient in the waking state, as proposed by Kilton Stewart, a highly original thinker. That would involve an attempt to weaken the negative images and strengthen the positive ones.

At any rate, we must keep in mind that the procedures I strongly recommend in this chapter are the indispensable basis for the subsequent work of the expert clinician.

At all times we have found statements that stronger and "healthier" dreams of a patient are a sure indication of progress. Furthermore, in recent literature they have been said to indicate that the patient has achieved a state of stable mental health and that treatment can be terminated. Again, utmost caution is advised. We have seen at the Foundation many former patients who had been dismissed as "cured" by their analysts or psychotherapists, in several instances based on the "improvement" of their dreams. It is true that progress in psychotherapy is reflected in the dreams. But it is also true that dreams are mere photographs or films of the events occurring in the unconscious.

You hold a beautiful hand-painted vase in your hands. It took a long time to create. It slips from your hands, and in a fraction of a second the vase is reduced to a pile of shards on the floor. Similarly, after a long time in therapy the patient may have built a stronger ego. Yet a traumatic event or a prolonged difficult period may cause serious psychic damage, and that is certain to show up in the dreams. I remember a woman who spent many years with a distinguished psychoanalyst. He did a commendable job, her life took a turn for the better, and her dreams were far more positive. Then, about six years later, the woman developed severe breathing problems. She was in constant fear of suffocation. She was unable to lie down in a bed; she always sat in a reclining chair. Her dreams were horrifying.

I have seen many other instances in which a sudden trauma, like the loss of a loved one, was reflected in a change in the nature of dreams. One should not consider either good dreams or bad dreams an absolute indication of mental health or disturbance. One must also take into account the other clinical factors and the current life situation of the individual.

If, however, we look on dreams as an X ray of the inner self, we have an invaluable treasure at hand.

Our emphasis on feelings, fantasies, and dreams results in many practical applications in psychotherapy. For example, when asked about their former treatment, specifically about any hostile feelings they had toward their therapists or any doubts they felt toward them, many patients admitted that they had never expressed their hostility or doubts. Some were surprised at the question. Their failure to communicate their feelings was, of course, a formidable impediment to their treatment.

The fear of expressing such negative feelings, though understandable, must be overcome. The therapist should make it his practice to initially advise the patients on the necessity of expressing all feelings, even though doing so may make them uncomfortable and apprehensive. In most cases the therapist's initial admonition is insufficient, and it needs to be reinforced. Often dreams are helpful in pointing to areas that the patient may be hesitant to touch on. In such cases the therapist has to make sure that the patient speaks not only about the sensitive matter but also about the apprehension he feels when approaching it.

A therapist who conducts a psychotherapy group should, in private sessions, encourage certain patients – those who appear hesitant to express any hostile feelings toward the therapist – to express their feelings. The reason for giving the advice privately is that patients who do not have an impediment to expressing such feelings may take the advice as encouragement to act out their feelings in prolonged and repetitive hostile tirades against the therapist. Furthermore, the advice to express all their feelings may incite the patients who have an abundance of surface feelings to constantly report on them. Those people have to be encouraged to refrain from repetitious reports of their feelings and to try to detect "deeper" feelings of which they are not so readily aware or that may be embarrassing.

At any rate, focusing on feelings does help open up access to the unconscious and brings about material and dreams from deeper emotional levels.

WORKING CONCEPTS

The emphasis on feelings and dreams also leads to a better formulation of the temporary working hypotheses we must form about each patient and to improved working concepts. The term "working concept," as used here, needs careful clarification. Even though such concepts are frequently used in the realm of theory, here we use them without theoretical implications. We use them strictly as practical concepts and tools for our clinical work. When we speak, for instance, about the unconscious or the superego we do so on the level of working concepts.

Actually, that is nothing new. For instance, as previously mentioned, therapists frequently use the terms of the topographical theory and the structural theory side by side. They may not call them working concepts, but that is what they are in practice, and they are useful in clinical work. It is only when we employ those terms in the context of theory that they become irreconcilable with each other.

Too many of our theories are so far removed from clinical reality that the abstractions and pseudoerudite intellectual discussion are not only useless but harmfully misleading. The theoreticians include or exclude whatever they wish. Their realm hardly ever touches on the uncomfortable realities and problems that are the priorities for the expert clinician. I referred to that when speaking about Dimensions II and III. I can only repeat that if the armchair theoreticians had even a little basic clinical expertise, they would be embarrassed to engage in such a pretentious exercise. The clashes between theoretical systems and the alteration of abstract concepts proclaimed as improvements have little to do with the real world the clinician faces. As indicated in this profound quote from Han Fei Tzu that Nathan Leites liked to use, it takes far more ability to establish a kernel of clinical truth than to create a mountain of theory:

> Once upon a time there was a traveler drawing for the King of Ch'i. "What is the hardest thing to draw?" asked the King. "Dogs and horses are the hardest." "Then what is the easiest?" "Devils and demons are the easiest. Indeed, dogs and horses are what people know and see at dawn and dusk in front of them. To draw them no distortion is permissible. . . . Devils and demons have no shapes and are not seen in front of anybody."

Not all working concepts are reserved for the therapist. Some can be fruitfully shared with the patient. They can help him crystallize certain problems. Here, too, it is important to stay close to the feelings and dreams of the patient and to use the appropriate, simple language.

As an example, let's select a simple working concept that applies to a number of patients who experience problems when another person shows love for them. The problems arise even when the other person is a desirable partner for them. We call that difficulty the Carmen complex. In the opera Carmen sings, "If you love me, I love you not!" As therapists know, there can be many reasons for resisting love and withdrawing. One or more reasons may apply in each case, and the patient may not know why he wants to remove himself from the situation. We will only mention three reasons: the patient may feel suffocated and panicky, fearing that he will lose his freedom; he may feel that he cannot carry the responsibility of taking care of another person; or if he has strong inferiority feelings, he may feel, perhaps only unconsciously, that since he is such an uninteresting and worthless person, anyone who loves him cannot be "such a big deal." As Groucho Marx said, "Any club that would accept me, I wouldn't want to belong to."

By probing with the patient his specific Carmen complex – and giving it that name – the therapist can help him become more familiar with the pattern and crystallize it in his own mind. It will be useful for the patient to be aware of its effect on his feelings, even though it may be a long time before those feelings are weakened.

Let me mention another advantage of the method I propose. Freud said that the task of psychoanalysis is to make conscious what has previously been in the unconscious. That certainly sounds impressive. However, many of us have seen people who were previously in analysis and can give an extended recitation of the supposed discoveries of their inner mechanisms. Some sound like "Dogma Incorporated." There was a time when psychoanalysts proudly reported such intellectual "insights" of their patients as proof of great improvement. Yet many of the patients did not improve much.

If, however, we stay close to the feelings and dreams of the patient and communicate with him on that basis, an emotional insight, not an intellectual insight, will occur, and improvement will ensue. The emotional insight occurs when the proper therapeutic work has reached the unconscious and has gradually brought it to change in the desired direction. The patient may not have conscious insight into the mechanisms that changed his inner structure; he may not even care about them. He just wants to feel stronger and more assured and to experience a feeling of well-being. Of course, some intellectual insight can also be achieved, but that is simply a fortunate by-product.

I have spoken of priorities and the clinical questions that the theoreticians appear to avoid at all costs. Let me pose a simple question from an area many of them know nothing about and most of them avoid, except when they are offering stereotyped answers. The area – this should come as no surprise to my readers – is dreams. I call the question simple because it is about something real, not about abstract concepts. There are, of course, also many difficult clinical questions in psychotherapy; we have dealt with a number of them elsewhere in this chapter.

My simple question refers to specific elements in these three dreams:

1. We encountered this dream earlier in this chapter. A gentle, somewhat timid, but highly intelligent and decent professor has been constantly annoyed by a vicious, sociopathic assistant. In his dream the professor tries to obtain clarification about a situation the assistant has handled badly. The professor is his usual thoughtful self in the dream, asking pertinent questions in a cautious and tactful way. The assistant answers rapidly and attacks the professor with his glibness and malice, twisting the whole situation to his advantage.

2. A man who cannot remember melodies in his mind, cannot carry the simplest tune, and had never previously had any dream involving music, dreams that he opens up the cover of a black piano and hears, for what seems to be about six minutes, beautiful music played by a full orchestra.

3. This is the last part of a longer dream. The dreamer is a man in his 70s who has been impotent since his late fifties and for many years had no sexual dreams in which he had physical contact with women. In this dream, however, he has intercourse with an attractive blond girl, experiencing intense pleasure such as he never felt before in his life. Consistent with his usual pattern of self-denial, the episode lasts only a few seconds.

The simple question is, how can such dreams occur? How, for example, can the unconscious of the professor produce the malicious actions and words of the assistant, behavior that is completely foreign to his nature? If the professor tried, in his waking state, to create the actions and words of the assistant, he would never come even close, no matter how much time he spent; it is simply not in him.

If the self-appointed experts really have the expertise they claim to have, they should be able to explain how the unconscious can produce dreams like the ones above, which appear utterly alien to the psychic makeup of the dreamer. Facile pseudoexplanations, as, for example, that we are dealing with "split-off" parts of the dreamer's personality, will not be accepted. Such terms explain nothing here.

Where does psychodynamic psychotherapy go from here? Even after a century of exploration, we are far from the desired goal. We have seen in this chapter what is most valuable in psychotherapy and what skills the therapist should master. But even at its best, intensive psychotherapy is a slow and difficult procedure, at present available only to the fortunate few. For the many people of limited means, the only hope on the horizon is that the intensive, extended group psychotherapy method described in this volume will become more widely available, thus helping a far broader patient population.

It has been said that while there are many people of goodwill, at any given time true civilization can be found in only a very small number of people dispersed over the globe. The same can be said of psychotherapists. As I have stated, our best experts know a great deal about which of our past and present practices are not valid. They know far less about what is truly valid and helpful. To transcend our present limitations, we need to look for areas insufficiently explored or not explored at all. We can only hope that clinicians of exceptional talent will bring new life to our craft.

We must also hope that the valuable knowledge we have acquired so far will not be drowned in an ocean of superficial thinking. I have stated that we are repairmen. The best in our field are humble and attend to the work at hand. They are an endangered species.

If knowledgeable people will try harder to be heard, the present trends can gradually be reversed. Conditions of training and the practice of psychotherapy vary greatly from place to place. If the new profession of psychotherapy comes into being somewhere, it may catch on and spread.

The choice is up to the psychotherapists. If they allow the present trends to continue, their destiny is already being structured for them. They will do shallow work as servants of the insurance companies. We hope, however, that they will bring meaning into their lives by serving, instead, the family of man.

> They are ill discoverers that think there is no land, when they can see nothing but sea.
>
> FRANCIS BACON

REFERENCES
As stated, this is not an academic paper, However, the reader may find some useful references below:

Abraham, K., Ferenczi, S., Simmel, E., & Jones, E. (1921). *Psychoanalysis and the war neuroses.* London: International Psychoanalytic Press.

Alston, T. M., Calogeras, R. C., & Deserno, H. (Eds.). (1993). *Dream reader: Psychoanalytic articles on dreams.* Madison, CT: International Universities Press.

Altman, L. L. (1975). *The dream in psychoanalysis.* New York: International Universities Press.

Berger, D. M. (1981). Psychoanalysis, dreaming and the REM state: A clinical vignette. *Canadian J. Psychiat., 26.*

Bibring, G. (1954). Training analysis and its place in psychoanalytic training. *Internat. J. Psycho-anal., 35.*

Blum, H. P. (1976). The changing use of dreams. *Amer. J. Psychoanal.*

Bonime, W. (1982). *The clinical use of dreams.* New York: da Capo.

Colby, K. M., & Stoller, R. J. (1988). *Cognitive science and psychoanalysis.* Hillsdale, NJ: Analytic Press.

de Schill, S. (Ed.). (1971). *Psychoanalytische Therapie in Gruppen.* Stuttgart: Ernst Klett Verlag.

de Schill, S. (Ed.). (1974). *The challenge for group psychotherapy.* New York: International Universities Press.

de Schill, S., Lebovici, S., & Kächele, H. (Eds.). (1997). *Psychoanalyse und Psychotherapie. Herausforderungen und Lösungen für die Zukunft.* Stuttgart: Georg Thieme Verlag.

de Schill, S., & Lebovici, S. (Eds.). (1997). *Le défi à l'égard de la psychanalyse et de la psychothérapie et les solutions pour l'avenir.* Paris: Presses Universitaires de France.

de Schill, S., & LaHullier, D. (1956). *The practice of mental health groups.* New York: AMHF – Brunner.

Erikson, E. H. (1954). The dream specimen of psychoanalysis. *J. Amer. Psychoanal. Assoc., 2.*

Erikson, E. H. (1958). *Young man Luther.* New York: Norton.

Evans, C. (1984). *Landscapes of the night.* New York: Viking.

Fisher, C. (1954). Dreams and perception. *J. Amer. Psychoanal. Assoc, 2.*

Flournoy, O. (1994). Metapsychoanalysis. In A. Haynal & E. Falzeder (Eds.), *100 years of psychoanalysis.* London: Karasu.

Fosshage, J. L. (1983). The psychological function of dreams: A revised psychoanalytic perspective. *Psychoanal. Contemp. Thought., 6.*

Fosshage, J. L., & Loew, C. A. (Eds.). (1987). *Dream interpretation: A comparative study.* New York: PMA.

French, T. M., & Fromm, E. (1964). *Dream interpretation.* New York: Basic Books.

Freud, A. (1965). *Normality and pathology in childhood: Assessments of development.* New York: International Universities Press.

Freud, S. (1895). Project for a scientific psychology. *Standard Edition, 1.* London: Hogarth Press, 1966.

Freud, S. (1900). *The interpretation of dreams. Standard Edition, 4 & 5.* London: Hogarth Press.

Freud, S. (1911). The handling of dream-interpretation in psychoanalysis. *Standard Edition, 11.* London: Hogarth Press, 1958.

Freud, S. (1937). Constructions in analysis. *Standard Edition, 23.* London: Hogarth Press, 1964.

Freud, S. (1940). *An outline of psychoanalysis. Standard Edition, 35.* London: Hogarth Press, 1969.

Fromm, Erich. (1951). *The forgotten language.* New York: Rinehart.

Fürstenau, P. (1977). Die beiden Dimensionen des psychoanalytischen Umgangs mit strukturell ich-gestörten Patienten [the two dimensions of psychoanalytic treatment of patients with structural ego disturbances]. *Psyche, 31.*

Fürstenau, P. (1979). *Zur Theorie psychoanalytischer Praxis* [on the theory of psychoanalytic practice]. Stuttgart: Klett-Cotta, 1992.

Fürstenau, P. (1970). *Z. Psychother. med. Psychol., 20.*

Gabel, S. (1985). Sleep research and clinically reported dreams: Can they be integrated? *J. Anal. Psychol., 30.*

Gaillard, J. M. (1990). *Le sommeil.* Lausanne: Payot.

Gay, P. (1988). *Freud: A life of our time.* New York: Norton.

Gedo, J. E. (1979). *Beyond interpretation.* New York: International Universities Press.

Gedo, J. E. (1981). *Advances in clinical psychoanalysis.* New York: International Universities Press.

Grawe, K., Donati, R., & Bernauer, F. (1994). *Psychotherapie im Wandel: Von der Konfession zur Profession* [psychotherapy in change: from confession to profession]. Göttingen: Hogrefe.

Greenacre, P. (1961). A critical digest of the literature on the selection of candidates for psychoanalytic training. *Psychoanal. Quart., 30.*

Greenberg, J. (1991). *Oedipus and beyond: A clinical theory.* Cambridge, MA: Harvard University Press.

Greenberg, R., & Pearlman, C. (1975). A psychoanalytic-dream continuum: The source and function of dreams. *Internat. Rev. Psychoanal., 2.*

Greenson, R. R. (1970). The exceptional position of the dream in psychoanalytic practice. *Psychoanal. Quart., 39.*

Grinstein, A. (1968). *Sigmund Freud's dreams.* Detroit, MI: Wayne State University Press.

Grinstein, A. (1990). *Freud at the crossroads.* Madison, CT: International Universities Press.

Grotjahn, M. (1977). *Art and technique of analytic group therapy.* New York: Aronson.

Grotjahn, M. (1978). Group communication and group therapy with the aged: A promising project. In L. F. Jarvile (Ed.), *Aging into the 21st century.* New York: Gardner.

Gutheil, E. A. (1951). *Handbook of dream analysis.* New York: Liveright.

Hall, C. S. (1966). *The meaning of dreams.* New York: McGraw Hill.

Hartmann, E. (Ed.). (1970). *Sleep and dreaming.* Boston: Little, Brown.

Hartmann, E. (1976). The changing use of dreams in psychoanalytic practice. *Internat. J. Psycho-anal., 57.*

Haynal, A. (1988). *The technique at issue.* London: Karnac. (Published in the U.S. as *Controversy in psychoanalytic method.* New York: New York University Press, 1989.)

Hirsch, I. (1992). Review of *Oedipus and Beyond,* by J. Greenberg. *Psychoanal. Books, 3.*

Hobson, A., et al. (1987). Dream bizarreness and the activation-synthesis hypothesis. *Human Neurobiol., 6.*

Holt, R. R. (Ed.). (1971). *New horizon for psychotherapy: Autonomy as a profession.* Madison, CT: International Universities Press.

Jeliffe, S. E. (1918). *The technique of psychoanalysis.* New York: Nervous and Mental Disease.

Jones, E. (1953–57). *The life and work of Sigmund Freud.* New York: Basic Books.

Karasu, T. B. (1987). The psychotherapy of the future: The 50-second hour. *Psychosomatics, 28.*

Karasu, T. B. (1992). *Wisdom in the practice of psychotherapy.* New York: Basic Books.

Kellerman, H. (Ed.). (1987). *The nightmare: Psychological and biological foundations.* New York: Columbia University Press.

Kohut, H. (1977). *The restoration of the self.* New York: International Universities Press.

LaBerge, S. (1985). *Lucid dreaming*. New York: Ballantine Books.

LaBerge, S., & Gackenbach, J. (Eds.). (1988). *Conscious mind, sleeping brain: Perspectives on lucid dreaming.*

LaPlanche, J., & Pontalis, J. B. (1967). *The language of psychoanalysis*. Paris: Presses Universitaires de France. (Reprinted, New York: Norton, 1973).

Mack, J. E. (1974). *Nightmares and human conflict*. Boston: Houghton Mifflin.

Masson, J. M. (1984). *The assault on truth*. New York: Farrar, Strauss & Giroux.

McCarley, R., & Hobson, A. (1977a). The neurobiological origins of psychoanalytic dream theory. *Amer. J. Psychiat.*

McCarley, R., & Hobson, A. (1977b). The brain as dream-state generator: An activation-synthesis hypothesis of the dream process. *Amer. J. Psychiat.*

Meissner, W. W. (1968). Dreaming as a process. *Internat. J. Psycho-anal., 49.*

Natterson, J. (Ed.). (1993). *The dream in clinical practice*. Northvale, NJ: Aronson.

Palombo, S. R. (1978). The adaptive functions of dreams. *Psychoanal. Contemp. Thought, 1.*

Paniagua, C. (1987). Can clinical psychoanalysis be scientific? *Amer. J. Psychiat., 41.*

Porret, J. M. (1987). Peculiarities and effects of the nocturnal psychological life of the child and the adolescent. In *Psychiatrie de l'enfant.* Lausanne: University of Lausanne.

Reiser, M. F. (1991). *Memory and brain: What dream imagery reveals*. New York: Basic Books.

Reppen, J. (Ed.). (1985). *Beyond Freud: A study of modern psychoanalytic theorists.* Hillsdale, NJ: Analytic Press.

Rycroft, C. (1981). *The innocence of dreams*. New York: Oxford University Press.

Shengold, L. (1989). *Soul murder: The effect of childhood abuse and deprivation.* New Haven, CT: Yale University Press.

Stewart, K. (1954). *Pygmies and dream giants*. New York: Norton.

Strunz, F. (1955). Die Aetiologie und Therapie der Alpträume. *Fortschr. Neurol. Psychiat.*

Thomä, H., & Kächele, H. (1989). *Lehrbuch der psychoanalytischen Therapie.* Heidelberg: Springer.

Valenstein, E. (1986). *Great and desperate cures*. New York: Basic Books.

Waldhorn, H. F. (1967). *Indications for psychoanalysis: The place of the dream in clinical psychoanalysis.* Monograph 2 of the Kris Study Group of the New York Psychoanalytic Institute, E. D. Joseph (Ed.). New York: International Universities Press.

Wallerstein, R. S. (Ed.). (1991). *The doctorate in mental health: An experiment in mental health professional education.* Lanham, MD: University Press of America.

Wisdom, J. O. (1949). A hypothesis to explain trauma reenactment dreams. *Internat. J. Psycho-anal., 30.*

Yalom, I. D. (1989). *Love's executioner.* New York: Basic Books.

Yalom, I. D. (1991). *The theory and practice of group psychotherapy* (3rd ed.). New York: Basic Books.

PART II

THE QUEST FOR AFFORDABLE AND EFFECTIVE PSYCHOTHERAPY

Intensive, Extended Analytic Group Therapy A Promise for Many

*Written in cooperation
with Denise LaHullier*

One of the foremost priorities of the American Mental Health Foundation is to develop effective, affordable forms of psychotherapy that will make quality treatment accessible to a far greater number of people. The focus on the quality of psychotherapeutic approaches and pertinent recommendations are presented in the publications of the Foundation. The improvements proposed pertain to both individual and group psychotherapy.

In this chapter we are dealing with a specific form of psychodynamic, interactive group psychotherapy, developed by Stefan de Schill at the Foundation over the course of 45 years. It offers considerably more treatment time to the patient and, owing to its special features, is considerably more intensive than the usual forms of group psychotherapy. Many patients who could not previously be placed into group psychotherapy can now derive great benefits from this treatment form.

We hope that the material presented in this chapter will not only allow therapists to become aware of this treatment form but also motivate them to use it.

Because we feel that the material is of such potential benefit to patients, we have taken the unusual step of publishing this chapter in both this book and the companion volume, thus making it available to the greatest number of readers.

Stefan de Schill is a Fellow of the American Group Psychotherapy Association.

Denise LaHullier
Coordinator, Group Therapy Sections
American Mental Health Foundation
International Institute for Mental
Health Research, Zürich and Geneva

1. A Parable

Even though mental health professionals like to portray themselves as ethical defenders of the public interest, their noble oratory is not always translated into action. Rather, a complacency, a lack of responsibility, and a tolerance for incompetence and questionable ethics are a frequent attitude among mental health professionals – as long as their own self-interest is not injured. They tend to shun decisive action that could answer the two most fundamental needs in psychotherapy: to ensure quality and adequate treatment time for patient care.

In spite of the concerns voiced, one encounters mental health professionals, such as Toksoz B. Karasu, who vociferously advocate shortening the treatment sessions, notwithstanding knowledge that the treatment time, in all too many cases, not only is of substandard quality but also has become shorter and shorter.

As we have pointed out, the promoters of "easy to learn" and "easy to apply" treatment, such as Karasu, Yalom, and Grotjahn (see Part I), find a great number of followers among professionals. The victims of such self-promotion and lack of interest in the public welfare are the patients and the students who truly seek to acquire knowledge rather than merely to enter a reasonably well-paying profession.

Our patients' great and compelling need for sufficient time and attention is seldom fulfilled. One would have hoped that some psychotherapists, despite the impediment of practical considerations, would have tried to be more generous with their treatment time. Sadly, we were unable to find concrete evidence of such efforts.

We pause here to relate a true story that may help us regain the human perspective that should imbue our work. The story was told to us by a friend.

A number of years ago, a girl in her early 20s and of modest circumstances arrived in New York from France. Coming from a desolate region of abandoned coal mines and rampant unemployment, the girl, whose name was Nicole, hoped to improve her knowledge of English and find some employment to pay for the bare necessities. Her mother, at great sacrifice, sent her a tiny monthly allowance to help her over the initial period.

To find employment, Nicole left her name with several French organizations and schools. Shortly thereafter she received a call requesting her presence at the home of a wealthy woman on the upper East Side. She was offered a job teaching French to the woman's two daughters, 8 and 12 years old, once a week for an hour. The remuneration per session was to be $3.00, which included the expense of transportation. Nicole, glad to have found a position, accepted immediately.

The two children seemed to enjoy the sessions immensely. Nicole, who had a lovely voice, would sing French songs, and the children would join in. No wonder the children did not want her to leave at the end of the hour, and Nicole always obliged. Soon the meetings were lasting three hours or more.

The mother, seldom home, was quite happy with the work and asked Nicole to come twice a week. She also invited the children of her friends to join the sessions, and within a short time six to eight children were usually present. The other mothers were delighted with Nicole's devotion and fine work; they congratulated and thanked her profusely.

That idyll continued for close to six months. Then one day in June, at the end of a session, the mother advised Nicole that this would be the last time and she need not return. The family would be leaving in a few days for their summer home.

Nicole went to a nearby park, sat down on a bench, and cried uncontrollably. That is where our friend noticed her. Only after much time and with considerable difficulty did our friend succeed in calming the distraught girl. Understandably, our friend then attempted to find out what the cause of her great sorrow was and learned of the lessons given to the children and of the other circumstances of Nicole's life.

Our friend was very moved and tried to console Nicole. She said, "I guess it is very hard to lose the only income you had." Nicole, still with tears in her eyes, looked at her in astonishment and said:

"Oh, no. They never paid me anything, and I did not want to ask. I felt too embarrassed. No, I am so sad because I will never see the children again!"

Our responsibility as health professionals is to look out for the welfare of the patients. We cannot hope to match the generosity of the girl who gave so freely of her time. There are stark realities that impose limitations on the goodwill of psychotherapists. Of course, psychotherapists should make a decent living. But we find too many instances where consideration of the patient's needs is grossly lacking.

Regarding the matter of professional fees and the treatment value our patients receive, let us restrict ourselves to the question of the length of therapy sessions. Obviously, the ratio of the professional fee to the length of the session is determined by the psychotherapist.

We previously discussed the question of the length and frequency of individual sessions. Originally set at 60 minutes, the standard "hour" has gradually been reduced to 50 minutes and then 45 minutes, and 40-minute sessions have already made their appearance. So far, only a few practitioners outside France have adopted the five-to-fifteen-minute kitchen timer sessions advocated by Karasu and other followers of Lacan.

Group therapy was also more generous to the patient in its early days. In the mid-1930s Paul Schilder placed into groups patients who had two or three individual psychoanalytic sessions with him per week. The groups met once a week. They consisted of no more than seven members and lasted about three hours. It is interesting to note that Schilder referred to them as "such large groups." Since then, the time allotted has been sharply reduced; the vast majority of groups meet once a week for an hour and a half.

In this chapter we want to acquaint the reader with a group psychotherapy method that allows generous time to the patients, does not entail a financial sacrifice for the group therapist, and can provide him with far greater satisfaction in his work than he has experienced in the past.

2. SOME FUNDAMENTAL CONSIDERATIONS

In this volume we have examined, at unusual length, the deterioration in the quality of psychodynamic psychotherapy. An even greater corrosion has afflicted group psychotherapy to a degree that we would have thought unimaginable in the 1960s and early 1970s.

In the present chapter we describe where the problems lie and what the remedies ought to be. Broadly speaking, we have divided the topic into two distinct areas: (1) the format, or the framework, within which group therapy must take place, and (2) the content, that is, the quality of the therapeutic work done within that context.

Our findings concerning psychodynamic group psychotherapy are based on more than 45 years of intensive study and practical work. As we have explained, one of the foremost priorities of the Foundation was to develop greatly improved treatment approaches in psychodynamic individual and group psychotherapy. The greatest need in the mental health field is to bring about far more effective treatment modalities at a cost affordable even to people of moderate means. While it was possible to increase the effectiveness of individual psychotherapy by applying the procedures described in the preceding chapter, "Working toward Clinical Expertise," the cost of two or more private sessions a week over a prolonged period of time was beyond the means of most people. For that reason, we needed to focus on group psychotherapy and to develop major modifications to achieve the desired goal.

The importance of the continued development of the form of group psychotherapy resulting from the efforts of the Foundation becomes even more obvious as we become more aware of the extent of emotional illness. The argument that more patients could be treated in a group setting is certainly sound. However, we have nowhere near enough group psychotherapists capable of adequately administering such a sophisticated treatment to the many who could profit from it.

There is a widespread tendency, uninformed and arrogant, among individual analysts and therapists to consider group therapy a sort of shabby relative, tolerated but not respected. Nothing could be less justified. To be an expert group psychotherapist, a professional must not only be an expert individual analyst and therapist but also have substantial additional talent and skills. Those who have a broad understanding of matters psychotherapeutic are aware that group psychotherapy has made a unique contribution by deepening, widening, and in some areas changing our understanding of psychological mechanisms and therapeutic processes, thereby allowing the formulation of better hypotheses specific to each individual. Through that individual focus the therapist avoids simplistic generalizing dogma and clichés, and his expertise and the patient's emotional health may be significantly improved.

There are many positive factors in group psychotherapy that are not available to individual therapists. Outstanding among them is the presence of multiple transferences, a factor of enormous importance. In the following paragraphs from Part I of this volume, attention was called to that matter:

> I believe we have the right to demand that those who wax so eloquent about the theories that should govern psychotherapy should have a solid basic knowledge themselves and do everything possible to enrich that knowledge, particularly where vital areas are concerned. There is much evidence, however, that many do not. As stated, many writers, staying safely in the realm of theoretical speculation, do not betray evidence of actual clinical expertise.
>
> To turn out book after book about therapy, those theorists should certainly have a measure of expertise in its basics. Again let us choose a simple example: transference. I assert categorically that individual therapy is insufficient for a full understanding of transference in all its dimensions. Analytic group therapy has been around for many decades. There is a vast literature concerning the multiple transferences in such groups and the crystallization of the transferences that allows for far more

understanding than individual therapy, where all transferences are projected on one analyst. For instance, claims by
the theorizers notwithstanding, an individual male analyst
cannot evoke sexual female transferences to the same
degree as can an attractive woman in the group.

No therapist has the complete understanding of
transference phenomena unless he has spent considerable
time in a group as one of its members and then conducted
psychodynamic groups himself. One would imagine that
the theorists who ooze therapeutic pontification would, in
their eagerness to help mankind, rush to acquire such
indispensable know-how so that they could better understand transference and thus psychotherapy. Alas, to the
best of my knowledge, none of them wishes to be thus
inconvenienced. That, of course, does not stop them from
writing further "fundamental treatises." Shrewd avoidance of clinical subjects that could become telltale signs of
ignorance, and a measure of writing ability, can successfully mask the lack of clinical knowledge.

We, however, maintain that one must fully understand certain fundamentals in psychoanalysis and psychotherapy before attempting
even the most rudimentary theorizing. And transference is one of
those fundamentals!

As Stoller masterfully points out his introduction to this volume,
however, such ethical restraint seems nonexistent in our field, where
freewheeling fantasy, readily accepted and acclaimed as "scientific" profundity, substitutes for clinical expertise.

There are other reasons that no psychotherapist – no matter how
gifted and accomplished – can rightfully claim full professional competence until he has studied and mastered the craft of group psychotherapy. He will not fully comprehend any of his patients until he has seen
them interact as members of a therapy group. For it is in that setting
that the therapist will get important additional clues that will lead him
to a broader view of his patients' behavior and personality, some of
which will be surprising.

At the beginning of this section, we mentioned that we need to divide the topic we are addressing into two areas, the first being the framework within which effective group therapy takes place.

Before we even touch on the components necessary for effective psychodynamic group psychotherapy, we must address the factor of treatment time. It is of crucial importance from both a clinical and an ethical point of view. No cheap rationalizations like Karasu's nor grandiose ravings like Lacan's should be permitted to obscure the basic needs of the patient.

We will, once more, cite some paragraphs that appear in Part I of this book. They are part of a small section disputing the assumption that one can treat seven or eight people successfully in a group by giving them an hour and a half once a week.

> On the basis of decades of experience, I am convinced of the value of group psychotherapy for many people who fall into a variety of clinical categories. However, it is valuable only if the groups are conducted by an expert therapist. Also, we must be very specific: what kind of group psychotherapy? Basically, we have to distinguish between analytic group psychotherapists, who focus on the individual, and group processors, who deal with the group as a whole. The reader will find the necessary details in the group therapy chapter in this volume. Unfortunately, most of the practitioners using those two modalities give their groups merely an hour and a half a week.
>
> It would be desirable for each patient in individual treatment to receive at least two sessions a week; that would constitute almost two hours a week. Alas, that is often not possible! Where in the world do all these geniuses come from who can perform the incredible feat of "curing" seven to nine people in group therapy with so little time; namely, one and a half hours a week? Some of those therapists are my friends – but they have never told me their secret!

It's like a barber chair
which fits all buttocks.

SHAKESPEARE

We assume that psychotherapists are paragons of insight and emotional wisdom, capable of leading their poor patients away from destructive errors such as rationalization and asocial behavior. However, having spent many years reading the group therapy literature and having attended far too many conferences and lectures, we have not once heard a therapist speak out in favor of according more generous treatment time to his groups. Yet lack of time per se could not have been the impediment, for some therapists gave a lot of time to the treatment of groups and conducted seven or more groups a week. One even had 15 groups a week. (An aside to the therapist who struggles to get referrals: As far as can be judged, in not one of those situations did a group therapist obtain many referrals because of his special expertise. It was usually a result of his position in a specific treatment entity or a privileged contact with a referring social worker.)

Since we are dealing with two distinct categories of psychodynamic group therapists, we are offered two distinct rationalizations for the paucity of time accorded.

First, the analytically oriented group therapists contend that merely attending group meetings for 90 minutes a week, even without actively participating, is of significant therapeutic value to a patient. Is it? And will 90 minutes a week of such attendance perform the miracle the poor patient is waiting for and – forgive us – paying for?

Second, the group processors contend that one can treat the group as a whole rather than arduously address the problems of the individual group members. In our companion volume Alexander Wolf cogently dissects the myth of such group process. We are not saying that group process and the postulation of a group mind (Grotjahn even commits the inanity of asserting that a group unconscious exists) were created as a rationalization for insufficient treatment time. We do, however, categorically state that the concepts of group mind and group process were eagerly picked up, consciously or not, by many therapists because those concepts offered them, on a silver platter, (1) a facile treatment method and (2) the convenient rationalization that if one is merely dealing with the group as a whole, an hour and a half a week is sufficient to take care of the whole caboodle. We have read innumerable treatises on the value of the work of group processors, both theoretical and clinical, most of them quite academic and intellectual, but when stripped of the verbiage and pretentious conceptualization, each one could be reduced by an expert and clear-minded clinician to a heap of scrap. We shall return to that later in this chapter.

We have been addressing the need for sufficient time for the psychotherapy patient since 1948, when one of us, de Schill, was appointed to join the ranks of the Foundation. In all our communications we stressed the importance of sufficient treatment time and of improved quality of treatment. Where are the results? Unfortunately, the clamor has been for shorter treatment sessions and shorter overall treatment time. The advocates of facile, virtually valueless treatment methods, clinicians who take superficial, generalizing positions, are increasingly capturing the attention of the insufficiently informed psychotherapists. The voices of such sages as Greenson, Stoller, and Leites, who insist on depth and quality, are lost in the crowd.

As we saw in Part I, too many psychotherapists, in spite of much sacrifice and effort, receive inadequate training, and the system for selecting students for the profession of psychotherapist does not select the best candidates. We also looked at concrete proposals for dealing with those problems. Since group therapists need to master skills in addition to those required for competent individual therapy, the question of selection and training are here of even greater importance.

3. FORMAT AND TECHNIQUES

Earlier we described why, in our endeavor to develop an effective psychotherapy method that most patients could afford, we had become convinced that only group psychotherapy could provide an adequate basis. Once we made that decision, a major question remained: Which method of group therapy, or which combination of methods, would provide the necessary foundation? Even in those days, the number of approaches was surprising, and the divergences were wide. None seemed particularly satisfying; many lacked clinical wisdom. It was not until a year later that a Viennese colleague and member of our Foundation, Joseph Wilder, called our attention to the efforts of Alexander Wolf.

Wolf's work was a partial base to build on: an intelligent, well-thought-out approach, demonstrating clinical acumen. We used Wolf's approach as one of the starting points for our goal, still very distant, of creating an effective, affordable, and widely applicable treatment method. It was a goal that most people considered – and rightly so – impossible to achieve, and the task proved to be as easy as transforming a passenger car into a ferryboat. It took more than 40 years of trial and error, and innumerable changes and innovations in technique and clinical rationale, to arrive at the stage described in this chapter.

To maintain the proper perspective, let us state once again the fundamental purpose of our endeavor: to increase the effectiveness of therapy and thereby reduce proportionately the total treatment cost to the patient. As the effectiveness of the procedure increases, the patient either will come for a shorter total treatment period, or, if limited by his financial circumstances, will be able to reduce his weekly expense by decreasing the number of sessions.

The urgent need for affordable treatment was originally demonstrated by a follow-up study by the Foundation, started in 1954 and conducted over a period of nine years. The study showed that within a year's time only about 1 percent of applicants for low-cost treatment were able to find therapy of at least two individual sessions a week. (It must be pointed out that treatment by trainees in the numerous training institutes was not considered acceptable therapy.) Information available to the Foundation does not any indicate improvement of the situation. Rather, it seems to have further deteriorated.

Let us begin our description of the group method developed by the Foundation with a point of greatest importance, the treatment time accorded to groups. We have mentioned that practically all group therapy meetings – analytic, group process, or whatever – are conducted once a week for an hour and a half. With groups averaging eight people, we found it impossible to do even a fraction of the necessary work in such a limited time. We doubled the group time to three hours and requested that the group members spend equal time in an alternate session, that is, one without the therapist's being present. Much credit should be given to Alexander Wolf for instituting that innovation. We have heard many theoretical and highly scholarly arguments condemning the use of such sessions, arguments claiming, for example, that therapy takes place only when the therapist is present. While such academic sophistry may sound impressive on paper, its proper place is in the wastebasket. The outstanding value of the alternate session is confirmed by the clinical experience of many expert group therapists over more than four decades. Attendance at the alternate sessions is necessary for any person wanting to participate in the intensive extended groups.

To proceed, we must briefly backtrack to the 1950s and 1960s. Perhaps only older psychotherapists remember how much hostility and derision group therapy encountered in those days. In many cases group therapy was accepted by an "established" analyst only when he wanted to get rid of a difficult patient. Frequently, either the analyst would state that the patient's problem was not psychological but medical, or if he was of a "modern" bent, he would advise the patient that group treatment was the indicated modality for his particular emotional problem.

At any rate, the essentials of psychodynamic group therapy were ignored by most mental health professionals and virtually all the medical profession. There was a time when the American Psychiatric Association refused to publish the announcements and advertisements of our group psychotherapy publications. Moreover, most patients felt antagonistic toward any suggestion to enter group treatment. Among their many arguments, the most potent and justifiable one was that they needed the fullest attention of the therapist and would under no circumstances allow their therapy to be diluted by sharing precious treatment time with a horde of other people.

The reader can well imagine our predicament. Here we were trying to disseminate knowledge concerning a treatment approach that we were convinced would help a great number of people, and apparently neither professionals nor patients wanted any part of it!

It was then that the Foundation decided to publish INTRODUCTION TO PSYCHOANALYTIC GROUP PSYCHOTHERAPY (de Schill, 1954), intended to offer professionals and patients detailed information regarding the treatment method. In view of the distrust and antagonism of professionals and patients toward group therapy, we anticipated that the publication would find a limited readership. We could not have been wronger. The first edition was published jointly by the Foundation and Robert Brunner, Inc., at the time the largest distributor of mental health publications in the United States. It was sold out within a few months. Between then and 1971 six editions were published.

The publication served two purposes: it allowed professionals to acquaint themselves with the fundamentals of the therapy method and, when given to prospective patients, greatly reduced their reluctance to enter group psychotherapy. In those early days of group therapy, most group patients were recruited from the individual patients of the therapist, and frequently the group therapy was in addition to regular individual sessions. Many therapists felt that the adjunct procedure would hasten improvement of the patients. Furthermore, many therapists were interested in the new method, as it allowed them to increase their revenue considerably. (That financial aspect was, of course, unrelated to the Foundation's reasons for promoting the method.)

Even though the demand for the text continued unabated, in 1972 the Foundation decided to temporarily stop its publication until two major problems could be overcome. The problems were called to our attention by patients to whom the publication had been distributed by clinics and psychotherapists. As we have explained, the Foundation stressed in all its communications the need for sufficient treatment time in group psychotherapy and for proper attention to individual group members. The complaints we increasingly received, however, lamented the fact that the techniques described in INTRODUCTION TO PSYCHOANALYTIC GROUP THERAPY were, owing to the brevity of the time offered, in actuality only sparingly used or, in the case of therapists who were "group processors," not used at all.

At the same time, we wanted to continue to inform the profession and the public of the benefits of the intensive, extended group therapy form the Foundation had developed. Eventually we decided to include the necessary information, as far as feasible, in all our publications while warning against the pitfalls mentioned.

Even now, after almost half a century of group therapy, it is astonishing how many professionals and physicians are unfamiliar with what we consider the most valid form of the treatment modality. While the following pages are addressed basically to psychotherapists and perhaps to prospective group members, they should also be instructive to a wider audience.

Before we start describing the intensive group method, however, we need to overcome the greatest single obstacle to its acceptance by psychotherapists, namely, the fear of loss of income. A therapist may ask why he should give twice the time to the treatment of a group, when it is unlikely that group members will be willing or able to pay twice the current fee. Surely, therapists need to make a reasonable living and are most unlikely to make an undue financial sacrifice.

The answer is simple; they don't need to, for these reasons:

—   While therapists cannot charge double for a double session, they can charge about a third more for the extended groups. Most patients will agree to make that extra sacrifice. And in cases of hardship the therapist may be willing to see a patient for the regular current group fee (it may be desirable to keep such an arrangement private).

—   With the extra time offered, the therapist can add one more patient to the group, allowing for an average of nine members. Since one or another patient may not show up for any given group session, the extra patient will not prove to be a burden.

- The greatest advantage is that the turnover in extended groups, owing to far greater patient satisfaction and loyalty to the group, is much smaller than in regular groups. That alone is of outstanding financial importance to the average psychotherapist, who does not have access to an unlimited pool of patients.
- The satisfaction of the group members results in a greater number of referrals to the competent therapist.
- A conscientious therapist spends time outside the group thinking about the problems and the dynamics of his patients. It takes far less time to have to think about nine patients than it does to think about two times eight.
- When third-party payers refuse to pay for this treatment modality and will pay only for a lesser, limited treatment form, the therapist can explain to the patient that it would be to his advantage to pay the relatively modest fee from his own pocket. The patient gets a good buy, and the therapist is relieved of considerable paperwork and the intrusive interference of third parties.
- As extended groups are considerably more effective, patients who could not otherwise have been placed into group therapy can now be included. That permits the therapist to draw from a wider circle of patients, including the ever-increasing numbers of the elderly.
- The extended groups are far more interesting and challenging than the usual short groups, which are necessarily more superficial.
- Most of all, the therapist has the satisfaction of being able to gain a far greater understanding of his patients and to see real progress in his patients while avoiding much frustration, self-doubt, and uncertainty.

Are there no drawbacks when proposing this procedure to prospective patients? Yes, there is one. Some people will be hesitant, or unable, to give six hours a week to therapy. But if they cannot afford two private sessions a week, what alternative is left for them? After all, this is the only intensive treatment form available at moderate cost.

The Foundation made major efforts to inform professionals of the benefits of the intensive, extended groups. We have already mentioned that in 1954 the first edition of Introduction to Psychoanalytic Group Therapy appeared. In 1956 the Foundation published The Practice of Mental Health Groups (de Schill & LaHullier), offering additional details on the method. Furthermore, the treatment was presented at many conferences. A few of the earliest ones were the Second International Congress of Group Psychotherapy in Zürich, 1957; the Sixth International Congress for Mental Health in Paris, 1961; the Sixth International Congress of Psychotherapy in London, 1964; the 23rd Annual Conference of the American Group Psychotherapy Association in Philadelphia, 1965; and annual meetings of the American Mental Health Foundation.

Of course, the principal purpose of this chapter is to acquaint psychotherapists with the intensive, extended group method in the hope that they will adopt the approach, and a great number of patients will eventually benefit from it. Many emotional disturbances, even those of a severe nature, previously not considered amenable to group psychotherapy, can now be treated in this particular therapy form. Since patients are seen almost exclusively in group sessions, those who can pay for only the equivalent of one individual session a week are able, for the first time, to receive intensive and extended psychotherapy. But let us for a moment put those important considerations aside. By far the most important factor is that if practiced by an expert psychotherapist, the treatment modality offers unique and unequaled possibilities for achieving success.

For the therapist to prepare prospective patients for group psychotherapy, he needs to give them detailed information about the procedure. Before 1954 about two-thirds of the people to whom the Foundation recommended group therapy either disliked the idea or rejected it outright, insisting on individual therapy. After that date, however, when the printed information was given to patients selected for the extended groups, less than a third of them objected. Acceptance of group therapy developed rapidly in the next 15 years or so. Between 1954 and 1972 some 80,000 copies of Introduction to Psychoanalytic Group Therapy were sold. In 1973 La psychotherapie de groupe, prepared by the American Mental Health Foundation and the International Institute for Mental Health Research in Switzerland, was published under the auspices of the Library of the Paris Psychoanalytic Institute by Presses Universitaires de France. Such an event would have been impossible just a few years before. Unfortunately, while analytic group therapy reached a high point during that period, quite a number of undesirable forms of group therapy also made their appearance.

Many people initially object to going into therapy with others because they dislike or fear people and because they feel that in a group they would not be able to speak freely about their problems. Such resistance is voiced even more frequently by patients who are being placed in the extended groups, because they will have fewer individual sessions.

The new patient who experiences anxiety needs to understand that his fears about entering a group are related to his problems and that it would therefore be advantageous for him to work those problems through in the group rather than avoid them. For most patients who receive the introductory printed information and whose anxieties and resistances are carefully handled, the initial period in the group is not difficult. The rare exceptions are the patients who become over-whelmed with anxiety when exposed to emotion-arousing situations that occur through interaction within the group. Such patients need the protection of the therapist to temper their anxiety and may be instructed not to attend the alternate meetings at first.

Whether or not a patient selected for group psychotherapy initially resists the idea of group work, his therapist must take on the necessary but often burdensome task of preparing him for it. One patient after another will ask the same questions about the principles and practices of group psychotherapy. The therapist who conducts the intake interviews of an organization or clinic may react to the repetitive questions by becoming less patient and explicit than is necessary to sufficiently diminish the patient's initial anxiety. Therapists in private practice who work with groups have the same problem.

Experience in individual treatment does not necessarily reduce a patient's questions about group therapy. In fact, anxiety over being placed in a new clinical situation and resentment against sharing the therapist's attention with other patients frequently induce strong resistance against group work. The resistance is manifested by the expression of innumerable questions and objections.

Since many of the applicants for referral through the Foundation were found suitable for extended group therapy, we gained considerable experience with the typical questions. As early as 1953, we felt that much unnecessary work could be eliminated for the therapist, whether he sees patients in a clinical or in a private setting, if he could give his patients literature explaining extended group therapy. Since patients frequently forget some of the information given them orally and tend to repeat questions, the literature is doubly useful.

Patients about to join extended groups receive only two private sessions with the therapist before entering the group. During those sessions the therapist collects data so that he can tentatively evaluate the psychodynamics and help the patient overcome fears and misapprehensions about joining the group. In addition to the two individual sessions before entering the group, the vast majority of patients require only two to eight private sessions a year. Exceptions are patients who are confronted with severely traumatic situations.

The information regarding format and technique that follows is principally directed to psychotherapists wanting to acquaint themselves with the procedure, but we have fashioned the text in such a way that a copy can be given to patients about to enter such groups. Part I can be given to patients to whom group therapy is being recommended. Part II can be given to patients who, after reading the first part, and possibly after further therapeutic assistance from their analysts, are willing to enter extended group therapy. For the convenience of the readers, the text has been arranged in question-and-answer form.

Introduction to Intensive, Extended Group Psychotherapy

Part I

1. How do I know that I need professional help with my emotional problems?
Everyone, no matter how stable and emotionally mature, can benefit from professional help to gain insight into his or her underlying emotional structure and functioning.

People with emotional disturbances often misunderstand, or even ignore, their manifestations and symptoms and do not take the proper steps to eliminate them. Some people hesitate to admit to themselves, much less to others, that they cannot cope adequately with their own emotional reactions. They may not realize that the inability to overcome emotional problems by oneself is by no means a sign of weakness or lack of intelligence. Direct application of will power for such a purpose tends to be useless. That is true even for those who know a great deal about psychology and psychotherapy.

The following are some of the problems that indicate a need for professional help: difficulties in interpersonal relations, marriage, and parenthood; loneliness and withdrawal; feelings of losing touch with reality; feelings of failure; general dissatisfaction with yourself or your life; inability to do things that you feel you should be able to do, such as concentrate, study, or work; feeling compelled to do things that you do not want to do; frequent feelings of unhappiness; expectations that something bad will happen; continual worries and anxieties of all sorts; nightmares; depressed moods and sadness; persistent feelings of being persecuted, blamed, or taken advantage of; pervasive feelings of hate or contempt; feelings of being inferior, of being disliked or rejected by others, or of disliking yourself; feelings of great tension, irritability, or excitability; persistent feelings of restlessness.

Because the human mind is intimately connected with the body, one may have physical complaints for which the physician is unable to find an organic cause. Such symptoms are often of psychological origin and may indicate a need for psychotherapeutic help. Examples are sleeplessness, headaches, sexual difficulties and dysfunctions, heart palpitations, excessive perspiration, fatigue, and digestive problems, such as frequent constipation, diarrhea, and stomach pain.

2. How do I know what type of help I need?
Many people try to select a form of psychotherapy merely on the basis of personal prejudice, hearsay, or pressure from others. A better way of finding the type of psychotherapy most suitable for you is to consult an experienced professional who is fully acquainted with the wide range of existing psychotherapeutic techniques. Many psychotherapeutic organizations and clinics also offer diagnostic services to determine your psychotherapeutic requirements.

Remember that any information you give a psychotherapist about yourself is strictly confidential. You should be as frank as possible in the diagnostic session to enable the interviewing psychotherapist to make a valid evaluation.

Clinical experience, gained in 45 years of research at the American Mental Health Foundation, has shown that most people in need of professional assistance can benefit greatly from a form of group treatment known as intensive, extended psychodynamic group therapy. It is a unique treatment form that offers considerably more time each week than other types of group therapy. It also allows for the requisite attention to the needs of each individual. That is in sharp contrast to many types of group therapy that attempt to treat the group as a whole. Many people who had emotional disturbances that did not yield in intensive individual treatment have had positive results in such intensive, extended group therapy.

These pages have been given to you because it is felt that this particular form of group treatment would be beneficial to you.

3. What is the setting of the group?

The group usually consists of eight or nine people, both men and women. Meetings last about three hours. Groups meet twice a week, once with the therapist and once without the therapist.

The meetings that are held without the therapist, called alternate meetings, are extremely valuable, since a person's feelings and attitudes in the group usually vary considerably depending on the presence or absence of the therapist. The difference may provide clues to self-understanding. Furthermore, alternate meetings pave the way to self-assertion and emotional independence.

Occasionally private sessions may take place. The therapist suggests when an individual session would be of benefit to a particular group member. Individual sessions may be indicated when feelings of reluctance toward psychotherapy or the therapist are strong. Such feelings of resistance occur in all forms of valid psychotherapy.

4. Why is intensive, extended group therapy so effective?

This form of psychotherapy is of outstanding value in attaining emotional insight and maturity. When practiced by a specially trained therapist, it draws on proven therapeutic techniques and utilizes all the psychodynamic fundamentals, such as transference and resistance analysis, free association, and dream interpretation. It has features that are all its own and cannot be duplicated in individual treatment. Among them are the following:

In a group the members work through their problems in a real situation of constant personal interaction. You will soon become aware of emotional difficulties in others. By understanding their feelings, you will gain insight into your own emotional problems and reactions. Your psychotherapeutic progress will be continually stimulated by observing and sharing in the reactions, experiences, and achievements of other group members.

Constant dynamic relations with the group will help you give up overdependency on the psychotherapist; such overdependency tends to prolong the process of recovery.

Another important element is that extended group psychotherapy is relatively inexpensive. Thus anxiety caused by the financial burden of treatment tends to be minor.

The many and varied interrelationships that take place in such groups are beneficial. If you see a therapist only for individual sessions, you can react merely to a single individual on whom you project emotional patterns established in childhood (transference). The emergence and understanding of those patterns and reactions are a prime factor in a successful treatment. Therefore individual therapy alone might be restrictive, since it cannot arouse the whole range of emotions buried deep within you. In group, however, the different personalities of the male and female members evoke a multitude of emotional reactions. They will help you understand your feelings, behavior patterns, and conflicts.

In the individual session the therapist is limited by the person's subjective reports of incidents and emotional reactions to them. In the group situation, however, the therapist and the group can objectively detect the manner in which each person's defensive and emotional patterns distort the perception of reality. Thus group members are helped gradually to achieve insight into their own deviations from objectivity.

People who have undesirable personality traits and behavior patterns can be better helped to overcome those shortcomings in groups than in individual therapy. After all, the psychotherapist cannot point out such flaws to the patient, since doing so might cause offense and harm the therapeutic relationship. However, through group interaction undesirable characteristics often become apparent, and group members can more freely point them out. The underlying causes can then be analyzed and worked through.

Because the group situation is more like the world we live in than the sheltered protection of a private session, any emotion expressed and worked through in a group constitutes a direct step forward. Personality changes thus achieved tend to be more definite and permanent.

5. Should I join a group even if I feel uneasy about it?
If you feel that you will not be able to speak about your problems with a group of people, or if you dislike or fear people, you should remember that such feelings and fears are directly connected with your problems. You should work through your fears rather than avoid them. They will very likely diminish after a few group sessions.

Some people have the erroneous impression that psychotherapy in groups – because it is less expensive – is more superficial than individual treatment. They may not want group sessions because they want to have the entire time and attention of the analyst, or they may not want to be bothered with other people's problems. In therapy, however, what seems to be more gratifying or less difficult is not necessarily what makes for the most effective treatment.

In the extended group sessions you will have ample opportunity to express yourself, but in fact the effectiveness of a psychotherapeutic technique is not directly proportionate to the amount of words a person utters. Speaking about problems of which you are already aware is only of minor significance. Far more important is bringing into consciousness the intense emotions that have been repressed since childhood. Only when you become aware of them can you focus on them and deal with them. In the ever-changing group situation created by the expressions, behavior, and interaction of the members, your deeper feelings will inevitably be elicited.

Thus the success of therapy greatly depends on the extent to which repressed emotions are stimulated, brought to awareness, expressed, and worked through.

PART II

1. What should I do in the group?

In the group you have an unusual opportunity to express your real thoughts and feelings. You need not force yourself to behave in any particular way. Some people participate actively from the beginning; others remain silent for a while. Whichever tendency you have, observe what the others do. Become aware of your feelings throughout the meetings. Watch for anticipatory feelings before the meetings and for reactions you have at any time afterwards. Sooner or later you will want to express those feelings in the group. If, however, you have difficulty verbalizing your feelings while you are experiencing them, you may be able to talk about them at subsequent meetings. Try to become aware of which feelings are difficult to express in the sessions with the therapist and which are difficult to express in the alternate sessions. If an inability to speak continues, it will be of value to express your feelings in an individual session with the analyst.

At any rate, going to psychotherapy is not like going to your dentist, where the necessary work is done for you. In psychotherapy your efforts can greatly facilitate the endeavor, resulting in earlier and greater benefits to you – and thus reducing the total time and cost of treatment.

The first phase in therapy includes the task of learning to identify feelings. As strange as it may seem, people are frequently unclear about what their real feelings are. Some may confuse them with opinions, values, and intellectual concepts, which are more often than not mere defenses against, and rationalizations of, their real feelings.

Four to six weeks of sessions will pass before you become fully aware of what is going on in the group. As you participate more and more, you will begin to sense what the group and the therapist are working toward, and you will gradually become emotionally involved. It is like watching people dance and then dancing yourself; only when you actively participate can you realize its essence. Be patient.

The initial sessions may be difficult. You may resent or dislike some of the members and want to abandon the group. No matter how strong those feelings are, do not give in to them. Discussing them in the group or in an individual session will provide valuable material that may lead to deeper insight and self-understanding.

You will notice that the group members do a number of things: speak about past and present experiences, problems, thoughts, and fantasies that are emotionally important to them; speak about feelings experienced at previous meetings, between meetings, and particularly during the present meeting; and state their feelings about each other and the therapist. Many of their emotions may appear irrational to you. However, you will soon realize that feelings have their own logic, and the group's tolerance of apparent irrationality will help you discover and express irrational feelings of your own. The group members also discuss dreams, since they are a vital factor in understanding a person's emotional problems and ways of dealing with them.

If you feel that you want to hide some of your thoughts and actions from the group because they seem shocking, embarrassing, or ridiculous or because you do not want to hurt another member's feelings or incur the dislike of anyone in the group, you should express your reluctance. The truthful expression of your feelings is absolutely necessary for your progress. A group meeting is not a customary social situation. Expressing your negative feelings here can help the other group members as well as yourself.

If you repeatedly feel blocked in the group and unable to express yourself, or if your mind goes blank, your therapist may suggest that you prepare a mental list of emotional experiences, dreams, and ideas that you previously experienced and that you intended to discuss but could not. If you go blank just the same, you might write the list down and refer to it in the group. However, spontaneous reaction will usually be of greater value than prepared material. As you gradually work through your tendency to block and find spontaneous expression easier, you will be able to dispense with such props.

You asked for professional assistance because of your emotional problems, not because you wanted to engage in intellectual discussions. Intellectual understanding alone does not bring about lasting change. Deep emotional understanding and progress will come about only by turning your attention inward and becoming aware of feelings and reactions that stem from childhood and adolescence. Therefore, it is most important that you be attentive to your reactions arising in the group and try to understand the emotional forces at work. That may require some concentration and effort. The continued expression of emotions will provide a basis for the necessary therapeutic work that will follow by weakening the unconscious forces that have hidden the deeply repressed feelings and conflicts. As they gradually emerge, they will become more understandable and manageable.

Some kinds of talk are fruitless in group therapy. First, intellectual discussions about abstract ideas and current events have no place here. This is not a high school debate. Second, try to avoid recounting outside situations. When you speak about your emotional reactions as they occur in the group, the therapist and your fellow group members can evaluate them and notice any distortions. But if you discuss at length your problems with your boss or your spouse, it is difficult to discern to what extent your report is emotionally colored.

"Symptom talk" is also of little value. For example, if there is a man in the group who feels inferior because of what he believes to be a physical shortcoming, it is certainly legitimate for him to speak of the problem, which quite possibly is what brought him to therapy. If, however, session after session, he speaks only about the one problem and never goes deeper, the therapist and the group members must point out his single-minded focus and direct his effort toward the necessary group work. Doing so will break the vicious circle in which he was caught and help him gradually clarify the underlying emotional factors.

Sometimes a person may fail to understand the rationale of therapy or may resent the procedure. Such feelings should be expressed when they occur rather than allowed to accumulate. At the same time, you should keep in mind that what happens in the group is not the result of arbitrary whims of the therapist. The therapist is forced to do, or not to do, what therapy requires. Though it may not be apparent, the group members have far more freedom of expression and action than the therapist does.

2. What will my relationship with the therapist be like?

It is vital that you bring up all your feelings toward the therapist, even though that may be difficult. Much of your psychotherapeutic advance will result from understanding the causes for the frequently changing feelings that are stimulated in your relationship with the therapist and the group members. Though your feelings may appear embarrassing, irrational, or hostile, their frank expression is of great value. If you cannot verbalize those feelings in the presence of the other group members, at least tell the group that you are experiencing that difficulty. You may discuss it in an individual session. Also, when you express your feelings about the therapist in the alternate session, be sure to bring them to the therapist's attention in the subsequent regular session.

Many times, seemingly against your will and without your conscious knowledge, inner mechanisms will work against your progress in therapy as painful areas are approached. Such reluctance to delve deeper may take the form of negative feelings against the therapist, the therapy, or both. Those feelings may be based on earlier attitudes toward parents and other people in authority. Your reactions may be so strong that unless the therapist is given a chance to work them through with you, they may actually induce you either to forsake professional help completely or, as an escape from the threatening situation, to seek another therapist. It may require a good deal of self-discipline not to give in to such feelings, which at the time may seem reasonable.

Doubts may also come up when you feel that you are not making visible progress. In all forms of psychotherapy periods of standstill and even setbacks occur. Such periods do not usually last long. Old patterns of feeling and behavior are tenacious, and progress does not occur in a straight line. Often an old pattern will recur when therapy touches on a hidden wound in your unconscious or when the next step forward seems frightening. Those difficult periods are an important part of psychotherapy and provide valuable material for further progress. Such resistance comes up in all types of therapy, and thus also in group therapy. In fact, working through the resistance is crucial to your progress.

3. What about my relationship to the other group members?

Become aware of your feelings toward your fellow group members and express them. Notice their reactions to you after you have expressed yourself, and see how their reactions affect you. Both what is said and how it is said are significant. People's behavior — always a significant clue to their unconscious drives and motivations — may reveal a discrepancy or may even directly contradict their spoken words. That may occur even when they believe they are being honest.

You may also notice a group member "acting out" an emotion; that is, expressing the emotion in an action rather than in verbalization.

Acting out can take the form of turning away from and ignoring a disliked group member or constantly interrupting that person. A group member may knowingly make false and malicious statements about another group member or about the therapist in order to hurt her or him or may falsely claim affection for other group members to win their alliance. It will make it much easier to understand the feelings underlying such actions, feelings that are often unconscious, if the behavior is interrupted and brought to the attention of the individual.

Soon you will become aware of the emotional patterns in some of the members as they react irrationally to certain situations. Your growing awareness will help you develop insight into your own behavior as well.

It is customary for group members to call one another by their first names. Everything said in the group by any of its members must be kept strictly confidential, and no knowledge gained about them, including their identities, may be divulged to any outsider.

4. Should I tell others that I am in group psychotherapy, and should I tell them what happens in the sessions?
You can decide for yourself whether to let others know that you are in psychotherapy. It is wise, however, to remember that some people still have prejudices against psychotherapy. Others may even try to use such knowledge to annoy or hurt you. Well-informed and mature people, however, will respect you for having chosen a path of self-improvement and inner growth.

It is always undesirable to speak with outsiders about what happens in therapy – private or group. First of all, the emotional reactions and evaluations you express to them should be saved for a session, from which you might derive therapeutic benefit. If you express the feelings to a person who is not a group member, you will be less inclined to bring them up in your next session, and valuable material may be lost. Furthermore, in the psychotherapeutic setting one is dealing with unconscious processes of all kinds, which an outsider will most likely misunderstand.

Another danger exists for those who regularly tell a friend or parent about the content of their sessions. A time may come when they will unconsciously refrain from bringing up certain material in the session just because they do not want to repeat it to their habitual confidant. The very process of the therapy thus becomes stifled.

5. What else can I do to help my progress?

Since your emotional structure and behavior patterns have been deeply ingrained since childhood, continued effort over an extended period of time is required to bring about positive and lasting changes. Conscientiously attending the regular and alternate sessions is only one factor necessary to your progress; your efforts to take notice of your emotions during and between the sessions are also of major importance.

The task of the psychotherapist is far from easy. An important part of the therapist's work, upon which much of the success of therapy depends, is to understand your unconscious conflicts and motivations. To that end, you must be completely honest. If you withhold information, change the facts, or embellish the truth, you will create a serious obstacle to effective therapy.

You may enjoy being in therapy and enjoy the group to which you belong. However, for a period of time you may dislike the group meetings. If so, you should bear in mind the therapeutic purpose of the sessions. Your discomfort during the sessions is a small price to pay for emotional gains that will enrich your life. Furthermore, the discomfort itself is a valuable clue to underlying emotional problems.

As you gain more and more insights, it is important that you attempt to make them meaningful in your life, applying them constructively to your battle against old patterns. If you content yourself with an intellectual understanding, you will have gained little, except perhaps an excuse for being neurotic.

You will observe that some insights you gain during a session, or between sessions, will slip away quickly, maybe after only seconds. If that occurs, it is important that you bring it to the attention of the therapist and the group, so that the causes of your forgetting will eventually be discovered. Make a conscious effort to remember any insights you gain during the sessions or between them. Write them down if necessary.

There is another way you can help your progress. Try to remember your dreams, your fantasies, and your daydreams and discuss them in the group sessions. Dreams are motion pictures of the forces moving in your unconscious; through psychotherapy you can decipher their meaning. When you wake up, lie still and attempt to recapture the dreams you had. Do not open your eyes until after you have recapitulated them. If you tend to forget dreams, in whole or in part, even though you recalled them upon awakening, write them down before the inner forces that work against deeper awareness erase them from your memory.

Just before a person falls asleep, the mind is in a suggestible state, and the unconscious tends to continue working with the impressions it receives at that time. Therefore, if you have difficulty remembering your dreams, try this technique: when you are falling asleep, tell yourself in an effortless way that you are going to have dreams and that you will recall them when you wake up. You may not achieve results the first few times, but chances are that you will soon.

6. How will I know when my therapy is finished?

During therapy you may experience a period of well-being such as you have never known before, or you may lose painful symptoms that you have had for some time. If that happens, you may consider yourself "cured" and decide to abandon therapy. Actually, deep and permanent structural changes may not yet have occurred in all areas where improvements are necessary. In many cases resistive forces are the underlying cause for the feeling of well-being. Unconscious resistance to anticipated anxiety and further change – and not the obvious satisfaction over improvement achieved – may be the real cause for the decision to leave. If you discontinue therapy at that point, you will avoid facing hidden painful feelings that are now ready to emerge. You will also avoid necessary further improvements that would strengthen your emotional stability.

You cannot be the judge of when your own therapy should terminate. Whenever you want to leave, discuss your intention frankly with your therapist and the group. They will be able to work with you to determine whether it is a result of resistance to further necessary change or a justified decision based on the solid ground of emotional health achieved.

From Therapist to Therapist

Some Characteristics of the Intensive, Extended Group

The method has a much different basis from present-day group therapy, a basis that results in marked improvement in interaction and other therapeutic factors. The greatly extended time permits far more attention to the individual member and thus allows better understanding of his psychic structure and dynamics, clearer emergence and crystallization of transferences, increased opportunity to work through resistances, and more opportunity for work with dreams. In short, the groups are characterized by greater depth and meaningfulness.

For the group therapist who is hesitant to venture into such unknown territory, we have a simple, practical suggestion: If he now conducts two groups or more, let him form one extended group as an experiment. Other therapists have tried that, and many of them now prefer the extended group.

It took many years of trial and error to arrive at the present stage of the intensive, extended group. Instead of recounting here the various steps in that process, we will limit ourselves to the elements that were found useful and are inherent parts of this group form today.

From the beginning, based on our experience with psychoanalytic group therapy, we carefully planned the composition of each extended group, emphasizing heterogeneity. As much as possible, each group member had personality traits and structures different from those of the other members. Patients with symptoms, forms, and degrees of emotional illness previously considered treatable only in individual psychotherapy were accepted in the extended groups. The only people not admitted were those whose emotional problems might render group work impossible, for example, psychotics who had no contact with reality, severe stutterers, and feebleminded people. As will be explained later, we also added sociopaths to the list of those excluded. Of course, there are also a few patients who, because of their special needs, should, at least temporarily, be seen only in individual sessions.

We had a wider choice in our selection of patients than therapists in private practice ordinarily have, because all patients applying to the Foundation for referral have a diagnostic interview with a psychiatrist expert in intake procedures. We studied the diagnostic reports and selected the more challenging and interesting cases for the extended groups.

Over the years, the ages of the group members ranged from 18 to 78. However, most of the members were between 22 and 60. The group therapist need not be afraid to include older people who are active and mentally alert. Many of them become valuable group members and benefit greatly from the procedure.

Each group had eight or nine members, with about an equal number of men and women. Whenever a member left, he was replaced by a new patient, selected with care to maintain the balance of the group.

Occasional private sessions proved a helpful component. Certain patients who were able to function in the group setting manifested anxiety when alone with the therapist. Others needed private sessions to reveal embarrassing material that they could not yet express in the group.

The three different situations – regular group sessions, alternate group sessions, and private sessions – often stimulate different conflict areas to be worked through. To them a fourth situation, also originated by Alexander Wolf, was advantageously added; the therapists suggested that the group members stay together for a while after sessions, perhaps over coffee at a nearby restaurant. In that social situation additional aspects of each person's reactive and defensive patterns could become apparent.

Some therapists tell the group members initially that they must help each other, that they will have to behave in a democratic way, or that they must relate in an adult manner to each other. Such demands tend to inhibit the patient and may obscure the emergence of his behavior patterns.

In the extended groups the patient must be made aware of the fact that the success of the procedure depends to a great extent on the patient's efforts toward awareness and honesty in revealing and understanding all his feelings and actions. Although primarily for his own benefit, such efforts on his part contribute to group work, even when the expressed emotions seem hostile, destructive, or embarrassing.

THE ROLE AND WORK OF THE THERAPIST

The extended time period is made necessary by some of these factors:

- Because there are few individual sessions, almost all the therapeutic work has to be done in the group. That includes the working through of difficult situations and problems.
- The handling of resistances is a challenging task, although it is greatly helped by the responses of the group members.
- To develop and maintain a feeling of participation and personal meaningfulness in the procedure, the therapist must relate to each patient during every session.

We concluded that it is essential for the therapist to know as much about each patient's psychodynamics as he would if the patient were in intensive individual therapy. To accomplish that, the therapist has to devote time outside the group to carefully rethinking what happened during the session. Also, new patients are asked to write down their dreams and fantasies so that the therapist can study them, even though they might not be reported during the session.

Traditional psychodynamic techniques – focusing on transference and the laying bare and working through of the various defense mechanisms and patterns – are applied. The therapist formulates tentative hypotheses concerning the unconscious forces and patterns active in each group member. As described in Part I, those hypotheses are based entirely on the productions of each patient and not on any rigid, dogmatic position. As group work progresses, significant material that is detected in the patients' defenses and transferences, expression of feelings, free associations, dreams, fantasies, and behavior makes possible continuous revisions of those hypotheses.

A major responsibility of the therapist is to clarify, at appropriate times, the direction of the efforts to be made by the patient. Thus the therapist channels group members toward meaningful exploration of the group interaction and understanding of underlying currents and mechanisms. He focuses the group's attention on emotions and behavior as they arise, establishing their significance and function within the individual psyche by linking them with the near and distant past. The patient's childhood gradually comes alive, and therapy is made an understandable, vital experience to the patient.

Such focusing diminishes the resistive digressions of the intellectual who tends to lose himself in theoretical speculations and of the patient who engages in long-drawn-out recitals of his life history or recent happenings. It also minimizes repetitive acting out of transferences and multiple transference reactions that do not result in any therapeutic exploration. As stated, acting out can take on many forms. Some group members may form seemingly warm, positive relationships that are, in effect, resistances to constructive therapy. Whenever the group fails to recognize such an impediment, the therapist needs to tactfully intervene; he is, after all, responsible for ensuring that precious group time is used appropriately.

Members are encouraged to express their reactions to group situations. Their reactions in turn serve as stimuli to the other patients. Therefore at any given time therapeutic possibilities exist for everyone, and the danger of merely having a series of individual sessions within the group setting is avoided.

As in any form of therapy, patients may conceal or act out resistances and frustrate the therapist's efforts to work through the problem. The difficulty is in direct proportion to the degree of hostility in the group. Even intense resistances can be worked through in the group, frequently with the help of other group members. The methods used often go beyond what is customary in individual and group therapy. Experiences in individual analysis and particularly in group psychoanalysis are increasingly forcing the abandonment of the concept that the analyst must be an impersonal constant and that interpretation is his only valid tool. It is becoming evident that the therapist's personality and experience are inevitably a factor of influence.

Going a step further, we are convinced that the therapist, guided by his knowledge and understanding, must use *all* possible techniques to bring about therapeutic progress. Furthermore, the therapist should apply different procedures and rationales to the various group members.

Patients come to therapy primarily for relief of pain and gratification of emotional needs, not for the kind of inner changes that the therapist knows are necessary to accomplish lasting results. Therefore when the analytic work is not sufficiently effective in working through a patient's resistance, the therapist may also have to use the patient's own drives, neurotic motivations, and secondary gains for that purpose. Such techniques include some strategic handling of the patient and the group, a principle that influences analytic work in any case, as for instance in the use of the so-called positive transference.

For example, a patient was on the verge of terminating therapy because of strong resistances. She had often spoken about her absent mother, on whom she had been extremely dependent. There was another group at the time that included an older woman who manifested characteristics similar to those the patient attributed to her mother. The patient was placed in the group with the older woman and became sufficiently involved to remain in therapy until she had worked through the resistance.

Another example: A patient who complained that his parents had been overprotective and doting was allowed as much freedom as possible by the therapist, who made only the most necessary comments in his direction. On the other hand, a patient who had experienced lack of paternal love in childhood was shown consideration and affection by the therapist. Any fears that such procedures interfere with the emergence of basic patterns are unfounded. The patient who was overprotected in childhood still complained that the therapist tried to control him, and the patient who was deprived of love accused the therapist of ignoring and neglecting him. Such distortions in the transference relationship are far more readily observed by the other group members than by the patient himself, and they are used to work through the problem.

The analyst again and again applies pragmatic procedures in chesslike moves to subtly maneuver the group toward interaction that will produce the desired insights. He is almost a subliminal orchestrator, eliciting responses from one group member to stimulate insights in another. The therapeutic process in the extended groups requires a balance of gratifying and frustrating the patient. By fostering and reinforcing properly timed ego-strengthening experiences within the transference relationships, the therapist brings about positive emotional changes. In other situations it is useful and necessary for the therapist to frustrate a patient's needs or desires. There are infinite applications of such techniques, and all of them require careful consideration by the therapist.

At best, the patient can acquire only partial cognizance of the processes involved. Conscious insight by the patient, while certainly sought, is usually far from complete and is but one of the factors that can bring about personality change.

Patients are continually urged to scrutinize their reactions to each situation in the group and *truthfully* report their feelings toward the situation and toward group members who stimulate feelings within them. They are prompted to describe accurately to the group significant behavior as well as their fantasies and dreams. The therapist stresses that afterreactions to each group session are important; members should carefully remember them and bring them up at the next meeting.

The therapist asks the group members to seek out the reason for each feeling, behavior pattern, dream, or fantasy by establishing the connection with similar feelings and memories from childhood. He makes them aware that childhood experiences are very important in analysis because they decisively influenced the development of deeply ingrained emotional patterns. He encourages the patients to relate all memories and associations, particularly those that are embarrassing. They may involve thoughts and feelings relating to the bodies of their father, mother, or siblings or their own bodies and physical functions, such as bowel movements or early sexual behavior. Eventually a comprehensive picture of the patient's early childhood should emerge.

As stated, the therapist also explains that a patient's progress in treatment may be hampered, or even completely thwarted, by his becoming superficial in therapy through avoidance of the requested efforts, by "acting out," by consciously presenting a false front to the group, or by engaging in actions within the group that are attempts to gratify himself yet conceal his real feelings. For instance, a patient may try to discourage a new member from continuing in the group instead of expressing his hostility directly toward the therapist.

The therapist encourages the patients to translate insights, gradually gained, into real-life experience by applying them constructively, first in the group and then in their daily battles against their old neurotic behavior patterns. For instance, patients who have unconsciously reacted to each interpersonal situation as fearful, helpless, and guilty children might gradually assert themselves in a more appropriate manner. However, the therapist should not expect miracles; in most instances, it will take time to notice tangible results.

No definite sequence of procedures or phases of progress are applicable to the group as a whole. Such techniques as "going around,"* in which a patient expresses his feelings and fantasies toward each of the other group members; dream interpretation; directiveness or nondirectiveness of the therapist; and others are used constantly in the group. Analytic as well as reeducative aspects of treatment are always present in group work. Furthermore, the group members are encouraged to attempt to understand the therapeutic procedure so that the time might be used advantageously.

The emotional reactions of the therapist are utilized as a helpful instrument for detecting the patient's unconscious and semiconscious motivations, such as attempts to control or manipulate the therapist, make him angry, or humor him.

A reflection on the treatment of sociopaths is in order, particularly since it can be difficult to recognize them and they can cause much damage to group work and disaster to individual group members. One needs to remember, however, that the fact that a person has committed a crime does not mean that he is a sociopath. In fact, most sociopaths will never be caught and convicted.

As is to be expected, work with such people is, while interesting, troublesome and unpleasant. Although those with the severest forms of sociopathy are not likely to come for treatment, there are many types of sociopathic personalities. We have had 11 such cases treated over a long period in these extended groups. Many more such patients dropped out after a short time in group therapy. Each of the long-term sociopathic patients made some progress in one or more areas, even though their aim in coming to therapy was to become more successful in their sociopathy rather than move toward a truly desirable goal.

Since sociopaths have not sufficiently developed a healthy, mature conscience, they often may appear admirably fearless, free, and

---

* In extended groups the original technique has been modified in such a way that after the person who is "going around" has expressed his feelings to a member, the member relates his reactions. "Going around" is one of the valuable but time-consuming techniques that can be applied only in extended groups.

authoritative to the neurotic group members, who are guilt-ridden, inhibited, and anxious. People who are not sociopaths themselves do not recognize that most sociopaths derive great pleasure from their asocial, destructive, and sadistic actions. Since it is the therapist's job to gradually elucidate the sociopathic, exploitative, destructive, and in some cases, self-destructive patterns, sooner or later a sociopath in the group almost invariably attempts to undermine the therapeutic group work and, in direct or devious ways, destroy the position of the therapist and discredit him. That becomes particularly evident when their attempts to exploit the therapist are thwarted by him.

Over the years, a number of neurotic patients were induced by sociopaths to leave the groups or were otherwise damaged by them. As a consequence, we consider it preferable not to include sociopaths in groups, even though such treatment, when properly conducted, is more effective for them than individual therapy alone.

A list of the traits prevalent in the sociopath may help the therapist and the group members identify them. The traits listed may appear in various combinations and degrees of intensity. The sociopath

- lives only for his own gratification
- although he may be extremely intelligent and cunning, may also be self-indulgent to the point of stupidity
- engages without hesitation in his gratification, regardless of the suffering it may bring to others
- exploits others without hesitation when it seems advantageous to him and rationalizes such actions (the guilt-ridden neurotic easily falls victim to him)
- finds meaning in the words "gratitude," "loyalty," and "duty" only if they refer to "obligations" of others to him
- in many cases presents a false front – charming and sincere – to cover the areas where his sociopathy is dominant
- will tell any lie to further his goals and create a good image; many are well spoken
- is convinced – or at least very hopeful – that his sociopathic acts will go unpunished
- often tries to get sympathy when in trouble or endangered, but returns to his old patterns as soon as he feels safe

- wards off any criticism either by attacking those who might realize or reveal the truth about him or by appearing to acquiesce
- often projects onto others his own sociopathy and selfishness
- is almost incapable of changing, has a marked inability to learn from his mistakes, and has no desire for socially constructive goals.

Many therapists nowadays speak of the "gestalt of the group" and the "group mind" as something above and beyond the individuals in the group. They attempt to deal therapeutically with the group as a whole in a global approach.

Our contention, however, is that the trends in a group that give the appearance of a "group mind" are actually resistance. As the transferences are examined, the resistive motivations of each group member causing such conformity become apparent. The therapist must analyze any neurotic submergence of the individual in the group and attack it until it is resolved.

Psychotherapists can accurately describe the relationships in the basic group without using terms such as "gestalt" and "group mind." The use of such terms is unnecessary and misleading.

We find that the patient's cooperation can counter some of the resistive and repressive forces that tend to destroy the constructive aims of therapy. The following techniques might be less necessary in individual analysis, where the patient is seen several times a week, than in the extended groups.

To prevent the patient's insights from slipping away, the therapist reminds him, at appropriate occasions and in simple terms, of his particular neurotic patterns, but only to the extent that they have become known to the patient in prior therapeutic work. The patient is encouraged to remember those formulations and, on occasion, to reinforce the insights by writing them down. For instance, an anxiety-ridden patient who unconsciously assumed the role of his dictatorial father was thus able to maintain his cognizance of the behavior and therefore avoid some of its pitfalls.

In other instances, where a group member is approaching awareness of a certain problem area – for example, hidden hostility,

fear of abandonment, a need to malign threatening figures – the therapist encourages him to search, even between sessions, for associations
and feelings, particularly those stemming from childhood experiences.
The therapist makes it clear that focusing on problem areas and on
already acquired insights and remembering such insights must not
become mere intellectual exercises but should involve real feelings.
Such suggestions, which are merely at the conscious level, are most
often followed only halfheartedly by the patients and are not as valuable as the traditional psychodynamic techniques. However, they
diminish some of the confusion and distortion into which the neurotic
patient regresses between sessions. They give him something to hold
on to outside the therapeutic situation that may help him deal more
realistically with threatening environmental situations.

It was the negative influences in the social world of the patient's childhood environment that originally gave rise to his fears, suffering, and
emotional imprisonment. It is now the social experience of the therapy
group, if the group is based on a valid therapy form, that helps him
enlarge his awareness of reality and gain emotional freedom and depth.

The therapist's communications with the patients are in simple,
nontechnical language, always expressed on their level of understanding and referring to their own dynamics and their own imagery, as evidenced in their dreams and fantasies.

As each patient is constantly made aware of his emotional reaction
to each group situation, he gradually arrives at a better understanding
of both outer reality and his own feelings.

DREAMS
The actual presentation and analysis of dreams occupy only about 20 percent of the extended group sessions. That is considerably more than is
possible in the usual brief groups. In fact, dreams are most important in
this type of group work. After a patient tells his dreams, the therapist
advises him to speak about the feelings experienced in them and to relate
any associations. The patient's understanding of his dreams is aided by
the associations, feelings, and interpretations of the other group members.

The therapist uses dreams to make the patient aware of the problem areas to which he must pay attention at each particular stage of his

therapy. Constant parallels are made in the group between a patient's dreams and his defensive and neurotic behavior. Furthermore, defenses and emotional reactions of the various patients are often compared, and similar, identical, and opposite patterns are pointed out. It is important to realize that the dream of a sociopath may mean the opposite of the same dream in a neurotic. For instance, a dream that would show progress in a neurotic may well mean a lack of change or even a hardening of the asocial tendencies in a sociopath.

Orthodox psychoanalysts who practice only individual analysis have expressed the fear that a premature interpretation of strongly repressed dream material by fellow group members could cause intolerable anxiety in a patient. We have not witnessed any such situation that could not be adequately handled. More often than not, it is sufficient simply to show no reaction to the correct but "dangerous" dream interpretation or, when appropriate, to probe its meaning for the "interpreting patient" rather than for the dreamer.

We know that at the beginning of therapy, dream material is often quite repressed and strongly symbolized; for example, patients may dream of animals, trucks, and so on, that threaten them. As therapy progresses, dreams become clearer, and significant human images appear. That process often happens more quickly for patients in the extended groups than for those who have only one individual session a week.

To achieve therapeutic effect, therapists who want to engage in this form of therapy should be skilled in the proper handling of dreams.

TRANSFERENCES

Psychoanalysts hold, and rightly so, that transference is a key factor in treatment. If so, then the extended group therapy method, far more than the usual group treatment, is indeed the psychoanalytic treatment form par excellence.

Consider this: A patient spends 180 minutes a week with the analyst, the equivalent of four 45-minute individual sessions. However, in the extended groups he would spend 360 minutes a week with his fellow group members. In individual therapy the transferences toward father, mother, brother, sister, and other childhood figures are projected onto a single person, the analyst. In the extended group those transferences are unscrambled and crystallized; that is, they are projected onto separate individuals. Assuming that for a specific patient the male therapist represents father and other members represent other family members, his transference reactions and distortions will be clearer in the group interaction, and in his dreams and fantasies as well.

All claims to the contrary notwithstanding, individual analysis does not and cannot offer such clear insight into the manifold transference factors operative in the patient. What may remain obscured in individual analysis has a good chance of being revealed here. The frequent difficulty in obtaining a satisfactory understanding of a patient's intrapsychic structure and functioning has been a prime factor in inducing the less gifted analyst to turn to the facile and superficial interpersonal and group-as-a-whole approaches. The conscientious and competent therapist, on the other hand, undertakes the more difficult task of gaining the full picture of the patient as an individual, a task without which no solid reconstructive work is possible.

As stated, to make possible the emergence of a variety of significant transference relationships, the therapist has to pay great attention to group composition. The transference relationships are allowed to develop and are elicited during the group session. Focusing on the transference involvements, the therapist asks the patients to associate to the feelings they are experiencing. Those associations are to both recent experiences and childhood experiences, especially within the original family. The procedure brings out the significance of the transference reaction: where it originated, how it has been reinforced, and why it results in defensive and resistive behavior.

ASSOCIATIONS AND FREE ASSOCIATIONS

Free associations in the group are generated under circumstances often different from the relative calm of individual sessions. Both procedures have their own validity and attraction for an analyst, but the group therapist must forgo the cherished and valuable tool of free association as practiced in individual analytic sessions. Thus, although the therapist will undergo an emotional loss, as if a dear friend has departed, he will find that the multitude of reactions and associations brought about by meaningful group interaction results in a wealth of significant material. In fact, free association as we know it in individual analysis is the only major element that cannot be duplicated in the extended groups. Yet the work in the extended groups proves that the group procedure does extremely well in eliciting meaningful associations.

There is a danger that a patient will not verbalize his associations because too much activity is occurring and that significant analytic material will be lost. The therapist must not take such an occurrence lightly, perhaps consoling himself with the hope that the lost affect will eventually become manifest again. He must try to prevent such loss, a difficult task indeed. He should attempt to observe the reactions of all group members and at the end of the session ask for unexpressed feelings, hoping that at least some will be remembered. Of course, the longer sessions provide the extended group members with more opportunity for self-expression.

> I get weary
> and sick of trying.
> I'm tired of living
> and scared of dying.
>
> OSCAR HAMMERSTEIN

THE ELDERLY

For many of our senior citizens in need of professional help, the extended groups are a most desirable form of treatment. Quite a number of the elderly experience a painful reduction of their social contacts. Friends have died, and there may be no one to take their place. The feeling of ever-increasing isolation can add greatly to existing depression and discouragement. Even though they are being placed in a group to help them overcome their emotional problems, the prolonged and regular contact with other human beings is an additional benefit.

Although we advocate heterogeneous groups, the elderly should be placed in a group compatible with their emotional status. Some of them feel uncomfortable with younger people, and some become sad when they are reminded of a lifestyle that is no longer available to them. For such people, homogeneous groups constituted by elderly people must be created. However, a surprising number do enjoy being with younger people and can be placed into the usual heterogeneous groups. In that case, one always has to make sure that the elderly person is not placed in a group where there is a group member who, owing to overwhelming hostility to a parental figure, will attack and harass the older member.

The topic of incorporating the elderly in groups was discussed at length in the chapter on the elderly that appeared in THE CHALLENGE FOR GROUP PSYCHOTHERAPY, the first volume of our present series.

SELF-EXAMINATION BY THE THERAPIST

Therapists tend to assume that everything they say and do is the result of their accumulated wisdom and therefore the best they can do. A therapist whose mind is already burdened with paying attention to the group members may not be inclined to take on the additional burden of self-examination. Furthermore, owing to psychological factors in his own makeup, which may range from grandiose arrogance to severe self-doubts, he may resist engaging in an endeavor that may turn out to be difficult and unpleasant.

At the same time, the therapist does want to help his patients and would like to see progress. For those reasons alone, he should ask himself a few simple questions about his feelings and reactions toward each of his patients. For instance, how does he feel about each of the group members who do not show much reaction toward him? It may actually be the patients who are not behaving in any unusual way toward the therapist that make him feel rejected, and he may not even realize it. Or does one or more of the patients represent parental or sibling figures to the therapist? If so, how does that influence his actions and reactions? Does he identify with one of the patients? If so, how does that make him feel toward the patient? Does he like him for it or dislike him? Does he feel sorry and protective toward the patient?

How does the therapist see the group in his mind? Does he see it as his family, or as the family he never had? How does he deal with his groups? Does he behave as his father or mother behaved, or perhaps in the opposite way?

Then there are the more complex questions, dealing with the patients who show strong reactions to the therapist. Here, too, we have many possibilities. The patient may be "loving," sexual, demanding, arrogant, critical, hostile. First the therapist must ask himself the questions we just suggested. Once he has become aware of his basic feelings toward a patient, he can then scrutinize his reactions to the feelings the patient expresses toward him. When a patient whom the therapist likes is aggressively hostile, that is quite a different matter from the same action by a patient for whom the therapist has negative feelings.

There is always the danger that the therapist will rationalize his feelings and possibly harm the patients. Thus this kind of self-interrogation can only have a salutary effect on the therapeutic work and stimulate increased insight in the therapist. The satisfaction of greater and valuable understanding will compensate for any temporary hurt to his ego.

4.   Quality of Treatment

So far in this chapter we have described the format of the intensive, extended groups and the techniques that can be most advantageously applied.

Yet all that amounts to an empty shell, devoid of value, as long as the core – the soul, if you will – is missing. And the soul is the quality of the work done within the framework we have outlined.

Previously in this volume we showed how psychotherapy has deteriorated. We also mentioned a decline in the last two decades in the overall quality of group psychotherapy, where the more thorough forms of analytic group therapy have been increasingly displaced by easy-to-practice, superficial approaches. At the same time, as Stanley Lesse and many others have consistently pointed out, selection and training of practitioners have greatly deteriorated. Intensive clinical training, which is indispensable, has been increasingly supplanted by academic course work that is of little value and is imbued with the freewheeling theories of professionals who have little clinical knowledge.

It is regrettable when a shoe repairman bungles his work. But it is a far more serious matter when a psychotherapist, who, after all, is supposed to be a repairman of emotional ills, does shoddy work. Countless people who could be helped are not obtaining relief from their suffering. It is for that reason that we have previously stated that group therapy is of value only when the therapeutic work is of high quality.

The responsibility for the care of the emotionally ill lies with the mental health profession. It is unconscionable to support systems and approaches that ignore the suffering of so many. Unfortunately, the trend has been for shorter treatment time and more superficial treatment procedures.

In the more than 70 years of its existence, the American Mental Health Foundation has vigorously opposed practices it considered detrimental to the public interest. We cannot politely look the other way while professional shortcomings or lack of interest prolong the ordeal of so many human beings. Many valid remedies are available, and we must not hesitate to apply them, even if doing so will inconvenience the professionals who are operating comfortably in the present system.

The reader, then, should not be surprised if we use strong language in objecting to approaches that we consider clinically unsubstantiated, irresponsibly superficial, and harmful to patients.

The trends of our times are so powerful that even well-meaning therapists are swayed by them unless their own clinical expertise and knowledge of psychotherapy are firmly established. Only the power of those trends can explain why so many professionals have become embroiled in flashy theories and scholarly ruminations far removed from the realities of the human psyche and of no interest to expert practitioners.

Let us present an example, one out of thousands, of the superficiality of present trends. In a paper published in 1984, Saul Scheidlinger, a former president of the American Group Psychotherapy Association and a widely quoted author, states:

> I foresee a continuation . . . toward pragmatism and eclecticism (the latter more in a sense of creative integration or pluralism rather than undisciplined subjectivity) in group-psychotherapy theorizing. With it will go a stress on devising specific methodologies for specific problems and conditions. . . .
>
> What kinds of changes are affected by what kinds of techniques, applied to what kinds of patients by what kind of therapists under what kind of conditions?[*]

We will address the second part of the quote first. It takes incredible naïveté to believe that those questions can be answered in that manner. The simplistic, pseudoscientific proposal reveals an utter lack of understanding of the human psyche, as well as of psychotherapy.

[*] S. Scheidlinger (1984), Group psychotherapy in the 1980s: Problems and prospects, *Amer. J. Psychother.*, 38.

Perhaps some mental health "scholar" will answer Scheidlinger's questions merely by referring to the myriad of writings dealing with one or more of the topics involved. Such a treatise would first ask which of the 20-odd categories of therapists would be suitable to deal with the clinical categories mentioned in DSM-IV and would then answer specifically the additional questions raised by Scheidlinger. The whole enterprise would cover many volumes but be devoid of any value.

An additional thought in regard to Scheidlinger's question "What kind of therapist?": Is there really any kind of psychotherapist other than the one who has the talent and the expertise to deal appropriately with the intrapsychic problems of the patient, whether in individual, group, or any other kind of treatment? Like surgeons, such therapists know what instrument to use, how to use it, and when to use it. Unlike surgeons, however, therapists have only one specialty: the vast and infinitely complex domain of the inner psychic structure and its functioning.

In the first part of the quote Scheidlinger speaks of the various trends in group psychotherapy. He insists on the need for ecumenism among the various creeds and condemns "undisciplined subjectivity." That may sound like democratic fairness to the credulous and the uninformed, and it is certainly a crowd pleaser, but it implies that something is valid simply because it exists. Scheidlinger includes everything, whether junk or not, in his populistic cocktail.

Scheidlinger does not seem to recognize that our craft requires a gifted psychotherapist who is sensitive to feelings and dreams and who feels that it is necessary to obtain a deeper understanding of each patient's unique inner universe and its workings. Doesn't it occur to him that he might be selling snake oil?

Ten years later it has still not occurred to Scheidlinger. In one of the least inspiring accounts of the history of group psychotherapy ever written, he still describes at length many superficial and one-sided approaches but merely allows a few lines, peppered with negative comments, for the comprehensive, in-depth intrapsychic psychodynamic group treatment forms.[*] None of his vaunted democratic fairness is

[*] S. Scheidlinger (1994), An overview of nine decades of group psychotherapy, *Hosp. Community Psychiat.*, 45.

shown here, when it comes to the most valid but more difficult and sophisticated group therapy methods.

As a supporter of the group-as-a-whole and group process approaches, Scheidlinger also speaks highly of the interpersonal, transactional approach, as represented by Yalom. We have analyzed Yalom's approach to a large extent in Part I of this volume and looked at its pretentious superficiality, lack of logic, and unfounded populistic claims. Yalom, like so many others, emphasizes the here and now and proclaims that psychoanalysis and analytic group therapy, like the one we are advocating, are lacking in that element. It is foolish for him to say so and foolish for anyone to accept such statements. What could be more in the here and now than the reactions of the analysand toward his therapist and the reactions of the group members to those present?

Scheidlinger states correctly that therapy groups are not the best place to study the so-called group process. He should have carried that statement a little further and said that any emphasis on group process has absolutely no place in therapy groups. What must happen in therapy groups, exclusively and at all times, is what psychotherapy commands, and that is an altogether different matter. Careful and skillful analytic work in the group will reveal, to a significant extent and in an impressive majority of cases, the child's world that operates in each patient. There are no "group processes" to be found in that world. The expert clinician is able to work with those clinically verifiable facts without the subterfuge of labor-saving intellectual constructs.

We started out by stating that the core issue is the quality of treatment, which depends on the talent and expertise of the therapist. In the hands of a therapist who does not have talent and expertise, format and technique are merely gimmicks.

How, then, can quality be achieved? In this volume we devote several hundred pages to answering that question. We show where the problems lie that must be avoided at all costs, and we give solutions for (a) obtaining far more adequate trainees for the profession of psychoanalysts and psychotherapists; (b) ensuring a far more fruitful, less wasteful course of study; and (c) explaining a vastly different therapeutic effort enabling therapists to obtain far better understandings of the individual psychodynamics of their patients and consequently to do quality work on a deeper level. The insistence on expert work will substantially alleviate the suffering of innumerable patients.

We also must not forget that a patient who pays for intensive, extended psychodynamic group therapy out of his own pocket will obtain better treatment than he would for lesser treatment modalities financed by third-party payers. In view of the ever-increasing and undesirable intrusion by managed care and third-party payers into the practice of psychotherapy, the treatment method described here may well become the only intensive psychodynamic therapy form that can be dispensed without unwarranted and damaging interference. That, of course, does not apply to the limited number of affluent patients who can afford costlier treatment procedures.

The required efforts described in the chapter "Working toward Clinical Expertise" in this volume apply equally to individual and group psychotherapy. If practiced by a psychotherapist who has the required talent and expertise, quality work will be the result. Moreover, considerable experience over many decades with intensive, extended groups has proved that this treatment method offers a hopeful solution to the most pressing problem in the field of mental health: effective, affordable treatment for a great number of the emotionally ill.

> If feeling fails you, vain will be your course.
> And idle what you plan unless your art
> Springs from the soul with elemental force
> To hold its sway in every listening heart.
>
> GOETHE
> TRANSLATED BY PHILIP WAYNE

BIBLIOGRAPHY
This brief, partial bibliography traces the origins and the development of the intensive, extended groups:

Wolf, A. (1949 & 1950). The psychoanalysis of groups. *Amer. J. Psychother., 3 & 4.*

Wolf, A. (1952). The psychoanalysis of groups: The analyst's objections. *Internat. J. Group Psychother., 2.*

de Schill, S. (1954). *Introduction to psychoanalytic group therapy.* New York: AMHF – Brunner. (6th rev. ed., 1971).

de Schill, S., & LaHullier, D. (1956). *The practice of mental health groups.* New York: AMHF – Brunner.

Wolf, A., & Schwartz, E. K. (1962). *Psychoanalysis in groups.* Orlando, FL: Grune & Stratton.

de Schill, S. (1969). *The dream in group, the group in dream.* New York: AMHF.

de Schill, S. (Ed.). (1971). *Psychoanalytische Therapie in Gruppen.* Stuttgart: Ernst Klett Verlag. (2nd ed., 1974).

de Schill, S., & LaHullier, D. (1973). Groupes de santé mentale: Une méthode intensive de traitement. In S. de Schill (Ed.), *La psychothérapie de groupe.* (Bibliotheque de l'Insitut de Psychanalyse). Paris: Presses Universitaires de France.

de Schill, S. (Ed.). (1974). *The challenge for group psychotherapy.* New York: International Universities Press.

de Schill, S. (Ed.). (1980). *Terapia psicoanalitica de grupo.* Milan: Feltrinelli Editore.

de Schill, S., & Lebovici, S. (Eds.). (1997). *Le défi à l'égard de la psychanalyse et de la psychothérapie et les solutions pour l'avenir.* Paris: Presses Universitaires de France.

de Schill, S., Lebovici, S., & Kächele, H. (Eds.). (1997). *Psychoanalyse und Psychotherapie. Herausforderungen und Lösungen für die Zukunft.* Stuttgart: Georg Thieme Verlag.

COMMENTS AND ACKNOWLEDGMENTS

In planning the introduction to the present volume and the contents of its companion volume, THE CHALLENGE FOR PSYCHOANALYSIS AND PSYCHOTHERAPY: SOLUTIONS FOR THE FUTURE, the members of the American Mental Health Foundation's editorial committee and its editorial consultants studied the writings of some 600 authors to determine which were best suited to cover the topics with which we wanted to deal.

We contacted the professionals we had selected and invited each of them to write on a specific topic within their area of expertise. In some instances, we indicated one of their previous writings on which to base the new writing. The resulting papers that appear in our volumes are, for the most part, significantly different from such earlier works.

Practically all the writings in our volumes are original papers, not based on prior writings. However, we thought it advisable, in the cases where a similar prior writing does exist, to secure the rights of reprint. We have therefore obtained such rights from Guilford Press of New York City for the introduction to this volume by John E. Gedo and from Jason Aronson, Inc., of Northvale, New Jersey, for the introduction by Robert J. Stoller.

We are also grateful to Robert Stoller and Paul E. Stepansky, editor-in-chief of the Analytic Press of Hillsdale, New Jersey, for the permission to quote extensively from the volume COGNITIVE SCIENCE AND PSYCHOANALYSIS, by Kenneth Mark Colby and Stoller.

At the beginning of the section "Earnestly Talking Nonsense," the procedure of recruiting Russian soldiers in Saint Petersburg is described. I read about it first in the early 1930s, in a history book. Years later I encountered a description of the procedure in one of the writings of the Austrian writer Alexander Lernet-Holenia. My account of the event is based on his narrative.

– S.deS.

APPENDIX

OTHER VOLUMES IN THE SERIES
THE SEARCH FOR THE FUTURE

Throughout this volume we have frequently referred to the other two volumes of the series THE SEARCH FOR THE FUTURE. The reader will find here some informative material about those volumes.

VOLUME I

THE CHALLENGE FOR GROUP PSYCHOTHERAPY

VOLUME II

THE CHALLENGE FOR PSYCHOANALYSIS
AND PSYCHOTHERAPY:
SOLUTIONS FOR THE FUTURE

VOLUME I

THE CHALLENGE FOR GROUP PSYCHOTHERAPY

Edited by Stefan de Schill
DIRECTOR OF RESEARCH
AMERICAN MENTAL HEALTH FOUNDATION

WITH CONTRIBUTIONS BY

RAYMOND BATTEGAY

STEFAN DE SCHILL

HELENE DURKIN

ADOLF FRIEDEMANN

JACK KRASNER

DENISE LAHULLIER

SERGE LEBOVICI

S. R. SLAVSON

JACOB SPANJAARD

JOSEPH WILDER

ALEXANDER WOLF

INTERNATIONAL UNIVERSITIES PRESS, INC.
NEW YORK, NEW YORK

This volume, first published in 1970, appeared in five major languages.
It is no longer in print.

"This work is brilliant, always carefully thought out. Mental health professionals throughout the world will be stimulated to fresh thinking and improved service for the emotionally ill. The French edition, appearing under the imprint of the Bibliothèque de l'Institut de Psychanalyse, Paris, constitutes a landmark in that it is the first book on group psychotherapy to be sponsored by a major psychoanalytic institute.

"Much attention is given to an outstanding achievement of the American Mental Health Foundation: the development of the first effective but inexpensive treatment method in psychotherapy, which promises to become an answer to our greatest health problem. This treatment form offers intensive and effective help to a wide spectrum of emotionally disturbed people at a fraction of the usual cost of treatment."

David Gerst, M.D.
Chairman
International Institute for Mental Health Research

"This volume is recommended without any reservations. In many years I have not come across any book or article that contained as many useful hints for my daily practice."

Die Heilkunst

"Group psychotherapy, a field constantly gaining in importance, has been given here a new standard reference work that conveys to both practitioner and student the latest knowledge of the theories, the methods, and the areas of application of psychotherapy. . . . Renowned practitioners and theoreticians of group psychotherapy provide the reader with a complete and up-to-date overall view of the present state of scientific knowledge in this field and of the specific methods used."

Ärztliche Forschung

"It is made clear that group psychotherapy has evolved into an established part of general psychotherapy and psychoanalysis. This could hardly be documented in a more convincing manner . . . the best compendium on psychoanalytic group psychotherapy at the present time."

Pro Medico

"Well-conceived, ambitious . . . recommended for . . . personality change in a group setting."

American Journal of Psychiatry

THE CHALLENGE FOR PSYCHOANALYSIS AND PSYCHOTHERAPY: SOLUTIONS FOR THE FUTURE

Edited
by
Stefan de Schill and Serge Lebovici

WITH CONTRIBUTIONS BY

STEPHEN A. APPELBAUM

STEFAN DE SCHILL

JEROME D. FRANK

MERTON M. GILL

ANDRÉ HAYNAL

HORST KÄCHELE

OTTO F. KERNBERG

DENISE LaHULLIER

SERGE LEBOVICI

MARGUERITE F. LEVY

WILLIAM W. MEISSNER

ROBERT MICHELS

JACQUES PALACI

MALCOLM PINES

RAINER RICHTER

HAROLD SAMPSON

STEVEN S. SHARFSTEIN

MONROE W. SPERO

MILTON THEAMAN

ROBERT S. WALLERSTEIN

IVAN WENTWORTH-ROHR

ALEXANDER WOLF

Jessica Kingsley Publishers
Taylor & Francis
1900 Frost Road, Suite 101
Bristol, PA 19007-1598

Jessica Kingsley Publishers
London

Les Presses Universitaires de France
Paris

Georg Thieme Verlag
Stuttgart

"THE CHALLENGE FOR PSYCHOANALYSIS AND PSYCHOTHER-
APY – SOLUTIONS FOR THE FUTURE is, by far, one of the most
consequential volumes to appear in years. It fulfills a much
needed, unique and important purpose: allowing us to hear
the voices of a substantial number of the recognized leaders of
our field, describing in detail the avenues which hold most
promise for the future of psychotherapy and mental health."

Valentine W. Zeitlin, M.D.
Chairman, Professional Board
International Institute for the Advancement of Psychiatry

"On many counts, this is a most exceptional volume. It unites,
for the first time, many of the foremost authors in psychoanalysis and psychotherapy, representing a diversity of approaches
while allowing for an unprecedented comparison of their basic
assumptions as well as expectations for the future and proposals
for improvement.

"Also of outstanding interest and value is the section which
describes a variety of treatment approaches that hold promise
for the future. Foremost among them is the psychodynamic
group therapy method developed by the American Mental
Health Foundation during 45 years. This treatment modality
offers the patient intensive, effective psychotherapy within
the framework of extended weekly treatment time, and at a
cost affordable to most people. The method does not require
a financial sacrifice on the part of the therapist, but it does
require an expert professional. In view of the ever-increasing
undesirable intrusion by third-party payers in the practice of
psychotherapy, this treatment method may well become the
only intensive psychotherapy form available that can be
offered without unwarranted and damaging interference."

Psychothérapies, Vol. IV, 1994

The table of contents and the list of authors included on the following pages show the basic structure for the volume. However, depending on the requests of the publishers, certain chapters may not appear in the English or foreign language editions.

The volume has been published in German by Georg Thieme, one of the two largest medical publishers in Germany. The French language edition of this work is being published by Presses Universitaires de France, the foremost academic publisher in that country, which also plans to promote Italian, Spanish, and Portuguese editions. The English language edition is being brought out by Jessica Kingsley Publishers of London and Philadelphia, a publishing company known for bringing worthwhile publications to the attention of mental health professionals.

THE CHALLENGE FOR PSYCHOANALYSIS AND PSYCHOTHERAPY
SOLUTIONS FOR THE FUTURE

appears in German under the title

PSYCHOANALYSE UND PSYCHOTHERAPIE
HERAUSFORDERUNGEN UND LÖSUNGEN FÜR DIE ZUKUNFT
Georg Thieme Verlag, Stuttgart, 1997

and appears in French under the title

A LA RECHERCHE DE L'AVENIR
UN DÉFI POUR LA PSYCHANALYSE ET LA PSYCHOTHÉRAPIE
Presses Universitaires de France, Paris, 1998

CONTENTS

Authors

Stephen A. Appelbaum
> Professor, University of Missouri at Kansas City School of Medicine; former Director of Psychology, C. F. Menninger Memorial Hospital

Stefan de Schill
> Director of Research, American Mental Health Foundation (since 1948); Vice President, International Institute for Mental Health Research, Zürich and Geneva

Jerome D. Frank
> Professor Emeritus of Psychiatry, Johns Hopkins University School of Medicine, Baltimore

Merton M. Gill
> Professor of Psychiatry, University of Illinois, Chicago; Supervising Analyst, Chicago Institute of Psychoanalysis

André Haynal
> Chairman, Department of Psychiatry, University of Geneva; former President, Swiss Psychoanalytic Society; former Vice President, European Psycho-analytical Federation

Horst Kächele
> Professor of Psychotherapy, University of Ulm

Otto F. Kernberg
> Associate Chairman and Medical Director, Westchester Division, New York Hospital, Cornell Medical Center; Professor of Psychiatry, Cornell University Medical College; Training and Supervising Analyst, Center for Psychiatric Training and Research, Columbia University, New York City

Denise LaHullier

Coordinator, Group Therapy Sections, American Mental Health Foundation and International Institute for Mental Health Research, Zürich and Geneva

Serge Lebovici

Professor Emeritus of Child and Adolescent Psychiatry, University of Paris North; Honorary Vice President, International Psycho-analytical Association; former Director, Paris Psychoanalytic Institute

Marguerite F. Levy

Professor, Queens College, Flushing, New York

William W. Meissner

Training and Supervising Analyst, Boston Psychoanalytic Society and Institute; former Clinical Professor of Psychiatry, Harvard Medical School, Boston

Robert Michels

Chairman, Department of Psychiatry, Cornell University Medical College; Psychiatrist-in-Chief, New York Hospital; Training and Supervising Analyst, Center for Psychoanalytic Training and Research, Columbia University, New York City

Jacques Palaci

Former President, National Psychological Association for Psychoanalysis, New York City; former Vice President, Theodor Reik Clinic for Mental Health and Research, New York City

Malcolm Pines

Consultant Psychotherapist, Tavistock Clinic, London; former President, International Group Psychotherapy Association

Rainer Richter

Professor of Psychotherapy, University of Hamburg

Harold Sampson
> Codirector, Psychotherapy Research Group, Mount Zion Hospital, San Francisco

Steven S. Sharfstein
> President and Medical Director, Sheppard Pratt, Baltimore

Monroe W. Spero
> President, International Institute for the Advancement of Psychiatry; Chairman, Professional Board, American Mental Health Foundation

Milton Theaman
> Former Executive Director, Psychological Service Center, New York City

Robert S. Wallerstein
> Chairman, Department of Psychiatry, School of Medicine, University of California, San Francisco; former President, American Psychoanalytic Association; former President, International Psycho-analytic Association

Ivan Wentworth-Rohr
> Professor Emeritus of Psychology, Pace University, New York City; former Chief of Behavior Therapy, Biofeedback Unit, St. Vincent's Hospital and Medical Center, New York City

Alexander Wolf
> Former Clinical Professor and Training Psychoanalyst, New York Medical College; former Supervising Psychotherapist, Postgraduate Center for Mental Health, New York City

The titles of the authors indicate the positions that they held when they wrote the chapters.

AMHF

The American Mental Health Foundation, organized in 1924, is dedicated to the welfare of people suffering from emotional problems and to the concerns of the elderly. The Foundation has devoted its efforts, with outstanding success, to bettering the quality of treatment and developing more effective methods, afforable even to low-income wage earners.

The Foundation's major therapeutic advances and improved training methods are described in its publications, considered by preeminent international mental health professionals to be of exceptional value for the essential improvement of psychotherapy and psychoanalysis. The Foundation, vitally interested in reaching the greatest possible audience for its findings, publishes in both the United States and abroad. Its publications appear in at least three languages.

None of the board members, officers, or professionals of the Foundation receives remuneration. Nevertheless, the costs of doing research, preparing publications and translations, and making the Foundation's findings known to the professions and the general public are very costly.

Because the Foundation has no endowment, all donations constitute a meaningful contribution to the public interest. Donations are tax-exempt.

AMERICAN MENTAL HEALTH FOUNDATION
1049 FIFTH AVENUE NEW YORK, NY 10028

NAMES INDEX

Subject Index

The terms *psychoanalysis, psychotherapy, concepts, theory, science, feelings,* and *dreams* are used innumerable times throughout the volume, particularly in the main chapter. For that reason the pages where they are mentioned in passing are not listed in the index. Only pages that treat those terms more extensively and pages that deal with a particular aspect of those terms — for example, *dreams* under *free association* — are listed.